Researching Operations Management

Researching Operations Management fills the growing need for a comprehensive textbook and reference on doing quality research in the field of Operations Management (OM). It addresses the particular problem—especially for advanced students and beginning researchers—that many academic departments specialize in just one or a few approaches to research. As a result, many students and researchers are not exposed to the breadth of possible research approaches in OM. Providing a concise overview of each of the most important research approaches in the field, the book enables researchers and students to understand and practice these methods, thus giving them a platform for choosing appropriate and complementary approaches to their research.

With contributions from an international group of leading thinkers in the OM research field, the book covers those methods frequently used in studies of OM as well as adjacent applied management areas such as management of innovation and R&D, logistics, and supply chain management. Included are chapters on surveys, case studies, action research, longitudinal field studies, and models and simulations together with chapters on planning, positioning, assessing, and publishing research. In addition, the contributors also consider ethical and cultural issues in researching Operations Management.

Christer Karlsson is Professor of Innovation and Operations Management and Dean for CBS Executive at Copenhagen Business School and also professor at the European Institute for Advanced Studies in Management (EIASM) in Brussels.

Researching Operations Management

Edited by Christer Karlsson

Routledge
Taylor & Francis Group

NEW YORK AND LONDON

First published 2009
by Routledge
270 Madison Ave, New York, NY 10016

Simultaneously published in the UK
by Routledge
2 Park Square, Milton Park, Abingdon, Oxon OX14 4RN

Routledge is an imprint of the Taylor & Francis Group, an informa business

Typeset in Bembo by
Swales & Willis Ltd, Exeter, Devon
Printed and bound in the United States of America on acid-free paper by
Sheridan Books, Inc.

Library of Congress Cataloging-in-Publication Data
Researching operations management / edited by Christer Karlsson.
p. cm.
Includes bibliographical references and index.
1. Industrial management—Research.   2. Production management—
Research.   3. Operations research.   I. Karlsson, Christer.
HD30.4.R478 2008
658.5'7—dc22
2008023707

ISBN10: 0–415–99055–6 (hbk)
ISBN10: 0–415–99056–4 (pbk)
ISBN10: 0–203–88681–X (ebk)

ISBN13: 978–0–415–99055–4 (hbk)
ISBN13: 978–0–415–99056–1 (pbk)
ISBN13: 978–0–203–88681–6 (ebk)

Contents

4   Surveys   84
Cipriano Forza

5   Case Research in Operations Management   162
Chris Voss

9   Concluding Remarks

Christer Karlsson

Acknowledgements

The book is based on a European Doctoral Educational Network (EDEN) program by the European Institute for Advanced Studies in Management (EIASM) in collaboration with the European Operations Management Association (EurOMA), with the editor as coordinator and the other authors as faculty. Some of the material has been published in a special issue of International Journal of Operations and Production Management, Vol. 22, No. 2, 2002 with this editor as guest editor.

We acknowledge the following:

EIASM for its development of the EDEN concept and providing the opportunity to develop and run this EDEN workshop on research methodology. At the time of publication of this book, the workshop has been run for more than 10 years.

EurOMA who have supported the development and operation of this workshop by providing faculty and making the event known in the EurOMA network as well as promoting its role as compulsory PhD programme in many business schools and universities.

International Journal of Operations and Production Management, which published the first research versions of a couple of the chapters in this book, hence making the workshop the key reference for research methodology in operations management.

Finally Routledge should be acknowledged for their support in bringing the wide scope of the thoughts of these authors together in a comprehensive research methodology textbook of this kind.

List of Contributors

This book is written by leading scholars in the field who describe how to carry out research at the very highest level with the aim of getting published. The authors have been chosen from scholars who have considerable experience in, doing and managing research, getting research published and review research in the field of operations management. Their details are given below in order of chapter appearance.

Christer Karlsson holds an MSc and PhD degree from Chalmers University of Technology, Gothenburg, Sweden in the area of industrial management. He is Professor of Innovation and Operations Management and Dean for CBS Executive at Copenhagen Business School and also Professor at the European Institute for Advanced Studies in Management (EIASM) in Brussels. For over 15 years he has been Director of the nationwide Swedish applied research institute IMIT, Institute for Management of Innovation and Technology. Among other positions held are vice chairman of the board of EIASM and member of division management of the Royal Swedish Academy of Engineering Sciences (IVA). He is a member of several editorial boards of professional journals including Journal of Product Innovation Management, International Journal of Innovation Management, International Journal of Operations and Production Management.

Simon Croom holds an MSc and PhD degree from the University of Warwick, Coventry in the United Kingdom in the areas of management science and supply chain management. He is Associate Professor of Supply Chain Management and Executive Director of the Supply Chain Management Institute at the University of San Diego in the US. He is a member of the editorial board for the International Journal of Operations and Productions Management (IJOPM) and Associate Editor of the International Journal of Value Chain Management. He was the organizing chair for the 4th Worldwide Symposium in Purchasing and Supply Chain Management and has served on the boards of both the European Operations Management Association (EurOMA) and the International Purchasing & Supply, Education & Research Association

(IPSERA). He was awarded a Chartered Institute of Purchasing & Supply (CIPS) Research Fellowship in 2007 for his work in supply chain management.

Cipriano Forza holds an MSc and a PhD degree from Padova University. He is Professor of Management and Operations Management at Padova University where he serves as coordinator of the PhD course in Management and Engineering. He teaches research methods at the European Institute for Advanced Studies in Management (EIASM) in Brussels. He has been visiting scholar at Minnesota University, London Business School and Arizona State University. He serves on the board of the European Operations Management Association (EurOMA). He is associate editor of Journal of Operations Management and member of the editorial board of Decision Sciences. He acts as a reviewer for several professional journals (International Journal of Operations and Production Management, International Journal of Production Research, International Journal of Production Economics, Production and Operations Management, International Journal of Technology Management). He has participated in the international survey-based research 'High Performance Manufacturing' since 1990. He has been published in various journals including the Journal of Operations Management, the International Journal of Operations and Productions Management, the International Journal of Production Research, and the International Journal of Production Economics.

Chris Voss gained a BSc(Eng) at Imperial College London, and an MSc and PhD at London Business School. He is Professor of Operations and Technology Management at London Business School where he has also held the post of Deputy Dean. He previously taught at the University of Warwick, the Australian Graduate School of Management and the University of Western Ontario. Professor Voss was founder and for many years chairman of the European Operations Management Association, and is a fellow of the Production and Operations Management Society (POMS) and the Decision Science Institute. He currently is president of the POMS service management college and is on the editorial advisory board of a number of journals including the International Journal of Operations and Production Management, the Journal of Product Innovation Management and the British Journal of Management.

Pär Åhlström holds an MSc and a PhD degree from Stockholm School of Economics in Sweden. He is Professor of Operations Management at Stockholm School of Economics, Sweden and Research Fellow at IMIT, Institute for Management of Innovation and Technology. He is currently a board member of European Operations Management Association and a member of the Scientific Council of the European Institute for Advanced Studies in Management. His publications appear in, among others,

International Journal of Operations and Production Management, Journal of Purchasing and Supply Management, European Management Journal, Journal of Product Innovation Management, International Journal of Innovation Management, Technovation and International Journal of Services Technology Management.

Paul Coughlan is Associate Professor of Operations Management and Director of Postgraduate Teaching & Learning (Research) at the University of Dublin, School of Business, Trinity College, Ireland where, since 1993, he has researched, taught and published in the areas of operations management and product development. Previous academic appointments were at Aalborg University, Denmark, London Business School, UK, and University College, Cork, Ireland. He holds a PhD from the University of Western Ontario, Canada, and MBA and BE degrees from University College, Cork. He is President of the Board of the European Institute for Advanced Studies in Management, and a member of the Board of the European Operations Management Association. He is a Director of Magnetic Solutions Ltd., a Dublin-based process equipment manufacturer which started as a Trinity College campus company.

David Coghlan is a member of the School of Business Studies at the University of Dublin, Trinity College, Ireland and is a Fellow of the college. He has an MSc from University of Manchester, an SM from Massachusetts Institute of Technology, a PhD from the National University of Ireland and an MA from University of Dublin. His research and teaching interests lie in the areas of organization development, action research, action learning, practitioner research and doing action research in one's own organization. He is a member of editorial review board of Journal of Applied Behavioural Science, Action Research, Systemic Practice and Action Research and the OD Practitioner. His most recent books include *Doing Action Research in Your Own Organization* (co-authored with Teresa Brannick, 2nd ed. Sage, 2005; 1st ed. 2001), *Changing Healthcare Organizations*, (co-authored with Eilish Mc Auliffe, Blackhall: Dublin, 2003) and *Managers Learning in Action* (eds. D. Coghlan, T. Dromgoole, P. Joynt and P Sorensen, Routledge, 2004).

J. Will M. Bertrand gained an MSc and PhD at Technische Universiteit Eindhoven. He is a Professor of Operations Planning and Control at the Department of Technology Management at Technische Universiteit Eindhoven. He has held a visiting position at Rutgers University in the US and has worked in managing positions for ASM-Lithography and for Philips in the Netherlands. He has served as member of the board of the Dutch Society for Logistics Management (VLM), and has been director of education for the postgraduate school for design of Management Systems, and scientific director of the PhD Research Institute (Beta)at Logistics Technische Universiteit EIndhoven. He is member of the editorial board of the International Journal of Operations and Production Management and the International Journal of Production Research.

Jan C. Fransoo is a Professor of Operations Management and Logistics at Technische Universiteit Eindhoven in the Netherlands. He holds an MSc in Industrial Engineering and a PhD in Operations Management & Logistics from Technische Universiteit Eindhoven. Following the completion of his PhD Thesis, he was awarded a fellowship by the Royal Netherlands Academy of Sciences. He specializes in operations planning and supply chain management in the process and FMCG industries, and is part of the Eindhoven Retail Operations group. He also serves as Research Director of the European Supply Chain Forum, a collaborative effort with about 20 large multinational companies. Professor Fransoo held various visiting appointments at US universities, including Clemson University, Stanford University, and the University of California at Los Angeles. He serves as Senior Editor of Production and Operations Management, Associate Editor of Journal of Operations Management, and has published over 30 papers in academic journals such as IIE Transactions, Production and Operations Management, Journal of Operations Management, International Journal of Operations and Production Management and European Journal of Operational Research.

1 Introduction to the Book

Christer Karlsson

Chapter Overview

- This book is both a textbook and a reference. It is especially aimed at PhD candidates, master thesis writers and young researchers but also the more experienced researcher will find the wide scope of research approaches helpful
- The book can be used as a complete text on research methodology in operations management (OM) and adjacent areas, or for consideration of general research issues combined with deeper focus only on the specialized chapter with the most relevant method. It can even be a lexicon of all the main approaches to OM research, suitably contained in one text
- The subjects covered are characteristics of good OM research, planning the research project, survey studies, case studies, longitudinal field studies, action research, and modelling and simulation. The foundation is laid in chapter 2 with a discussion of what is research, what is good research and what is typical for research in the areas of OM. Chapter 3 focuses the research process, mapping existing literature and then addresses the choice of method or methods to deal with the research questions. Chapter 4 is about surveys using questionnaires, but also covers many general issues on sampling, validity, reliability and other issues common to all approaches. Chapter 5 addresses case research, both for studies with a few or multiple cases. The importance of rigour and how to achieve it in case research is underlined. Chapter 6 is on longitudinal field studies, in-depth studies of change processes inside organizations. Chapter 7 is on action research where the researcher enters the organization with the combined aim of making changes in the organization while studying it. Chapter 8 discusses modelling and simulation with the possibilities of analysing rather holistic perspectives and trying out 'what if' analyses—i.e. examining the effect of different managerial interventions. Chapter 9 is a

summary of the book. After considering what good research is, the reflections in this text conclude with thoughts about the ethics and morality of research

1.1 Introduction

The aim of this book is to be a comprehensive textbook and reference for how to do good research in the field of operations management (OM). First the book is intended as a core textbook for master and PhD students and young researchers. It is a comprehensive textbook and handbook for researchers in the field, giving basic knowledge about the different research approaches in the field. The primary focus of the book is to support PhD students in their first or second year of study as well as master thesis writers and students on higher-level courses that contain some research methodology.

However, the book is aimed not only at young researchers. More experienced researchers can benefit from a comprehensive description of all the most common research approaches in the field of OM. All the authors involved in this book have benefited from repeated acquaintance with each other's deeper knowledge in the different approaches. Several faculty members have sought to participate in the series of methodology seminars on which this book is based, indicating that not even faculty members can be expert in all of the wide range of research methodology knowledge represented here.

A particular problem, especially for PhD students and young researchers, is that many departments tend to specialize in one or few approaches to research, so they are not exposed to the breadth of possible research approaches. The book covers enough of each of the most important research approaches to allow students at least to practise different approaches and set them in relation to other approaches, but is not intended to be a specialized text on any single method or methodology. Thus it gives a platform, which few research settings can provide, to enable the individual researcher to choose appropriate and complementary approaches, as well as helping her or him to develop a stronger argument for their own research choices.

The subject of the book is the different research methods frequently used in studies on OM as well as adjacent applied management areas such as management of innovation and R&D, logistics, supply chain management, etc. Typical courses the title is intended for would incorporate the topics of research methodology and thesis writing. Typical course levels are final part of bachelor's programmes, master's programmes, and first or second year of PhD programmes.

1.2 How to Use the Book

The chapters of the book have a logical sequence but can also be used as stand-alone references. The second chapter is aimed at developing the reader's capability of enhancing the level of scientific contribution in her/his research and the skills in positioning the research. The third chapter gives a hands-on approach to planning a research project in a way that is 'complete'. Five chapters on different research approaches follow with descriptions, discussions and cases with references and analytical comments. Research tools are defined, described and demonstrated with examples. Substantial references to published articles and a brief bibliography are provided at the end of each chapter. At the end of the book you will find an index with subjects, issues and authors.

There are at least three different ways of using this book. Firstly, it can be used as a complete text on research methodology in OM and adjacent areas. Chapter 2 sets out to help with consideration of what research is, what it produces, issues to consider before and during conducting the research, and what is quality in research. Then the reader moves on to Chapter 3 to be assisted in planning the research and considering appropriate research approaches to use. Chapters 2 and 3 are intentionally written in a dialectic style with the purpose of helping researchers consider all of the issues in the research planning phase. Chapters 4 and following are more specialized in tone, with a less dialectic but still practice-oriented style. Chapter 4, in particular, not only describes survey research but also goes into detail regarding how research questions are formulated, how data is selected and gathered, and the important issues of validity and reliability. Subsequent chapters follow the same format, with different research approaches as presented in some more detail below.

A second way to use the book, especially for the reader who is already a bit into a project, with a main chosen method, can be to study the general parts and then focus only on the specialized chapter with the most relevant method. In addition, other chapters can be used as references, remembering the strength of combining approaches. Thirdly, the book can be a lexicon of all the main approaches to OM research, suitably contained in one text. Chapters are summarized with the most important points made in bullet point listing.

1.3 Plan of the Book

The subjects covered are characteristics of good OM research, planning the research project, survey studies, case studies, longitudinal field studies, action research, and modelling and simulation.

The logic of the structure is such that it should be fairly easy to navigate. The text is structured and formatted in a manner intended to allow searching and referencing and with a certain intended sequence of research methods.

The foundation is laid in Chapter 2 with a discussion of what is research, what is good research and what is typical for research in the areas of OM. A fundamental perspective here and throughout the book is that the key aim of research is to contribute by adding to existing knowledge. A second fundamental perspective is that research has to be of high quality so the reader can trust the results. Research needs and quality are discussed together with how to get research published and how to assess published research.

Chapter 3 focuses on how to plan a research project. It takes mapping of existing literature as a starting point in the research process, and then addresses the choice of method or methods to deal with the research questions. The quality dimension is taken further through a discussion of different aspects of validity.

Following the overview provided by Chapters 2 and 3, subsequent chapters deal with individual research approaches in specific detail.

Chapter 4 is about surveys using questionnaires, but also covers many general issues on sampling, validity, reliability and other issues common to all approaches. Because of this, Chapter 4 is important not only in itself, but also because of many fundamental issues valid across the subsequent chapters on specific approaches. As a starting point, it takes conceptualizing the research issue through the development of a theoretical model and discusses the unit of analysis and definitions. The reader is then taken through the steps of detailed research planning. Special attention is given on how to analyse and interpret data, further discussing validity issues.

Chapter 5 addresses case research, for studies with either a few or multiple cases. The importance of rigour and how to achieve it in case research is underlined. The importance of and approach to developing a research framework with clearly defined constructs and research questions is explained. Case studies should not be just visits to organizations. Precision is achieved through research instruments and protocols. The analyses should be well structured and systematic. Analysis can be both within case and across case analyses. A common result of case studies is generation of hypotheses and achieving this in a reliable manner is examined in some detail.

Chapter 6 is on longitudinal field studies, in-depth studies of change processes inside organizations. Longitudinal field studies are case studies but are distinguished by studying a phenomenon over time, in real time, often for extended periods of time. To gain access to organizations to conduct a longitudinal field study, it can be set up as clinical research, where the researcher participates in and studies organizational change. The chapter discusses how to design and execute a longitudinal field study, including some hints on the often laborious task of analysing longitudinal case data.

Chapter 7 is on action research where the researcher enters the organization with the combined aim of making changes in the organization while studying it. Hence there is a thorough discussion of what action research is, how it developed and how to plan it. It is often said that this is an approach for the more experienced researcher, which may be true, but younger researchers may also collaborate with a senior advisor in action research programmes. What skills are needed and how to actually do action research is discussed. How action research can contribute to knowledge and what should be thought of to achieve research quality and not just a study visit report are given special attention.

Chapter 8 discusses modelling and simulation with the possibilities of analysing rather holistic perspectives and trying out 'what if' analyses—i.e. examining the effect of different managerial interventions. The focus here is on quantitative models and causal relationships between variables of the model. These can be descriptive as well as prescriptive and are valuable in both understanding and solving OM problems. Setting up model-based quantitative research is described step by step and a practical example of model-based empirical research is demonstrated.

Chapter 9 is a summary of the book. That is if a very wide-reaching text book on research methodology can be summarized! Hence this is a brief summary of learning from the different chapters. The possibilities of generalizations of the text in this book into areas adjacent to OM are discussed. This is followed by overall reflections related to important basic values behind the book. One is on the strength of combining methods, methodological triangulation as it is called. Another is on the importance of doing high-quality research that is good in different ways. This is an expectation that society has of academic researchers. So, after considering what is good, the reflections in this text conclude with thoughts about the ethics and morality of research.

2 Researching Operations Management

Christer Karlsson

Chapter Overview

- What is operations management?

  - The OM field
  - The OM perspective and fields of research
  - Research issues and approaches
  - A European research focus

- Characteristics of good operations management research

  - The aims and scope of research
  - Concurrent markets of academia and practice

- Research as contribution to knowledge

  - The concept of knowledge
  - Existing knowledge and research contribution
  - From exploration to knowing how and why
  - Creating and developing knowledge
  - Research outputs and knowledge contribution

- Building the research contribution

  - Starting with the intended contribution
  - Reverse logic
  - Building the chain of evidence
  - The problem–method–contribution fit
  - Value of the contribution—generalizability
  - A comprehensive view on contribution

- Research needs and quality

  - The concept of research quality
  - Contingencies in demands on research

- Research ethics and ethics for researchers

- ○   What are ethics and morals?
- ○   Ethics for researchers

- Characteristics of good research presentation

  - ○   Different media, their value and quality
  - ○   How research texts differ from other texts
  - ○   Common characteristics of good presentations

- Getting published

  - ○   Academic publishing
  - ○   Targeting the publication
  - ○   Publishing process
  - ○   Writing the manuscript
  - ○   Review process and editing

- Analysing research and research contribution

  - ○   Reviewing research
  - ○   The role of external assessments and reviewing
  - ○   A tool for reviewing research

- Summary
- References and bibliography

This chapter deals with the meaning of research, how it contributes to theory and practice, why is research done and what is good research. It examines the fundamental standpoint that research aims at the creation and development of knowledge. The aim of this chapter is to establish a context for the theme of the book through discussions of what is meant by research and what is the area of operations management (OM), as well as what qualifies as good research. The chapter deals with fundamentals of research concepts and philosophies addressing mainly the potential, new or early-stage researcher. As such it is an introduction to research and to how to do research. However, the concerns of experienced researchers and professionals are also addressed in relation to the contributions of research and how quality is assessed.

2.1 What is Operations Management?

Research in OM addresses issues relevant both for academics and practitioners. Hence OM research can contribute to the knowledge of academics and development of the field as well as to the knowledge of practitioners and development of skills in managing operations. In this section we will give a very brief introduction and overview of the field of OM and the research. One aim is to establish a common frame of reference for the area in which we will discuss how to do research. Another aim is to consider in what way research methods applied to OM are also useful in other areas with similar characteristics.

2.1.1 The Operations Management Field

Operations are the way in which products, that is, goods and services are produced. Operations are a transformation activity: transforming resources convert inputs into outputs. Within this general definition we all perform operations and operations go on all around us. Operations take place not only in manufacturing but also in sales, services, administrative processes and much more. Hence, what is described in this book is applicable to many functions in an organization. However we often take a starting point in the production function, either of goods or services.

What then is OM? There is a strategic part putting operations in the context of a business and developing the strategy for the operation. There is then a resource creation and organizing part. Financial, physical and human resources are accessed to build a production system with resources to transform the inputs. Designing the production system involves organizing these resources in ways that will give the production system desired characteristics. A management system controls and audits the transformation system and also assesses and continuously improves it.

There are some characteristics of the OM field that influence how we deal with it. It is an applied field with a managerial character. It deals with issues and problems encountered in the so-called real world. It is cross-disciplinary drawing on disciplines such as economics, finance, accounting, organizational behaviour, marketing, mathematics and more.

If OM uses these different disciplines, is it then a 'necessary' or even separate field of research? The answer lies in the fact that our cross-disciplinary approach in itself creates and defines an area and where our concepts have relevance and value. About one third of the activities of the leading management consultancy firms in the world deal with OM. The focus on operations not only creates a discipline in itself but also new perspectives. A large area of supply chain management comes from an integrated perspective of internal and external operations; broadening the view of managing material flows has lead to logistics; and focusing operations has resonated with the resource-based view in strategy.

As researchers in the field we have concurrent customers. We direct our results not only to the academic world but also to practitioners. We are out there studying operations in the commercial world looking for best practices and new patterns out of which come new models for management.

2.1.2 The OM Perspective and Fields of Research

Research in OM covers many issues and is carried out using several different research approaches. Although there is some correlation between the issues and the research approaches it still leaves us with high and, sometimes, confounding variation within the field.

The scope of OM is wide, based on the perspective of operations as transforming resources. First there is the strategic perspective focusing on the role of and the objectives for the operations function. An important aspect here is how operations are related to and play a role in the mission of the organization. This leads to a strategy for operations and for how the operations help the firm to compete on the market. Operations systems are designed concurrently with the products that the operations system is supposed to produce. Here, design of the system will include external systems in procurement and distribution. Design involves planning information and material flows as well as physical layouts and choice of process technologies for the transformation activities. Operations design also involves designing an organization, its processes and structures, and staffing it with human resources. There is a need to choose and develop planning and control of capacity, inventory, and transformation activities in the internal as well as the external production system, and to design and build different support systems for quality assurance, system maintenance and system improvements.

An important contribution is that there are operations and thus OM in almost any function of a business or organization. The resources that are gathered, structured, processed and controlled can be human, material or information and they may appear in organizational units dealing with marketing, manufacturing, after sales service, financial control and so on. Hence, most of the research methods dealt with in this book apply to most of what goes on in organizations.

In each of the areas we find research on different issues conducted with different research approaches and with the perspectives from different disciplines. There are surveys with questionnaires and interviews, there are single and multiple case studies, there are longitudinal field studies, there is action research, and there is modelling and simulation. We address each of these important research approaches in the following chapters of this book.

2.1.3 Research Issues and Approaches

To understand the issues and approaches in OM, we first take a historical perspective. A striking observation when looking into the documented history of research in OM is that the history seems to be short. It is often argued that the history started around 1980, with the inauguration of the *Journal of Operations Management* in the US and the *International Journal of Operations and Production Management* in the UK (Voss, 1995; Filippini, 1997). Another frequently held view is that the history of OM started with Taylor (see for instance Chase, 1980). In more recent times, an important event was the start of the manufacturing strategy field by the publishing of Skinner's (1969) seminal article *Manufacturing: missing link in corporate strategy*. Let us undertake a brief overview of fields and approaches. The aim is not to give a precise description of the development of OM but rather to give some ideas about what issues are dealt with and in what ways.

For the 1980s very similar research agendas were put forward both in the US and in Europe. Main areas were labelled operations policy, operations control, service operations, productivity and technology, and quality (Miller and Graham, 1981; Voss, 1984). Later surveys of the focus of OM research in the 1980s listed production planning and inventory control, purchasing, facilities, product and process design, process technology, job design, work organization, organization structure, management of technical change, maintenance and reliability, quality control, work measurement, manufacturing policy, cost estimation, systems approaches, physical distribution and service operations as most common fields of research. The pattern was similar in both Europe and the US (Voss, 1995). From the 1980s to the 1990s less attention was paid to inventory control, aggregate planning and forecasting. Purchasing received less attention although to some extent replaced by supply chain management. Strong growth areas were strategy and quality (Filippini, 1997).

In contrast research approaches differed between the US and Europe. An overview of 1980s research papers found that the most common approach in the US was modelling followed by simulation, conceptual, survey, and case and field research. In contrast in Europe the most common were conceptual studies followed by field, survey, case, modelling and simulation methods (Voss, 1995; Karlsson and Åhlström, 1998). For the 1990s in the US a tendency of less modelling and simulation and more survey and conceptual studies could be seen (Filippini, 1997).

In this book we cover the most common approaches to OM research. However, there is a particular focus on what could be called European OM research style. Hence we start with surveys and continue with case studies, longitudinal field studies, action research and conclude with modelling and simulation.

2.1.4 A European Research Focus

The history of thought in OM (Karlsson and Åhlström, 1998), since World War II, has been heavily influenced by the US. The 1970s saw the development of a strong quantitative orientation towards production and material control problems (Buffa, 1980; Chase, 1980) This quantitative orientation also influenced European ideas and practices in OM, especially since American textbooks, i.e. mostly Buffa, were used both in academic courses and as reference texts for managers.

However, there were new ideas coming out of Europe, which influenced the rest of the world:

- Work organization and worker conditions had been important in Europe, at least from the Industrial Revolution and maybe even earlier.

This focus had been the basis for many important contributions, most importantly socio-technical systems theory (Trist and Bamforth, 1951), which still influences production system design and work organization, among other things

- Although referring mainly to general management, the concepts of organic and mechanistic systems of management (Burns and Stalker, 1961) also had implications for operations

- The contingency theory school, which developed in the mid-1960s, was a major new way of thinking in European management. A clear link with OM was the classic work of Woodward (1965) who addressed different aspects of production management and technological contingencies in production organization. Some issues included span of control, separation between line and staff, organizational levels, organizational consciousness, definition of positions and ratios of direct to indirect personnel

- The further development of contingency theory was influenced by the Aston studies (Pugh et al., 1968). In a series of influential papers, a group of UK researchers investigated the relationship between an organization's technology and organization structure

- On the more technology-based side, group technology (Burbidge, 1975) developed simultaneously in the UK and the Soviet Union. Group technology opened a wide range of layouts and other aspects of production system designs between the functional and the product workshop

The focus on different issues and the difference in research approaches is to a large extent influenced by the academic setting. Academic organizations and their history are different in Europe compared with the US and even within Europe the history of academic organizations is different enough to form an important discriminating factor. One aspect of the academic setting is the existence in Europe of specialized organizations for higher academic teaching and research, for instance the German 'Hochschule' and the French 'Ecole Supérieure'. These schools are often translated as universities of technology or business schools within a university. However, the organizations are not to be likened to universities. In most cases, the intention has been to educate and train students to become elite practitioners. The organizations often focus on management, while universities focus on disciplines in the social and behavioural sciences. The degrees are equally difficult to translate. Master of science is frequently used for differently structured programmes that may be called 'Diploma' in German or 'Civilingenjör' in Swedish. The contribution of these specialized organizations to OM thinking in Europe has been considerable. Up to 1998, seven of the top ten contributing schools to OM conferences in Europe were linked with universities of technology (Karlsson and Åhlström, 1998).

Different schools of thought within OM have developed in different academic organizations. The European 'university of technology' has focused often on the needs of engineers in future managerial positions. Important subjects in the curriculum include production system design, layouts, production technology, the control of material flows, statistical quality control, allocation and utilization of plants and equipment, planning techniques, managing the production function, organization of line and staff in production, wage systems, productivity measures, product cost calculations, work organization and worker safety. Business schools within Europe have, on the other hand, focused on the needs of the general manager. Important subjects in the curriculum include investment calculations, product cost calculations and allocation and utilization of plant and equipment.

There are also many research institutes which add to the rich picture of OM in Europe. Applied research institutes are often closely connected to specialist universities (such as 'Hochschulen' in German). These institutes attract research funding as well as researchers who split their time between academic research institutions and the institutes. In addition to problem solving for industry, the research output is new knowledge, particularly on applications and implementation procedures, often developed through the deep insights gained through close contact with a few cases.

There are clear differences between OM research traditions in Europe and the US. These can be characterized along three dimensions: integration versus reductionism, qualitative versus quantitative, and people versus technology orientation (Drejer et al., 2000). In a categorization of research along these three dimensions, American research has often been based on large surveys of phenomena in industry with an effort to reach statistical significance and reliability. There are often narrow research questions that are studied in great detail. Methods are often quantitative with large databases. Although the research may focus on both technology and people issues there is a tendency to focus on observable identities such as tools and systems (ibid). In contrast, European research has often been based on the researcher working in or close to industry. Issues are often cross-disciplinary with a focus on the whole plant or worksite. The studies are often based on a small sample, are usually wide in scope and may be longitudinal. The outcome can be rather descriptive and hypothesis generating rather than hypothesis testing. The people dimension is quite important with focus on work organization and the workforce.

A further school of research is the Scandinavian approach, a subset of the European tradition (Drejer et al., 2000). It is typically conducted in small countries with small populations but with researchers even more integrated in organizations than elsewhere in the European. In the Scandinavian approach a very broad view of operations is taken in 'production systems' (ibid; Karlsson, 1996). It led to concepts such as 'the extended operations concept' and 'the manufacturing extraprise'. Another feature is the strong contingency view emphasizing that different production systems originated in different contexts. The research developed based on longitudinal field studies and clinical management research with the researchers developing academic knowledge and within-company knowledge simultaneously (ibid; Åhlström and Karlsson, 1996).

It is with a focus then on the general European and the particular Scandinavian approach that this book is written. Further, with the aim of serving all OM researchers there is a clear focus on integrative rather than reductionist perspectives, qualitative in addition to quantitative approaches, and a considerable focus on people along with technology.

2.2 Characteristics of Good Operations Management Research

The aims of research in OM are often related to good practice. The close connection to practice makes relevance a major criterion for good OM research. Since research also needs to contribute to the academic world in OM research, we often face the problem of concurrent needs for practical relevance and academic contribution.

Another fundamental characteristic of good research is that there is significant contribution to knowledge. New knowledge may be significant in different ways. Typically research contributions consist of additions to pre-existing knowledge. Research results can also be more or less significant in terms of their size of contribution to theory or to practice. For example results may deal with phenomena not previously observed, or they may contradict earlier knowledge. An important factor is the potential value that can be created when applying the research results. This factor has particular importance in applied areas such as OM. Results may be related to and will have to take into account the extent to which they apply to industries, maturity or size of the organization and geographical or cultural setting.

The choice of target group has particular significance. At whom are the contributions to knowledge aimed? There is a range of targets from the individual firm to OM practitioners, and OM researchers as well as other management researchers and policy makers. A common risk for the young researcher is to formulate the aim and research questions too generally and not to frame a researchable question. But there is also an alternative risk, of being too narrow. For example, the problem may have no general value beyond the studied case. Solving a specific problem for an individual organization using existing well-established knowledge may be of limited value to both the research community and to the practitioner community. It risks being consultancy rather than research.

The generally thought of most significant characteristic of good research is that, methodologically, it is well done. Research is expected to provide trustworthy knowledge since it is done by independent knowledgeable scholars trained to develop knowledge using rigorous processes. The quality of research is dealt with in section 2.4.

2.2.1 The Aims and Scope of Research

The aim of research is the creation and development of knowledge and the output is contribution to knowledge. Research output is published and presented mainly in the form of research articles in professional scientific journals, as well as in books, especially anthologies and more applied texts. Student textbooks seldom contain previously unpublished knowledge but may combine and transfer pre-existing knowledge in new and accessible ways.

Research may have different purposes; in broad terms confirmation, falsification and exploration. Often the initial thought of purpose would be confirmation. Building on existing research is one obvious path to follow. Previous findings may be confirmed in other organizational, industrial, technological or cultural settings. One reason for choosing confirmation may be a quest for finding truths. Another reason may be that OM research models are often based in the natural sciences with facts based on physical phenomena. However, general truths are hard to reach in behavioural research. The second purpose, falsification, offers many more opportunities. While confirmation will need a rather extensive study, falsification only needs to identify the rejection of the earlier hypothesis or theory. This is not to say that it is easy to achieve falsification but there are many alternatives in studying different activities, business environments or cultures. The third purpose, exploration, offers endless opportunities. There are always issues and problems from different empirical situations that have not been studied before. However the researcher should ensure that the research contribution is substantial and not too specific to one unique situation.

2.2.2 Concurrent Markets of Academia and Practice

A challenge for the OM researcher is to create contributions and value for both academia and practice. This challenge will promote the often empirically based research approaches used in OM. The field of OM to a large extent deals with applied and cross-disciplinary issues and research is often carried through in close relation to industry. However, practice should be seen in a wider perspective than the firm. OM research has potential to contribute on many levels: society, industry, organization, group, individual.

Even if researchers in OM face a quest for contributions both to the academic and to the practitioner's world, the degree and extent of involvement in practice may vary substantially from gathering data to taking action. For example, there are low degrees of involvement when mailing questionnaires or modelling processes on a computer. With interviews there is somewhat more but still a small amount of interaction. Staying a bit longer in the field observing what is going on in practice enables observations, which may be more or less participative and longitudinal. The researcher may even intervene, taking on a helping and treating role in relation to the studied object, leading to a clinical approach. The researcher may have an objective to improve the studied object and, so, engage in action research. Furthermore the researcher may create, possibly together with an organization, a set up for experiments and a laboratory. Eventually the researcher may build and run the studied object himself.

The role of the researcher is, however, not limited to supplying the markets of academia and direct practitioners. As well as the basic roles of research and teaching, researchers are responsible for the dissemination of their research output. In addition researchers are increasingly expected to discuss knowledge and to develop it together with users. Knowledge should be interpreted together with practitioners and implications developed. Researchers are expected to participate in 'next tier' activities. For example, through research parks, incubators and other organizational forms, researchers are increasingly required to observe and facilitate knowledge becoming action.

The demand on universities and, correspondingly, their demand on researchers are increasingly rooted in the economic context of the research. Increasingly, universities are requested to contribute to economic growth in general as well as regional development. Research funding applications now include a section on relevance in terms of possibilities for commercialization. This requirement derives from shorter development time scales for impact in industry and, in particular, leads to shorter cycle times in research.

2.3 Research as Contribution to Knowledge

In the previous section the role of research has been defined as the creation and development of new knowledge and the value of research as the contribution it makes to academia and practice. The concepts of knowledge and contribution, and the types of contribution, will now be discussed.

2.3.1 The Concept of Knowledge

The concept of knowledge is complex. It is not the purpose of this book to examine it in depth, and there is a whole range of literature on knowledge and knowledge management. However, a shared understanding of what is meant by knowledge is needed to discuss contribution to knowledge in the context of researching in OM. A few definitions of knowledge provide some perspectives. 'Knowledge is information that has been organized and analyzed to make it understandable and applicable to problem solving and decision making' (Turban, 1992). 'Knowledge consists of truths and beliefs, perspectives and concepts, judgment and expectations, methodologies and know-how' (Wiig, 1993). 'First, knowledge, unlike information, is about beliefs and commitment. Knowledge is a function of a particular stance, perspective, or intention. Second, knowledge, unlike information, is about action. It is always knowledge to some end. And third, knowledge, like information, is about meaning. It is context-specific, and relational' (Nonaka, 1995). There are many other ways of defining and classifying knowledge. A popular classification in the management area has been the distinction between tacit and explicit knowledge. To some extent one can say that theoretical development in research is about explicit knowledge while the practice involves considerable tacit knowledge.

More distinct perspectives can be found by going further back in history to classical philosophers such as Socrates, Plato and Aristotle. First the distinction between knowledge (*epistêmê*) and craft or skill (*technê*). Episteme or knowledge is built on rational formula or 'logos'. Techne or skill or craft can be called the know-how. An individual can have knowledge without skill or skill to do something without the (theoretical) knowledge. One may know the law of impact but not possess the skill of playing snooker, or the possess skill of playing snooker without knowing the law of impact. Having distinguished craft from scientific knowledge, Aristotle also distinguishes it from virtue (*aretê*) or attitude. By virtue Aristotle meant the attributes, attitudes or basic values of an individual. One may have different approaches to the same thing. Playing soccer one may be a defender or an attacker. Different value systems will guide different behaviour, for example risk aversion or entrepreneurship. If these three dimensions can exist to any extent with or without the existence of the other one can say that they are orthogonal. But the existence of each of them will contribute to the competence of the individual. Hence, competence is a more general term and can be said to consist of knowledge, skills and attributes.

2.3.2 *Existing Knowledge and Research Contribution*

Contributing to knowledge requires that there is an existing field of knowledge to contribute to. To qualify as a contribution the candidate knowledge shall not have been published anywhere in any respected publication. Thus it is necessary to know what has already been published. Early on, the research must include a careful scan of the existing published knowledge. There are of course at least two more reasons for this scan. One is that the research literature gives inspiration to research issues and in many cases contain suggestions for further research beyond what has been studied in the individual study. Another reason is that a lot can be built on and used, such as constructs, research protocols and references to other relevant literature.

The scope of the field of OM knowledge is almost unlimited. There are different kinds of issues and different perspectives on the area, for example, in operations strategy, management, or control. There are disciplines that support OM research such as finance, organizational behaviour, or control theory providing different perspectives. With the development of knowledge production and ease of access over the Internet, relevant areas have had to be narrower and the knowledge limited to 'most relevant'. Nevertheless it is a requirement to cover all relevant adjacent knowledge when scanning the literature. The next chapter will discuss how to do a relevant mapping of existing literature depending on the research issue.

That the result of the research is supposed to contribute to existing knowledge does not mean that it has to be a major breakthrough. In the global world of knowledge production, most contributions are, in practice, minor. So what is then the size or scope of a contribution?

An important measure of a contribution is how general it is, either in theory or in practice. A theory that applies to many situations is of higher value than one specific to one situation. A model that applies to many concrete situations is more valuable the more general the situation is. Here is a special challenge in the kind of research that OM represents. It may be difficult to generalize at all outside the studied objects. There are many external and internal factors to control for. The study may have been made in certain industries, countries, cultures, economic situations, competitive situations and so on. Further, rather than generalization based on statistical evidence, the researcher will often have to make analytical or theoretical generalization, which will be discussed later under basis for claims.

2.3.3 From Exploration to Knowing How and Why

When contributions to existing knowledge are produced, the field expands and matures. The knowledge base becomes more solid and gradually different development patterns can be observed. Seeing new knowledge as contributions also acknowledges that knowledge is cumulative. Even when new knowledge is destructive of or contradicts existing knowledge, the total knowledge area is expanding. Studies that show that what was expected (hypothesized) could not be demonstrated also add to existing knowledge. It is said that Edison, when criticized for a thousand unsuccessful experiments before eventually he succeeded, responded by saying that they were not mistakes, 'I demonstrated what did not work and why'.

Developing knowledge in a field may go through different phases depending on the volume and maturity of existing knowledge. With little to base the theoretical development on, the study will by necessity take on an explorative character. Hence early phase research will often be explorative. A warning can be issued here. If an issue or problem is defined in too specific a way the field will seem to be little researched. However, the possibility of generalization may be meagre and the result will have little scientific or practical value. Such a narrow definition may signal that the researcher needs to study the area more.

After many explorative studies with different perspectives and approaches, a base or platform identifying components of the field emerges. An increasingly better description of the field is created by more systematic studies covering the explored area. More complete coverage of the field emerges and the research can be said to have entered a descriptive phase. Descriptive research results will typically identify components, patterns, systems and structures.

Good descriptive research creates a good foundation for analytical research.

Analysing the relations between the pieces starts with a good understanding of components and structures in the field of knowledge. Analytical research finds correlations between variables and identifies how independent variables influence dependent variables. Findings will typically be of the contingent, if–then, character.

Good analytical models create understanding of how one condition or variable will cause a certain effect. The ability to synthesize develops as causal analyses suggest what causes what. If contextual variables and different background variables can be controlled for, there is a possibility of foreseeing and forecasting what will happen in certain situations. Eventually the researcher may produce normative models and give advice.

A major reason for discussing the sequence of knowledge development based on a cumulative perspective is that attempts to do all in one study contain considerable risks. To explore an area, build an analytical model, conclude on causal effects and eventually provide a set of recommendations may not be possible within a limited scope, given the pattern of knowledge development. Research should typically explore before being able to describe a field of knowledge, know the components before understanding the relations, and know the relations before foreseeing the effects.

The cumulative and sequential development of knowledge creates one possible basis for a classification of knowledge: know what, know how and know why. Research will initially ask questions about what is in the area. With more knowledge the researchers will try to find out how it is and eventually ask why is it so; what causes this?

2.3.4 Creating and Developing Knowledge

In conducting research the researcher should consider also that there are different levels of knowledge. A comparison may be made with the educational system where the same areas may be studied at different school and university levels so increasing the individuals' understanding and skills with the help of analytical tools and theory. The empirical base may contain data, information and knowledge. Data (from *datum*, something given) are those facts that can be gathered and for which there are measures. When data are put in a system or context they create meaning and form information. With information somebody can be informed or enlightened. The information can then be put into a context and used and, so, add experience. This experience enables an interpretation of the information, its applicability, effects and other strengths and weaknesses. Knowledge is developed as a result.

The knowledge development process does not have to proceed with the classic conceptual and theoretical development followed by empirical studies. In 'grounded theory' the researcher starts with collecting data and then tries to find categories in a process called coding. The categories can then be given properties. This enables conceptualization, which allows the researcher to define different phenomena he wants to study and discuss. The developed knowledge gives a framework for describing and mapping knowledge. Complex structures of concepts can now be built, which can be used for the research. These built-up structures of concepts may be called constructs and can form a base for know-what research.

By considering the concepts or constructs in relation to each other the possibility for analysing data and information emerges. In analysing the pieces in terms of concepts and constructs the researcher looks at patterns and how the pieces are related to each other. This exploration opens the possibility for understanding but also a first level of concluding. After breaking down the knowledge one may also find new ways of putting the pieces together in a process called synthesizing. A way of doing this is to create a model in terms of a representation of a more complex reality. If a model with general validity can be created it may embody a theory in terms of a systematic statement of principles. A basis for know-how research has been reached. It may, for example, say something about how things work.

An understanding of how things work provides the possibility of studying cause–effect relations. The developed model of how things work may form the base for hypotheses on what causes what, where the researcher will look for if–then relations. This hypothesizing opens the possibility for normative conclusions and recommendations. In practice, not actually knowing the causal relations does not always hinder individuals from drawing normative conclusions from just correlations, but this is another discussion. With causal knowledge, a know-why level of knowledge is reached.

2.3.5 Research Outputs and Knowledge Contribution

Because of the cumulative character of knowledge and the sequential development of the field discussed above, different research outputs in different phases of the development of the field of knowledge will be seen. A common picture of this is that a research project will start with collection of facts without prior assessments of them, then an analysis of those facts, then generalizations from them, and eventually tests of those generalizations. However, as Hempel (1966) pointed out, this is both a too narrow and restricted inductive view of scientific research. In reality the researcher will have to define a problem or issue and collect 'relevant' data.

In the early phase of development of a field or area of knowledge characteristics of the explored phenomenon will be observed. Explorative research will be done and there will be results in terms of concepts and constructs, classifications and definitions. These may be, for example, transforming and transformed resources, production technology, supply chain, or operations strategy. Then there will be descriptions of phenomena in the area. Descriptions and overviews of patterns and structures will emerge. Research results may take the form of production systems, production control systems, procurement functions, or production organization structures. Further on the researcher will develop models explaining how components are related to each other. Research results in the form of analytical models may, for example, explain how the flow of material can be controlled, how quality can be measured and audited, how the supply chain can be managed and how to promote innovation. This will enable the researcher to build models which managers can use for understanding the production system and taking informed decisions. Continuing the logic, through causal studies the researcher should eventually reach normative knowledge. He will understand causal effects and be able to foresee effects of different actions/measures. For normative knowledge, the typical research outputs could include handbooks with checklists and other kind of tools for implementation in practice. In reality this final outcome is hard to achieve with reasonable validity. Therefore, case-based research uncovering causal relations in specific situations is more likely to take place. Typical examples could be Toyota Production System or Lean production, Six Sigma, or even scientifically more doubtful books such as Built to Last or In Search of Excellence. This is not to say that such books do not have great impact. On the contrary, as we see in executive education for example, spectacular well-known cases have greater impact than well-grounded theory.

2.4 Building the Research Contribution

The key task in doing research is to make the contribution. Going through a number of steps of building the research contribution will facilitate the process of generating knowledge through research. The discussion here will be conceptual while the issue of planning the research project will be dealt with in Chapter 3. The logic and discussion in the next section of this chapter is illustrated in Figure 2.1. When we talk about research we often think of the right-hand side of Figure 2.1, a research report that is the outcome and final product of the research. It has a logical sequence starting with the problem and ending with the result. However, from the start we will take a holistic perspective of research and engage in iterative thinking and planning of the intended contribution and how will we get there through an analysis, what data will be needed, what method, the precise problem and the relevant existing literature as described in the left-hand side of Figure 2.1.

It is important that the researcher has a mental image of the end-point so that the research can be planned in a comprehensive way. This task can be compared with project management with its clear goal. The activities on the way that lead to the goal are thought through and the relations between them are considered. This does not mean that the researcher will have to or can stick to a detailed plan but the cohesiveness of the product and process will help and is paramount for quality. So think holistically and apply a 'logic of end to end' perspective.

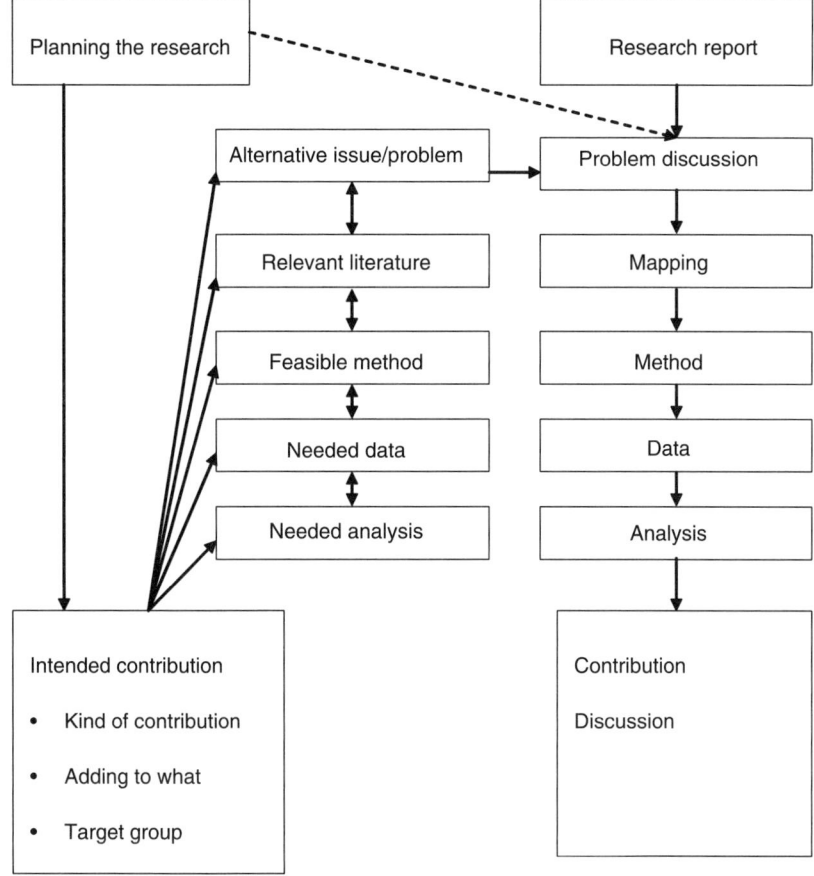

Figure 2.1 Building the Research Contribution.

2.4.1 *Starting with the Intended Contribution*

Since the researcher is supposed to create a contribution it is a good idea to start defining the intended contribution. The researcher may not know exactly what the contribution will actually be since that will depend on the outcome of the research. However, an aim is needed and can be expressed in a theoretical model, hypotheses, or other general outcome of the intended research: what approximately does the researcher envision as the final result or contribution? Furthermore what is this contribution supposed to do? Will it describe something, find clusters or characteristics, explain relations between something, or demonstrate causal effects from something? What kind of contribution is it? What existing knowledge is it that this contribution will add to? At whom is the contribution directed, what are the potential target groups? What kinds of results, conclusions and discussion of implications can be foreseen?

2.4.2 Reverse Logic

Starting with the intended research contribution it is practical to enter a form of reverse or backward logic considering what has to be done to reach the intended contribution (see the left-hand side of Figure 2.1). The contribution initiates demands on what to do and how to do it. It is not unusual that the intended research question has to be changed because of lack of empirical material or resources. When the researcher knows what he expects to contribute and to which existing knowledge base, he can start the more thorough mapping of the existing knowledge, analysing the areas of practice and research literature. He can then start to find the necessary or feasible way to achieve the knowledge development and plan a study or other effort, e.g. simulation, creating a reliable and robust way of doing the research (method), analysing methodology, and creating an empirical and/or theoretical foundation. He can also plan how to analyse, synthesize, conclude and set the contribution in the research field context.

2.4.3 Building the Chain of Evidence

An important aspect of research quality is that the reader can follow the logic of the study and report (see the right-hand side of Figure 2.1). The logic should ideally allow the reader to be able to repeat the study and come to the same results. This is not always realistic outside the natural sciences, but in OM researchers also have to make what is done and found trustworthy.

There are two important issues to deal with. First, that all the research steps fit together and that it is possible to see how one step follows the other. Second, that the elements of research created in each research step fit so that, for example, the available empirical material will suffice for answering the research question, that the analytical approach will give valid outcomes and so on.

Although when planning the research doing reverse or backward logic planning as described above is helpful, in the report the researcher will and should have a forward chain of evidence. A research report is expected to start with a problem discussion based on the relevant problem from practice and the theoretical formulation. Out of this discussion, the researcher should develop a clear problem definition, with reference both to practice and literature. Then there should be a thorough mapping of the literature to develop a picture of the relevant knowledge and gaps in the knowledge. The researcher should then be able to formulate the research questions. These may be explorative, hypothesis generating, or hypothesis testing, for example. In this connection one would expect a theoretical development resulting in a conceptual model of what will be studied. This model or framework will then be used in data gathering and analysis. This brings us to considerations of methodology. What should be studied and with what methods can the researcher do the study in order to achieve valid results. In reality the researcher will often find that he has to reformulate the research question here because of available resources but this may be or may not be seen in the final report. In the considerations of methodology it should also be made clear how the analysis is intended to be done. A discussion integrating the research question, the theoretical and empirical base, data gathering, analysis, and kind of expected results is especially expected here. Following this, the data and the analysis will be presented. Finally, after the analysis the synthesis can be made and conclusions can be reached.

To make the study repeatable and able to be followed, it is an advantage to separate data analysis and the creative thinking by the researcher in a synthesis. On the other hand research approaches such as action research are built upon an ongoing sequence of observation, analysis, and making changes so it is hard to separate the analysis from the synthesis. The sequence of analysis, synthesis and conclusions may not exactly fit all research approaches but should be seen as a general target. Details of the different approaches are discussed in later chapters.

2.4.4 The Problem–Method–Contribution Fit

Not all research questions can be answered by all research methods and one particular method can not answer all types of research question. A wish to find out about common practice in an industry is not well answered by an action research project in one firm and a mailed questionnaire survey may not give deep insight in causal relations in implementation projects.

There are some typical situations we may consider. We may want to study a rather unexplored issue. For that purpose we will search rather openly in available data in practice as well as in literature that can give meaning to the issue. We will identify patterns and come up with hypotheses or propositions or in the best of cases generate theory. An opposite situation and research aim is when we test more precise research questions and hypotheses. Typically large sample surveys by questionnaires, possibly triangulated with interviews, may be used to reach statistically significant validation or falsification of hypotheses. One approach is not in itself better than the other but there should be a fit between what we want to contribute, what study we should and can do and the formulated research aim.

The fit between problem, method and contribution is often reached in an iterative manner. It may turn out that the research question could not be answered with the available data and research resources, or data may be suitable for answering another and more interesting research question than was first defined. Often a research project, especially for a young researcher, will start with a given methodology. There may be a school of thought at the institution or there may be certain available data and nothing more.

The feasible type of research question and hence method is related to the advancement of the research field. Early stage research will be explorative and inductive while mature stage research will be focused and deductive (Edmonson and McManus, 2007). Developing the fit between research questions, methods and data can start with either. Conventional thinking may start in problem definition, followed by choice of method, analysis, synthesis and generated results. As an alternative, empirical studies may also start in the data and choosing it to enable sense-making and to theorize. The connections between the pieces in problem definition, method, data and conclusion give quality to the research (van Maanen et al., 2007). A prerequisite for getting it right may be that we are aware of our own view on epistemology and ontology, something we will discuss in Chapter 3.

2.4.5 Value of the Contribution—Generalizability

The desired outcome of the research is to reach a possibility of claiming that both the researcher and the reader have learnt something in general rather than only the particular researcher in relation to the particular situation. This means that the researcher will in some way or another generalize around what has been found. Generalizability is a standard aim in all research but will mean different things in different approaches and related research issues. In quantitative research generalization is achieved by statistical sampling. Adequate sampling will increase the representativeness of the empirical base and broaden the area for which the researcher can claim validity. The question is of course 'generalizable in relation to what?' Is it a matter of industry, organization size, geographical location, or what? In qualitative research the issue is different and sampling or selection of cases will have the aim of finding cases of particular interest for the research issue. The researcher can either do a purposive sampling if the research question is related to a certain population, or theoretical sampling finding cases that are specific in relation to the theory area the research is grounded in. Generalization can then be done by comparisons with similar cases and with theory in what is called analytical generalization. The demand for generalizability will vary with the perspective: if it is positivist there is an objective reality, if it is constructivist then that reality is socially constructed by interpretation. For more positivistic case studies there is some need for generalizability while interpretative studies have less such requirement. See further discussions in Chapter 3.

2.4.6 A Comprehensive View on Contribution

The ultimate criteria for assessing the research will be the value of the contribution and the quality of the research. The final part of a research report should discuss the contribution and relate it to earlier existing knowledge. It should also discuss the approach and qualities of the study. There are always limitations and shortcomings and it is important for the demonstration of quality that the researcher shows ability to discuss these issues.

2.5 Research Needs and Quality

Demands on research have many dimensions related both to content and form. Sometimes in the discussion of research quality there is only a focus on how well the study is done. However, the content and its relevance should not be forgotten.

A first question any producer may ask himself is if there is a need for the product and will it be demanded. For the researcher this means, does the OM research deal with issues that are important to operations managers or those involved in managing operations, and/or are the results valuable for the research community so that knowledge is taken forward and the results can be built on further. Even if the issue is of importance, the researcher should ask himself if this is an issue that needs to be or is suitable for research? The issue may be trivial and hence not needed, either by practitioners or by academics (except for the researcher).

Then there are all the questions about the form or how well the research has been done. Research quality will be discussed further in each chapter because what is good research is partly approach dependent. Here only some general aspects that are well known to readers of research methodology are mentioned. A deeper discussion of these concepts will be dealt with in the following two chapters on planning research (Chapter 3) and survey research (Chapter 4).

The reader should be able to evaluate if the research has been done in a reliable way. A general, but hard to fulfill aim, is that the reader should be able to repeat the study and see if the same results are achieved. This is of course much more difficult in behavioural sciences with their unique and con-textual specific cases than in natural sciences, but the principle is worth considering. At least the reader should be able to follow the text, understand the chain of logic and come to the same conclusions or at least understand how they are reached.

For these reasons a number of questions should be raised. One question is whether appropriate methods of data collection have been used? Another question is if appropriate methods of data analysis have been used? Are sound and logical conclusions derived and based on the data and the analysis? Are conclusions that are drawn and recommendations that are made thoughtful and reasonable given the study?

2.5.1 The Concept of Research Quality

The general criterion for research quality must be trustworthiness. There are four particular requirements used in social sciences that are of relevance to OM research: construct validity, internal validity, external validity and reliability. Construct validity means that the operational measures used to measure the constructs actually measure the concepts they are intended to measure. Internal validity means that the study actually measures what it is meant to measure and that demonstrated relationships are explained by the factors described and not by other factors. External validity means in a similar way that the results are valid in similar settings outside the studied objects. Reliability means that the study is objective in the sense that other researchers should reach the same conclusion in the same setting. In positivistic research this is important for stating that the study demonstrates 'the truth'. Hence reliability has become the most important criterion in many research communities. Other criteria concerning the quality of the research include systematic, rigorous, repeatable and ability to follow.

The ultimate objective is to be credible or trustworthy. The important question is if the research is done well or not. The role of a methodology section in a research report serves to describe how well the research is done and to convince the reader that he can trust the results. Sometimes methodology chapters seem more aimed at demonstrating that the author has read certain books on research methodology. The methodology section should not be a literature survey but should show that the research is done well. The utmost request is that research, irrespective of approach, is done with rigour. That requirement will be developed throughout this book.

Research quality also refers to value. How significant is the claimed contribution to the advancement of management knowledge, management skills or both? Is the contribution major or minor?

2.5.2 *Contingencies in Demands on Research*

Different research communities establish specific criteria for good research. In an early stage of a new academic area, researchers tend to borrow from more established areas. For example, with a background in factory management OM researchers have borrowed a lot from natural sciences. With a background in organizational behaviour and human resources they borrow from organizational studies in social sciences. Hence the approaches become dependent not only on the issues and problems of study but also on the different research communities. The research is credible to the extent that appropriate methods for the research aim and questions are used, that the research is rigorous in its execution, and uses appropriate methods for data gathering, analysis and drawing of conclusions.

2.6 Research Ethics and Ethics for Researchers

Doing research in a way that is technically of high standard is not enough. There are also ethical issues a researcher should consider.

2.6.1 *What are Ethics and Morals?*

Ethics refers to a system or code of morals. Moral means relating to, dealing with, or capable of making the distinction between right and wrong in conduct (Webster, unabbreviated dictionary). Ethical issues may always have been important but have been much more observed in a time of concerns about humanity, animals, environment and the whole earth.

2.6.2 *Ethics for Researchers*

Ethical issues for researchers deal with communicating benefits and risks, protection of identity, privacy, obtaining informed consent and much more (European Commission, 2007).

There are four areas where the European Commission has defined principles of research ethics for European research: the principle of respect for human dignity, the principle of utility, the principle of precaution and the principle of justice. Some of the important issues for the OM researcher may be the following.

Researchers should exercise strict requirements for consent procedures. Justification for involvement of vulnerable individuals or groups must be made. Data must be fairly and lawfully processed for limited purposes, and be adequate, relevant and not excessive, accurate, not kept longer than necessary, processed in accordance with the data subject's rights, secure and not transferred to countries without adequate protection. Each participant in a research project should be informed clearly of its goals, its possible adverse events, and the possibility to refuse to enter or to retract at any time with no consequences. Moreover, no inducement should justify participation in a research project (ibid). Although this principle is developed with research on individual human beings the same can be said for individuals and groups of individuals forming an organization. Especially in such situations it should be taken into account that not all individuals are able to understand a contract with such rules. An explanation in terms suitable for the targeted individuals should follow.

Researchers should exercise strict requirements for utility. The researcher must be able to prove that the benefit from the research justifies the burden put on the population. This is especially sensitive if the rights of human individuals are affected.

Researchers should exercise strict requirements for precaution. Each research project should be preceded by a careful assessment of predictable risks and burdens in comparison with foreseeable benefits for the subject to others. A specific issue is the issue of dual use, for example that a research output may serve for peaceful as well as aggressive aims.

Researchers should exercise strict requirements for justice. There should be an analysis of benefits sharing. Intellectual property rights issues should be considered, identified and inducements to research participants, empirical data sources and researchers justified. Compensation for negative effects on participants and issues of equality should be considered.

For these ethical considerations, with whom should the researchers contract and who will follow up on it? There are reasons why the researcher should make a contract with the world, humanity, environment and each concerned individual. There is a lack of contracting partners but each governing body, being it the university or the granting body should develop and demand a contract with at least some of the points mentioned above. Increasingly research granting organizations include articles on ethics in the contracts. For European Union projects refer to cordis.europa.eu.

2.7 Characteristics of Good Research Presentation

Being able to report on the research is of paramount importance to the researcher. One could claim that reporting is important to all studies but research has an extra strong requirement. It is well expressed by the old saying 'Publish or perish'. If you do not publish you do not exist! It is therefore important to learn how to get published. What is a good research report differs from discipline to discipline and from area to area but there are many common characteristics. The requirements are well established in each research community. The standards are also maintained through the peer review process.

2.7.1 Different Media, their Value and Quality

There are many media or channels through which the researcher can get publication including scientific journals, professional journals, edited books, business journals, research report series, conference proceedings and working papers. The most prestigious are leading scientific journals and the best professional journals. What determines the value of publication in the various media is to a large extent based on values in the particular research community, not least because of the review processes in which established researchers are reviewers. Important factors influencing value of publication are frequency of appearance in citation indexes or impact factors as well as whether they are included in the business press ranking systems. For the researcher the most academically valuable publication will generally be in scientific journals. Within them, as within the other channels, there is a more or less established hierarchy of values given to each publisher and specific journal. In the next sections there is a focus on journal articles as a medium, though most of the discussion is also relevant for other forms of publication. How to get articles published in scientific journals is then dealt with in detail in section 2.8.

2.7.2 How Research Texts Differ from Other Texts

Different publications have different purposes and target groups. The research paper has a particular aim in presenting and disseminating a contribution to knowledge to the academic research community in the respective field. The readers, and before that the reviewers, will ask questions such as what is the purpose of the research, what is the contribution and what does the author claim, how well is the claim supported, what is the theoretical framework and does the author know the area well enough, is the method adequate, is the report well structured and easy to follow, and is it well written? The criteria the reviewer will use are those established in the publication in question and in the research community. In this respect the researcher is in a different position from the journalist or novelist. The assessment criteria are much stricter giving little freedom for innovative forms of presentation.

2.7.3 Common Characteristics of Good Research Presentations

Some criteria regarding the form of the text are more or less common for all media. The report should be written for the reader, not for the author. Remember the target group and that the reader does not know any of the 'extras' from the project that are known by the author. This is one of many reasons why it is so important to regularly present outlines to colleagues in the university department or other organizational environment. A report is built up from many parts and it is important that the line all through the report is clear to the reader. See the former section on how to build a chain of evidence.

An aspect of particular importance in research reports is how the arguments are built. There are three sets of logic: deduction, induction and abduction. All three are built on the same three components or factors. One component is the rule. It is about how the world is structured and functions. It says that a precondition that can be observed implies a result or conclusion. A second component is a condition that has been empirically observed: the database or the research material. A third component is the result or conclusion. The three ways of arguing differ on where they take their starting point and how then the logic goes on. A deductive argument starts by taking a position in a rule, applying it to data to reach a conclusion. An inductive argument starts with something observed empirically, trying conclusions to find the rule. An abductive argument starts in the result or conclusion, testing rules to find out about the precondition. See Figure 2.2.

The difference can be demonstrated by the following brief example:

- Deduction:
  - Rule: With low flexibility in the production system we are not good at making to order

Logic of argument		
Components		
Rules	Observations	Results
Argumentations		
Deduction	Induction	Abduction
Rule	Observation	Result
⇩	⇩	⇩
Observation	Result	Rule
⇩	⇩	⇩
Result	Rule	Observation

Figure 2.2 The Logic of Argument.

- ○ Observation: Our production system has low flexibility
- ○ Result: Hence we are not good at making to order
- Induction:
  - ○ Observation: Our production system has low flexibility
  - ○ Result: We are not good at making to order
  - ○ Rule: The reason why we are not good at making to order is that our production system has low flexibility
- Abduction:
  - ○ Result: We are not good at make to order
  - ○ Rule: A reason why we are not good at make to order is that our production system has low flexibility
  - ○ Observation: Let us check if our production system has low flexibility

The three perspectives of deductive, inductive and abductive argument apply not only to the way text is built but also to the whole study and the research report.

Readability is important in scientific publications. The following questions address this criterion. Is the organization of the manuscript clear, is it well structured and is the flow of argument logical and clear? Is the language appropriate to the target group or groups? Note that in OM, researchers often address themselves to academics and practitioners simultaneously. How is the text style? Is it direct, fresh and thought provoking, and does it create interest in the reader? Is the length relevant in relation to the contribution and to the format and standards of the publication? How are different kinds of exhibits used? Are figures clear and explained in the text? Does the abstract give a good comprehensive summary of the report or does it only mention indirectly what the report is about? Does the title give appropriate information about the content and contribution of the report? How is the overall readability?

Following these standards for a report on research is important not only in getting the message through but also for being accepted in research publications. There is literature on how to write reports and it is helpful to learn from it. For the writer of academic journals and books, there are also standards from the publishers, normally available from the editor or the publication's website.

2.8 Getting Published

Getting published has always been important for a researcher and it is getting more so. The old saying 'Publish or perish' says most of it. I tend to say 'If you don't publish you don't exist', at least in the scientific community. But there are many more reasons than just being recognized. Publications and the quality of the publication weigh heavily in academic promotion both internally and when seeking new positions elsewhere. It is also an important factor in the popular ranking and hence earns points in the research assessments and accreditation processes that have become important for institutions. Regardless of all those systems, the personal satisfaction may be the most important. To see the article printed, to create a domain to be known within, and to have impact on other research and researchers is rewarding.

2.8.1 Academic Publishing

There are many outlets for publishing academic work but the most important and rewarding from an academic perspective is in scientific journals. International journals count much higher than local or regional ones. This may be unfair to researchers who do not have English as a mother tongue but it is difficult to get around. There are numerous journals at different levels and it may be difficult to choose. Indexes such as citation index and impact index give a good idea. A general classification does not exist but many institutions have A, B and C journals or similar lists. Consult your own organization.

A paper will often go through many stages. It may start as a working paper discussed at the department, be presented after development at some conference, be developed more and be submitted to a journal. Try to find a journal in which there is a reasonable possibility of being accepted but do not start too low. A good review feedback may help you to get in there or elsewhere later.

2.8.2 Targeting the Publication

To get published there are two basic demands, one of content and one of quality of research. Is the contribution significant enough and relevant for the channel and target group? Is the research quality up to the standards of the research community at which the publication is targeted? In addition to these general questions dealt with earlier, under research quality and common characteristics respectively, it is important to study carefully and analyse the publication policies of the potential publication.

Publications such as journals, books and reports series for academic research do have publication policies. Get hold of that before you design the manuscript. In scientific journals they are mostly published in the journal together with rules for submitting a manuscript and information about the review process. Normally there are specifications of target groups, type of contributions and styles of manuscripts. Sometimes there are calls for special issues and then there will be a special definition of the type of contributions expected. Note that special issues do not mean lower levels of standard for acceptance but the limited focus might make it easier to get in if the submitted manuscript fits within the scope.

There are, in addition, some practical points to follow to improve the chances of getting published. Read the publication policy carefully. There are many guidelines and following them will considerably increase the chances of publication. Study some of the published manuscripts. They are not all role models but they give a good idea of the standards and formats wanted. Read papers authored by members of the editorial board. It gives a very good idea of what they think is good research and what is publishable. Study their references to find out what is important for your literature mapping. Use references to members of the editorial board. With a more distinct plan, contact the editor or associate editor for your sub-area, find out about plans and additional policies or value systems carried by the editor(s).

When targeting, you should not only see the value of your contribution from your perspective. Journals want contributions that fit their mission and they have plans. Look out for announcements of special editions and editors attending conferences.

2.8.3 Publishing Process

There is almost always a long path from planning the paper to getting published. A good idea is to envision a few alternatives when planning the paper. Maybe when planning the research consider when and where this can be published. The following steps should be considered: which working papers should be written when, what papers should be submitted to which conferences and, eventually, what can be published in which journals? Planning the research is the issue in Chapter 3; here we will focus writing the paper for publication.

Before submitting the paper see to it that it is a complete paper with a theoretical chance of being accepted after development. Reviewers can get very annoyed if the author has not done her/his best. Test your own manuscript against how papers are reviewed. See section 2.9.

2.8.4 Writing the Manuscript

There are different kinds of papers. Most common are theory-testing and theory-development papers. Other alternatives may be conceptual papers, literature reviews, and papers on methodology. The focus in this book is on empirically based papers, either deductive, testing theory, or inductive, generating theory. However, this book does not focus on writing reports and dissertations; there is a whole range of literature specializing in that. Each of the following chapters on different research approaches discusses aspects of publishing that type of research. There are just a few general remarks on the writing here.

First, write about something interesting, not only to yourself, but to the target group. It should contribute new knowledge and have relevance. A good way to start is by writing a synopsis, which is the whole article in three pages or so. Test that there is a real problem or issue, a research approach that is relevant with an investigation model and plan, empirical data, a framework for analysis, a synthesis leading to the contribution and results that can be put in relation to existing knowledge. The title must be attractive and mirror the contribution.

In discussing the research problem or issue the author has to make clear that he knows what is already published, what he wants to contribute and why it is relevant. Mapping the literature does not mean a survey but analysing what there is that is relevant. Develop a clear aim for the paper. In the methodology section, remember that it is there to ensure the research is well done, not that the author has read all popular books on methodology. A fundamental principle is that the reader should be able to follow the article and trust the thought process. Therefore, it is often good to keep data, analysis, synthesis and conclusions separate. Finally check that conclusions are in line with the aim, explain the importance and relations to earlier research, discuss limitations and suggest further research. Before submitting the paper to any journal, have it reviewed by colleagues, discussed in seminars and, maybe, tested as a conference paper. Then the paper can be submitted.

2.8.5 Review Process and Editing

The first step in the review process will be an assessment by one or more editors, one of which may be an area editor. An area editor may cover a subfield or a geographical area. There are often also invited guest editors, especially for special issues. Many submitted papers are rejected at this stage. With the increasing pressure on researchers to get published and the globalization of management research it is not uncommon that first round rejections exceed 50%.

If the paper passes the first screening, it will go for a so called double-blind review, meaning that authors will not know the identity of the reviewers and the reviewers will not know that of the authors. Two or three established researchers may do the review and respond in anything between 2 and (in bad cases) 6 months. The editor will put the reviewers' comments together and hopefully comment on what has to be done and what may be done to the paper. There will be demands such as rework and resubmit, major revisions, minor revisions. Rarely the response will be 'publish as is'.

Then there is time for revisions. Take every comment from reviewers into careful consideration and do whatever sounds relevant. In most cases the reviewer will check what is done. Always go through each comment from the reviewer and write clear comments about how you have responded or why you have not. After resubmitting there may be another round if there are some minor issues, but ensure that you have done all that you can or you may be rejected.

Finally there will hopefully be a manuscript sent for proofreading. This may be a boring activity and has to be done in a few days but gives a sense of being close to fulfillment. It should be said that several journals have skipped this phase, relying on automatic typesetting.

2.9 Analysing Research and Research Contribution

In learning what is good for publication an effective route is to review what is already published and submitted for publication. The idea of studying published articles in the targeted publications has already been mentioned. But one can go further and systematically review them in the way they are reviewed in the double-blind review processes. The author has run a formal course in reviewing with his PhD candidates and sometimes masters students. It is of course also helpful to review own manuscripts in such a systematic way and even better to do it for each other in a group of researchers or students.

2.9.1 Reviewing Research

The aim of reviews is both to guarantee the published scientific material regarding quality and to contribute to the amelioration in the process from early manuscripts to publication. The standard approach is a peer review in which established researchers review submitted manuscripts. This may take place either in open, blind or double-blind processes. Many journals follow a double-blind review process as described in the previous section. In this way there is supposed to be a high level of integrity and independency. However, sometimes it is evident who the author is and a one-way blind or open process is used.

2.9.2 The Role of External Assessments and Reviewing

Reviewing manuscripts for scientific journals is a task and an activity that may not be taken lightly. It is a responsibility to the academic community to be an assessor of research quality. Research and research reports that do not have enough credibility must not be let through. At the same time it is a considerable and delicate job to assess in a short time the research and research report it has taken one or several researchers maybe years to complete. The reviewer should be tactful. Characteristics of the manuscript should be given. Strengths and weaknesses should be analysed and commented upon. Negative remarks should be mild and weaknesses should be followed by suggestions on how to improve (Lee, 1995).

It is the role of peer reviewers and editors to help advance the research and its quality. Scientific manuscripts are typically intended for circles, sometimes many, of continuous improvement. Many manuscripts submitted to journals will be accepted conditionally, accepted after revision, or rejected but accepted for resubmission after rewriting.

2.9.3 A Tool for Reviewing Research

Let us imagine we have a manuscript to review. A well-done review should contain both general aspects and careful examination. The general overview should bring up what has been discussed in quality of research and especially analyse the chain of evidence. Start with the title, the abstract, the aim, and then go to the end and see what the actual contribution is. Is there a fit on this level? If so, study the chain of evidence a bit closer. Is there a problem discussion anchored in practice and theory? Does it end with a clearly defined problem? Is there a solid mapping of the literature? Are research questions clearly stated? Is there a theoretical development of a research model? Is there a methodology discussion connecting the problem, research question, empirical data and form for analysis, so that the research approach is appropriate for the research question, the empirical data is sufficient for the empirical base, and the analysis is appropriate for answering the research question? Are data, analysis and synthesis/conclusion clear and distinct to enable external assessment? Do the conclusions answer the research question? These questions should be addressed in the general overview and then the reviewer can go into detail following the manuscript page by page.

Finally in this chapter there is a set of questions provided in Table 2.1 with the aim of helping researchers review their own or a reviewed manuscript, asking the most important questions. It may be a good idea to develop a proposal for a manuscript and ask colleagues to comment on these questions in relation to the manuscript.

2.10 Summary

- **What is OM?** Operations concern transforming human, physical and information resources into products and services. OM exists in and applies to all functional areas of a company or other organization. Research in OM draws on many disciplines and has become its own discipline. Research in OM has several perspectives and approaches beyond being just quantitative or qualitative. Perspectives and approaches vary with academic and other heritage
- **Characteristics of good OM research.** Research aims at the creation and development of knowledge. Research in OM addresses both

Table 2.1 Questions to Ask in Reviewing a Manuscript

Theory
Theoretical foundation
Are choices of theoretical foundations discussed regarding appropriateness?
Are all necessary and appropriate concepts included and discussed?
Are there concepts discussed but not later used? Why?
Conceptualization
Which are the key concepts and constructs? Which are the ones used in aim, research question, hypotheses, etc?
Are there theoretical definitions of concepts? There may be different ways of defining a concept.
Is the meaning of the concepts discussed?
Are the meanings of concepts used consistently?
Are there operational definitions of variables?
Are similar phenomena that could be included in the concepts discussed?
Are there similar concepts and definitions used by other authors with the same theoretical meaning?
Characters and consequences of aims and research questions
Which type of questions are the research questions and how can they be answered?
Is there a discussion of what it means to the intended contribution and the possibilities to do different kinds of generalizations?
Is there a discussion of what the research questions imply to delimitations of the study?

Method
Choices concerning methodological approaches
Are choices well described? Should be with analytical discussions, not only descriptions.
Are choices discussed and motivated in relation to aim and research questions?
Are the choices discussed and motivated in relation to alternative approaches?
Description of the research process
Are the different steps and the choices made in the different steps presented and discussed?
Choice of methods and techniques
Are chosen techniques for data collection and gathering discussed?

Empirical observations
Data matrix
Are the choices of indicators, variables described, discussed and motivated?
Alternative empiric
Are alternative data points, data sources, empirics discussed?
Data quality
Are the qualities of data in terms of credibility, trustworthiness, reliability, and validity discussed in an adequate manner?

Analysis
Analytical approach
Is the chosen way of doing the analysis in line with research question, methodological approach, and available empiric?
Transparency
Is the analysis easy to follow? Is it evident which part of the analysis aims at answering which questions and what answers are provided?

Exhaustiveness
Does the analysis cover all essential questions that are possible to respond to based on existing theory?
Is the available empiric used in a way to give exhaustive answers to the questions?
Are there motivations when essential questions are not discussed or the analysis is not exhaustive?

Conclusion and discussion
Generalizations
Are the conclusions logical and sound following the analysis?
Are conclusions generalized in a correct way?
Own theory
Do the conclusions and the discussions related to them relate to the theoretical model, framework and questions that have been stated?
General theory
Are conclusions and discussions related to them discussed in relation to existing theory and results from other studies?

Format and formalities
Figures and tables
Have figures and tables headings and explanations so they can be understood without reading the text?
Are figures and tables correctly designed?
Are figures and tables explained and discussed in the text?
References
Are references in the text designed in a correct way according to the publication?
Do all the references in the text appear in the list of references?
Is the list of references correctly designed according to the publication?
Language
Is it easy to follow the presentation and argument?
Is the text well structured?
Is the structure of chapters, sections and paragraphs linked so the reader can follow from paragraph to paragraph?
Is there a correct and consequent use of tense?

---

academics and practitioners. Hence there are often concurrent needs for practice relevance, and academic contribution. Research can have different aims such as exploration, confirmation and rejection. The degree and extent of involvement of the researcher varies not only with the research project but with the research approach. Research is increasingly expected to have economic impact

- **Research as contribution to knowledge.** Competence can be said to consist of knowledge, skills, and attributes. The result of the research should be to contribute to existing knowledge. This means adding something that was not known in the research community. Research can be explorative, descriptive, analytical, causal and normative, in relation to the state of existing knowledge. There are different levels of knowledge in terms of know-what, know-how and know-why. Results will be constructs, system descriptions, analytical models, forecasts and recommendations

- **Building the research contribution.** The key task in doing research is to make a contribution to knowledge. To plan the research apply a holistic and 'final logic' perspective on the whole research. Start with the intended research contribution and enter a form of reverse logic. There must be a fit between research issue, method, data and results. A chain of evidence should be clear. Make claims for generalizability and discuss forms of generalization. Check that the contribution matches the aim. Demonstrate the contribution by relating results to earlier existing knowledge
- **Research needs and quality.** A first question to ask is if there will be a demand for the research results? Will academics find it worth considering and will it advance knowledge? Will practitioners be helped in understanding and dealing with the issues they face? The key issue in research quality is that of credibility or trustworthiness. There are requests for validity and reliability. The demands vary with research approach. The research must be done rigorously (which is not rigidly)
- **Research ethics and ethics for researchers.** Ethics refer to a system or code of morals. There are ethical issues about humanity, animals, environment and the earth. Research ethics include respect for human dignity, utility, precaution and justice. Consider setting up a contract. It can be done with different stakeholders without necessarily meeting them, but be prepared to do so
- **Characteristics of good research presentation.** For many researchers it is 'publish or perish'. There are many outlets; international scientific refereed journals are the crown. Remember to make a contribution, not only a text. Logic of argument can be deductive, inductive, or abductive. Readability is important for reaching out
- **Getting published.** Plan for publication early during the research process. Target the publication or possible alternatives. Start by writing a comprehensive synopsis. That will make you think of the whole article. Repeatedly present to and get reviews from colleagues; use your research group or network. The review process will probably be long with several steps but getting published is worth the effort
- **Analysing research and research contribution.** Reviewing provides intensive learning on what is good research. This goes both for the reviewer and the submitter. Being accepted for review normally provides a lot of good critique that helps you develop your research. Reviewing is refereeing but also assisting in getting to publication. Peer reviews are of highest importance to guarantee the quality of research. Making good reviews is an obligation for members of the scientific community. Journals have schemes for reviewing; a lot can also be learned from them for submitters. Use checklists and maybe develop your own

References and Bibliography

Amoako-Gyampah, K. and Meredith, J.R. (1989) The operations management research agenda: an update. *Journal of Operations Management*, Vol. 8 No. 3, pp. 250–262.

Babbie, E.R. (1973) *Survey Research Methods.* Belmont: Wadsworth.

Bartunek, J.M., Bobco, P. and Venkatraman, N. (1993) Toward innovation and diversity in management research methods. *Academy of Management Journal*, Vol. 36 No. 6, pp. 1362–1373.

Becker, H.S. (1998) *Tricks of the Trade: How to Think About Your Research While You're Doing it.* Chicago: University of Chicago Press.

Bickman, L. and Rog, D.J. (eds.) (2000) *Handbook of Applied Research Methods.* Thousand Oaks, CA: Sage.

Boyatzis, R.E. (1998) *Transforming Qualitative Information: Thematic Analysis and Code Development.* Thousand Oaks, CA: Sage.

Buffa, E.S. (1980) Research in operations management. *Journal of Operations Management*, Vol. 1 No. 1, pp. 1–7.

Burbidge, J.L. (1975) *The Introduction of Group Technology.* UK: Heinemann.

Burns, T. and Stalker, G.M. (1961) *The Management of Innovation.* London: Tavistock Publications.

Campbell, D.T. and Stanley, J. (1966) *Experimental and Quasi-experimental Designs for Research.* Chicago: Rand McNally.

Campbell, J.P., Datt, R.L. and Hulin, C.L. (1982) *What to Study: Generating and Developing Research Questions.* Beverly Hills, CA: Sage.

Chase, R.B. (1980) A classification and evaluation of research in operations management. *Journal of Operations Management*, Vol. 1 No. 1, pp. 9–14.

Cochran, W.G. and Cox, G.M. (1957) *Experimental Designs* (2nd ed.). New York: John Wiley.

Cooper, H.M. (1984) *The Integrative Research Review.* Beverly Hills, CA: Sage.

Cooper, H.M. and Hedges, L.V. (eds.) (1994) *The Handbook of Research Synthesis.* New York: Russell Sage Foundation.

Crabtree, B.F. and Miller, W.L. (eds.) (1999) *Doing Qualitative Research* (2nd ed.). Thousand Oaks, CA: Sage.

Creswell, J.W. (1998) *Qualitative Inquiry and Research Design: Choosing among Five Traditions.* Thousand Oaks, CA: Sage.

Denzin, N.K. and Lincoln, Y.S. (eds.) (1994) *Handbook of Qualitative Research.* Thousand Oaks, CA: Sage.

Drejer, A., Blackmon, K. and Voss, C. (2000) Worlds apart?—a look at the operations management area in the US, UK and Scandinavia. *Scandinavian Journal of Management*, No. 16, pp. 45–66.

Dubin, R. (1969) *Theory Building.* New York, NY: The Free Press.

Edmonson, A.C. and McManus, S.E. (2007) Methodological fit in management field research. *Academy of Management Review*, Vol. 32 No. 4, pp. 1155–1179.

Eisenhardt, K.M. (1989) Building theories from case study research. *Academy of Management Review*, Vol. 14, No. 4, pp. 532–550.

Emory, W.C. (1985) *Business Research Methods.* Homewood, IL: Irwin.

European Commission (2007) *Ethics for Researchers—Facilitating Research Excellence in PF7.* Luxembourg: European Commission, Office for Official Publications.

Feagin, J.R., Orum, A.M. and Sjoberg, G. (Eds.) (1991) *A Case for the Case Study*. Chapel Hill: University of North Carolina Press.

Filippini, R. (1997) Operations management research: some reflections on evolution, models and empirical studies in OM. *International Journal of Operations & Production Management*, Vol. 17 No. 7, pp. 655–670.

Flynn, B.B., Sakakibara, S., Schroeder, R.G., Bates, K.A. and Flynn, E.J. (1990) Empirical research methods in operations management. *Journal of Operations Management*, Vol. 9 No. 2, pp. 250–284.

Gahan, C. and Hannibal, M. (1999) *Doing Qualitative Research using QSR NUD.1ST*. Thousand Oaks, CA: Sage.

Ghauri, P. and Gronhaug, K. (2002) *Research Methods in Business Studies: a Practical Guide*. Harlow, England: Pearson Education.

Glaser, B. and Strauss, A. (1967) *The Discovery of Grounded Theory: Strategies for Qualitative Research*. Chicago: Aldine.

Hedrick, T., Bickman, L. and Rog, D.J. (1993) *Applied Research Design*. Newbury Park, CA: Sage.

Hempel, C.G. (1966) *Philosophy of Natural Sciences (Foundations of Philosophy)*. Englewood Cliffs, New Jersey: Prentice-Hall.

Jorgensen, D. (1989) *Participant Observation: a Methodology for Human Studies*. Newbury Park, CA: Sage.

Karlsson, C. (1996) Radically new production systems. *International Journal of Operations & Production Management*, Vol. 16 No. 11, pp. 8–19

Karlsson, C. and Åhlström, P. (1998) The history of thought in operations management. *POMS Annual Conference*, conference paper.

Lee, A.S. (1995) Reviewing a manuscript for publication. *Journal of Operations Management*, Vol. 13 pp. 87–92

Marshall, C. and Rossman, G.B. (1989) *Designing Qualitative Research*. Newbury Park, CA: Sage.

Meredith, J.R. (1993) Theory building through conceptual methods. *International Journal of Operations & Production Management*, Vol. 13 No. 5, pp. 3–11.

Meredith, J.R., Raturi, A., Amoako-Gyampah, K. and Kaplan, B. (1989) Alternative research paradigms in operations, *Journal of Operations Management*, Vol. 8 No. 4, pp. 297–326.

Miles, M.B., and Huberman, A.M. (1994) *Qualitative Data Analysis: an Expanded Source Book*. Thousand Oaks, CA: Sage.

Miller, J.G. and Graham, M.A.W. (1981) Research in operations management: an agenda for the 80's. *Decision Science*, Vol. 12 No 4, pp. 547–581.

Nonaka, I. and Takeuchi, H. (1995) *The Knowledge Creating Company: How Japanese Companies Created the Dynamics of Innovation*. London: Oxford University Press.

Pugh, D.S., Hickson, D.J., Hinings, C.R. and Turner, C. (1968) Dimensions of organizational structure. *Administrative Science Quarterly*, Vol. 13, pp. 65–105.

Schatzman, L. and Strauss, A. (1973) *Field Research*. Englewood Cliffs, NJ: Prentice Hall.

Sieber, S.D. (1973) The integration of fieldwork and survey methods. *American Journal of Sociology*, Vol. 78, pp. 1335–1359.

Silverman, D. (2000) *Doing Qualitative Research: a Practical Handbook*. Thousand Oaks, CA: Sage.

Skinner, W. (1969) Manufacturing—missing link in corporate strategy. *Harvard Business Review*, May–June, pp. 136–145.

Strauss, A., and Corbin, J. (1998) *Basics of Qualitative Research: Techniques and Procedures for Developing Grounded Theory* (2nd ed.). Thousand Oaks, CA: Sage.

Sullivan, R.S. (1982) The service sector: challenges and imperatives for research in operations management. *Journal of Operations Management*, Vol. 2 No. 4, pp. 211–214.

Sutton, R.L. and Staw, B.M. (1995) What theory is not. *Administrative Science Quarterly*, Vol. 40, 371–384.

Swamidass, P.M. (1991) Empirical science: new frontier in operations management research. *Academy of Management Review*, Vol. 16, pp. 793–813.

Trist, E. and Bamforth, K. (1951) Some social and psychological consequences of the long wall method of coal-getting. *Human Relations*, Vol. 4, p. 1.

Turban, E. (1992) *Expert systems and applied artificial intelligence*. New York: Macmillan.

van Maanen, J., Dabbs, J.M., Jr., and Faulkner, R.R. (1982) *Varieties of Qualitative Research*. Beverly Hills, CA: Sage.

van Maanen, J., Sørensen, J.B. and Mitchell, T.R. (2007) The interplay between theory and method. *Academy of Management Review*, Vol. 32 No. 4, pp. 1145–1154.

Voss, C. (1984) Production/operations management: a key discipline and area for research. *Omega International Journal Of Management Science*, Vol. 12, No. 3, pp. 309–319.

Voss, C. (1995) Operations management—from Taylor to Toyota and beyond. *British Journal of Management*, Vol. 6, Special issue, pp. 17–29.

Wax, R. (1971) *Doing Field Work*. Chicago: University of Chicago Press.

Webster's New Twentieth Century Dictionary, Unabbreviated (1979). Simon & Schuster.

Whetten, D.A. (1989) What constitutes a theoretical contribution? *Academy of Management Journal*, Vol. 14, No. 4, pp. 490–495.

Wiig, K. (1993) Knowledge management: Where did it come from and where will it go? *Expert Systems with Applications*, Vol. 13, pp. 1–14.

Woodward, J. (1965) *Industrial Organization: Theory and Practice*. London: Oxford University Press, London.

Yin, R.K. (1981a) The case study as a serious research strategy. *Knowledge: Creation, Diffusion, Utilization*, Vol. 3, pp. 97–114.

Yin, R.K. (1981b) The case study crisis: some answers. *Administrative Science Quarterly*, Vol. 26, pp. 58–65.

3 Introduction to Research Methodology in Operations Management

Simon Croom

Chapter Overview

This chapter provides an introduction to the process of research. It addresses the basic questions and issues necessary when setting out to plan and design a research project. The chapter concentrates on eight core aspects of the research process:

- **An overview of the research process.** Much of the output of management research may seem to imply that the research conducted followed a clear, uncomplicated process. The reality is that this is rarely the case. Consideration is given to the 'messiness' and iterative nature of many research projects and programmes
- **The nature of operations management research.** Building on chapter 2, the focus is on 'positioning' research, that is, understanding the influences and implications of a research project within the context of the field as a whole
- **Structured literature review.** Understanding the role of the literature in shaping the research process and specifically exploring useful tools, techniques and methods for conducting and developing a cohesive and comprehensive literature review
- **Research methodology**. Understanding the philosophical and conceptual considerations in the choice of research perspective and the nature of research and the researcher
- **Qualitative and quantitative methods.** An overview of the nature of each category of method
- **Methods.** A discussion of the more common methods serving as an introduction to the methods examined in this text
- **Positioning OM research methods.** Provides an understanding of when to use certain methods and methodologies
- **Ensuring quality and evaluating your research.** Validity and reliability are critical concerns for researchers. The chapter examines the main issues that need to be considered in addressing research quality

- **In conclusion** there is a reflection on the pragmatic concerns in research design

This chapter examines the research process by providing an overview of the key elements of a research project. Whilst primarily focusing on doctoral research, the majority of the discussion is intended to be equally valid to academic research in general.

The academic research process can be thought of as analogous to detective work—researchers and detectives alike are *investigators* and their success is largely achieved through dedication, insight, attention to detail and a steady, methodical approach to the organization of their work. It may help to keep this analogy in mind when considering the design of the research process. Gathering data as evidence, interpreting that evidence and concluding on the basis of a clear, sound and supportable methodology is the prime purpose of any research investigation. A cohesive and logical approach is critical to the success of any research study and this will be the underlying message of this chapter as we discuss methods for investigating the literature and developing the research design.

3.1 An Overview of the Research Process—
a Seven-stage Model

Gill and Johnson (1991:3) warn that '. . . the research process is not a clear-cut sequence of procedures following a neat pattern but a messy interaction between the conceptual and empirical world, deduction and induction occurring at the same time.' There are many well-established methods, processes and protocols used in conducting academic research, but because research can be such a 'messy' process, there is real need to adopt a disciplined and structured rationale to the research programme in order to guide and integrate the various activities involved in the project.

Very few research projects or doctoral projects follow a neat, linear project plan. Research can be a very individual and personal process, subject to the vagaries of inspiration and motivation and the opportunities that may arise (and dissolve) at any time during the study. Reviewing, revising and revisiting your methods and data will be a critical and often frustrating element of the process, but one that brings with it opportunities to ensure that the primary aim is to conduct 'good' research.

Despite the iterative nature of many projects, it is important to have an appreciation of the sequencing of the main elements of a research project, which is outlined here in Table 3.1 (Bryman, 1988:20).

Starting with a broad area of interest and a fairly open research question is not uncommon—the 'messy' nature of research cited by Gill and Johnson above does include the development of the research question, which often evolves as a direct consequence of continual literature review. It will also be

Table 3.1 A Simplified Overview of the Research Process (Bryman, 1988:20) Reprinted from *Doing Research in Organisations*, A. Bryman, Taylor and Francis Books, 1988, with permission from publisher

Section in this chapter		
Section 1: Positioning your research	1. Identify a broad area of study	Based on the mapping of the literature, what is the general area of the research?
Literature searching Writing the review	2. Select the research topic	Having an idea of the possible gaps in the literature and issues raised elsewhere, what is the central research question?
Section 2: Research philosophy	3. Decide the approach	What is the general philosophical position of the research?
	4. Formulate the plan	What is the project plan or research design?
Section 3: Research methods and methodology	5. Collect the data or information	Based on the philosophical position, what data should be collected?
	6. Analyse and interpret the data	What methods of analysis are being applied to quantitative and qualitative data analysis?
	7. Present the findings	Are the findings supportable? In other words, are they valid?

likely that the research question will change at various stages during the study. The iterative nature of research is discussed by Mingers and Brocklesby (1997:494), who claim that there are four clear phases in the iteration of the research process:

- *Appreciation* (of the situation)
- *Analysis* (of the underlying structure/constraints)
- *Assessment* (of the ways in which the situation could be different)
- *Action* (to bring about a desirable change)

In elaborating on each of these phases, Mingers and Brocklesby contend that real world problem situations are messy and complex and thus are best considered by incorporating three contrasting perspectives or 'worlds' in order to deal with the richness of real world situations. They describe these 'worlds' as the social, personal and material worlds. The *social* world refers to shared social systems, the *personal* world being an individual's thoughts, emotions, experiences and beliefs and the *material* world being outside of, and independent of, humans. Researching in each of these 'worlds' or perspectives typically addresses different phenomena and concerns and implies the use of different methods and methodologies. Table 3.2 provides an overview

Table 3.2 A Framework for Mapping Methodologies (Mingers and Brocklesby, 1997:501)

	Appreciation of:	*Analysis of:*	*Assessment of:*	*Action to:*
Social	Social practices, power relations	Distortions, conflicts, interests	Ways of altering existing structures	Generate empowerment and enlightenment
Personal	Individual beliefs, meanings, emotions	Differing perceptions and personal rationality	Alternative conceptualiza- tions and constructions	Generate accommoda- tion and consensus
Material	Physical circumstances	Underlying causal structure	Alternative physical and structural arrangements	Select and implement best alternatives

of the different characteristics of the three alternative 'worlds' and the four phases in their research.

Essentially Mingers and Brocklesby's framework is intended to illustrate that there are not only different phenomena that will be of interest (social, personal, material), but at each stage of the research study the focus of study will be on different characteristics of those phenomena. For example, examining the behaviour of a continuous process may start with 'appreciation' of the size, capacity and flow rate of the plant, followed by an 'analysis' of the determinants of resource flow and utilization. 'Assessment' could then compare different plants' configurations and technologies for the same (or similar) products and materials. 'Action' may involve determination of the 'best' or optimum configuration. As the research progresses, increased data and information and greater awareness of existing knowledge and research (through literature study and empirical analysis) will facilitate a narrowing of the focus of the study through increasing attention to one or a few specific variables of interest.

Thus the research process is one in which it is frequently necessary to adapt and amend the original plan in order to respond to both challenges and opportunities that arise as the process evolves, as the illustration, on the following page, from the author's doctoral research may help to illustrate.

The influences on the iterative process of this research were both internal, arising from the researcher's reflections, literature study and data analysis, and external, resulting from changes in the research client. It should not be surprising therefore to realize that due to the impossibility of controlling some external variables in many types of organizational research, one should expect and, as far as possible, plan for the iterative and changing nature of the research as it progresses.

Text Box 3.1

'The Management of Dyadic Capability in New Product Development: A Qualitative Analysis of Customer-Supplier Relationships during the Jaguar X300 Vehicle Development Programme.' S. Croom 1996. PhD Thesis, University of Warwick, UK.

During my PhD research into supplier collaboration into new product development in the auto industry I experienced the consequences of evolution and iteration in the project. Over the four-year duration of my project the focus of my research shifted three times.

Firstly, after examining my pilot study during the last quarter of my first year I identified a new opportunity—to examine four specific design cases. This moved me away from an interview-based survey approach to a mixed method case approach.

The second change arose due to a major shift in Jaguar's organization's approach to new vehicle development through the direct adoption of Ford's product development system.

Finally, as I completed my first phase of field work my analysis of the data and reflection on the growing body of literature I was reviewing identified the significance of supplier design autonomy—this was a direct consequence of 'discovering' the importance of a previous paper by Banri Asanuma, 1989. My research question was refined to emphasize supplier design autonomy as a variable of interest.

3.2 The Nature of Operations Management Research

This book focuses on research within the operations management (OM) field, an evolving subject area with foundations in factory management, production engineering and industrial engineering. As we saw in Chapter 2, current OM research incorporates a broadening agenda, encapsulating operations and manufacturing strategy, service operations management, innovation, design and supply chain management. It has been observed from comparative analysis of OM publications (Pannirselvam et al., 1999) that the field is expanding. In particular, two main developments in the last 10 or so years have been the growth of research into new product development and an increase in integrative studies between OM and other disciplines, notably marketing. It has been debated (Swamidass, 1991; Sower et al., 1997; Pilkington and Liston-Heyes, 1999) whether this evolution now means that OM can in fact be considered as a distinct academic discipline.

Whilst delineating the OM field may be an interesting and important one for authors, from the perspective of OM research, a more prosaic consequence of the evolution of OM for doctoral research is the increasing eclecticism of such research and, as a result, the broadening of the theoretical *antecedents* used as the basis for development of OM theory. 'Antecedent' theories provide the basis for the investigation of a phenomenon (see also Section 2.1.1). The intellectual antecedents have likewise expanded from a heavy reliance on theories and concepts founded in the technical/economic areas of mathematics, statistics, operations research and econometrics, to include social/institutional theories from such disciplines as sociology, psychology and anthropology.

There is also a wider incorporation of OM theory in other management and organizational disciplines, for example, in research concerned with the resource-based or competency view of strategy. This area in particular has emerged over the last decade to be a significant development in 'mainstream' management literature and draws on recognizable OM core areas of asset utilization and resource alignment. As OM research also has a strong *applied* nature, it has been argued (Meredith et al., 1989) that if OM research is to be of practical value to managers then researchers will also need to consider new research *methods* from *paradigms* used in other fields.

There are three direct implications of the broadening of the OM agenda for the discussion of research planning and methods:

1   The range of topics and subject fields now being researched within the OM field is broadening the domain of research. Not only is more research concerned with, say, service operations and inter-organizational operations, but also the topics considered to be germane to OM encompass issues previously considered outside the bounds of OM, such as organizational learning and knowledge (Germain et al., 2001)

2   The influence of OM research on broader social science and management science research in other disciplines is undoubtedly increasing, leading others outside of the OM community to examine and interrogate OM research

3   The incorporation of 'new' OM topics will require awareness of a broader literature base, incorporate previously 'non-OM' theoretical ideas and require a different and wider variety of methods of investigation

This chapter is concerned with the changing scope of the OM discipline in two respects. Insofar as one must be aware of the influences of antecedent literature on OM theory development, to this end guidance is provided on structuring and utilizing the literature when undertaking OM research. Guidance is also provided for the development of methodological approaches and issues which OM researchers may deploy in order to stimulate the development of a more catholic OM discipline.

3.2.1 Positioning your Research

As the field of OM has broadened, it has been necessary to look beyond 'traditional' OM literature in order to gain insights into existing research, theories and hypotheses in previously 'alien' fields of research. It is imperative that the subject of the research is defined and understood, which involves identifying the current theoretical and empirical state of knowledge in the subject. In conducting doctoral or other research it is important to review up-to-date literature and evaluate the seminal influences and strong antecedents on the chosen field of study. It is useful to reflect on the focus of research by asking the following questions:

- What research already exists in the chosen topic?
- Is the theory of this topic well developed?
- Are there gaps in current research?
- Will the research be applied or fundamental research?
- Who will be the customers of the research?
- Is the topic of current concern to managers?
- Is the topic of current concern to researchers?
- Is the topic of current concern to policy leaders and funding bodies?

The answers to these questions can be clarified through literature study and interviewing key actors in the academic, managerial and policy arena. It is usually rare for anyone to choose a research topic without having some familiarity with the topic area, either through previous academic studies or firsthand experiences. For starting doctoral researchers, the research supervisor or sponsor is likely to play a major role in guiding the direction of the study. However the research topic emerges, academic research is dependent upon the researcher having a clear and, most importantly, *critical* knowledge of the literature, which in essence means being able to identify why the research addresses gaps in existing knowledge through carrying out a structured review of existing literature. In the next section of this chapter we will explore the purpose of literature reviews and examine some methods for searching, managing, mapping and writing the review.

3.3 Structured Literature Review

3.3.1 Purpose of the Literature Review

A fundamental part of any academic research is to review the existing academic literature in the field of interest. This helps to establish the authority and legitimacy of the research, but more importantly it ensures the 'researchability' of the topic before the empirical analysis begins. In other words, it helps to clarify the possible contribution of the proposed research and helps to constrain the research to a feasible scope. It is a common characteristic of many research proposals that they initially have a rather broad and ambitious intent. As discussed previously regarding the 'messy' or iterative characteristic of many doctoral research projects, by examining the existing publications in an area of interest the research question will evolve and hopefully focus on a question of interest that also meets the need to address limitations in current knowledge. In other words, it meets the criterion for an 'original' piece of research which is typical for doctoral work. The literature review thus plays a central role in helping to narrow down the scope of the research into a manageable project.

Conducting a review of the literature is also a critical component for the development of research skills and capabilities. Particularly at the doctoral level, constant exposure to published research, critical evaluation of that literature and continual refinement of the written literature review over a period of many months helps to develop a rigorous approach to the research process. In addition to gaining greater subject knowledge, reviewing the literature in a particular field will increase awareness of how to frame and structure academic research questions, will provide considerable insight into the research methods and data analysis which result in published articles and will help to inform knowledge of the traditions in particular research fields.

For doctoral research, the literature review must be a wide-ranging search, be sensitive to pertinent literature across a range of different, but allied, disciplines and provide a high level of critical (i.e. systematic) and conceptual discussion of the research problem and the relevant philosophical traditions related to it. At the master's level, the review should be analytical, incorporating not only the topic but also methodological issues.

The literature review contributes to the research process and development of the researcher in four broad areas:

1 It helps to inform the researcher's understanding of the existing state of knowledge relating to their phenomenon of interest. This is typically demonstrated through the production of a detailed map of the literature which underlines the researcher's familiarity of the subject area. It is one of the key elements of a doctoral thesis that will be evaluated by the examiners and the wider community

2 The review guides the development of the constructs, hypotheses and questions employed in the study of the chosen topic—in essence it serves to justify the choice of topic

3 It generates the detailed philosophical justification for the choice of research methodology, typically by enabling the researcher to provide a sound basis for the evaluation of previous research

4 Finally, the process of undertaking a rigorous literature review helps to develop and refine important research skills, such as information handling, classification and ability to employ a critical, yet non-partisan, stance in the evaluation of existing knowledge

Text Box 3.2

The following is an example of how the literature may be used in the formulation of the research proposal.

The fundamental problem addressed in this study is the relationship between organizational slack and innovation. There are a number of studies that have investigated this relationship on an overall firm level by looking at public financial information (see for instance Singh, 1986; Zajac et al., 1991; Nohria and Gulati, 1996). In these studies the focus has been on identifying a level of slack that eventually lead to a specific outcome in innovation. There have also been studies on the relationship between knowledge and innovation (see for example Bartezzaghi et al., 1998; Magnusson, 2000). The focus of these studies has been to establish a relationship between knowledge and innovation. By managing central knowledge processes the firm is able to create new innovations. This study differs from previous studies in three ways.

First, the focus is not on the relationship between slack and innovation or knowledge and innovation, but instead on slack and knowledge. Organizational slack in this study is viewed as something necessary for organizational learning. This relates to the work by Geppert (1996) and Lawson (2001), who argues that slack is important for producing knowledge.

Second, the unit of analysis is not the firm, but instead different projects inside the firm. To be able to identify how and why slack influences knowledge processes it is necessary to meet people that are affected by changes in slack over time.

Third, the area of interest is product development. The relationship between slack and knowledge processes can be found in different areas such as operations, marketing and product development. In order to be competitive over time the firm needs to come up with new ideas and products. This implies that product development activities are of crucial importance. Handled correctly it can give a firm significant advantage in the marketplace (Wheelwright and Clark, 1992). Due to its importance in organizations the area of interest in this study is product development. These three differences lead to the purpose of the study.

The purpose of the study is to investigate how and why organizational slack influences the creation and exploitation of knowledge in product development processes.

In Anders Richtnér's PhD thesis, the research statement given in Text Box 3.2 provides a strong and very clear description of precisely where the research will focus and helpfully where it will not. Clarifying the antecedent literature and identifying the main influences on the development of the research question will also serve to identify the contribution being made by the research. In Figure 3.1 the focus of the research is stated along with some of the more relevant theories.

Here, Richtnér's use of a simple map or schematic model of the research topic helped to clarify the main topics of interest on the study of the relationship between slack and knowledge, as well as providing some contextual positioning in relation to firm level analyses of innovation. The succinct and clear nature of such maps is an effective way to clarify the research domain.

In addition to providing the context for positioning the research within existing literature, reviewing the literature makes important contributions to other vital aspects of the process. For example, Hart (1998:27) summarized the role of the literature review in the research process as shown in Table 3.3.

Reviewing does not just involve identifying what literature exists, but interpreting the literature in order to provide a robust foundation for further developing knowledge in the field. An academic researcher needs to be able to see the logic in the argument of existing research as a prerequisite to proposing and delivering progress in knowledge in any field. In this respect, there has been heavy criticism of management literature reviews by Tranfield et al. (2003), commenting in particular that they are '. . . usually narrative and have been widely criticized for being singular descriptive accounts . . . often selected for inclusion on the implicit biases of the researcher. . .'. There is thus a very real danger that the literature review fails to provide either a

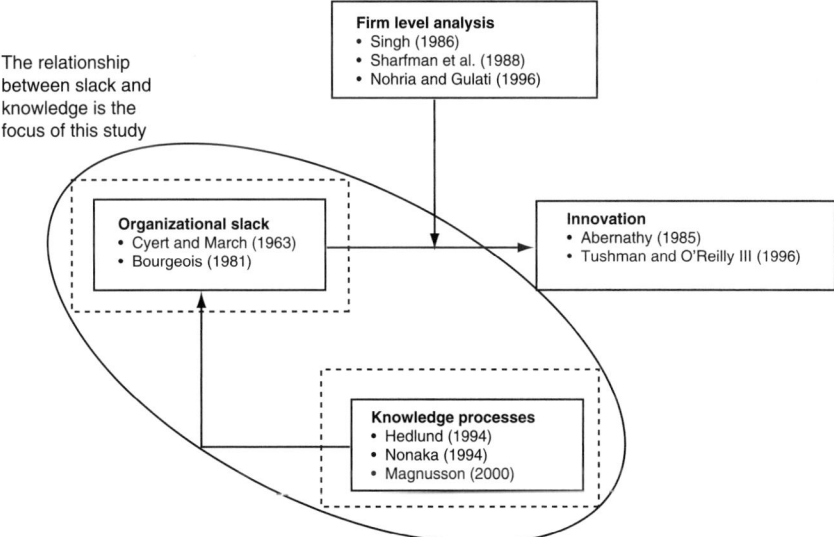

Figure 3.1 Extract from Doctoral Research Proposal by Anders Richtnér (2004). Doctoral Thesis, Stockholm School of Economics, Sweden 'Managing Knowledge Creation. Examining organizational slack and knowledge in product development projects'.

Table 3.3 The Role of the Literature Review (Hart 1998:27)

Distinguishing what has been done from what needs to be done
Discovering important variables relevant to the topic
Synthesizing and gaining a new perspective
Identifying relationships between ideas and practice
Establishing the context of the topic or problem
Rationalizing the significance of the problem
Enhancing and acquiring the subject vocabulary
Understanding the structure of the subject
Relating ideas and theory to applications
Identifying the main methodologies and research techniques that have been
  used
Placing the research in a historical context to show familiarity with state-of-the-art
  developments

sufficiently robust analysis of the existing state of the 'intellectual territory' or a valid foundation for the development of the research hypotheses and questions. The need for a structured, systematic approach to literature review is proposed by Tranfield et al. (2003) in their comparison between the method of literature review in medical science and those of management research, which provides a useful contrast between the two fields of literature.

3.3.2 Searching for Literature

The literature review process thus typically begins as a broad overview of existing texts which are often broad in scope and may only dedicate a small section to the research phenomenon of interest. This stage of the process provides the entrée to the area and helps to locate the topic in the broader field. So, for example, starting with the leading texts in production and OM may only offer a superficial discussion of a topic (such as the product development process), but it will provide a clear view of where the topic 'fits' into the OM field. Furthermore, many texts provide a short bibliography on each topic. The bibliographies and reference lists contained within published works (including texts, monographs, journal papers, conference papers and theses) will be the main source of intelligence in the first stages of the literature review. Exploiting existing published literature reviews, identifying which papers and materials are most commonly referenced and how others have critiqued the literature can be a definitive part of clarifying the research topic and question. There should be no reluctance to consume others' reviews of the literature and to capitalize on existing reference lists, nor should the need to make several 'sweeps' of the literature be overlooked.

This leads on to the process of reading. It may sound strange, but reading research literature for the purposes of review is a distinctive process. Unlike recreational reading or reading to study at undergraduate level, reviewing a piece of literature typically involves several iterations, often over a period of several months.

The first stage of reviewing any piece should be simply to browse through the materials primarily to become familiar with the content and format of the source. Secondly, speed reading or scanning should help to clarify the salient parts of the paper and identify useful information—for example, academic journal papers can contain lengthy discussion of the quantitative analysis undertaken, yet this may not be relevant in the initial stages of the research programme; instead, the objective in the early stages of the review is simply to identify what sources others use when conducting a study into the chosen topic and what references they cite. It is rarely useful at this stage to studiously read and annotate every sentence, paragraph or section. Indeed, it would be far too time consuming and uneconomic to do so, given the potentially enormous volume of literature that is so readily accessible through Internet searching and academic databases. Thirdly, identify which parts of the materials are pertinent to the research. Often it takes some time to develop the critical faculties to effectively evaluate a research paper, so in the early stages just try to get a 'feel' of the literature and the scope of the existing literature. It is advisable to simply dip into the literature even during a spare 5–10 minutes. It is surprising how one can gain a pretty thorough insight into a body of literature purely by scanning and speed reading. Finally, make notes that will form the centrepiece of the review. Again, in the early stages of the review these may be fairly eclectic and wide ranging, at least until one has a good perspective on the existing body of literature and the key issues salient to your research. Hart (1998) again provides a very useful summary of the phases of literature review (Table 3.4).

3.3.3 Managing Literature Materials

Over the course of any research project one is likely to access several hundred references. Managing this vast database will involve some of the rather more mundane aspects of research, namely developing abilities to search for pertinent references, filing materials for easy access and maintaining full records of the references. One cannot be expected to immediately recall every article, so a system of cross-referencing back to the source is critical from the very outset as it will undoubtedly be necessary to refer back to many articles and sources a number of times during the course of the research project. A key piece of advice here is not to ignore a key resource in any literature research—the university subject librarian—who will invariably provide a good overview of existing sources and perhaps some guidance about filing and classifying materials.

In maintaining a literature database, using one of the more common bibliographic software packages such as EndNote (www.endnote. com), Procite (www.procite.com), Biblioscape (www.biblioscape.com), Bookends (for Mac) (www.sonnysoftware.com), ReferenceManager

Table 3.4 A Summary Flow Chart of the Literature Search (Hart, 1998:34)

Stages	Sources	Outcomes
Background information and ideas search	Encyclopaedias Dictionaries Text books Library catalogue (OPAC)	Initial mapping of the topic area. A search vocabulary of concepts. Provisional list of key authors/works
Begin mapping topic		
Focus topic and analyse information needs	Subject librarians Guides to the literature	Identification of sources of information and guides to the literature
Detailed search of sources	Abstracts Indexes Electronic sources Bibliographies Dissertation abstracts Conference proceedings	Identification of articles, reports, work in progress. Lists of monographs/text books/anthologies. Lists of dissertations from theses and conference papers
Construct initial bibliographies		
Secondary evaluations of the literature	Review journals Indexes to reviews Citation indexes	Identification of review of items. Citation map of the topic

(www.refman.com), Bookwhere (www.webclarity.info/products/book-where.html) or LibraryMaster (www.balboa–software.com) is highly advisable, not least because it is now common accepted practice. Such database packages are specifically designed for the management of academic literature references and many incorporate quite extensive search facilities linking to the major online reference database such as Proquest, Business Source Premier, Science Direct, Ebsco and Emerald. It is not the purpose of this chapter to provide detailed instruction in the use of any of these packages. However, whatever system is chosen, it is important to be aware of the need to maintain personal 'library copies' of materials for future use. Again, it is increasingly feasible to do this electronically using pdf (portable document format) files. Most of the bibliographic databases mentioned above allow comprehensive record entry of all source literature materials and link the facility directly to stored electronic source files for ease of retrieval (typically this involves entering the full file location in to the URL field in the database).

Despite the widespread domination of the personal computer and networked resources, many researchers still prefer to have paper or 'hard' copies of their materials for ease of reading and review. Again, it is useful to be able to access these readily and it is recommended that a separate record identifying number is used for each item—such as the one allocated by your bibliographic system. Even if this is simply in numerical order according to the (random) sequence in which you enter the record, it will ease the management of the database as the review develops.

Managing and maintaining the bibliography will be an important part of the literature review process throughout the research programme and it is worth investing time early on to choose an appropriate package, learn how it is used and ensure data and records are kept 'clean'.

3.3.4 Note Taking, Annotating and Summarizing

The key challenge for the literature review is to be both effective and efficient. Capturing the essence of published materials is pertinent to the development of the research argument, supports the research design, is central to the development of knowledge relating to the field of study and is vital for the rigour of the final literature review either in the doctoral thesis or in published research. Since the review will be conducted over a lengthy period and revisited numerous times, it is again important from the outset to adopt a clear process for note taking. This section examines a number of techniques commonly used to help the note taking process.

The temptation to highlight, underline or annotate large tracts of an article is one that should be avoided simply because it may well distract from important concepts or findings when returning to the piece later in the research project. As we saw above, the literature review has a number of specific roles and they must be taken into account when making and recording notes. For example, reviewing a piece in order to identify its antecedent literature is quite different from comparing its findings to other published research. Keeping notes separate from the source material is thus one of the primary mechanisms used to enable collation and synthesis of all of the notes, summaries and commentaries produced during the review of the literature.

Some commonly used methods for recording analysis of an item are outlined below.

3.3.4.1 Using 'Post-It' / 'Sticky Notes'

One of the great advantages of using 'post-it' or 'sticky notes' is that they are easy to manipulate and can be stuck on the source material without causing damage. Particularly when reviewing a library book, it is not desirable to make notes on to the page, so compiling notes during reading, then having an easy way to retain them, can be extremely useful and achievable by writing short notes and extracts onto 'post-it' or 'sticky' notes. These can be affixed to the relevant page of the text or article during review, different coloured notes can be used for different purposes (such as yellow for key empirical findings, green for methodology and red for citations) and subsequently transferred onto larger sheets of paper or card for collating and organizing into topic and themed groups. Each note should have a reference to the exact source (i.e. record number and page), allowing both cross-referencing and ease of return to source. It also allows the reading and note taking activity to be decoupled from the literature *analysis*.

Once the notes have been made the synthesis of the literature is achieved by organizing each note and compiling a detailed summary review. In essence, this is a somewhat time-consuming task involving sorting and organizing all of the post it notes according to predetermined or emergent themes —it may be useful to spend some time just reviewing all of the notes in order to gain a good overview of these themes.

Whilst this is a very portable and 'low-tech' method, it still allows for a high degree of flexibility and manipulation of notes throughout the research process.

3.3.4.2 Using Record Sheets and Worksheets

Employing a form or table for mapping the literature helps to build the review using common fields and themes. The use of tables also allows comparison across various fields—for example by author, theme, theory or citation. Furthermore, the content of such tables can readily be transferred into a spreadsheet such as Excel to allow greater manipulation and control over the content of the review.

Figures 3.2 and 3.3 are examples of a record sheet and a worksheet that are typically used to summarize the review at various stages of progression.

By constructing a clear structure for reviewing literature, comparisons

Topic/Theme/Concept:					
Author/date	Theory/ standpoint	Evidence	Argument	Core citations	Misc.

Figure 3.2 Record Sheet (Hart, 1998:146).

	Author/date	Author/date	Author/date
Topic/Theme/Concept			
Description			
Antecedents			
Evidence/Data			
Consequences (therefore)			
Part of (major category)			

Figure 3.3 Worksheet (Hart, 1998:150).

between articles are much easier, the critical analysis of articles will be consistent because information is clear and the review will be comprehensive. Using these tables enables identification of the salient points from each work reviewed, allows cross-reference and comparison of different works and provides a robust insight to the nature of a topic, particularly how it has been researched and how knowledge has developed.

As the literature review develops, it helps to highlight the relevant and important keywords and phrases that can be used to classify the body of literature. It will then be relatively easy to cut and paste the main elements of the review into a bibliographic database which increases the flexibility and quality of the literature records. Furthermore, the ability to be able to collate and organize the literature using keywords, phrases and themes will be a vital step in the construction of a map of the literature (see Figure 3.4 later in this chapter).

3.3.5 Using Citation Searches

Being able to trace where particular works are referenced by others is a key aspect of the literature searching and reviewing process as it shows how ideas have been disseminated, discussed and critiqued within a particular field.

In addition to using published bibliographies and literature reviews, there are a number of online databases available thorough university libraries such as the 'Web of Knowledge' and the 'Web of Science' that allow quite extensive, yet very quick, citation searches. Searches are conducted by taking a particularly significant piece and entering the full reference into the citation search engine—the resulting list shows all published works that have referenced that work.

In many ways this allows for 'two-way' literature searching. For example, if a publication is very closely aligned to the chosen topic, it is extremely useful to find other work that has referenced the piece to help identify very quickly a focused body of literature. Whilst citation searches are really only useful for publications that are typically over 2 years old—simply because the lead time for many journal articles is approximately 18 months and thus it can take that time before a paper appears as a reference—they are a vital tool in refining the reference map. A citation search will often open up areas of the literature that have not been encountered before and provide different disciplinary perspectives on the chosen topic. Consequently, citation searches are best used once the literature review reaches a relatively mature stage containing clear identification of the seminal works in the field.

3.3.6 Mapping the Literature

Once satisfied that the review contains a significant number of resources and a key citation search has been undertaken, the production of a map showing the topography of the field is an extremely valuable way to encapsulate the field and will be useful in the final write-up of the report or thesis. By using graphical representation it is easy not only to define how one sees the current body of knowledge, but it will allow others to understand how the field has been defined in the research. This can be particularly useful for supervisors, who will then be able to provide much more focused guidance and direction. Furthermore, it helps provide a much clearer view of the main influences on research in the chosen field.

Having developed keywords and phrases during the progression of the initial review of the literature, a widely used technique to help map the literature is to use a relationship tree or network diagram. The purpose of such diagrams is to show how the research topic has been informed by the antecedent literature over time. Often it is useful to start by using a diachronic approach (i.e. one which maps the progression and changes in the literature over time) to show the links between key works. It is not necessary to include every source—indeed the ability to identify the most salient and seminal works pertaining to the research is a key measure of the quality of a doctoral thesis. Having conducted citation searches, the construction of a citation tree should be relatively straightforward—the example shown in Figure 3.4 is simply an indicative one to show how such a tree is presented. In this, the main references across a related section of a literature search are connected according to the use of one reference in the citations of another and the apparent influence of one article or reference on another (which is usually determined when reviewing the piece).

3.3.7 *Writing the Review*

Doctoral theses in particular all contain a review of the existing knowledge associated with the chosen research topic, thus producing the written review is a critical part of any doctoral project. It is also a key element of academic publications, research monographs and other forms of scholarly output. As with all forms of writing, planning and pre-writing are vital first steps. The literature review will undoubtedly evolve frequently throughout the study— do not be surprised to even have to revisit and edit the review immediately prior to submission—this is a normal part of the process of iteration for many research theses.

The citation map of the literature provides a framework around which to plan the structure of the review section, and the bibliographic database and record sheets will provide much of the initial content for the critique. Ideally, write a plan of the literature review addressing some of the following key issues.

First define the topic—a single statement is often most effective, but at the same time many doctoral students find this notoriously difficult to do in the first few years. However, it is always worth trying to be as succinct as possible in the problem statement and ensure clarity over the issue of the 'theory'

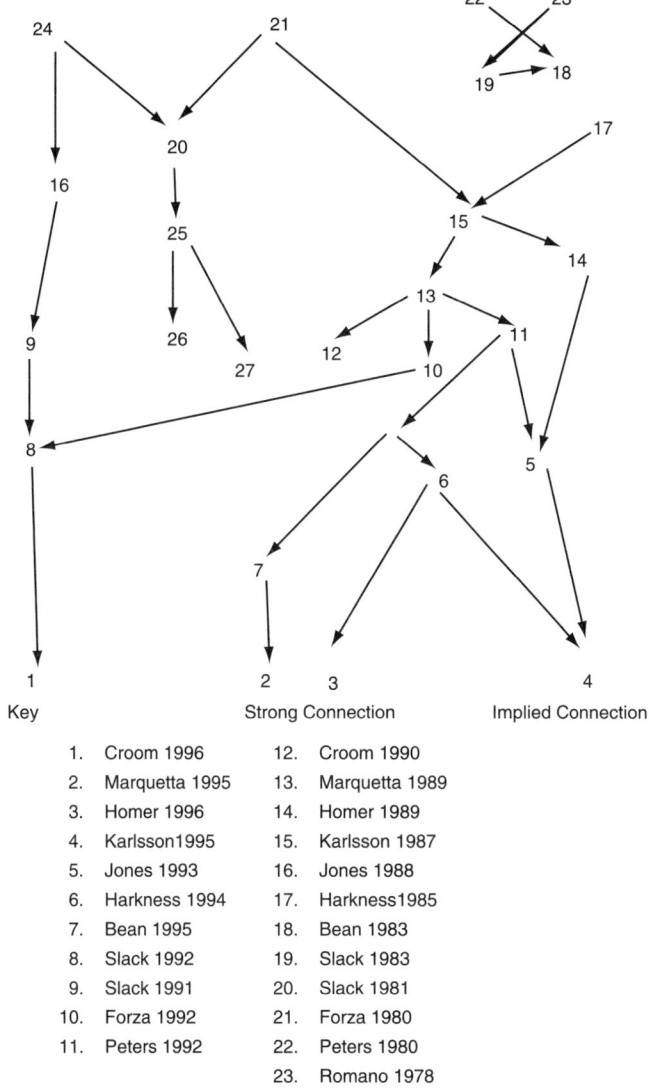

Key   Strong Connection   Implied Connection

1.	Croom 1996	12.	Croom 1990
2.	Marquetta 1995	13.	Marquetta 1989
3.	Homer 1996	14.	Homer 1989
4.	Karlsson1995	15.	Karlsson 1987
5.	Jones 1993	16.	Jones 1988
6.	Harkness 1994	17.	Harkness1985
7.	Bean 1995	18.	Bean 1983
8.	Slack 1992	19.	Slack 1983
9.	Slack 1991	20.	Slack 1981
10.	Forza 1992	21.	Forza 1980
11.	Peters 1992	22.	Peters 1980
		23.	Romano 1978

Figure 3.4 Illustration of Citation Tree.

with which the research is concerned. (See also the section 'How to Define the Research Topic' later in this chapter.)

Secondly, the majority of the review will present an overview of the existing work on this topic—here the use of diagrams and charts from the initial research proposal or plan are extremely helpful. Try as much as possible to avoid 'listing' in the review, that is, merely providing a superficial bibliography of the literature. A more viable approach is firstly to discuss the main research methods used in existing research, define the main issues that have been explored, give an overview of the definitions used and concepts developed in the literature and then draw links between complementary concepts and methods as well as contrast opposing views.

It is expected that the review is *critical* in nature by providing a systematic expression of opinion and judgment about both individual pieces and the overall existing body of literature. The review should identify what is considered to be seminal work, address the strengths and weaknesses of the work, and articulate the specific contribution to the field made by such work.

Finally, the literature review must have a *conclusion* which relates the general development of the literature to the perceived gaps and opportunities in the field, specifically linking such gaps to the research topic being examined in the study.

Remember that not only doctoral examiners, but journal article reviewers, editors and most readers want a succinct review. It is obviously accepted that not only is it impossible to cover everything in the literature, but there are clear limits regarding the length of the papers, theses and reports which are increasingly being enforced. The objective of the literature review is to show knowledge and synthesis of the literature, demonstrate the ability to make critical comments about the important aspects of that literature, and, most of all, show how existing research informs the current research project.

3.4 Research Methodology

3.4.1 How to Define the Research Topic

As we have already seen, the literature review plays a major role in helping to identify and clarify research topic and questions. The development of a valid research proposal thus needs an inherent logic to its research *design*—i.e. a clear definition of the chosen topic and of the methods to be employed to investigate the topic.

Typically, the research design begins with some statement of the problem, system or domain in the form of research questions, propositions or constructs that define precisely what will be investigated. Further, any academic research project can be considered to have as its objective some element of either (at one extreme) the development of a theory (*inductive research*) or at the other extreme to test a theory (*deductive research*). But, what precisely is a 'theory'?

3.4.1.1 The Components of a 'Theory'—an Overview
of the Terminology

Many researchers become confused in their use of language and expression when trying to describe their research, particularly in trying to present the theoretical frame of reference. So, it is important to have a clear understanding of the terms most commonly used in the expression of a research topic or question (see also Wacker, 2004).

A *theory* is an attempt to explain how a system or phenomenon works by identifying the constituent elements of the system and how they interact and relate to each other—for example, ancient Greek philosophers, most notably Ptolemy, proposed a theory of 'geocentricity' to explain the behaviour of the bodies within the Solar System. Their view (and the foundation of the Ptolemaic system) was that the Earth was very near to the physical centre of the Solar System and that all of the heavenly bodies—moon, planets and sun—rotated around the Earth. Theories consist of a collection of logically interrelated *propositions* that aim to explain a set of phenomena—in the case of the Ptolemaic system one of the main propositions concerned the movement of the planets in relationship to the 'equant' or imaginary centre of the Solar System. Thus, a *proposition* is a statement in which some relationship between two or more concepts or variables is proposed. Propositions are typically made in the form of declarative statements (e.g. war causes death—which is an example of a univariate proposition), bivariate (e.g. war causes death and poverty), or multivariate (war causes death, poverty and environmental destruction which lead to economic decline). A *law* is a proposition about which we have sufficient evidence to believe that it is probably true in social science. Laws are typically statistical in nature; that is, they only hold in a probabilistic sense of being true most of the time or in most circumstances.

A *concept* is a mental image or perception, either of real things (such as a product) or of things that cannot be observed (such as morality). Concepts that can only have one value are constants; those that can have more than one value are *variables*.

Constructs are a special kind of concept in that they are abstract and deliberately invented for a special scientific purpose, and they often change their meaning or are discarded as theories develop. The 'equant' or imaginary centre of the solar system is an example of such a construct, as are measures such as customer satisfaction, IQ and general personality behaviours such as Machiavellianism.

Many research proposals include *hypotheses* (see also section 4.3.2.3 in the next chapter) which are simply propositions that state a predicted or assumed relationship between two or more variables (e.g. employee satisfaction + service quality = customer satisfaction). It is crucial that any hypotheses must be stated in a form that can be clearly tested through field research. Hypotheses must be phrased as clearly and simply as possible and provide the answer to the problem or question that initiated the inquiry (hence, there should be a *problem statement* such as: What is the relationship between employee satisfaction, service quality and customer satisfaction?).

In statistical studies, research is often conducted to try to find support for a *null hypothesis*, that is, a hypothesis that there is no relationship among the variables of interest. Many statistically orientated studies (e.g. large surveys) try to find evidence against the null hypothesis as this allows you to accept the research hypothesis simply because it is the only available alternative.

3.4.2 Research Philosophy

Research philosophy is concerned with the fundamental challenge for any form of research, namely to adopt an approach to a study that will provide insight into the phenomenon or process of interest. This in itself is a particularly problematic objective for any researcher, as the study of knowledge and truth (i.e. epistemology and philosophy) has at its heart the dilemma that truth may be conceived as being either objective or subjective. This highlights a fundamental and critical challenge for the researcher, namely, *are we really seeing what we think we see?* The issue of whether truth and fact is only ever value-laden versus the notion that truth is innate, the product of pure reason and therefore perspective-free, is at the heart of the philosophical debate and thus central to the methodological considerations of your research (Habermas, 1972).

Much of the research methodology literature in management and organizational studies employs Burrell and Morgan's (1979) seminal work on *paradigms.* They contested that the four paradigms (see Table 3.5) identified were mutually exclusive and based on contradictory assumptions (Mingers, 2001). However, although there is a fundamental distinction made in many management research texts between apparently opposing paradigms (Bryman 1989a, b; Easterby-Smith et al., 1991; Gill and Johnson, 1991; Creswell, 1994), many writers now advocate the use of not only mixed *methodologies,* but take the debate further by presenting a case for the use of several methodologies from different *paradigms* (Hassard, 1988; Mingers, 2001). It is argued that such an approach is desirable in order to 'make the most effective contribution in dealing with the real world' (Mingers and Brocklesby, 1997). There are those who view the use of mixed-paradigm methodologies as untenable, unacademic, illogical or just 'bad research'. However, there is not a black and white case for either a multi-paradigm or a single-paradigm based approach. The first step is to be aware of contrasting paradigms.

3.4.2.1 Positivism and Constructivism (Interpretivism)

Various writers on research methodology start by setting out a dichotomous view of the researcher's choice of philosophical position. Bryman (1988, 1989a), for example, discusses the two general approaches to organizational research as being concerned with either quantitative or qualitative *methodologies,* whilst both Easterby-Smith et al. (1991) and Gill and Johnson (1991) characterize the debate in terms of two main *paradigms*: positivism and phenomenology. Meredith et al. (1989) view the epistemological choice as being between rational and existential *paradigms,* whilst Hirschman and

Holbrook (1992) adopt a similar view, contending that research *paradigms* exist on a continuum between material determinism (empiricism) and mental determinism (rationalism). A good starting point in this discussion is thus to examine the distinctions between the underlying positions of positivism and constructivism.

To put it bluntly, the *positivist* or *rational* stance is one of empirical validation—a belief in objective reality. For the positivist, the world is external to the individual. The emphasis is on observable facts, derived from valid, reliable measurement, and providing results and conclusions which are replicable (verifiable) and generalizable (Bryman, 1988:40–41). Truth is viewed as an objective, innate product of pure reason. On the other hand, *constructivism* (or interpretivism) takes an opposite stance, one in which the researcher considers all observation and analysis to be socially constructed, that is, dependent upon the researcher as a participant; and they hold the view that actions and phenomena are dictated by the specific circumstances found in the situation.

So, a positivist position is one in which research is regarded as a process to find out the 'facts', whilst a constructivist position is more concerned with research that attempts to make sense of, and to provide an interpretation of, the research phenomenon. Between these two extremes lie other positions, the most commonly cited being *post positivism* and *critical theory*. Table 3.5 provides a summary of the alternative research paradigms, from the objective, rational stance of positivism to the subjective, contingent and interpretative stance of constructivism.

Table 3.5 A Spectrum of Research Paradigms

Positivism	Postpositivism	Critical theory	Constructivism (interpretivism)
Reality exists as truth Knowledge is context-free. Research can reveal the 'true' state of affairs Basic posture is reductionist and deterministic Verification is how validity is ensured	Reality exists as truth, but can only be very imperfectly apprehended Objectivity is valued and achieved through overall resemblance of findings to pre-existing knowledge Concern for validity is with falsification	Reality is determined by social and historical values, becoming reified as time passes Validity is supported by clear description of assumptions and values Research is seen as a form of social or cultural criticism	Reality is dependent upon the individual (existential) Research aims to see the world from the viewpoint of the subject In order to understand, one must interpret Concerned with matters of knowing and being, not with method per se

In their discipline note, Pannirselvam et al. (1999) found that OM research had remained very much positivistic in nature. Specifically, their comparative analysis of OM journals and conference publications between the 1980s and 1990s found that surveys and simulation were the predominant methods used, indicative of a strong, positivistic (or at least a *post positivistic*) position. They also noted that there is often a strong relationship between the research topic, the philosophical position employed and the methodology used in the publications (commonly known as the 'what', the 'why' and the 'how' of research design).

Whilst addressing one's own philosophical position is important to address concerns for the underlying logic of the research, it often causes much confusion early in the process when doctoral students try to determine which 'type' of researcher they are. There are a number of reasons why it may be particularly difficult to clarify this. Firstly, relative inexperience may mean that one has insufficient firsthand experience of research to have settled on any specific 'world view'. Secondly, the research problem may not sit comfortably within the description for any single paradigm. Thirdly, it is often after one has conducted a large element of the research that it is really possible to define one clear position.

3.4.2.2 Choices about the Type of Researcher

Often a real challenge in planning research will be to determine precisely how to gather data and how to interpret it. Whilst the issues surrounding the philosophical paradigm behind the research are important, it is often far more practical to start with some personal reflection using Eilon's (1974) paper about the 'faces' of research which provides a useful classification of contrasting approaches to the whole process of research.

Eilon suggested that it is possible to identify seven 'archetypes' of research worker, each archetype described with specific reference to two issues, the main approach to research and the level of interaction with the 'system or problem domain' (Table 3.6). These archetypes serve as quite a useful guide to the nature of the research process and can be a good foundation for thinking about how the project will develop and what tasks will be involved. For example, one may be really attracted by the opportunity to work inside an operation for an extended period of time, which opens up the possibility of getting to know the routines, methods and character of the 'problem domain'. Alternately, one may be more fascinated by the opportunities to explore an analytical method or develop a simulation programme. So, depending on personal preferences, skills, experience and aspirations, the way any research project is conducted relies quite heavily on the preferences of the key researcher(s).

In reality, one is likely to identify with at least two, if not more, of the archetypes; but at least this helps one to think about the *operationalization* of any chosen research programme.

Table 3.6 Seven Archetypes of Researcher

Archetype (Self-image)	Approach	Interacts with the 'system' or problem domain?
Chronicler: A detached observer whose function is to record a series of facts or patterns of behaviour 'for posterity'	Attempts to study the phenomenon of interest without prejudgment and by adopting a passive role outside of the process	No
Dialectician: A participating observer who aims for an objective view through dialogue	Engages the actors in the process by questioning, debate and argument rather than passive observation	Yes
Puzzle-solver: Primarily interested in the intellectual activity associated with *solving* a well-structured problem than the process of data collection	Often content to engage in problem suggested by others, being more interested in the degree of abstraction	No
Empiricist: Employs 'scientific' models	Focuses on experimentation, and is thus mainly interested in the conduct of simulations, trials, tests and comparative studies	Yes
Classifier: Attempts to interpret existing knowledge and research	Concerned with the organization and categorization of data but not its collection, frequently based on own value judgments	No
Iconoclast: Challenges existing knowledge	Employs critical interpretation of current thinking and theories and, though primarily a critic, may propose alternative theories	No
Change-agent: Prime objective is to change the system There are two types of change agent: the catalyst and the activist	Catalyst Is careful not to impose own views but to reach consensus through facilitation and moderation	Yes
	Activist Attempts to direct change towards own views and solutions	Yes

Having some ideas about the *archetype* of researcher with which you feel most affinity will help you to bring clarity to decisions about the choice of methodology and methods.

3.5 Qualitative and Quantitative Methods

Whilst quantitative and qualitative *methods* are distinctive, they are not incommensurate with each other (Burrell and Morgan, 1979). For example, case research often involves both quantitative and qualitative methods in the research design (see Chapter 5). Here, we briefly discuss the nature of each in order to provide a basis for our examination of the choice of research design.

3.5.1 Quantitative Approaches

The use of mathematical and statistical tools to manage the analysis of numerical data has long been associated with a more positivistic approach to research. Bryman (1988b:12) described quantitative research as being generally underpinned by a natural science model. At its extreme, quantitative research adopts a *deductive* approach, setting out to test hypotheses in order to build upon an existing body of knowledge in the particular sphere of interest. The validity of a quantitative research approach is adjudged to be attained through the logic of a common, structured process, much akin to the 'seven-step scientific method' commonly used in physical sciences such as chemistry. In this method, concepts are examined and tested through the clear delineation of indicators (variables) which are observable, tangible and clearly defined. Testing of causality between variables is achieved through controlled measurement, using laid down procedures and protocols. Thus, the results of such research are evaluated in terms of the validity of the *process* of research (did it follow a 'scientific' method?) and will frequently incorporate some statement of confidence in the results (such as statistical level of significance). The ability to replicate, and thus verify, quantitative research is seen as a critical indicator of the validity of the research.

Quantitative methods can be viewed as ones which basically incorporate a process of observation; with data collection achieved through such processes as laboratory controlled experiments or structured surveys.

3.5.2 Qualitative Approaches

Qualitative approaches, by contrast, are at their extreme concerned with constructivism, interpretation and perception, rather than with identification of a rational, objective truth. The emphasis is upon a socially constructed nature of reality. Qualitative methods variously recognize and attempt to account for the significance of interpretation, perception and interaction in the process of defining, collecting and analysing research evidence. Perhaps in stark contrast with the established scientific disciplines of quantitative

members of the organization. A distinctive characteristic of action research is the focus on problem resolution and change management in an organization or group of organizations. Considerable attention has to be paid to the influence and impartiality of the researcher as this often presents a challenge in dealing with the validity of any action research programme.

3.6.5 Qualitative Axiomatic Research—Modelling and Simulation (Chapter 8)

Axiomatic research, also described as 'rational' research, represents in some sense a 'classic' theoretical approach to research (Stigum, 1990). Mathematical models are the basis of axiomatic research, which are developed to examine the behaviour of systems under controlled or bounded conditions using 'abstract' (as opposed to empirically observed) data. One of the primary objectives of axiomatic research is to provide predictive instruments for the operation of a system under a range of conditions. A typical application of axiomatic modelling in the OM field has been stochastic modelling of inventory systems, although there is an established history of axiomatic research in a wide range of OM topics.

3.6.6 'True' Experiments

Setting up highly controlled situations in which to test relationships between variables is a trait of the true experiment. Such 'true', 'classical' or scientific experiments require that a researcher is able to manipulate in some way the independent variable of the research hypothesis in order to observe the influence of particular variables upon the dependent variable under examination. In behavioural studies, typically an experiment would involve establishing two separate groups of participants. Suppose one wished to identify the impact of a particular reward scheme on the efficiency of a production line. An experiment could be established in a laboratory setting where two identical production lines are set up. One would then randomly assign a group of participants to not receive a reward ('non-treatment group') whilst a second group of operators are randomly assigned to receive the reward (the 'treatment group'). The intention would be to ensure that all other variables likely to impact efficiency are the same for both groups, which is why it is important to randomly assign individuals to the two groups. Any differences in efficiency between the two groups can then be analysed statistically to determine if the reward had a significant effect. By manipulating and monitoring just one variable in a system it is possible to build a strong case to verify or dispute a hypothesis concerning the relationship between the independent and dependent variables. Using statistical tests to measure the confidence level (i.e. the mathematical likelihood of the existence of a relationship between two variables) will enable the researcher to support or reject the claimed relationship.

Using experiments in general management research can be difficult when dealing with social systems because of a range of problems. It may be difficult to control for variables other than the independent and dependent variables of interest and thus there may be 'noise' in the system which impacts on the data collected. Participants in an experiment may change their behaviour simply because they are being observed (the Hawthorne effect). It can also be problematic to apply objective measures to behaviour of individuals or groups. However, in OM, laboratory experimentation and product simulation are two OM research methods which could be classified as 'true' experiments.

3.6.7 Quasi-experiments

To counter some of the problems faced in constructing experiments, it still may be possible to conduct a 'quasi-experiment'. Due to the inability of the researcher to control all the conditions surrounding the activity being observed, often it is necessary to accept natural restrictions and amend the research method to be as close as possible to laboratory control conditions. For example, when trying to evaluate the impact of a particular process management technique in a real-life setting, it may not be feasible to randomly assign individuals to treatment and non-treatment groups. Instead it may be possible to identify two different groups due to some already occurring circumstances. For example, one production line may be operated only by women and another only by men. If the aim was to evaluate if gender had an impact on the adoption of certain practices on a production line such a naturally occurring situation would present an opportunistic grouping.

There is a limitation in quasi-experiments to the extent that generalization from the research is restricted by the highly contrived or controlled nature of the study. It is difficult to control the groups; one is merely able to observe the differences between them. The lack of an ability to control the situation and the possibility that one makes an incorrect conclusion about the cause and effect relationships can seriously restrict the contribution of quasi-experiments. However, the primary contribution of quasi-experimental research is considered to be for theoretical rather than managerial advancement in that it can help to build one's hypotheses and test out relationships as a major step in theory building.

3.7 Positioning Operations Management Research Methods

Meredith et al. (1993) presented a framework that related four alternative philosophical paradigms to the choice of appropriate research methods by linking the source of information used and the approach taken to generate knowledge (Figure 3.5). Recognizing that issues regarding data gathering are often a core consideration is an important and helpful consideration in academic research design.

		SOURCE AND KIND OF INFORMATION USED IN THE RESEARCH		
		NATURAL		ARTIFICIAL
KNOWLEDGE GENERATION APPROACH		**Direct observation of object reality**	**People's perceptions of object reality**	**Artificial reconstruction of object reality**
RATIONAL	**Axiomatic**			Reason/logic theorems Normative/descriptive modelling
	Logical positivist/empiricist	Field studies Field experiments	Structured interviewing Survey research	Prototyping Physical modeling Laboratory experimentation Simulation
EXISTENTIAL	**Interpretive**	Action research Case studies	Historical analysis Delphi/expert panel Intensive interviewing Introspective reflection	Conceptual modelling

Figure 3.5 A Generic Framework for Classifying Research Methods (from Meredith et al., 1989).

The value of Meredith et al.'s framework is not simply to direct the researcher to one cohesive set of methods (e.g. to chose between either case or action research) but to clarify the paradigmatic influences upon different methods. Again, exercising the multi-paradigmatic possibilities (Mingers and Brocklesby, 1997) one may consciously choose a range of methods from differing paradigms in order to enrich the study and analysis of the phenomena.

3.7.1 Choice of Method

In the previous sections we have concentrated on the connections between research method(s), the philosophical position of the researcher and the nature of the question or problem being investigated. However, there are many pragmatic issues that need to be addressed in developing your research design. One of the most important concerns in considering empirical field research is the question of access—in other words, will you be able to gather the data you need? Gummesson (1991) discusses access as one of the core concerns that needs to be clarified when undertaking research. Table 3.7, developed by Professor Henrique Corrêa (now of the *Fundacao Getulio Vargas, Sao Paulo, Brazil*, this table was published in his 1992 doctoral thesis at the University of Warwick), provides a useful framework for matching some of the more practical questions related to access faced by researchers when developing their research design.

The ten research characteristics listed by Corrêa in the first column are

Table 3.7 Summary of the Research Design Choice (Corrêa, 1992)

Research requirements/ characteristics	Axiomatic and experimental research	Survey research	Case study	Action research
Presence of the researcher in data collection	Possible	Unusual/ difficult	Usual	Usual
Small sample size	Possible	Unusual	Usual	Usual
Variables difficult to quantify	Possible	Possible	Possible	Possible
Perceptive measures	Possible	Possible	Possible	Possible
Constructs not predefined	Unusual	Difficult	Adequate	Possible
Causality is central	Adequate	Possible	Adequate	Possible
Need to build theory— to answer 'how' question	Possible	Difficult	Adequate	Possible
In-depth understanding of decision-making process	Difficult	Difficult	Adequate	Possible
Non-active role of researcher	Possible	Possible	Possible	Impossible
Lack of control over variables	Difficult	Possible	Possible	Possible

useful illustrations of some of the common concerns that are often faced. Relating each of these characteristics to the four methods listed helps in selection of both method(s) and maybe refinement or reassessment of the research question. For example, the opportunity to have a researcher actively collecting data is not a trivial matter—in a proposal to conduct international comparisons of operations practices, lack of fluent speakers in relevant geographical locations will constrain such studies to those where a researcher does not need to be present (e.g. questionnaire data collection). Another illustration using Corrêa's framework would be faced when attempting to study a new phenomenon in operations (such as the role of Web 2.0 in mediated project teams); there may be very few valid examples of users and thus a small sample size would be a serious constraint to conducting a questionnaire survey, but would not be problematic for case or action research.

Whilst Corrêa's framework helps researchers to clarify which methods are feasible, it does not determine which methods are *appropriate*. Of significance in this respect is giving regard to issues of quality of the research.

3.8 Ensuring Quality and Evaluating Your Research

3.8.1 What Makes a Good Theory?

In order to contribute to knowledge, your research project must demonstrate that it has characteristics of good theory. There are three basic rules that define a good theory:

- Theory must be *consistent* with the underlying views of 'reality' of the research—in other words, there must be consistency between the ontological, philosophical and analytical approaches employed in the research. If theory and reality are not consistent then either the theory is wrong, the measurement of reality is wrong or both are wrong. This is why it is vital that one can show that the research methods and findings are *valid*
- Theories must be testable. Typically this is achieved by setting out hypotheses and conducting an investigation to test the hypotheses
- Theories are never *proven* to be true, but they can be falsified (if proven, they are no longer theories, but facts). Since theories cannot be proven to be correct because one negative instance will disprove the theory (and we can never exhaust all instances), the aim of science is to eliminate rival theories. Then we have some reason to believe that the one theory (or more in some cases) that we are left with is probably correct until we can come up with a better theory

Wacker (2004) provided a useful overview of the characteristics of what constitutes a good theory in OM, as summarized in Table 3.8.

The eight 'virtues' listed here should be used to help guide one's evaluation of whether any theory developed in the study reflects a good theory. So, when taking decisions about the quality of one's research, great care must be given to issues surrounding the validity of the approach taken, otherwise the veracity and accuracy of any conclusions will at best be questionable, at worst be indefensible. In other words, without valid research one cannot expect to develop a 'good' theory.

3.8.2 Validity

In simple terms, a good piece of research meets accepted standards of *validity* in a range of dimensions.

3.8.2.1 Internal Validity

Internal validity refers to the extent to which the conclusions regarding dependency between factors of a relationship are certifiable, in other words, are we confident that the cause and effect identified are actually supportable

Table 3.8 Characteristics of a 'Good' Theory (from Wacker, 2004:644)

Virtue	Key feature	Why important for 'good' theory and for the development of the field
Uniqueness	The uniqueness virtue means that one theory must be differentiated from another	If two theories are identical, they should be considered a single theory. Although it applies to all criteria for theory, this virtue directly applies to definitions since definitions are the most elemental of building blocks for theory
Conservatism	A current theory cannot be replaced unless the new theory is superior in its virtues	Therefore, current theory is not rejected for the sake of change. This criteria is needed so that when a new theory is proposed, there is a good reason to believe all other theories are lacking in some virtue (Quine and Ullian, 1980; Kuhn, 1980; Popper, 1957)
Generalizability	The more areas that a theory can be applied to makes the theory a better theory	If one theory can be applied to one type of environment and another theory can be applied to many environments, then the second theory is a more virtuous theory since it can be more widely applied. Some authors call this virtue the utility of the theory since those theories that have wider application have more importance
Fecundity	A theory which is more fertile in generating new models and hypotheses is better than a theory that has fewer hypotheses	Theories which expand the area of investigation into new conceptual areas are considered superior to theories which investigate established research areas.
Theory parsimony, theory simplicity, theory efficiency, Occum's razor	The parsimony virtue states, other things being equal, the fewer the assumptions the better	This means if two theories are equal in all other aspects, the one with fewer assumptions and the fewer definitions is more virtuous. This virtue also includes the notion that the simpler the explanation, the better the theory. This virtue keeps theories from becoming too complex and incomprehensible

Internal consistency	Internal consistency means the theory has identified all relationships and gives adequate explanation	Internal consistency refutation means that the theory *logically* explains the relationships between variables. The more *logically* the theory explains the variables and predicts the subsequent event, the better the theory is. This *internal consistency* virtue means that the theory's entitles and relationships must be *internally compatible* using symbolic logic or mathematics. This *internal consistency* means that the concepts and relationships are logically *compatible with* each other
Empirical riskiness	Any empirical test of a theory should be risky. Refutation must be very possible if theory is to be considered a 'good' theory	If there are two competing theories the theory that predicts the most unlikely event is considered the superior theory. In the opposite case, if the theory predicts a very likely event then it is not seen as being very valuable theory. This criteria is sometimes put in a different way: 'Every good theory has at least one prohibition; it prohibits certain things from happening' (Popper, 1957)
Abstraction	The abstraction level of theory means it is independent of time and space. It achieves this independence by including more relationships	The abstraction level means it is better to integrate many relationships and variables into a larger theory. If one of two competing theories integrates more internally consistent concepts, it is more virtuous than a theory that integrates fewer internally consistent relationships

rather than extraneous consequences of some other significant relationship. Internal validity is of particular concern in causal and explanatory studies when one may be interested in making tentative statements about cause and effect.

There are three useful strategies to use if one is interested in trying to identify cause and effect:

- Methods triangulation (which involves using multiple research *methods*, such as interviews and questionnaires)
- Data triangulation (in which one will gather *data* from several different sources, such as through face-to-face interviews with several different types of people, collection of quantitative performance measures and conducting observations in several different settings)
- 'Researcher-as-detective' (e.g. carefully thinking about cause and effect and examining each possible 'clue')

A strong argument for the use of case studies in terms of their contribution to research quality is made, not surprisingly, by Eisenhardt (1989:542) who claims that the qualitative data obtained through case research helps '. . . inform understanding of the relationships identified', and that this is '. . . crucial to the establishment of internal validity'.

3.8.2.2 *External Validity*

External validity relates to the general applicability of the conclusions; in other words do they truly reflect reality and consequently can they be demonstrated elsewhere? Three distinct types of external validity can be considered:

- **Population validity.** This refers to the ability to be able to generalize about particular phenomena from surveying or examining a sample and then extrapolating the observed causal behaviour to the whole population of interest. This is an important concern for survey research and is often addressed by using random selection techniques for sampling
- **Ecological validity.** This refers to the degree that a result generalizes across different settings. For example, let's say that a pull scheduling system has been shown to improve material flow in a medium-volume manufacturing operation; in order to be able to make a similar assertion about material flow in low-volume manufacturing operation, it would be necessary to test the hypothesis in the low-volume setting. Even then, before making any valid claims about the generalizability of pull scheduling, one must be very careful to restrict claims to those contexts for which evidence exists
- **Temporal validity.** This is present to the degree that a research finding generalizes across time. For example, assume that a certain shop floor improvement technique tends to work well with many different kinds of

operators and in many different process contexts. To make claims for the temporal validity of your findings, one would have to provide supporting evidence over a period of time, for example by repeating a survey on an annual basis

3.8.2.3 Construct Validity

Construct validity relates to the extent to which an observation measures the concept it is intended to measure; in other words, are we measuring what we are looking for? Since construct validity has more to do with logical than empirical correspondence, construct validity is likely to be the most difficult to establish. Eisenhardt (1989:542) states that by using multiple sources of data and iterating between constructs and data in case research, the '. . . researcher is attempting to establish construct validity'.

The problem is that usually there is no single behaviour or operation available that can provide a complete representation of the construct. Therefore, one must clearly specify the way the construct was represented in order for others to understand what was done and to evaluate the quality of the measure. Clear and thorough discussion of the development of the constructs used in the research is often based on a critical analysis of the literature, developed through iterative empirical data analysis or a combination of both of these approaches. In demonstrating construct validity, the intent is to show that the patterns of behaviour anticipated in the theory or model proposed in the research are precisely those patterns observed in the empirical data. In many cases of research using quantitative methods, construct validity is addressed using statistical methods (such as ANOVA) whilst in qualitative research we often see the use of triangulation (the use of more than one method for collecting and analysing qualitative data) to address concerns for the construct validity of the study.

3.8.2.4 Descriptive Validity

Descriptive validity refers to the degree that the account reported by the researcher is accurate. One very useful strategy for obtaining descriptive validity is *investigator triangulation*—that is, using a number of different investigators in the collection, analysis and interpretation of the data. The intention in using investigator triangulation is to demonstrate that the observed phenomenon is represented by the data collected and using more than one observer/analyst provides evidence of the independence, integrity and, most significantly, the replicability of the study.

3.8.2.5 Interpretive Validity

Interpretive validity is present to the degree that the researcher accurately portrays the *meaning* given by the participants to what is being studied. It is all too easy to impose your or others' interpretations on participants' or respondents' perceptions. Addressing concern for interpretive validity requires one to demonstrate that the study has, in essence, 'got into the heads' of the participants and that there is an accurate documentation of their viewpoints and meanings.

Two useful strategies for obtaining interpretive validity are to discuss the findings with participants to see if they agree and to use 'low-inference descriptors' in the report—that is, using terminology relating to the variables, phenomena, experiences, etc. of interest to the study that are gathered using verbatim descriptions from participants' accounts. For example, one may be interested in asking questions about cycle time whereas the organization you are studying makes far wider use of the term 'takt' time (output rate). To address interpretive validity one would either use *takt* time as a classification or ensure that a glossary of terminology is given and discussed with all participants.

In the postmodern or constructivist research paradigm, there is acceptance of multiple interpretations and as such the approach used of interpretive validity often focuses more on documenting and critiquing the nature of the discourse between researchers or between researchers and subjects.

3.8.2.6 *Theoretical Validity*

Theoretical validity is present to the degree that a theoretical explanation provided by the researcher fits the data. Four helpful strategies for ensuring theoretical validity are:

- Extended fieldwork (collecting data in the field over an extended period of time)
- Theory triangulation (using multiple theories and perspectives to help you interpret the data)
- Pattern matching (making several predictions at once and seeing if they occur)
- Peer review (discussing your interpretations and conclusions with your peers or colleagues)

3.9 In Conclusion—Thinking about the Three Main Elements of Research Design

Gummesson (1991) provided a very useful and pragmatic overview of management research by summarizing three main concerns that researchers face —those associated with access, pre-understanding and quality. These neatly link to the three main elements of any research project.

3.9.1 Access

Whether one is undertaking data collection in the 'real world', or conducting experiments with 'artificial' data but using proprietary software, one will often encounter issues relating to difficulties and opportunities over access to the data or to the means of data analysis preferred in the study. This is why some of the 'gaps' that exist in current literature are so evident for a very simple reason—it is (or has been) very difficult to gain the required access to the problem domain to conduct the necessary research. OM research is often concerned with issues that are commercially sensitive; topics relating to issues of new product innovation, process technology investment and strategic sourcing are frequently considered by organizations to be very confidential. This can present some difficulties for the researcher in terms of obtaining access and disclosing data and findings. It may be possible to resolve this by observing strict confidentiality in the research report, but even so there are many situations where even agreement to anonymity will be insufficient in the eyes of the sponsoring or participating organization.

It is important to be practical about access—if one has difficulty getting to the data or analysis, rethink the research question or method. A great example of where researchers conducted an investigation that was hampered by lack of access was the study conducted by Garrahan and Stewart (1992) into aspects of worker flexibility at Nissan's Sunderland (UK) plant. The two authors conducted their study of vehicle assembly workers' conditions without ever entering the plant, creatively choosing to interview workers outside of the plant—in social clubs, in their home and other settings. This overcame the apparent critical problem they encountered at the outset—the organization's refusal to allow admission to the plant.

Access may also be dictated by the time available to conduct the field work and the costs associated with different research designs. It is immensely frustrating when meetings are cancelled, interviews curtailed or funding is not renewed—so it helps to have contingencies in place, even if this means resetting research questions and downgrading objectives.

3.9.2 Pre-understanding and Understanding

Pre-understanding for many doctoral researchers is largely founded on the literature, since they may have had little or no practical organizational experience. However, whilst the literature section undoubtedly shapes pre-understanding for the empirical research, the more time spent in any organizational setting, the greater will be the level of pre understanding that is brought to the problem being researched. It is true to say that by the end of the research one has become an expert in that area! For experienced (post-doctoral) researchers, pre-understanding can be shaped by practical experience, previous research and an extended exposure to the problem domain.

Gummesson (1991:60) usefully distinguishes between understanding which comes from our own experiences and observations and that provided by intermediaries—the latter being pertinent when interviewing participants to key decisions, assessing the impact of participant perceptions and trying to gain insights into the strategic rationale underpinning decisions.

Since research frequently follows an evolutionary process, with reflection between the definition of the topic and research questions, existing literature and your data and its analysis, your understanding will likewise evolve. Keeping an open mind, being prepared to change direction and, most importantly of all, being aware of the boundaries and limitations of the research, are all vital aspects of successful research that emerge as understanding of the topic evolves.

3.9.3 Quality

> Science is much closer to myth than a scientific philosophy is prepared to admit. It is one of the many forms of thought that have been developed by man and not necessarily the best. It is conspicuous, noisy and impudent but it is inherently superior only for those who have already decided in favour of a certain ideology or have accepted it without ever having its advantages and its limits.
>
> (Feyerabend, cited in Gummesson, 1991:146)

Knowing the strengths and weaknesses of one's research methodology allows for far greater clarity in the claims that can be made relating to the research conclusions. Many authors promote a mixed-method approach as providing a greater degree of understanding, depending on the specific aspect of the research subject being investigated. For sure, research that incorporates mixed methods of collection and analysis will offer richer opportunities than confining research to quantitative or qualitative methods, but the key question will always be: 'What are the most *appropriate* methods of collection and analysis?'

This chapter has set out to provide some guidance on this question.

3.10 Summary

- **Designing research in OM.** Designing research in OM needs to take into account the 'messy', iterative nature of a typical management research project. Things can, and will, go wrong. Or at least, they may not go according to your initial plan
- **The process of research**. The process of research enables you to discover issues, theories, literature sources, phenomenon, characteristics and variables that you will not have considered at the outset. This is probably one of the most exciting parts of any research project—you cannot always anticipate what you will find

- **Manage the process.** What you can do is manage the process of 'asking the right questions'. This is essentially what research design is all about. Recognize that your research is likely to evolve; as you read the literature your ideas, understanding and interests may change; as you undertake your investigation some things will work, others will not; your original ideas will change, new ideas will emerge and your focus will shift
- **Position your research and take concrete steps.** In the face of apparent uncertainty you can, however, take clear concrete steps to ensure the process you adopt is a rigorous and reliable one. This chapter addressed these steps by concentrating on how you position yourself and your research. 'Positioning' is at the heart of successful research and this chapter set out to provide consideration and practical guidance on how to consider the key decision in research design
- **Follow fundamental rules:**

  ○ Know the literature—read, reflect and annotate
  ○ Understand where your research fits into the 'big picture'—i.e. where your research is located within the subject field
  ○ Reflect on yourself as a researcher—both your 'philosophical position' and the type of researcher you consider yourself to be
  ○ Be conversant with the range of research methods and methodologies available before deciding on your research design
  ○ Recognize the utility and approaches that may support mixed methods and methodologies
  ○ Design validity and reliability into your research and constantly review and revise
  ○ Know what 'good' research looks like

References and Bibliography

Bartezzaghi, E., Corso, M. and Verganti, R. (1998). 'Managing knowledge in continuous product innovation'. Paper presented at the 5th International Product Development Management Conference, Como, Italy

Bryman, A. (1988) *Doing Research in Organisations*. London: Routledge.

Bryman, A. (1989a) *Quantity and Quality in Social Research*. London: Unwin Hyman.

Bryman, A. (1989b) *Research Methods and Organisational Studies*. London: Unwin Hyman.

Burrell, G. and Morgan, G. (1979) *Sociological Paradigms and Organisational Analysis*. London: Heinemann.

Corrêa, H.L. (1992) *The Links Between Uncertainty, Variability of Outputs and Flexibility in Manufacturing Systems*. PhD Thesis. University of Warwick, UK.

Croom, S.R. (1996) *The Management of Dyadic Capability in New Product Development: A Qualitative Analysis of Customer-Supplier Relationships during the Jaguar X300 Vehicle Development Programme*. PhD Thesis. University of Warwick, UK.

Creswell, J.W. (1994) *Research Design. Qualitative and Quantitative Approaches*. London: Sage.

Denzin, N.K. and Lincoln, Y.S. (1994) *Handbook of Qualitative Research*. Thousand Oaks: Sage Publications.

Dyer, W.G. and Wilkins, A.L. (1991) Better stories, not better constructs, to generate better theory: a rejoinder to Eisenhardt. *Academy of Management Review* 6(3) pp. 613–619.

Easterby-Smith, M., Thorpe, R. and Lowe, A. (1991) *Management Research: An Introduction*. London: Sage Publications.

Eilon, S. (1974) Seven Faces of Research. Editorial in *OMEGA The International Journal of Management Science* 2(1) pp. 1–9.

Eisenhardt, K. (1989) Building Theories From Case Research. *Academy of Management Review* 14(4) pp. 532–550.

Garrahan, P. and Stewart, P. (1992) *The Nissan Enigma: Flexibility at Work in a Local Economy*. London: Mansell.

Geppert, M. (1996) Paths of managerial learning in the east German context. *Organization Studies* 17(2) pp. 249–268.

Germain, R., Dröge, C. and Christensen, W. (2001) The mediating role of operations knowledge in the relationship of context with performance. *Journal of Operations Management* 19 pp. 453–469.

Gill, J. and Johnson, P. (1991) *Research Methods for Managers*. London: Paul Chapman Publishing.

Gummesson, E. (1991) *Qualitative Methods in Management Research*. California: Sage Publications Inc.

Habermas, J. (1972) *Knowledge and Human Interests*. London: Heinemann.

Hart, C. (1998) *Doing a Literature Review*. London: Sage Publications

Hassard, J. (1988) Overcoming hermeticism in organizational theory: An alternative to paradigm incommensurability. *Human Relations* 41 pp. 247–259.

Hirschman, C.H. and Holbrook, M.B. (1992) *Postmodern Consumer Research: The Study of Consumption As Text*. Newbury Park: Sage Publications Inc.

Kuhn, T.S. (1980) Theory choice: In Klempe, E.D., Hollinger, R., Kline, A.D. (eds.), *Introductory Readings in the Philosophy of Sicence*. Buffalo, New York: Prometheus Books.

Lawson, M.B.B. (2001) In praise of slack: time is the essence. *Academy of Management Executive* 15(3) pp. 125–135.

Magnusson, M. (2000) *Innovation and Efficiency—A Knowledge-Based Approach to Organizing Industrial Firms*. Doctoral Thesis, Chalmers University of Technology, Göteborg.

Meredith, J.R., Raturi, A., Gyampah, K.A. and Kaplan, B. (1989) Alternative research paradigms in operations. *Journal of Operations Management* 8(4) pp. 297–326.

Mingers, J. (2001) Combining IS research methods: Towards a pluralist methodology. *Information Systems Research* (INFORMS) 12(2) pp. 240–259.

Mingers, J. and Brocklesby, J. (1997) Multimethodology: towards a framework for mixing methodologies. *Omega: International Journal of Management Science* 25(5) pp. 489–507.

Nelson, C., Grossberg, P.A. and Treichler, L. (1992) *Cultural Studies*. New York: Routledge.

Nohria, N. and Gulati, R. (1996) Is slack good or bad for innovation? *Academy of Management Journal* 39(5) pp. 1245–1264.

Pannirselvam, G.P., Ferguson, L.A., Ash, R.C. and Siferd, S. (1999) Operations management research: an update for the 1990s. *Journal of Operations Management* 18 pp. 95–112.

Pilkington, A. and Liston-Heyes, C. (1999) Is production and operations management a discipline? A citation/co-citation study. *International Journal of Operations and Production Management* 19(1) pp. 7–20.

Popper, Sir K. (1957) Philosophy of science: a personal report. In Mace, C.A. (ed), *British Philosophy in Mid-Century*. London: Allen.

Quine, W.V. and Ullian, J.S. (1980) Hypothesis. In Klempe, E.D., Hollinger, R., Kline, A.D. (eds.), *Introductory Readings in the Philosophy of Sicence*. Buffalo, New York: Prometheus Books.

Richtnér, A. (2004) *Managing Knowledge Creation. Examining Organizational Slack and Knowledge in Product Development Projects*. Doctoral Thesis, Stockholm School of Economics, Sweden.

Singh, J.V. (1986) Performance, slack and risk taking in organizational decision making. *Academy of Management Journal* 29(3) pp. 562–585.

Sower, V., Motwani, J. and Savoie, M. (1997) Classics in production and operations management. *International Journal of Operations and Production Management* 17(1) pp. 15–28.

Stigum, B. (1990) *Toward a Formal Science of Economics: The Axiomatic Method in Economics and Econometrics*. Cambridge, MA: MIT Press.

Swamidass, P. (1991) Empirical science: new frontier in operations management research. *Academy of Management Review* 16(4) pp. 793–814.

Tranfield, D., Denyer, D. and Smart, P. (2003) Towards a methodology for developing evidence-informed management knowledge by means of systematic review. *British Journal of Management* 14 pp. 207–222.

Wacker, J.G. (2004) A theory of formal conceptual definitions: developing theory-building measurement instruments. *Journal of Operations Management* 22 pp. 629–650.

Westbrook, R. (1995) Action research: a new paradigm for research in production and operations management. *International Journal of Operations and Production Management* 15(12) pp. 6–20.

Wheelwright, S.C. and Clark, K.B. (1992) *Revolutionizing Product Development: Quantum Leaps in Speed, Efficiency and Quality*. New York: The Free Press.

Yin, R. (1993) *Application of Case Study Research*. London: Sage Publication.

Zajac, E.J., Golden, B.R. and Shortell, S.M. (1991) New organizational forms for enhancing innovation: the case of internal corporate joint ventures. *Management Science* 37(2) pp. 170–184.

4 Surveys [1]

Cipriano Forza

Chapter Overview

- When to use survey research
- The survey research process
- What is needed prior to survey research design:

  - The theoretical model
  - Defining the unit of analysis
  - Developing and testing the operational definitions
  - Stating the hypotheses

- Designing a survey

  - Considering constraints and information needs
  - Planning the activities
  - Designing the sample
  - Choosing the data collection method
  - Developing the measurement instrument
  - Defining how to approach companies and respondents

- Pilot testing the questionnaire

  - Handling non-respondents and non-response bias
  - Inputting and cleaning data
  - Assessing the measurement validity and reliability

- Survey execution
- Data analysis and interpretation of results
- What information should be reported in articles

4.1 Introduction

If we compare contemporary research in OM with that conducted in the early 1980s, we notice an increase in the use of empirical data (derived from field observation) to supplement mathematics, modelling and simulation in order to develop and test theories. Many authors have called for this empirical research since OM became an established field of study (such as marketing, management information systems, etc.) within the management discipline (Meredith et al., 1989; Flynn et al., 1990; Filippini, 1997; Scudder and Hill, 1998). The rationale was to reduce the gap between management theory and practice, to increase the usefulness of OM research to practitioners and, more recently, to increase scientific recognition of the OM field. Survey research is one of the methods widely used to perform this empirical research in OM.

4.1.1 *What Survey Research is and For What Purposes it can be Used*

In OM, as in other fields of business, research can be undertaken to solve an existing problem in a work setting. This chapter focuses on survey research conducted for a different reason—to contribute to the general body of knowledge in a particular area of interest. In general, a survey involves the collection of information from individuals (through mailed questionnaires, telephone calls, personal interview, etc.) about themselves or about the social units to which they belong (Rossi et al., 1983). Usually information is collected only about a subset (a sample) of elements belonging to the entire group of people, firms, plants or things that the researcher aims to investigate. The selection of the sample is made according to certain rules so that the researcher can obtain information about large populations with a known level of accuracy (Rea and Parker, 1992).

Survey research, like the other types of field study, can contribute to the advance of scientific knowledge in different ways (Kerlinger, 1986; Babbie, 1990). Accordingly, researchers often distinguish between exploratory, confirmatory (theory-testing), and descriptive survey research (Pinsonneault and Kraemer, 1993; Filippini, 1997; Malhotra and Grover, 1998).

Exploratory survey research takes place during the early stages of research on a phenomenon, when the objective is to gain preliminary insight into a topic, and provides the basis for more in-depth survey research. Usually, there is no model and concepts of interest need to be better understood and measured. In the very preliminary stages of inquiry, an exploratory survey can help researchers to determine the concepts to measure in relation to the phenomenon of interest, the best way to measure them and how to discover new facets of the phenomenon under investigation. Subsequently, an exploratory survey can be used to uncover or provide preliminary evidence of association among concepts. Later, it can help researchers to explore the validity boundaries of a theory.

In OM, new topics continuously arise that have been scarcely researched or not researched at all in the past, thus requiring exploratory research. Product configuration is an example of such an issue brought to the attention of the OM community recently. In framing exploratory survey research on this issue and specifying its intended contribution, Salvador and Forza (2004) write as follows:

> As a whole, the examples present in the literature suggest that engineering a company's operations in order to get the maximum potential benefits out of product configuration might be a challenging task for a company. We do not know, however, where and to what extent the issues reported in individual cases may be generalized to a larger population of companies . . . Because of the embryonic stage of published research on the impact of product configuration on operations, the nature of our empirical inquiry is exploratory . . . we chose to run a large-scale survey in order to assess whether or not the case-based information present in the literature can be generalized to companies facing the customization–responsiveness squeeze . . . This allowed us to collect evidence of widely perceived managerial issues relating to product configuration . . . Future works may build on the insights we provided, articulating a theory of the interdependency between a company's operations and the adoption of configurable product structures. Based on theoretical advances, multi-items measures tapping some relevant constructs underlying the studied phenomenon may be developed.
>
> (Salvador and Forza, 2004)

Sometimes exploratory survey research is carried out using data collected in previous studies in order to gain new insights into a topic at low cost before embarking on a new ad hoc survey. In such cases survey research may be used easily to explore associations between concepts or boundaries of validity in these associations. For example, Corbett and Whybark (2001), in presenting their research on the relationship between manufacturing practices and performances, state:

> The first objective of this paper is to explore the relationship between a manufacturing practice index and a performance index using data gathered by the Global Manufacturing Research Group (GMRG) to see if the results are the same as found in the other data {surveys . . .}. The larger the number and intensity of the practices used, the greater the performance of the firm. When the entire GMRG data set is used, however, there is still a great deal of scatter in the data; more than in the results of some of the other researchers . . . It was possible to identify two groups of firms that differed significantly on their performance indices, but that had the same practice scores . . . Still, it is clear that the managers in some firms extract greater performance from a given set of practices than other managers can. Finding out why should be a high research priority.
>
> (Corbett and Whybark, 2001)

Confirmatory (or theory-testing or explanatory) survey research takes place when knowledge of a phenomenon has been articulated in a theoretical form using well-defined concepts, models and propositions. Some established OM subfields (such as manufacturing strategy, quality management and, more recently, supply chain management) have been researched extensively, in part through survey research, and the corresponding bodies of knowledge have been developed enough to allow researchers to engage in theory-testing survey research (Handfield and Melnyk, 1998). Here, data collection is carried out with the specific aim of testing the concepts developed in relation to the phenomenon, the linkages hypothesized among the concepts and the validity boundaries of the model. Correspondingly, all of the potential error sources have to be considered carefully. Narasimhan and Kim (2002), in a typical example of OM theory-testing survey research, clearly present the theory that they are going to test and keep a tight connection between each part of their work and this theory:

> The focus and thrust of this paper mirrors what has been said in the literature. The premise . . . is that coordination between marketing strategies (diversification) and SCI {Supply Chain Integration} strategies will lead to better performance than when the two strategies are pursued independently . . . In short, most empirical studies have either ignored or failed to fully address how diversification strategy affects performance. This paper posits that SCI moderates the relationship between diversification and performance, by potentially reducing the importance of interaction effect between product diversification (PD) and IMD {International Market Diversification} on performance . . . The remainder of the paper is organized as follows. The next section discusses the literature review leading to the development of a research model to be tested. The following section discusses the sampling frame, measures and data collection. This is followed by a discussion of the results of model testing. In the final section we present implications and conclusions.
>
> (Narasimhan and Kim, 2002)

Sometimes, before embarking on a confirmatory survey to test a theory, OM researchers use secondary data to expose a theory to empirical tests that can allow for theory refinement and better design of the survey. This approach is different from exploratory survey research based on available data, in that theory is, in this case, already well formalized. Even so, secondary data usually have a number of limitations that the researchers should mention openly. Anderson et al. (1995) make an exemplary use of this kind of survey research:

> Only recently has such a theory of quality management to describe and explain the effectiveness of the Deming Management Method been articulated by Anderson, Rungtusanatham, and Schroeder . . . In this

paper, the proposed theory . . . is empirically examined. The constructs
. . . are operationalized using measurement statements developed by the
World-Class Manufacturing research project team . . . It is important to
note that this paper does not claim to present formal conclusive tests of
the proposed theory; the secondary nature of both the constructs operationalization and the data limits the ability to do so.

> (Anderson et al., 1995)

It should be noted that hypothesis generation and testing can be achieved
both through the process of deduction (i.e. develop the model, formulate
testable hypotheses, collect data, then test hypotheses) and the process of
induction (i.e. collect the data, formulate new hypotheses based on what is
known from the data collected and test them). This chapter follows a traditional post positivistic perspective and, therefore, refers to the first approach.
However, a researcher who follows a different epistemological approach
can disagree. Bagozzi and Phillips (1982), for example, state that the two
approaches can be applied in the same research. They proposed a new methodological paradigm for organizational research, termed holistic construal.
This approach 'is neither rigidly deductive (or formalistic) nor purely
exploratory. Rather it subsumes a process by which theories and hypotheses
are tentatively formulated deductively, tested on data and, later, reformulated
and retested until a meaningful outcome emerges.' This approach 'is
intended to encompass aspects of both the theory-construction and theory-
testing phases'. Therefore, in research following this approach we can observe
a starting model and a refined model, as illustrated by Forza and Filippini's
(1998) article on total quality management (TQM):

> The proposed model contains seven dimensions: orientation towards
> quality, human resources, TQM links with suppliers, TQM links with
> customers, process control, customer satisfaction and conformance . . .
> The p-value of the hypothesised model turned out to . . . {have} a very
> high goodness-of-fit . . ., but an analysis of the t-value revealed that the
> relation between 'human resources' and 'process control' is not statistic-
> ally significant . . . The theory on SEM {structural equation modelling}
> suggests the suppression of the non-significant relation in this case
> . . . Since the link between 'orientation towards quality' and 'human
> resources' is statistically significant . . ., a fact that supports the import-
> ance attributed to human resources by the theory on TQM, an attempt
> was made to see whether 'human resources' have a direct influence on
> performance . . . A second attempt was made by hypothesising a relation
> between 'orientation towards quality' and 'customer satisfaction', medi-
> ated by 'human resources' {. . . Both attempts lead to not significance in
> newly hypothesized relationships between 'human resources' and other
> constructs. The article at this point discusses the theoretical and practical
> meaning of eliminating the construct 'human resources'.} Therefore . . .

in order to obtain a more parsimonious and better fitted model . . .
human resource construct {has been dropped . . .}. The modified
model {thus obtained is tested and results discussed in detail. It should
be noted that this modified model has been developed deductively
(using available knowledge) and inductively (using empirical evidence
emerged from the data being analysed)}.

(Forza and Filippini, 1998)

Descriptive survey research is aimed at understanding the relevance of a phenomenon and describing the incidence or distribution of the phenomenon
in a population. The primary research objective is not theory development,
although through the facts described it can provide useful hints both for
theory building and theory refinement (Dubin, 1978; Malhotra and Grover,
1998; Wacker, 1998). Many issues, interesting to practitioners, policy makers
and academics, can be researched through descriptive survey. Examples
include the level of adoption of best practices or the investigation on the
performance objectives pursued by companies in different sectors or countries. The following passages taken from an article written by Husseini and
O'Brien (2004) clearly illustrate the content and the structure of a paper
based on descriptive survey research:

> This paper aims to investigate manufacturing strategies and practices in
> . . . newly industrialising countries (NICs) . . . A vast amount of litera-
> ture exists in the manufacturing strategy area. We review those related
> to our discussions . . . Data from the first round of the International
> Manufacturing Strategy Survey (IMSS) . . . constitutes the main source
> for our study . . . We consider a comparative analysis of manufacturing
> strategy and practice data between a group of NICs, referred to as
> Group 1, and the two benchmarks which we define for this purpose . . .
> Group 1 consists of four countries: Argentina, Brazil, Chile and Mexico
> which are the four largest economies in Latin America . . . Benchmark 1
> represents average data for the two industrially leading countries, Japan
> and USA . . . Benchmark 2 represents the average IMSS data for the UK,
> Germany and Italy . . . The results . . . help in identifying some general
> characteristics for the firms in NICs as compared to those in more
> developed countries . . . {Firms operating in NICs} are facing a con-
> siderable amount of under-investment in process technology, . . . disec-
> onomies of scale due to their much limited markets . . . Due to the
> complexity of manufacturing strategy formulation for the kind of less
> stable and or less supportive environment, and also due to its particular
> difficulties in implementation, we believe a hybrid use of both planning
> and adaptive (or incremental) modes for manufacturing strategy process
> could be more appropriate for the firms in NICs. However, such a
> hybrid approach needs to be more elaborated.

(Husseini and O'Brien, 2004)

4.1.2 When to Use Survey Research

Theoretical constraints associated with the state of the art of knowledge on the researched issue and practical constraints associated with the intended kind of contribution may limit survey applicability. As a consequence, survey research may be not the best choice or may need to be combined with other methods.

When the available knowledge on a research issue is very limited, then concepts are not well defined, measures are not available, lessons from previous empirical research may not be available, associations between concepts and explanations of these associations may be unknown, and so on. Exploratory survey research and, to a certain extent, descriptive survey research are the available survey choices. They provide new insights on the phenomena, their strengths, the contexts in which they take place and on how to measure them. These kinds of survey complement the knowledge gained though case studies, overcoming the limited generalizability of cases and pushing towards the development of measures that can be used in different contexts. However, they do not effectively support the discovery of subtle or complex relations or really new aspects. The highly structured questionnaires and the limited presence of open questions, necessary to perform good quantitative analyses, limit the exploration capability in comparison with cases. Therefore, cases and survey should be seen as complementary in exploration and theory-building research.

When knowledge on a topic is widely available and theory-testing research is to be carried out, then theory-testing survey research should be considered. Survey is one of the preferred methods in this situation, as it allows for testing if the hypothesized relationships or differences hold in different contexts. This generalization capability is one of the main strengths of the survey method, together with the relatively limited effort required to collect and analyse data compared to other methods. However, if the aim of the researcher is to investigate the mechanisms that explain the hypothesized relationships, then survey research may present some limitations on its own and, so, its use in combination with case studies may represent a better methodological alternative. Likewise, if the researcher aims to give detailed prescriptions for practice, for example to implement a postponement initiative in order to reduce inventory costs, then survey research falls short on precision or simply may not be feasible due to the need for detailed information on the context and on the relevant variables. In this case, simulation or mathematical modelling is preferable, although survey may help in providing parameters or other empirical data for use.

Therefore, survey is a suitable method when knowledge of the phenomenon is not too underdeveloped, when generalization is an important intended contribution, when the variables and the context can be detailed, when the empirical evidence sought concerns 'how variables are related', 'where the relations hold' and 'to what extent a given relation is present'.

When research needs depart from these conditions, survey research needs to be complemented by other methods.

4.1.3 What OM Topics have been Researched by Means of Survey

Survey research has been used (sometimes in combination with other methods) to investigate phenomena in different OM subfields (see Table 4.1). The researcher interested in a given OM subfield can gain valuable insights into the possibility of survey use by considering whether survey research has been employed previously in that subfield. No previous use of survey research may suggest the existence of severe constraints, while previous use may suggest that survey research is applicable, albeit with careful scrutiny of previous experience.

Quality management, operations strategy and supply chain management (and in particular purchasing) are three OM subfields widely researched through survey. Even though survey is widely used in these OM subfields, there are discussions concerning survey appropriateness and how survey research should be designed in a specific subfield. Some researchers address such points in a systematic way, thus paving the way to a better understanding of possible contributions and shortcomings of each research method applied to a specific research issue. For example Barnes (2001), while discussing the use of survey to investigate the manufacturing strategy process, writes:

> It is also extremely doubtful whether survey research would provide the rich data set required . . . Survey research risks superficiality, and may be unreliable if reliant on a single respondent from one organisation (Bowman and Ambrosini, 1997). This problem might be particularly acute when investigating the strategy process, as the perceptions and interpretations of events by individuals are likely to play a key role . . . Surveys seem best suited to large scale data gathering, especially where factually based data is required, as would be the case when investigating the content of operations strategy (e.g. Flynn et al., 1997) . . . Notwithstanding Hill et al.'s (1999) criticisms of their use in operations management research, questionnaires have been used to investigate aspects of the operations strategy process (e.g. Anderson et al., 1991; Tunalv, 1990). Questionnaires invariably have the benefit of greater efficiency for the researcher. Key issues in their use centre on what questions to ask, in what form and of whom. It is generally agreed that questionnaires are best suited to asking specific rather than general questions, and for closed rather than open questions (Robson, 1993). As such they are best aimed at collecting data to test theories, hypotheses or propositions . . . The effectiveness of the method depends entirely on the quality of the questionnaire responses obtained. This in turn relies on the diligence, goodwill and level of understanding of respondents.

Table 4.1 Survey Research in OM Subfields. Adapted from Pannirselvam et al. (1999) The review considers 1,754 OM articles which appeared in the period 1992–1997 in the following journals: Decision Sciences (DS), IIE Transactions, International Journal of Operations and Production Management (IJOPM), International Journal of Production Research (IJPR), Journal of Operations Management (JOM), Management Science (MS), Production and Operations Management (POM)

	Survey	Modelling and survey	Theoretical conceptual and survey	Case study and survey	Simulation and survey	Total survey	Total topic	% survey
Strategy	77	3	6	2		88	213	41%
Quality	51	2	5			58	222	26%
Process design	33	3	2			38	221	17%
Inventory control	16		1	1		18	317	6%
Purchasing	15					15	39	38%
Scheduling	13	1				14	500	3%
Services	11	1		1		13	53	25%
Distribution	7					7	61	11%
Facility layout	2	3			1	6	149	4%
Project management	3					3	34	9%
Aggregate planning	3					3	13	23%
Work measurement	3					3	10	30%
Quality work life	3					3	4	75%
Maintenance	2					2	40	5%
Facility Location		1				1	21	5%
Forecasting	1					1	20	5%
Capacity Planning						0	41	0%
Count total	240	14	14	4	1	273	1958	14%
Article total	206	11	10	3	1	231	1754	13%
Double count number	34	3	4	1	0	42	204	21%

Foregoing the opportunity of personal contact with respondents is less time-consuming for the researcher. However, it prevents respondents from seeking clarification from the researcher and the researcher from responding to non-verbal communications. Interviewing a key respondent in the organisation might alleviate these dangers, but this reduces efficiency.

(Barnes, 2001)

4.1.4 How Survey Research has been Used in OM

Recognition of the value of empirical research in OM has led to an increase in both the number and the percentage of studies based on empirical research and, especially, on survey research (Rungtusanatham et al., 2003). The number of survey-based articles increased steadily from the mid 1980s to the early 1990s, and then increased sharply from 1993. By 1996, empirical research-based articles accounted for approximately 30% of the research published in the main OM outlets, and survey-based articles accounted for 60% of this empirical subset. As survey research has been used more widely, rigour has also increased. Several studies have helped the discipline to achieve this outcome. In the late 1980s and, again, in the late 1990s a number of articles contrasted the use of survey and other research methods in OM, thus providing insights into when and why to use survey research (see Table 4.2). In 1990, Flynn et al. provided general indications on how to use survey in OM and subsequently, in the second half of 1990s, a number of studies analysed how survey research both had been and should be used in OM (see Table 4.3). After 2000 a number of articles have focused on very specific aspects of survey research in OM and on the application to specific OM subfields (see Tables 4.3 and 4.4). All of these articles constitute a valuable body of knowledge on and capitalize on the experience of survey research in OM.

Yet, in spite of the progress made, there are still many opportunities to improve the application of survey research. These opportunities are noted in papers reported in Tables 4.2, 4.3 and 4.4 and are recognized by journal reviewers. Sometimes reviewers have a hard job to push authors to improve the quality of their survey-based articles. Further, some authors have the bad habit of quoting methodological articles almost without using their suggestions. This habit does not help the improvement of OM survey research and is not respectful of reviewers.

Improvement opportunities relate to several aspects of survey research and increase in number, detail and required effort as the time goes by. However, they may be grouped around the following general issues:

- Framing the survey research in terms of theoretical contribution (thorough usage of available theoretical background, clear statement of the intended theoretical contribution, use of clearly defined concepts, clear consideration of the boundaries of validity of the results etc.)

Table 4.2 OM Survey Research Usage Compared to the Usage of Other Methods

Article	Content related to survey research
Amoako-Gyampah and Meredith, 1989	They analyse (in terms of research content and methods) both the papers published in 10 journals over the period 1982–1987 and the papers in the pipeline (published in the Proceedings of the Annual Meeting of the Decision Sciences Institute, 1986 and 1987)
Meredith et al., 1989	They present and discuss alternative research paradigms in OM. Subsequently, they classify the articles published in DS and MS in 1977 and the articles published in the same journals plus JOM in 1987. The incidence of survey-based articles is 0% in 1977 and 4% in 1987
Wacker, 1998	He discusses what a good theory is, compares different approaches (among which survey) to contribute to theoretical development, analyses the application of these approaches across JOM, MS, IJPR, IJOPM, POM, Harvard Business Review (HBR), DS, Product Innovation Management (PIM) in the period 1991–1995.
Scudder and Hill, 1998	They review and classify empirical research in OM by considering 13 journals (traditional outlets of OM research) in the decade 1986–1995. They provide evidence of the growing usage of survey research in OM
Pannirselvam et al., 1999	They assess the state of research in OM by examining the research topics addressed and the methodologies used. The considered articles were published in DS, IIE, IJOPM, IJPR, JOM, MS, POM in the period 1992–1997. They provide detailed information about the use of survey research (eventually in combination with other methods) to study the various OM topics
Gupta et al., 2006	They review and evaluate more than 150 empirical research papers published in POM journal over the period 1992–2005. They classify the empirical research articles based on their primary purpose, data collection approach, data analysis technique and operations topics

- Use of scientific (i.e. reliable and valid) measurement instruments, possibly shared across OM researchers (if a measure cannot be trusted, no empirical result deriving from that measure can be trusted)
- Rigour in survey design and execution phases (sampling, administration, data analysis etc.)
- Clarity and explicitness in reporting information on the survey execution (these are basic requirements if critical use of results, comparison and replication are to be possible)

The rest of this chapter is devoted to presenting the overall structure of a

Table 4.3 Specific Analyses of Survey Research in Operations Management

Article	Content related to survey research
Flynn et al., 1990	They provide the foundation of empirical research in OM. They present various empirical research designs with a special focus on survey. They provide several useful prescriptions and tools for survey research. A list of scales usable in OM surveys is provided, exemplified and discussed. A list of empirical researches in OM is provided with the specification of topic investigated and analytical method used in each research
Verma and Goodale, 1995	They discuss the importance of statistical power analysis in field-based empirical research in OM and related disciplines. They analyse the statistical power of 28 survey-based articles published in JOM and DS in the period 1989–1992. They draw implications for OM survey research
Filippini, 1997	He traces the evolution of OM topics and research approaches in the period 1986–1996. He analyses the Proceedings of the Annual Meeting of the Decision Sciences Institute, 1996 and compares the results with those of Amoako-Gyampah and Meredith (1989). He draws attention to the need for improving the quality of survey research in OM
Flynn et al., 1997	They provide an overview of the first round of the survey-based World Class Manufacturing (WCM) research project. In a subsequent round this project was conducted at an international level. It is characterized by great attention to the measurement issue and by the wide coverage of OM issues. This project is currently on its third round involving 10 countries
Whybark, 1997	He provides a detailed view of the GMRG (Global Manufacturing Research Group) survey research. This is one of the longest established survey research programmes in OM. This project involved many countries and provided knowledge on the international usage of manufacturing practices
Van Doselaar and Sharman, 1997	They present the details of the survey process and procedure of a successful survey in the transportation and distribution sector. Such a detailed information is usually not reported in survey-based articles due to space constraints
Collins and Cordon, 1997	They identify and discuss methodological issues surrounding the design and administration of large-scale surveys. They compare the design and execution of two survey research studies on manufacturing strategy that led to insights concerning sample selection, respondent preparation, bias, etc.

(Continued Overleaf)

Table 4.3 (Continued)

Article	Content related to survey research
Forza and Vinelli, 1998	They present the opinions of 89 OM scholars on the desirable characteristics of survey research as well as the expected contribution of future survey researches
Forza and Di Nuzzo, 1998	They analyse the possibility of combining results of different surveys and provide suggestions in order to allow future meta-analyses on OM issues
Malhotra and Grover, 1998	In order to bridge the gap between survey research and theory development they provide a normative perspective on what constitutes 'good' survey research, developed a list of 17 ideal survey research attributes. They then applied these 17 attributes to evaluate 25 survey-based OM papers from four journals between 1990 and 1995 to evaluate OM survey research and provide suggestions for its improvement
Rungtusanatham, 1998	He draws attention to content validity. This is one of the first articles that address this topic
O'Leary-Kelly and Vokurka, 1998	They provide an in-depth review of different methods available for assessing the construct validity of measures. They provide some examples taken from OM research on manufacturing flexibility
Handfield and Melnyk, 1998	They reflect on the theory-building process of an empirical OM research. They exemplify their thought by means of OM research on TQM. They provide indications for reviewers of empirical theory driven research
Hensley, 1999	He focuses specifically on the development and use of reliable and valid measurement scales in OM research. He reviews six studies in terms of the approaches to the development and validation of multiple-item measurement scales. He identifies and discusses strengths and weaknesses of these six studies in order to evaluate methods of scale development used in OM, discusses why OM researchers encounter difficulties in developing scales and advises on when and why OM researchers may want to develop scales
Klassen and Jacobs, 2001	They assess the different effectiveness of mail, fax, PC disk-by-mail and Web mail survey (combined with e-mail notification). They used a total sample of 118 respondents from both small and large companies and from both manufacturing and service companies. They compared the different surveys against cost, coverage error, response rate, item completion rate and systematic respondent bias
Forza, 2002	He presents in detail the survey research process in the OM research context. He provides indications for each phase of the survey research process in order to improve research quality and efficiency

Frolich, 2002	He analyses the 233 single manager surveys published in DS, IJOPM, IJPR, JOM, MS, PIM, POM in the period 1999–2000. He investigates answer rates and the dependence by the survey planning. He reviews techniques to improve answer rates of OM surveys
Boyer et al., 2002	Though a controlled experiment they compare print versus electronic surveys
Rungtusanatham et al., 2003	They consider six major OM journals (DS; MS; JOM; IJPR; IJOPM; POM) and analyse in detail all the survey-based articles published in these journals over 21 years (1980–2000) for a total of 285 articles. The historical analysis provides an overview of the issues researched through survey and of several methodological aspects
Ketokivi and Schroeder, 2004	They conduct a multitrait–multimethod analysis of perceptual performance measures to investigate item-specific trait, method and error variance
Tsikriktsis, 2005	He discusses the research implications of missing data and types of missing data. He provides recommendations on which techniques should be used under different circumstances to improve the treatment of missing data in OM survey research
Shah and Goldstein, 2006	They review applications of structural equation modelling (SEM) in MS, JOM, DS and POM till August 2003 and provide guidelines to improve the use of SEM in OM research
Rungtusanatham et al., 2007	They discuss when it is appropriate to pool data provided by key informants with transparently different demographics across units of analysis so as to create a single larger data set for statistical manipulations. They provide guidelines for pre and post data collection actions to assure measurement equivalence
Roth et al., 2008	They provide a compilation of multi-item scales and objective items derived from published empirical OM articles. Each measure is presented in detail, providing description of the construct, of the measure and of its validity and reliability. Examples of questionnaires are provided

survey research process (section 4.2), to provide a detailed road map of this process and prescriptions on how to conduct it (sections 4.3–4.8) and to illustrate the properties of well-performed survey research (section 4.9) in order to reduce the shortcomings that OM survey research is likely to encounter. The chapter should help OM researchers, especially those engaging in survey research for the first time, by providing an overview of the survey research process.

Table 4.4 Survey Research in Specific Subfields of Operations Management

Article	Content related to survey research
Boyer and Pagell, 2000	They investigate a number of methodological issues regarding measures used in operations strategy and advanced manufacturing technology
Barnes, 2001	He reviews the methodological options for the empirical investigation of the operations strategy process thus including survey. The advantages and disadvantages of each, together with circumstances in which they might be used best, are identified. He focuses on the practical implications for researchers
Dangayach and Deshmukh, 2001	They examine manufacturing strategy articles published in refereed journals until January 2001. They provide some information on the use of survey on the manufacturing strategy topic
Ho et al., 2002	They address several issues relevant for supply chain management survey research such as construct definition, construct validity and modelling choice
Davies and Kochhar, 2002	They address methodological issues (several related to survey) which can improve the quality of findings from manufacturing best practice and performance studies

4.2 The Survey Research Process

Survey research is a long process which requires a pre-existing theoretical model (or conceptual framework). It includes a number of related sub-processes: the process of translating the theoretical domain into the empirical domain; the design and pilot testing processes; the process of collecting data for theory testing; the data analysis process; and the process of interpreting the results and writing the report. This survey research process is illustrated in Figure 4.1.

The required level of sophistication of the conceptual model differs among the different types of survey research. Exploratory survey research, in the most exploratory fashion, can be carried out without a theoretical model. However the definition of a sketchy framework that at least classifies the variables measured (for example levers and performance) will improve the quality of the survey and will increase the contribution of subsequent data analysis and interpretation. Theory-testing survey research puts great importance on the model since, by definition, it is not theory-testing if, from the outset, it is not based on a theoretical model. Any flaw in the modelling undermines the contribution of such theory-testing survey research. Descriptive survey research does not necessarily require a model, since only a rigorous definition of the concepts to be measured is required. However, again in this case, the availability of a model will facilitate a

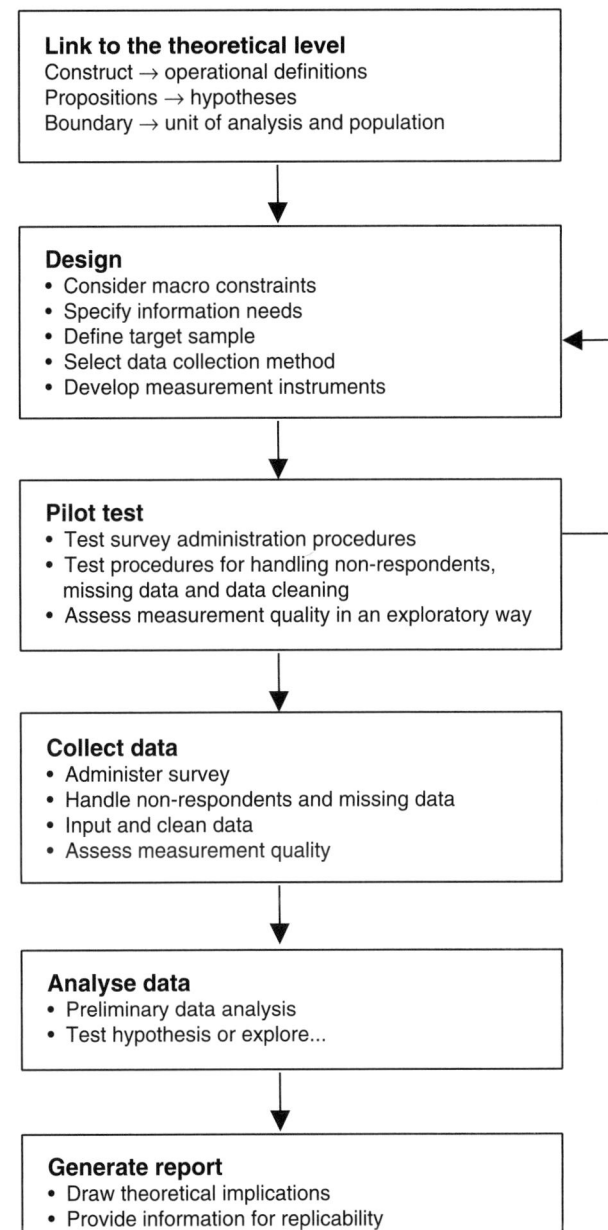

Figure 4.1 The Survey Research Process.

meaningful presentation of the results, a reduction in the length of the questionnaires, and will improve the usability of the resulting data for other purposes. Therefore, the rule is 'the more well developed the model, the better' for any kind of survey research, although the minimum acceptable level is different.

The analyses performed when data are available differ among the different types of survey research. Exploratory survey research uses more descriptive analyses, fewer model-based analyses (for example it uses exploratory factor analysis instead of confirmatory factor analysis). Furthermore it may perform many different trials to gather new insights from the available data. A proposed model can be the result of the data analysis. Theory-testing survey research carries out the previously planned analyses and, even, post-hoc analyses to better interpret the obtained results. Relational analyses are used more than descriptive analyses in such theory-testing survey research. Eventually, the tested model can be modified and retested. Descriptive survey research uses descriptive analyses, however it can also use data reduction techniques (such as factor analysis) to present a more parsimonious view of the phenomenon being described.

The care and rigour with which the various steps of survey research are performed varies across survey research types. Exploratory survey research does not put stringent constraints on measurement. Single item perceptual measures may be acceptable, if knowledge on that aspect is limited. Theory-testing survey research requires extreme rigour in all analyses. For example, measures must satisfy all the requirements of good measurement. Descriptive survey research requires rigour in representing the population under study but less rigour than theory-testing survey research in terms of measurement.

In summary, different types of surveys place different emphasis on the model, require different rigour in measures, imply different sophistication of data analysis, need different theoretical efforts, etc. All of these differences may place different emphases on the various phases of the overall survey research process even though all of these different phases are present.

The following sections focus on theory-testing survey research, as it is the most demanding type of survey research. In this way it is easier to increase awareness both of possible shortcomings and of useful preventative actions that can be taken. However, in the various sections some consideration is paid to the other types of survey research as well, especially in section 4.8 where the main differences between theory-testing survey research and other types of survey research are synthesized.

4.3 What is Needed Prior to Survey Research Design

Before starting survey-based research, the researcher should have taken the steps previously recalled in this text by Karlsson (Chapter 1) and Croom (Chapter 2). First, the researcher should have a clear idea of what the problem is about and should discuss it in depth. Secondly, the researcher should map the problem in the existing literature, so as to be cognizant of what is already known and what is still unknown. This activity might reveal that the original idea of the researcher is not feasible or has been pursued already by some-body else. Thirdly, the researcher should clarify the intended contribution. For all of these points, a thorough literature review is crucial.

The contribution of a survey research project depends on how well it is based on existing knowledge, since in survey research, as distinct from case studies or action research, the structured and specific data collection procedures make it difficult to recover missing information. In exploratory survey research a careful consideration of available knowledge allows the researcher to perform the most rigorous survey permitted by the state of the art of knowledge on the phenomenon. In theory testing it facilitates the reuse of measures, explanations and previous results, thus enabling surveys that do not suffer the limitations encountered in the previous ones. To clarify this point, consider the differing motivations of both exploratory and theory-testing survey-based research.

Exploratory survey research may pose several problems in framing the research, as little support is provided by the available literature. Appropriate framing and positioning of the research is important to focus the research and to open up a discussion, thus paving the way to further research. This effort clearly emerges in the Salvador and Forza (2004) exploratory survey-based article, where they write:

> The management scholar addressing the topic of product configuration has to confront two key issues: (1) is product configuration really a management topic, or should be left to knowledge engineers and design theorists? (2) in case it has some managerial implications, how relevant are these implications in the business world? In addressing the first question, we defined an appropriate operational context for product configuration, i.e. the customization–responsiveness squeeze. Then, we synthesized what product configuration is from a technical standpoint, by drawing on past research by Artificial Intelligence and Design Theory scholars. Finally, we conceptually explained why it is relevant from a management standpoint. We addressed the second question by means of a hybrid quantitative–qualitative exploratory research design.
>
> (Salvador and Forza, 2004)

In contrast, theory-testing survey research is based on more established knowledge and, therefore, it is easier to communicate clearly the focus of the research. This excerpt from Anderson et al. (1995) illustrates this positioning of theory-testing survey research:

> Only recently has such a theory of Quality Management to describe and explain the effectiveness of Deming Management Method been articu-lated by Anderson, Rungtusanatham, and Schroeder . . . In this paper,

the proposed theory of quality management underlying the Deming Management Method is empirically examined.

(Anderson et al., 1995)

4.3.1 The Theoretical Model

Before starting survey-based research, the researcher has to (when conducting a theory-testing survey) or may find it more convenient (when conducting an exploratory or descriptive survey) to establish the conceptual model. He complies with this requirement (Dubin, 1978; Sekaran, 1992; Wacker, 1998) by providing:

- *Construct names and nominal definitions*: clear identification, labels and definitions of all the constructs (i.e. 'theoretical concepts' or, in a somewhat looser language, 'variables') considered relevant
- *Propositions*: presentation and discussion of the role of the constructs (independent, dependent, intervening, moderating), the important linkages between them, and an indication of the nature and direction of the relationships (especially if available from previous findings)
- *Explanation*: a clear explanation of why the researcher would expect to observe these relationships and, eventually, linkages with other theories (within or outside OM (Amundson, 1998))
- *Boundary conditions*: definition of conditions under which the researcher might expect these relationships to hold; it includes the identification of the *level of reference* of the constructs and their statements of relationships (i.e. where the researcher might expect the phenomenon to exist and manifest itself—individual, group, function or organization)

Developing good nominal definitions (sometimes termed formal conceptual definitions) is a major issue in order to advance OM theories. In this field, there are concepts that have been defined ambiguously and whose scope has so widened in use that they are vague and overlap with other concepts. This is the case of terms such as world class manufacturing, lean production, agile production, lean–agile production or dynamic manufacturing. These concepts have been used for a long time with a lot of overlapping in their meanings. Are they really different things? What do they have in common and what differentiates them? A different problem is represented by terms that are used with different meanings. Take for example the term form postponement. In some cases it is used to refer to a specific process configuration while in others to refer to a change in a process configuration, sometimes it is referred to physical activities while other times to decisions. Different meanings lead to different operationalizations and different relationships to other concepts.

Currently, OM research does not pay enough attention to developing good formal conceptual definitions. It is crucial to understand that without a clear and unambiguous definition of a concept we cannot assess the content validity of a measure of the concept, since we have not determined the content before. Without an agreement on what a concept does mean, it is meaningless to assess face validity (in this case we would end up using face validity assessment as a tool to develop concepts instead of as a tool to develop a measure of a concept). Further, if we have two concepts that overlap, it would be meaningless to test for discriminant validity between the corresponding measures. Finally, if we put a performance outcome within the definition of a practice, then it is meaningless to test the predictive validity of a measure of this practice by using the same performance as a criterion variable. Fortunately, now we can find some guidelines (see Table 4.5) on how to provide a good formal conceptual definition (Wacker, 2004) and we have some examples of articles devoted to identifying the domain of a specific concept as a preliminary step of measure development (see, for example, the work of Koste and Malhotra (1999) on manufacturing flexibility).

Very often the theoretical framework is depicted through a schematic

Table 4.5 A Summary of the Rules for a 'Good' Formal Conceptual Definition (Wacker, 2004)

Rule 1: Definitions should be formally defined using primitive and derived terms. Formal conceptual definitions should differentiate between formal concepts and non-formal measurable terms. All definitions should follow the 'rule of replacement'

Rule 2: Each concept should be uniquely defined. It should exclude (as many as possible) shared terms with other definitions to reduce confusion with related concepts. This rule means that the formal conceptual definitions denotation matches as closely as possible match its connotation

Rule 3: Definitions should include only unambiguous and clear terms. Put another way, do not use vague or ambiguous terms

Rule 4: Definitions should have as few as possible terms in the conceptual definition to avoid violating the parsimony virtue of 'good' theory

Rule 5: Definitions should be consistent within the production/operations management field. That is, formal conceptual definitions should be as similar as possible between studies

Rule 6: Definitions should not make any term broader. New definitions should not expand the concept to make it broader and less exclusive

Rule 7: New hypotheses cannot be introduced in the definitions. In production/operations management, the definitions should not include instances where only 'good' events happen

Rule 8: Statistical tests for content validity must be performed after the terms are formally defined. These empirical tests are not tests of the conceptual validity of a concept but rather are used to test if the formally defined concepts sample the conceptual domain diagram. While not being a requirement, it may be useful to facilitate communication. The researcher can find valuable support for this task in methodological books in social sciences (such as Dubin, 1978; Kerlinger, 1986; Emory and Cooper, 1991; Miller, 1991; Sekaran, 1992) or in OM (Anderson et al., 1994; Flynn et al., 1994), and in methodological articles in OM (Meredith, 1998; Wacker, 1998).

Theory-testing survey-based articles must be particularly clear in presenting the theoretical model. Anderson et al. (1995), for example, recall the theoretical model that they are going to test in the following way :

> . . . seven constructs or the 'Whats' of a theory . . . The seven constructs are: (1) Visionary Leadership, (2) Internal and External Cooperation, (3) Learning, (4) Process Management, (5) Continuous Improvement, (6) Employee Fulfillment, and (7) Customer Satisfaction . . . Nominal definitions for the seven constructs are shown in Table . . . Visionary Leadership, for example, is defined as 'the ability of management to establish, practice, and lead long-term vision for the organization, driven by changing customer requirements, as opposed to an internal management control role' . . . The formal statement {that specifies the relationships among the seven constructs} is depicted as a path diagram in Figure . . . and can be stated as follows: 'The effectiveness of the Deming Management Method arises from leadership efforts toward the simultaneous creation of a cooperative and learning organization to facilitate the implementation of process-management practices, which, when implemented, support customer satisfaction and organizational survival through sustained employee fulfilment and continuous improvement of processes, products, and services.' In the final stage of theory development, Anderson . . . juxtaposed the resulting set of relational elements and statements shown in Figure . . . in order to determine the level of support for the proposed constructs and relationships, essentially responding to the question of 'Why'—'Why are the constructs related as proposed?' . . . A second comment concern the generalizability of the proposed constructs and relationships {. . . the validity of the proposed theory} across different national cultures {is debated} . . . the empirical study reported in this paper marks a beginning towards addressing this issue by exploring the validity of the articulated theory using both American-owned and Japanese-owned plants in the U.S.
>
> (Anderson et al., 1995)

Sometimes, OM surveys are carried out with multiple purposes, so that several papers can be derived from a single data collection initiative, some descriptive, others theory-testing and others explorative. In this case, the researcher may rely on several theoretical models to design the survey. Whybark's (1997) words mentioned below make this point well with reference to the GMRG survey. To maintain clarity, however, it is recommended that a single piece of research that uses data collected through a multipurpose survey pursues only one objective, either exploratory or descriptive or theory-testing. It is also recommended that theory-testing and descriptive purposes are investigated in depth before survey design, so that variable operationalizations and the sample are satisfactory.

> There is no single, specific theory, hypothesis, or process model behind the GMRG surveys. Instead, much of what is included was suggested because it is associated with one or more general operations management theories. These theories were not pulled together into a specific meta-theory for guiding the design, however. This general descriptive design is consistent with the objective of the project, yields results that permit some theory testing and serves as the basis for some theory building. Many operations management theories have been tested with the GMRG data, but the concepts that guided the development of the questionnaire were very broad. One of these concepts was that there would be differences in manufacturing practices among the countries in which the survey was administered. Thus one of the objective was to develop a questionnaire that could be used to document manufacturing practices in many countries. More narrowly focusing on specific hypotheses might unnecessarily restrict the opportunity to gather general data . . . Another concern that broadly guided the GMRG project was the need to control for potential industry differences. There was a strong a priori assumption that there would be fairly significant differences between industries that could mask country differences if they were not controlled . . . Literature and consultants have suggested that certain practices are associated with good performance. These contentions did influence the design of the questions in the second questionnaire so that some of these hypotheses on the relationships between practices and performance can be tested.
>
> (Whybark, 1997)

Unfortunately, for many OM topics formal theory is underdeveloped. For many years OM has developed implicit theories and the lack of explicitness has hindered the testing of these theories. As a consequence, before embarking on theory-testing survey research, the OM researcher is often obliged to develop a theoretical framework. This development activity itself can be publishable (as for example Anderson et al., 1994; Flynn et al. 1994; Forza, 1995).

4.3.2 From the Theoretical Model to Hypotheses

Once the constructs, their relationships and their boundary conditions have been articulated, then the propositions that specify the relationships among the constructs have to be translated into hypotheses, relating empirical indicators. For example, the researcher might propose the following: 'the adoption of TQM in organizations would have positive effects on organizational performance'. Such a statement is at the conceptual level. At the empirical level (i.e. at the level of hypotheses), the following hypothesis might be tested: 'ROI {return on investment} would be positively correlated with the degree of TQM adoption'. In this hypothesis the 'degree of TQM adoption' is an empirical and numerically based measure of how extensive the adoption of TQM is or how committed the organization is to TQM. In other words, before the researcher can talk about how to collect data it is necessary to:

• Define the unit of analysis corresponding to the level of reference of the theory
• Provide and test the operational definitions for the various constructs
• Translate the propositions into hypotheses

4.3.2.1 *Defining the Unit of Analysis*

The empirical parallel of the 'level of reference' of the theory is the 'unit of analysis'. The unit of analysis refers to the level of data aggregation during subsequent analysis. The unit of analysis in OM studies may be individuals, dyads, groups, plants, divisions, companies, projects, systems etc. (Flynn et al., 1990). OM researchers should pay greater attention to specifying clearly both the level of reference and the unit of analysis. Unfortunately, many empirical works do not state clearly the level of reference and subsequently do not defend the choice of the unit of analysis.

It is necessary to determine the unit of analysis when formulating the research questions. Data collection methods, sample size, and even the operationalization of constructs may sometimes be determined or guided by the level at which data will be aggregated at the time of analysis (Sekaran, 1992). Not having done so in advance may mean that, later, appropriate analyses for the study cannot be performed.

When the level of reference is different from the unit of analysis the researcher will encounter the cross-level inference problem, i.e. collecting data at one level and interpreting the result at a different level (Dansereau and Markham, 1987). For example, if data are collected, or analysed, at group level (for example at plant level), and conclusions are drawn at individual level (for example at employee level), the researcher will encounter the ecological fallacy problem (Robinson, 1950; Babbie, 1990). The issue of cross-level inference becomes more important when more than one unit of analysis is involved in a study (Babbie, 1990). Discussion of methodological problems associated with the level of analysis (plant, strategic business unit (SBU), company) can be found in Boyer and Pagell (2000), with reference to operations strategy and advanced manufacturing technology, and in Vokurka and O'Leary-Kelly (2000), with reference to manufacturing flexibility.

The definition of the unit of analysis is not obvious in some researches. Defining it at a theoretical and empirical level is important to avoid the cross-level inference problem and even the possibility that a reader might fail to understand the level to which the research refers. An exemplary case of definition of the unit of analysis is provided by Rungtusanatham (2001):

> The unit of analysis in this study is, at a theoretical level, a transformation process, and, at an empirical level, a process operator. The job of a single process operator in a manufacturing environment is, itself, a transformation process, complete with inputs and outputs. Therefore, one can arguably equate, as Cantello et al. (1990, p. 62) did, a process operator's job to a transformation process. As such, individual-level data about the deployment of SPC {Statistical Process Control} with respect to an individual's job and the individual employee's perceptions about, and affective reactions to, his or her job would be appropriate for conducting empirical examinations of Propositions 1 and 2.
>
> (Rungtusanatham, 2001)

4.3.2.2 Developing and Testing the Operational Definitions

This section focuses mainly on the 'what' part of an operational definition (the list of observable elements), while leaving the 'how' part (the specific questions, etc.) to section 4.4.5, 'The Measurement Instrument'.

DEVELOPING THE OPERATIONAL DEFINITIONS

The first problem that the researcher faces is to translate the theoretical concepts into observable and measurable elements. If this work is not done well, the nominal definitions will not match the operative definitions. In this case, all the rest of the research may not be trusted. Some articles are done well in terms of data processing and are clearly presented but show a considerable misalignment between nominal definitions and operative definitions (sometimes they do not even provide a clear nominal definition). These articles may be considered as examples of 'garbage in—garbage out' so diminishing any contribution provided by the empirical analysis.

If the theoretical concept is multifaceted, then all of its facets have to find corresponding elements in the operational definition.

> Operationally defining a concept does not consist of delineating the reasons, antecedents, consequences, or correlates of the concept. Rather, it describes the observable characteristics of the concept in order to be able to measure it. . . . Learning is an important concept in educational setting. {In order} to measure the abstract concept . . . {of} learning we need . . . to break it down to observable and measurable behaviors . . .

The dimensions of learning may well be as follows: 1. Understanding 2. Retention 3. Application . . . Terms such as understanding, remembering, and applying are still abstract {Each dimension can be further decomposed in observable elements. Understanding is specified in:} answer questions correctly, give appropriate examples. {Retention is specified in:} recall material after some lapses of time. {Application is specified in:} solve problems applying concepts understood and recalled, and integrate with other relevant material.

(Sekaran, 1992)

The list of observable elements of each construct facet should be developed before writing the items/questions that constitute the measure. The separation of the two tasks will help the researcher focus on the content instead of on the wording. A careful literature review, the collection of all measures previously used for the concept under investigation and a conceptual analysis of the content must be performed. The works of Koste and Malhotra (1999) and Koste et al. (2004) are good examples of such a practice.

This action of reducing abstract constructs so that they can be measured (i.e. construct operationalization) presents several challenges: alignment between the theoretical concepts and the empirical measures; the choice between objective and perceptual questions; the choice of the number of questions for the construct, for a dimension of a construct or for an observable element. These problems can be alleviated by using operational definitions that have already been developed, used and tested. The availability of such operational definitions is rapidly increasing in OM and, recently, those published in top OM journals have been collected in a handbook (Roth et al., 2008). In spite of that improvement, the researcher may be forced to develop new measures or to improve existing ones: here, research reporting previous experiences and giving suggestions on measure development may be useful (see for example Converse and Presser, 1986; Hinkin, 1995; Hensley, 1999).

The translation from theoretical concepts to operational definitions can be very different from construct to construct. While some constructs lend themselves to objective and precise measurement, others are more nebulous and do not lend themselves to such precise measurement, especially when people's feelings, attitudes and perceptions are involved. When constructs, such as 'customer satisfaction', have multiple facets or involve people's perceptions/feelings or are planned to be measured through people's perceptions it is recommended to use operational definitions which include multiple elements (Lazarsfeld, 1935; Payne, 1951; Malhotra and Grover, 1998; Hensley, 1999). In contrast, when objective constructs are considered, a single direct question would be appropriate.

Sometimes constructs may be measured both though perceptual and objective measures. In this case, the properties of the two methods should be compared. One important case is that of operational and financial performance which, in OM surveys, are investigated through perceptual measures. Ketokivi and Schroeder (2004) show that this approach is acceptable but requires caution.

The process of identifying the elements to insert in the operational definition (as well as the items (questions) in the measure) may include both contacting those in the population of interest to gain a practical knowledge of how the construct is viewed in actual organizations, and to identify important features of the industry being studied. 'The development of items using both academic and practical perspectives should help researchers develop good preliminary scales and keep questionnaire revision to a minimum' (Hensley, 1999).

TESTING THE OPERATIONAL DEFINITIONS FOR CONTENT VALIDITY

When the operational definition has been developed (i.e. when the set of items of a multi-item measure has been developed), the researcher should test it for content validity. The content validity of a construct measure can be defined as the degree to which a measure's items represent a proper sample of the theoretical content domain of a construct (Nunnally and Bernstein, 1994)[2]. Stated otherwise, it is the degree to which the measure spans the domain of the construct's theoretical definition (Rungtusanatham, 1998).

Two conditions are to be satisfied by a measure's items in order to confirm content validity. First, each item should fall within the concept's theoretical domain. Secondly, the set of items should capture the different facets of a construct in a balanced way. If the items are too similar to each other, then important facets of the constructs are probably not covered. If the items touch only one aspect of a multifaceted construct, then the measure does not span the entire domain of the construct.

Evaluating the face validity of a measure (i.e. assessing whether the measure 'on its face' seems a good translation of the theoretical concept) can indirectly assess its content validity (Rungtusanatham, 1998). Face validity is a matter of judgement and must be assessed before data collection. In order to highlight the importance of such assessment before heavy data collection, Menor and Roth (2007) present, and perform, the development of a new measurement instrument as a two-stage process. They iterate the first stage four times in order to reach enough agreement between experts.

The assessment of face validity in OM surveys is quite rare, but it has increased over the last few years. Even in more established disciplines such as marketing, however, the assessment of face validity has involved various approaches, procedures and metrics (see Hardesty and Bearden (2004) for a review and a systematic but synthetic presentation).

One possible approach to assessing face validity involves a panel of subject-matter experts (SMEs) which are exposed to individual items and are asked to judge the degree to which these items are representative of the construct's conceptual definition. Subsequently, for each *i*th candidate item in the measure, Lawshe's (1975) content validity ratio (CVR_i) is calculated. Mathematically, CVR_i is computed as follows:

$$CVR_i = \frac{n_e - \dfrac{N}{2}}{\dfrac{N}{2}},$$

where n_e is the number of SMEs indicating the measurement item i as 'essential' and N is the total number of SMEs in the panel. Lawshe (1975) has also established minimum CVR_i for different panel sizes. For example, for a panel size of 25 the minimum CVR_i is 0.37. As an alternative to CVR_i, other metrics/criteria are available (see Hardesty and Bearden, 2004).

Another approach to assessing face validity is to give judges both the list of items and the definition of each construct or construct dimension. Subsequently, judges are asked to map the items into the constructs' definitions or, for multifaceted constructs, into the construct dimensions' definitions (Hardesty and Bearden, 2004). Cohen's (1960) *k* index as well as other inter-rater agreement indices are also used to assess face validity and, if necessary to improve it, through identifying which items to discard. An interesting example of an application of this approach can be found in Menor and Roth (2007). A combination of the two approaches can be found in the following excerpt.

> Assessing face validity . . . can be accomplished by having the constituent measurement items evaluated by subject-matter-experts, under the condition that the experts have been briefed as to the dimension's research definition . . . For this research, seven subject-matter-experts on SPC volunteered to participate in evaluating the face validity of the 66 measurement items for the 14 SPC implementation/practice dimensions . . . Each expert was asked to complete . . . two tasks . . . For task A {attributing each item to the closest dimension as for the meaning}, we provided the seven experts with the operational definitions for each of the 14 dimensions and a random listing of the 66 measurement items. The sorting results from task A were then used to compute Cohen's (1960) k, an index . . . the overall degree of inter-expert agreement as to the placement of the measurement items . . . We then asked the subject-matter-experts to evaluate, in task B, how adequately each measurement item measures the dimension to which it has been assigned. For each measurement item, the experts were asked to respond to a seven-point scale with '1' anchored as 'barely adequate' and '7' anchored as 'almost perfect' . . . From the experts' input for task B, we computed and evaluated the average adequacy score and the

standard deviation of adequacy scores for each individual measurement item.

(Rungtusanatham et al., 1999)

This phase of preliminary checking for content validity may prevent subsequent problems with reliability and convergent/discriminant validity (see section 4.5). The researcher has the opportunity to identify and to modify ambiguous or difficult-to-interpret items, which in turn improves reliability. If multiple constructs are investigated, the use of a Q-sort procedure may help to identify the convergent/discriminant capability of a given set of items. If an item is mapped by some experts into one construct and by others into another, it means that the item does not contribute to discriminating between the two constructs. If the researcher adds an additional category named 'other constructs' and an item is mapped into this category by some experts, then the item may be problematic for convergent validity.

4.3.2.3 Stating Hypotheses

A hypothesis is a logically conjectured relationship between two or more variables (measures) expressed in the form of testable statements. A hypothesis can also test whether there are differences between two groups (or among several groups) with respect to any variable or variables. These relationships are conjectured on the basis of the network of associations established in the theoretical framework and formulated for the research study. Hypotheses can be set either in the propositional or the if–then statement form. If terms such as 'positive', 'negative', 'more than', 'less than' and 'like' are used in stating the relationship between two variables or comparing two groups, these hypotheses are directional. When there is no indication of the direction of the difference or relationship, they are called non-directional. Non-directional hypotheses can be formulated either when the relationships or differences have never been explored previously, or when there are conflicting findings. It is better to indicate the direction when known.

The null hypothesis is a proposition that states a definitive, exact relationship between two variables. For example: a) the correlation between two variables is equal to zero; or, b) the difference between the means of two groups in the population is equal to zero.

In general the null statement is expressed as no (significant) relationship between two variables or no (significant) difference between two groups . . . What we are implying through the null hypothesis is that any differences found between two sample groups (or any relationships found between two variables based on our sample) is simply due to random sampling fluctuations and not due to any 'true' differences between the two population groups (or relationship between two variables). The null hypothesis is thus formulated so that it can be tested for possible rejection. If we reject the null hypothesis, then all permissible alternative hypotheses related to the tested relationship could be supported. It is the theory that allows us to trust the alternative hypothesis that is generated in the particular research investigation . . . Having thus formulated the null H_0 and alternative H_a hypotheses, the appropriate statistical tests, which would indicate whether or not support has been found for the alternate, should be identified.

(Sekaran, 1992)

A clear example of how to pass from a theoretical model to hypotheses is provided by Rungtusanatham et al. (1998). In that work the difference between propositions and hypotheses as well as the difference between constructs emerge clearly:

> Proposition 1: Visionary leadership enables the simultaneous creation of a cooperative and learning organization . . .
>
> The theoretical constructs {i.e. visionary leadership, cooperative organization, and learning organization} were operationalized as multi-item measurement scales . . .
>
> Stated in standard null form, Proposition 1 suggests the following two hypotheses . . . Hypothesis 1: Visionary Leadership {intended as the specific measure of the construct} is not positively related to Internal and External Cooperation {idem} . . . Hypothesis 2: Visionary Leadership {idem} is not positively related to Learning {idem}.
>
> (Rungtusanatham et al., 1998)

In formulating an hypothesis on the linkage between two variables, the OM researcher should be conscious of the type of relation being tested. For example, if the researcher tests a relation between two variables by means of r Pearson coefficient, a linear relationship is implicitly assumed. If results are not statistically significant, the researcher cannot conclude that there is no association. It can only be stated that in the sample considered there is no evidence of a linear relationship between the two variables considered. However, an exponential relation could exist and, if tested, emerge. In summary, when stating the hypotheses and, later, when choosing the appropriate test, the researcher should think carefully about the kind of linkage being assumed/tested. Narasimhan and Kim (2002) are very clear on that point, as demonstrated by the following:

> Hypothesis 3a. The moderating effect of IMD {International Market Diversification} on the curvilinear relationship between PD {Product Diversification} and performance is insignificant, as the level of internal integration across the supply chain increases.
>
> (Narasimhan and Kim, 2002)

4.4 How a Survey should be Designed

Survey design includes all of the activities that precede data collection. In the following presentation of this phase of the survey research process it is assumed that the researcher has already performed all of the activities recalled in section 4.2, namely problem focusing, literature review, etc. In this stage the researcher should consider all the possible shortcomings and difficulties and should find the right compromise between rigour and feasibility. Planning all the future activities in a detailed way and defining documents to keep track of the decisions made and the activities completed are necessary to prevent subsequent problems.

4.4.1 Considering Constraints and Information Needs at the Macro Level

Before embarking on a survey, the researcher should consider the suitability of the survey method and the overall feasibility of the research project. If a well-developed model is not available then the researcher should consider how much time and effort will be required to develop such a model. Time, costs and general resource requirements can constrain a survey project, forcing a less expensive type of survey or, in the extreme, making it impracticable. Other possible constraints are the accessibility of the population and the feasibility of involving the right informants.

In survey research, there is a trade-off between time and cost constraints, on the one hand, and minimization of four types of error, on the other hand:

- *Sampling error:* a sample with no (or unknown) capability of representing the population (because of inadequate sample selection or because of auto-selection effects) excludes the possibility of generalizing the results beyond the original sample
- *Measurement error:* data derived from the use of measures which do not match the theoretical dimensions, or are not reliable, make any test meaningless
- *Statistical conclusion error:* when performing statistical tests there is a probability of accepting a conclusion that the investigated relationship (or other effect) does not exist even when it does exist
- *Internal validity error:* when the explanation given of what has been observed is less plausible than rival ones, then the conclusions can be considered erroneous

While dissatisfaction with the above-mentioned constraints could halt the survey research, failure to minimize all of the above four errors 'can and will lead to erroneous conclusions and regression rather than progress in contribution to theory' (Malhotra and Grover, 1998).

To evaluate adequately the tightness of the constraints, the researcher should identify the main information needs (such as time horizon, information nature, etc.) which flow from the stated hypotheses and, ultimately, from the various purposes of the study. For example, if the study aims at a very rigorous investigation of causal relationships, or if the theoretical model implies some dynamics, then longitudinal data may be required (i.e. data on the same unit at different points in time). Boyer and Pagell (2000) have called for such an extended time horizon when researching operations strategy issues. Similarly, if the study requires information which is considered confidential by the respondents, then the cost and time to get the information is probably high and a number of survey design alternatives are not viable. Finally, a study may aim not only to test a theory but also to perform additional exploratory analyses, while reducing the cost of the research and increasing the speed in generating knowledge. In this case, the problem is to satisfy questionnaire length constraints: classifying information items by priority can be of help in subsequently choosing what questions to eliminate (Alreck and Settle, 1985; Babbie, 1990).

It is useful at this point to give an example of what it means to consider a survey project at the macro level. Collins and Cordon (1997), while reporting on and comparing their survey experiences, clearly highlight the importance of the macro-level choices for a survey project:

> A comparison of the different approaches taken in the two studies, and indeed the differences in approach taken by the IMD and IBM researchers in the 'Made in Switzerland' study raises a number of {methodological} issues . . . sample (sector) selection, respondent preparation, quality assurance for data input, the elimination of bias and the gathering of data complementary to that of survey instrument. The first study, 'Manufacturing strategies in western Europe', included an initial set of interviews with 16 companies followed by a mailed questionnaire answered by 121 companies. The second study, 'Made in Switzerland', while also obtaining data from 116 manufacturing site/plants, was conducted exclusively by interviewing company executives. While the second approach requires more resources, it has . . . the following advantages: a) the preparation of the respondents seems more rigorous, b) higher quality and more consistent data—furthermore, apparent inconsistencies point out interesting new hypotheses, c) blatant bias is eliminated, d) the gathering of complementary data to that of the questionnaire allows for the testing of face validity and the testing of hypotheses that were not made explicit at the beginning of the study, e) much higher response rate.
>
> (Collins and Cordon, 1997)

4.4.2 Planning Activities

Survey research is a process with a series of steps that are linked to each other (see Figure 4.1). Carefully planning this process is crucial to preventing problems and to assuring the quality of the research process. For this reason the design phase should be detailed, and followed by a pilot-testing phase aimed at ensuring that the survey instrumentation and procedures are adequate.

However, in planning the activities it should be recognized that the decisions made during the early steps affect the choices available at later steps (see Figure 4.2). For example, if the researcher decides to use a phone survey, subsequently this choice will limit the number and the sophistication of the measures that can be employed.

It is not possible to proceed step by step: constraints and limitations in the later steps should be considered in the earlier steps. For these reasons, major decisions about data collection (telephone, interview, Web and mail) and time horizon (cross-sectional, longitudinal) must always be made prior to designing and selecting a sample and constructing the questionnaire and the other material. It is important to match the capabilities and the limitations of the data processing methods with the sampling and instrumentation. For more details on project planning see Alreck and Settle (1985).

4.4.3 The Sample

Before discussing the sample we need to define the following terms: population, population element, population frame, sample, subject and sampling. *Population* refers to the entire group of people, firms, plants or things that the

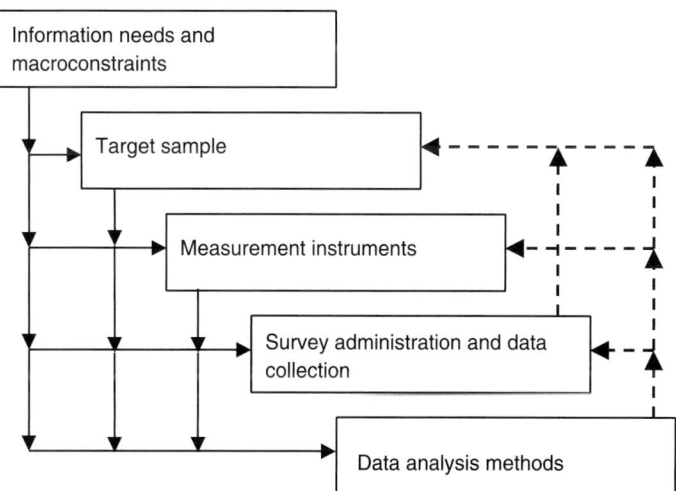

Figure 4.2 Linkages between Decisions in Survey Planning (adapted from Alreck and Settle, 1985).

researcher wishes to investigate. An *element* is a single member of the population. The *population frame* is a listing of all the elements in the population from which the sample is to be drawn. A *sample* is a subset of the population: it comprises some members selected from the population. A *subject* is a single member of the sample. Finally, *sampling* is the process of selecting a sufficient number of elements from the population so that by studying the sample, and understanding the properties or the characteristics of the sample subjects, the researcher will be able to generalize the properties or characteristics to the population elements. Sampling overcomes the difficulties of collecting data from the entire population which can be impossible or prohibitive in terms of time, costs and other human resources.

Sample design is a step usually overlooked in OM surveys (Forza and Di Nuzzo, 1998; Rungtusanatham et al., 2003). Many articles do not report adequately on how their sample was constructed, and do not provide sufficient information on the resulting sample. The majority of survey-based OM articles (approximately 88%) do not rely on a probabilistic sampling approach (Rungtusanatham et al., 2003). Poor sample design can constrain the application of more appropriate statistical techniques and the generalizability of the results. Two issues should be addressed: randomness and sample size. Randomness is associated with the ability of the sample to represent the population of interest. Sample size is associated with the requirements of the statistical procedures used for assessment of measurement quality and hypothesis testing.

4.4.3.1 Population Frame

The population frame should be drawn from widely available sources to facilitate the replication of studies. The industry classification (specified through International Standard Industrial Classification (ISIC) or other standard codes) is an important aspect of framing the population. Even though ISIC codes can provide a useful starting point, they were not designed for OM research. Therefore, the classification may need to be modified to fulfil the needs of an OM researcher (see Flynn et al., 1990). Additionally, in some countries ISIC codes are not available or having the list of companies with their ISIC codes may be too expensive and other classifications, if available, cannot always be trusted. The GMRG survey has solved these problems by using product descriptions as the industry selection criterion (Whybark, 1997). To facilitate control of industry effects, a good practice is, therefore, to consider four-digit ISIC codes to describe products when building the frame and then the research sample. This issue should not be underestimated since 'controlling industry effects can compensate for variability between industries, in terms of processes, work force management, competitive forces, degree of unionisation, etc.' (Flynn et al., 1990).

There are other justifiable ways of choosing a sample, based on specific aspects (for example common process technology, position in the supply chain, etc.) which should be controlled for in the investigation of the phenomenon under study. For example, Dun's databases are useful sources since they provide such information (in some countries at plant level) as products made, number of employees, addresses and others (see http://www.dundb.co.il/). Other than industry, another important variable to be controlled for is company size: number of employees and sales are easily available and can be incorporated in the sample selection process.

4.4.3.2 Sample Design

There are several sample designs, which can be grouped into two families: probabilistic and non-probabilistic sampling. In probabilistic sampling the population elements have some known probability of being selected, unlike in non-probabilistic sampling. Probabilistic sampling is used to ensure the representativeness of the sample when the researcher is interested in generalizing the results. When time or other factors prevail on generalizability considerations then non-probabilistic sampling is usually chosen. Table 4.6 shows some basic types of sampling approaches (for more details see Babbie, 1990).

Table 4.6 Sampling Approaches

Representativeness	Purpose is mainly	Type of sampling
Essential for the study => probabilistic sampling	Generalizability	Simple random sampling Systematic sampling
	Assessing differential parameters in subgroups of population	Proportionate stratified random sampling (for subgroups with an equal number of elements)
		Disproportionate stratified random sampling (for subgroups with a different number of elements)
	Collecting information in localized areas	Area sampling
	Gathering information from a subset of the sample	Double (or multistage) sampling
Not essential for the study -> non-probabilistic sampling	Obtain quick, even if unreliable, information	Convenience sampling
	Obtain information relevant to and available only from certain groups	Judgement sampling (when looking for information that only a few experts can provide)
		Quota sampling (when the responses of special interest minority groups are needed)

Stratified random sampling is a very useful type of sampling since it provides more information for a given sample size. Stratified random sampling involves the division of the population into strata and a random selection of subjects from each stratum. Strata are identified on the basis of meaningful criteria like industry type, size, performance, or others. This procedure ensures high homogeneity within each stratum and heterogeneity between strata. Stratified random sampling allows the comparison of population subgroups and allows control for factors like industry or size which very often affect results.

4.4.3.3 Sample Size

Sample size is the second concern. It is a complex issue which is linked to the significance level and the statistical power of the test, and also to the size of the researched relationship (for example association strength or amount of difference).

When making statistical inference, the researcher can make either a type I error (reject the null hypothesis H_0 when it is true) or a type II error (H_0 is not rejected when the alternative hypothesis H_a is true). The probability of making a type I error (α) is called *significance level*. Typically in most social sciences (OM included) α is taken to 0.05, however in several cases $\alpha=0.01$ and $\alpha=0.001$ are used. The null hypothesis is rejected if the observed significance level (p-value) is less than the chosen value of α (McClave and Benson, 1991). The probability of a type II error is β, and the *statistical power* is equal to $1-\beta$. A high statistical power is required to reduce the probability of failing to detect an effect when it is present. A balance between the two types of errors is needed because reducing any one type of error raises the likelihood of increasing the probability of the other type of error. Low power leads to a study which is not able to detect large size effects, while high power leads to committing unnecessary resources only in order to be able to detect trivial effects. Methodologists are only now beginning to agree that a power of about 0.8 represents a reasonable and realistic value for research in social/behavioural sciences (Verma and Goodale, 1995). This means that only 20% of the repeated studies will not yield a significant result, even when the phenomenon exists.

Even though the power of a statistical test depends on three factors (α, effect size and sample size), from a practical point of view only the sample size is used to control the power. This is because the α level is effectively fixed at 0.05 (or some other value) and the effect size (for example the size of the difference in the means between two samples or the correlation between two variables) can also be assumed to be fixed at some unknown value (the researcher may wish not to change the effect but only detect it). The required sample sizes, with desired statistical powers of 0.8 and 0.6, are shown in Table 4.7 as a function of effect size (and significance levels). One can see that the required sample size increases while increasing the

Table 4.7 Effect Size, Statistical Power and Sample Size

	Stat. power = 0.6		*Stat. power = 0.8*	
	α=0.05	*α=0.01*	*α=0.05*	*α=0.01*
Large effect (e.g. strong association)	12	18	17	24
Medium effect (e.g. medium association)	30	45	44	62
Small effect (e.g. small association)	179	274	271	385

statistical power, and/or decreasing the significance level, and/or decreasing the size of the effect researched. Verma and Goodale provide more detail (and selected bibliography) on this issue. They also provide some figures of the statistical power evident in OM articles published in the Journal of Operations Management (JOM) and Decision Sciencs (DS) in the period 1990–1995.

4.4.4 Data Collection Method

Data can be collected in a variety of ways, in different settings and from different sources. In survey research, the main methods used to collect data are interviews and questionnaires. Interviews may be structured or unstructured. They can be conducted either face to face or over the telephone. Questionnaires can be administered personally, by telephone (in person or through interactive voice responding systems) or through the Web, can be mailed or e-mailed to the respondents.

Each data collection method has merits as well as shortcomings. The choice of the best method cannot be made without taking into account the needs of the specific survey as well as the time, cost and resource constraints. Different methods can be used in the same survey to compensate for the weaknesses of each method. However, the use of mixed approaches may raise difficult issues, the most important of which is represented by the fact that the same respondent may give different answers to the same question administered through different methods. Problems and possible solutions are discussed by Dillman (2007:217–244).

In a mail survey, questionnaires are printed and sent by mail. The respondents are asked to complete the questionnaire on their own and to send it back. Mailed questionnaires have the following advantages: cost savings; they can be completed at the respondent's convenience; there are no time constraints; they can be prepared to give an authoritative impression; they can ensure anonymity; and they can reduce interviewer bias. On the other hand, mailed questionnaires have a lower response rate than other methods, involve longer time periods, and are more affected by self-selection, lack of interviewer involvement and lack of open-ended questions.

In a face-to-face survey, the interviewer solicits information directly from a respondent during personal interviews. The advantages are: flexibility in sequencing the questions, details and explanation; possibility of administering highly complex questionnaires; improved ability to contact hard-to-reach populations; higher response rates; increased confidence that data collection instructions are followed. On the other hand, disadvantages include: higher cost; interviewer bias; the respondent's reluctance to co-operate; greater stress for both respondents and interviewer; less anonymity.

Telephone surveys involve collecting information through the use of telephone interviews. The advantages are: rapid data collection; lower cost; anonymity; large-scale accessibility; higher confidence that instructions are followed. The disadvantages are: less control over the interview situation; less credibility; lack of visual materials.

Recently, a new way to approach companies and administer questionnaires has appeared. The researcher can send a questionnaire through e-mail or ask respondents to visit a web site where the questionnaire can be filled in without the need to return the questionnaire, since data input is done directly by the respondent. One advantage is the minimal cost compared with other means of distribution (Dillman, 2007). However, potential problems lie in sampling and controlling of the research environment (Birnbaum, 1999; Dillman, 2007).

Table 4.8 summarizes the relative strengths of the different methods. Here, '1' indicates that the method that has the maximum strength and '4' the minimum with respect to each factor considered. Dillman (1978:74–76) and Rea and Parker (1992) provide a more detailed comparison.

Electronic surveys deserve some additional words, since there is a lot of discussion on, and a fast development in, their use. Klassen and Jacobs (2001) report the first systematic experimentation and comparison in OM (of Web-based, mail, fax and PC disk-by-mail technologies), providing many insights into this issue:

Table 4.8 Comparison of Data Collection Methods (adapted from Miller, 1991:168)

Factors influencing coverage and secured information	Mailed	Personal interview	Telephone survey	E-survey
Lowest relative cost	2	4	3	1
Highest response rate	4	1	2	3
Highest accuracy of information	2	1	4	3
Largest sample coverage	1	4	3	2
Completeness, including sensitive materials	3	1	2	4
Overall reliability and validity	2	1	3	4
Time required to secure information	4	2	1	3
Ease of securing information	1	4	3	2

If a survey was to be conducted only using the Web-based technology, respondents are unlikely to be truly representative of the population . . . Moreover, if Web surveys become commonplace, reviewer expectations for response rates may need to be adjusted downward from 20% (Malhotra and Grover, 1998) to possibly 10% (i.e. Web response rate was approximately half that of other technologies). Second, while the return rate of the Web survey was lower than other survey technologies, the item completion rates of surveys completed using Web, fax and disk-by-mail technologies were significantly higher than with the mail survey. Third, the limited evidence of systematic bias with the application of computing technology in forecasting characteristics can be viewed as either a threat to data validity or an opportunity to collect data from a different subgroup . . . This finding indicates that a sub-sample of best practice users in operations management can be tapped who otherwise might be underrepresented. At the present time, a combined approach of using Web and fax technologies to survey managers offers significant benefits over the sole use of mail for establishment-level, self-administered surveys.

(Klassen and Jacobs, 2001)

Boyer et al. (2002) provide further evidence on electronic surveys properties in OM:

In general, our study confirms the findings of Klassen and Jacobs (2001) . . . and extends their findings . . . electronic surveys offer important capabilities in terms of contingently coding questions . . . Electronic surveys are much more challenging to develop . . . require different handling procedures . . . {but lead to} greater efficiency {in data entry} and greater data accuracy . . . Both methods {electronic and mail surveys} had statistically similar response rates, scale/construct means and inter item reliabilities . . . Electronic surveys have substantially fewer missing responses . . . Electronic surveys provide an important capability to design surveys in a contingent manner.

(Boyer et al., 2002)

The Web survey technique has made impressive improvements in the last 4 years. On one hand, researchers have gained a better understanding of its requirements in terms of visual design and consideration of computer logics (constraints and opportunities) (see Dillman, 2007:352–497). On the other hand, respondents continuously increase their confidence with Web instruments and communication technologies continuously increase speed and friendliness. All of these changes together make the Web-based survey much less problematic in terms of response rate and non-respondent bias. These improvements lead to a need to reassess the findings of Klassen and Jacobs (2001) and Boyer et al. (2002). One important aspect to investigate is the possibility of having multiple respondents from the same organization by using a Web-based survey. With multiple respondents, we may improve response rate, reduce missing data, decrease costs, increase speed, reduce inputting errors but at the expense of having potentially uncontrollable method (respondent) bias.

4.4.5 The Measurement Instrument

One of the main characteristics of the survey is that it relies on structured instruments to collect information. Once the researcher has decided the content of a measure (the specific empirical aspects that have to be observed), several tasks remain in order to develop the measurement instrument, namely:

- Defining how the questions are to be formulated to collect the information on a specific concept (see subsection 'Wording')
- For each question, deciding the scale on which the answers are to be placed (see subsection 'Scaling')
- Identifying the appropriate respondent(s) to each question (see subsection 'Respondent Identification')
- Putting together the questions in questionnaires that facilitate and motivate the respondent(s) to respond (see subsection 'Rules of Questionnaire Design')

The main issues related to each task are discussed in the following subsections. It should be noted, however, that the actual design of the survey questionnaire depends on whether the questionnaire is to be administered by telephone interview, on site through interview, on site using pen and paper, or by mail using pen and paper.

4.4.5.1 Wording

In formulating the questions the researcher should ensure that the language of the questionnaire is consistent with the respondent's level of understanding. If a question is not understood or is interpreted differently by respondents, the researcher will get unreliable responses to the question, and these responses will be biased. The researcher also has to choose between an open-ended (allowing respondents to answer in any way they choose) or closed question (limiting respondents to a choice among alternatives given by the researcher). Closed questions facilitate quick decisions and easy information coding, but the researcher has to ensure that the alternatives are mutually exclusive and collectively exhaustive. Another choice in formulating the questions is the mix of positively and negatively worded questions in order to minimize the tendency in respondents to circle the points mechanically toward one end of the scale.

The researcher should replace double-barrelled questions (i.e. questions that have different answers to its subparts) with several separate questions. Ambiguity in questions should be eliminated as much as possible. Leading questions (i.e. questions phrased in a way that lead the respondent to give responses that the researcher would like to, or may come across as wanting to, elicit) should be avoided as well. In the same way loaded questions (i.e. questions phrased in an emotionally charged manner) should be eliminated. Questions should not be worded to elicit socially desirable responses. Finally, a question or a statement should not exceed 20 words of full line in print. For further details on wording, see for example Converse and Presser (1986), Dillman (2007).

4.4.5.2 Scaling

A second task in developing the measurement instrument concerns the scale to be used to measure the answers. The scale choice depends on the ease with which both the respondent can answer and the subsequent analyses will be done. There are four basic types of scale: nominal, ordinal, interval and ratio (see Table 4.9). The sophistication of the application for which the scales are suited increases with the progression from nominal to ratio. As the sophistication increases, so also does the information detail, the ability to differentiate the individuals and the flexibility in using more powerful tests. For a more detailed treatment of the use of scales in OM, see Table 4.10 and Flynn et al. (1990).

When addressing data analysis later in this chapter, we will note the importance of considering two basic kinds of data—non-metric (qualitative) and metric (quantitative):

> Non-metric data includes attributes, characteristics, or categorical properties that can be used to identify or describe a subject. Non-metric data differs in kind. Metric data measurement is made so that subjects may be

Table 4.9 Scales and Scaling Techniques

Basic scale type	What it highlights	Scaling technique
Nominal	Difference	Multiple choice items, adjective checklist, stapel scale
Ordinal	Difference, order	Forced ranking scale, paired comparison scale
Interval	Difference, order, distance	Likert scale, verbal frequency scale, comparative scale, semantic differential scale
Ratio	Difference, order, distance with 0 as meaningful natural origin	Fixed sum scale

Table 4.10 Scaling Techniques in OM (adapted from Flynn et al. 1990)

Scaling technique	Example	When to use	Benefits	Limitations
Multiple choice items	Which of the following philosophies concerning quality are used by your plant? Please check *all* that apply. __ Total quality control by all employees __ Continuous improvement of quality __ Statistical process control __ Zero defects as a goal for all employees	Entire range of response should be classifiable into a limited number of discrete, mutually exclusive categories	Simple, versatile. Can be used to obtain either a single response or several	Respondents may not always follow directions when a single response is desired. Should not be used for numeric (continuous) data, where a direct question is more appropriate. Limited statistical analysis is possible due to nominal data
Forced ranking scale	Please rank the importance of the following objectives or goals for manufacturing at your plant over the next five years. Rank #1 the most important objective, #2 for the next most important, and so on. You may rank several objectives the same if they are of equal importance. Rank __ Low unit cost __ Ability to rapidly introduce new products or make design changes __ Ability to make rapid volume changes __ Consistent quality __ High performance products __ Fast deliveries __ Dependable delivery __ Low manufacturing cycle time	Used when researcher seeks to obtain standing of the items relative to each other	Obtain most preferred item, as well as the sequence of the remaining items. Relativity between items is measured	Absolute standing of an item is not measured, nor is the interval between items. Response task rapidly becomes tedious for respondents if more than a few items are included

	Example	When to use	Advantages	Cautions
Likert scale	We emphasize good maintenance as a strategy for achieving schedule compliance. — Strongly agree — Agree — Neither agree nor disagree — Disagree — Strongly disagree	Use when it is necessary to obtain people's 'position' on certain issues or conclusions	More readily analysed and interpreted than open-ended attitude questions. Flexible, economical and easy to compose items. Can obtain a summated value in order to measure a more general construct	Respondents may be lulled into marking the same response for each item, therefore, care should be taken so that some of the items are inclined towards the pro side of the issue and the rest toward the con side
Ratio scale	How many engineering change orders occurred last year?	Used when exact figures on objective (as opposed to subjective) factors are called for	Allow to identify not only the magnitude of the differences but also the proportion of the differences	Precise figures may not be available to respondents and may be more likable perceived as confidential information. Different respondents may respond using different unit of measures due to their habit

identified as differing in amount or degree. Metrically measured variables reflect relative quantity or distance, whereas non–metrically measured variables do not. Non-metric data is measured with nominal or ordinal scales and metric variables with interval or ratio scales.

(Hair et al., 1992)

4.4.5.3 Respondent Identification

Very often the unit of analysis in OM research is the plant or the company. However the plant (company) cannot give the answers: it is the people who work in the plant (company) that provide information on that plant (company).

Due to the functional specialization and hierarchical level in the organization, some people are knowledgeable on some facts while others know only about others. The researcher should therefore identify the appropriate informants for each set of information required. Increasing the number of respondents, however, increases the probability of receiving only some completed questionnaires, leading to incomplete information, which can impact on the results of relational studies. On the other hand, answers from respondents who are not knowledgeable cannot be trusted and increase random or even bias error.

Further, if perceptual questions are asked, one can gather a perception which is personal to that respondent. In order to enhance confidence in findings, the researcher can use some form of triangulation, such as the use of multiple respondents for the same question or the use of multiple measurement methods (for example qualitative and quantitative). These actions reduce the common method/source variance, i.e. potentially inflated empirical relationships which can occur when the data have been collected using the same method or have been provided by the same single source (Rungtusanatham et al. 2003). Vokurka and O'Leary-Kelly (2000) and Boyer and Pagell (2000) discuss this issue in relation to research on manufacturing flexibility, operations strategy and manufacturing technology.

4.4.5.4 Rules of Questionnaire Design

Once the questions have been developed and their associations to respondent(s) have been established the researcher can put together the questionnaire (Converse and Presser, 1986). There are some simple things that the researcher should keep in mind. Some basic rules of courtesy, presentability and readability are essential for successful data collection. An attractive and neat questionnaire with an appropriate introduction, instructions, and a well-arrayed set of questions with good alignment and response alternatives will make it easier for the respondents to answer the questions. Coloured questionnaires (especially bright ones) remind the respondent about the request to complete the questionnaire.

For both the researcher and the respondent, related questions (for example 'what is the percentage of customer orders received by EDI?' and 'what is the percentage of customer order value received by EDI?') closely placed facilitate cross-checks on the responses. Mixing items belonging to different measures contributes to avoiding stereotype answering. The presence of reversal questions keeps attention high. The length of the questionnaire affects the response rate and attention in filling in the questionnaire. Finally, codes can facilitate subsequent data input.

Recently, questionnaire design has introduced the so called principles of visual design. These principles consider the appearance of the questionnaire not only as a manifestation of care and professionalism, but also as a communicating instrument whose importance is close to that of wording. The underlying reason is the observation that respondents, before reading a question, make a number of visual interpretations based on visual processing, which may lead them to skip a question or to misinterpret instructions on how to answer. Even when they are reading a question, they do not put equal attention on each word of the question thus risking misinterpretation of the question. Visual aids greatly reduce this kind of error. Dillman (2007) illustrates the principle of visual design and provides a number of useful examples.

4.4.6 Approaching Companies and Respondents

To increase the probability of the success of data collection the researcher should plan the execution of survey research carefully and provide detailed instruction on the following: 1) how sampling units are going to be approached; and 2) how questionnaires are going to be administered. In other words, the protocol to be followed in administering the questionnaire has to be developed.

Increasingly, companies and respondents are being asked to complete questionnaires, and are becoming more reluctant to collaborate. Researchers, therefore, must find ways to obtain the collaboration of companies and specific respondents. Dillman (1978, 2007) underlines that the response to a questionnaire should be viewed as a social exchange, suggesting that the researcher should:

- Reward the respondent by showing positive regard, giving verbal appreciation, using a consulting approach, supporting his or her values, offering tangible rewards, making the questionnaire interesting
- Reduce costs to the respondent by making the task appear brief, reducing the physical and mental efforts that are required, eliminating chances for embarrassment, eliminating any implication of subordination, eliminating any direct monetary cost
- Establish trust by providing a token of appreciation in advance, identifying with a known organization that has legitimacy, building on other exchange relationships

A peculiar problem of OM survey research is the difficulty in reaching the right respondents. Very often researchers send a questionnaire to a company without knowing the name of the respondent. In this case, there is a high probability that the questionnaire will be lost or delivered to a person who is not interested in, or knowledgeable about, the subject. The contact strategy should take this problem into account and vary the approach based on such influencing variables as, for example, the company size, which can influence the presence of certain professional/managerial positions.

In OM, Flynn et al. (1990, 1997, 1999) suggested—and also successfully implemented—a contact strategy based on contacting potential respondents and obtaining their commitment to questionnaire completion prior to distribution. When respondents understand the purpose of a study, lack of anonymity may not be so problematic. This approach allows for the provision of feedback to respondents, which may serve as an incentive to participation. This method also establishes personal contacts, which facilitates a reduction of the possibility of missing data.

> The plant manager of each sampled plant was contacted by telephone to solicit the firm's participation. Participating plant managers each appointed a plant research coordinator to serve as liaison with the research team. The packet of questionnaires was sent to the plant research coordinator. It included 21 questionnaires, targeted at various respondents in the plant. For example, the accounting questionnaire requested performance information, while the direct labor questionnaire contained a set of scales designed to determine workers' perceptions of practices and culture at the plant. The research coordinator distributed to questionnaires to the named managers and a random sample of 10 direct laborers. Respondents were asked to return their questionnaires to the plant research coordinator in sealed envelopes. When the entire set had been received, the plant research coordinator returned the packet of sealed envelopes to the research team . . . In return for participating, each firm was provided with a detailed profile of its practices and performance, as well as benchmark data on practices and performance in its industry. This yielded a response rate of 60% of the firms that were contacted. Analysis of the industry, size and location of responding and nonresponding firms did not indicate any significant differences; although it was not possible to question nonrespondents on items more relevant to the hypotheses, there was not a respondent bias indicated in this basic analysis.
>
> (Flynn et al., 1999)

Approaching companies and respondents is a process. The number and sequence of the steps, the means used at each step and the decisions taken at each step all have an effect on answer rate and data reliability. The experience of Collins and Cordon (1997) is exemplary:

The approach used by IMD and IBM in contacting the companies/sites differed and is worthy of comment . . . The initial contact with a prospective respondent was made by phone. The project was described in detail, with a particular emphasis being placed on the benefits accruing to the company/division/site/executive through participation as well as the time commitment that was required. The executive was finally asked if he or she would agree to receiving a letter, essentially summarizing the telephone conversation, together with copies of the questionnaire in the desired language or languages. It was only after the receipt of the letter and questionnaires that the executive was asked to decide whether or not to participate. A few days after receipt of the letter executive was contacted to determine his/her reaction and, in the case of an affirmative response, to fix a date for the plant tour and interview. An affirmative response solicited a letter to the executive confirming the time and date of the visit as well as designating those members of the research team who would participate. Additional questionnaires were forwarded if necessary. Of the 36 individuals contacted whose sites met the a priori criteria for participation, 35 agreed to participate in the study—a response rate of 97.2 per cent . . . Of the 35 executives ultimately interviewed by the IMD team, 26 were known beforehand to the IMD researchers . . . The others were referred to the researchers by individuals in the aforementioned group.

(Collins and Cordon, 1997)

Even though reference contact procedures in OM, such as those presented above and others summarized by Frohlich (2002), do exist, the researcher has to rely on his experience and knowledge of the context being investigated. An adaptation of the contact procedures described in the literature is needed. This is consistent with the tailored approach proposed by Dillman (2007).

4.5 Pilot Testing the Questionnaire

4.5.1 Purpose and Modality of Pilot Testing

Once the questionnaires, the protocol to follow in administering these questionnaires and the identity of the sample units are defined, the researcher has to examine the measurement properties of the survey questionnaires and to examine the viability of the administration of these surveys. In other words, the researcher has to test what has been designed. It is remarkable the number of problems that testing can highlight even when all the previous steps have been followed with maximum attention.

The pre-test of a questionnaire should be done by submitting the 'final' questionnaire to three types of people: colleagues, industry experts and target respondents. The role of colleagues is to test whether the questionnaire accomplishes the study objectives (Dillman, 1978). The role of industry experts is to prevent the inclusion of some obvious questions that might reveal ignorance of the investigator in some specific areas. The role of target respondents is to provide feedback on everything that can affect answering by and the answers of the targeted respondents. The target respondents can pre-test the questionnaire separately or in a group. If the questionnaire is to be mailed, it can be sent to a small pre-test sample. Telephone questionnaires must be tested by telephone, as some aspects cannot be tested in a face-to-face situation (Dillman, 1978). This type of questionnaire is easy to test and the researcher can modify and use the revised questionnaire the same day.

Based on my experience, I propose that the best way to pre-test a self-administered questionnaire is to proceed in two phases, each with completely different but complementary objectives.

In the first phase the researcher fills in the questionnaire with a group of potential respondents (Fowler, 1993) or when visiting three to four potential respondents. The respondents should complete the questionnaire as they would if they were part of the planned survey. Meanwhile the researcher should be present observing how respondents fill in the questionnaire and recording the feedback. Subsequently the researcher can ask 1) whether the instructions were clear, 2) whether the questions were clear, 3) whether there were any problems in understanding what kind of answers were expected, or in providing answers to the questions posed, and 4) whether the planned administration procedure would be effective.

In the second phase (not always performed in OM surveys) the researcher carries out a small pre-test sample (for example 15 units) to test the contact–administration protocol, to gather data to perform an exploratory assessment of measurement quality and to obtain information to better define the sample and the adequacy of measures in relation to the sample. In this phase the researcher can also carry out a preliminary analysis of the data to investigate 1) whether the answers to certain questions are too concentrated due to the choice of scale, 2) whether the content of answers differs from what was expected, and 3) whether the context modifies the appropriateness of questions (for example, a question can be meaningful for business-to-business (B2B) companies but not for business-to-consumer (B2C) companies, or can be appropriate for medium-size companies but not for very small or large companies). Furthermore, it may be possible to observe the effects of missing data and non-response bias in order to define appropriate countermeasures. This pilot study can help to better define the sample and to plan for a 'controlled sample' instead of the 'observational one' which is generally more problematic but unfortunately more common in OM. In summary, this pilot test should resemble as closely as possible the actual survey that will be conducted for theory testing.

4.5.2 Handling Non-respondents and Non-response Bias

Non-respondents alter the sample frame and, therefore, can lead to a sample that does not represent the population even when the sample was adequately designed for that purpose. Non-respondents, as such, can limit the generalizability of results. In the pilot-testing phase the researcher should identify a way to address this problem.

From 1995–2000 the answer rate in the top seven OM journals varied typically from 20–40%, with an average of 32% (Frohlich, 2002). Some OM scholars state that it is important to reach a response rate greater than 50% (Flynn et al., 1990), as is found in the other social sciences. Other researchers set the limit at 20% (Malhotra and Grover, 1998). This point is much debated, since many researchers find it hard to agree on these response rate percentages. However, especially for theory-testing survey research, response rate in combination with non-response bias is a major issue. The example provided by Fowler (1993:43)—and reported in Table 4.11—is instructive.

Fowler estimates the presence of blond-haired persons in a population of 100 persons with 25 blond-haired individuals. If response rate is 70% and 75% of non-respondents have blond hair, it means that out of the 30 non-respondents 0,75*30~22 have blond hair and therefore only 25–22=3 blond-haired individuals respond. Therefore, the estimate is 3 blond-haired persons in the population while, in reality, there are 25 such individuals. Table 4.7 shows that when there are major biases (such that non-respondents have characteristics—e.g. blond hair—systematically different from the respondents) even studies with response rates of approximately 70% produce considerable errors in estimates. When response rates are lower, estimates are not very good even when bias is modest. The problem is that 'one usually does not know how biased non-response is, but {it} is seldom a good assumption that non-response is unbiased' (Fowler, 1993).

OM researchers could consider articles from other disciplines in order to increase awareness on non-respondent causes (see Roth and BeVier, 1998; Greer et. al., 2000) and effects (see Wilson (1999), who underlines the

Table 4.11 Effect of Biased Non-response on Survey Estimates (Fowler, 1993:43)

Response rate (%)	Bias level (percentage of non-respondents with characteristics (blond hair))						
	(10)	(20)	(25)	(30)	(40)	(50)	(75)
90	27	26	25	24	23	22	19
70	31	27	25	23	19	14	3
50	40	30	25	20	10		
30	60	37	25	13			

resulting lack of external validity). To calculate the response rate, the researcher can refer to Dillman (1978:49–52).

The non-response effects on results can be addressed in two ways: 1) by trying to increase response rate and 2) by trying to identify the non-respondents to control whether they are different from the respondents.

Response rates can be increased considerably when a subsequent follow-up programme is applied. Dillman (1978) proposes that 1) after 1 week a postcard is sent to everyone (it serves as a reminder and as a thank you), 2) after 3 weeks a letter and a replacement questionnaire are sent only to non-respondents, 3) final mailing similar to the previous one (or even a telephone call). Dillman (2007) suggests a combination and tailoring of modalities to approach respondents and remind them to fill in the question-naire and return it. Based on my experience, I think that a phone call is more useful, since it makes it possible 1) to ensure that the target respondent has received the questionnaire, 2) to establish a personal contact, 3) to have some time to explain the research, 4) to help the respondent and 5) to gather some information on non-respondents.

Researchers should at least keep track of the non-respondents. They should survey some of them (even using a condensed questionnaire or using a telephone call) to understand whether and how much bias has been intro-duced (see for example Ward et al., 1994). An alternative method is to check for differences between the first wave of respondents and later returns (Lambert and Harrington, 1990). Even though this approach provides useful information, the researcher should keep in mind that he is still comparing respondents that, in the end, provided a response.

Personally I think that the researcher may trade sample size for sample representativeness. He can follow two opposite strategies: 1) devote a great effort for a limited number of contacts and 2) devote small effort for a great number of contacts. The former strategy leads to higher response rate, known sample bias and higher data reliability and completeness. The latter may lead to larger samples but with unknown representativeness and data quality.

Since OM tends to rely on small sample sizes, it would be useful at this point to check the credibility of the available sample. Sudman (1983:154–163) provides a scale to evaluate the credibility of a small sample. This scale, reported and commented on by Forza (2002), is based on the following considerations. Usually a sample taken from a limited geographic area repre-sents the population less than a sample taken from multiple locations. Articles which discuss possible sample bias are more credible than those that do not. The use of a special population in some cases is a powerful tool to test a theory but if used for convenience it can introduce obvious biases. It is possible that sample sizes are satisfactory when the total sample is considered but, after breakdowns, the resulting subsamples may be not adequate in size for more detailed analyses. When the response rate is poor, it is very likely that some bias has been introduced by self-selection of respondents.

Sometimes the researcher is pressed by lack of time or cost or resources; even in this case some sample designs are more effective in using the available resources than others.

4.5.3 Inputting and Cleaning Data

The first step in processing data usually entails transcribing the data from the original documents to a computer database. In this process, about 2–4% of the data can be transcribed incorrectly (Swab and Sitter, 1974:13). The errors arise from two situations: 1) the transcriber misreads the source document but correctly transcribes the misinterpreted data (86% of transcription errors are of this type); and 2) the transcriber reads the source document correctly but incorrectly transcribes the data (Karweit and Meyers, 1983). Independent verification of any transcription involving the reading and interpretation of hand-written material is therefore advisable.

When an error is detected, the researcher may choose between the following options, singly or in combination, to resolve the error (Karweit and Meyers, 1983):

- Consulting the original interview or questionnaire to determine if the error is due to incorrect transcription
- Contacting the respondent again to clarify the response or obtain missing data
- Estimating or imputing a response to resolve the error using various imputation techniques
- Discarding the response or designating it as bad or missing data
- Discarding the entire case

In the last 20–30 years, progress has been made in the way in which data are collected and cleaned. Optical-scanning and Web-based questionnaires allow automatic inputting of data, thus reducing errors. Computer-assisted personal (CAPI) or telephone (CATI) interviewing allow interviews to be completed with answers entered directly in databases thus reducing intermediate steps and errors. The data input programmes can perform checks on the data (ensuring, for example, that the values are within a certain range, or that other logical constraints are satisfied). New techniques are available not only for inputting data but also for distributing and even developing questionnaires. 'Integrated' software applications, such as SPSS Data Entry Survey Software or Sphinx Survey, assist in questionnaire development and questionnaire distribution (on the Web for example), as well as in building the database and analysing of the collected data.

4.5.4 Assessing the Measurement Quality

4.5.4.1 Importance of Ensuring and Assessing Measurement Quality

Section 4.3 has already highlighted the fact that researchers, when moving from the theoretical level to the empirical one, must operationalize the constructs present in the theoretical framework. Carmines and Zeller (1979) note that 'if the theoretical constructs have no empirical referents, then the empirical tenability of the theory must remain unknown'. When measurements are unreliable and/or invalid, analysis can possibly lead to incorrect inferences and misleading conclusions. Without assessing reliability and validity of measurement it would be impossible to 'disentangle the distorting influences of {measurement} errors on theoretical relationships that are being tested' (Bagozzi et al., 1991).

Measurement error represents one of the major sources of error in survey-based research (Biemer et al., 1991; Malhotra and Grover, 1998) and should be kept at the lowest possible level. Furthermore, as measurement error affects the results of survey-based research, it should be assessed not only during the research, but also reported in the report or articles derived from the research.

When we address the issue of measurement quality, we think of the quality of the survey instruments and procedures used to measure the constructs of interest. However, the most crucial aspect related to measurement quality concerns the measurement of complex constructs by multi-item measures, which is the focus of the remainder of this section. The presentation of the fundamental aspects of measurement quality assessment is illustrated, throughout this section, with an example taken from OM literature (Ahire and Dreyfus, 2000). This example highlights the fact that measurement quality assessment is becoming much more sophisticated in OM.

> The current research instrument consisting of 30 items {to measure 6 constructs . . .} was refined prior to testing the proposed model. For this purpose, a confirmatory factor analysis {CFA} of the initial measurement model was conducted using LISREL . . . The initial measurement model with all 30 items resulted in an inadequate fit . . . The initial measurement model was refined using standard CFA refinement procedures . . . as follows. The items with excessive standardized residuals and modification indices were identified and eliminated one at a time . . . we stopped refinement upon attaining generally acceptable model fit thresholds without a substantial reduction in the content validity of constructs. Four items were eliminated from the original 30 items . . . Most of the loadings {of individual retained items on corresponding constructs} are above 0.6 suggesting that the items align well with their respective constructs . . . Thus, considering the large size and heterogeneity of our sample, the model fit indices . . . demonstrate that the

refined model fits the data well. {Correlations between scales (i.e. measures of constructs) are reported.} . . . Considering the high scale intercorrelations, several reliability and validity indices were computed to ensure that the refined scales represent reliable and valid measurements of the underlying constructs.

(Ahire and Dreyfus, 2000)

4.5.4.2 Measure Quality Criteria

The quality of measures is evaluated in terms of validity and reliability. Validity is concerned with whether we are measuring what we intend to measure, while reliability is concerned with stability and consistency in measurement scores. Lack of validity introduces a systematic error (bias), while lack of reliability introduces random error (Carmines and Zeller, 1979).

RELIABILITY

Reliability indicates dependability, stability, predictability, consistency and accuracy, and refers to the extent to which a measuring procedure yields the same results on repeated trials (Kerlinger, 1986; Carmines and Zeller, 1979). Reliability is assessed after data collection, although some actions to reduce reliability problems may already be taken while assessing face validity (see section 4.3). The four most common methods used to estimate reliability are: 1) test–retest method, 2) alternative form method, 3) split halves method, 4) internal consistency method (see Table 4.12). Fundamental readings on this issue are Nunnally (1978) and Carmines and Zeller (1979).

The most popular test within the internal consistency method is the Cronbach coefficient alpha (Cronbach, 1951). Cronbach's α is also the most used reliability indicator in OM survey research. Cronbach's α can be expressed in terms of $\bar{p}$, the average inter-item correlation among the n measurement items in the instrument under consideration, as follows:

$$\alpha = \frac{n\bar{p}}{1 + (n-1)\bar{p}}$$

Cronbach's α (is therefore related to the number of items, n, as well as to the average inter-item correlation $\bar{p}$. Nunnally (1978) states that new developed measures can be accepted with $\alpha \geq 0.6$, otherwise $\alpha \geq 0.7$ should be the threshold. With $\alpha \geq 0.8$ the measure is very reliable. These criteria are well accepted in OM. Computation of Cronbach's α coefficient is well supported by statistical packages.

Two scale reliability indices are reported: Cronbach's α . . . and

Table 4.12 Methods to Assess Reliability

Method	Procedure	Meaning
Test–retest	It calculates the correlation between responses obtained through the same measure applied to the same respondents at different points of time (e.g. separated by 2 weeks)	It estimates the ability of the measure to maintain stability over time. This aspect is indicative of the measure stability and low vulnerability to change in uncontrollable testing conditions and in the state of the respondents
Alternative form	It calculates the correlation between responses obtained through different measures applied to the same respondents in different points of time (e.g. separated by 2 weeks)	It assesses the equivalence of different forms for measuring the same construct
Split halves	It subdivides the items of a measure into two subsets and statistically correlates the answers obtained at the same time to them	It assesses the equivalence of different sets of items for measuring the same construct
Internal consistency	It uses various algorithms to estimate the reliability of a measure from measure administration at one point in time	It assesses the equivalence, homogeneity, and inter-correlation of the items used in a measure. This means that the items of a measure should hang together as a set and should be capable of independently measuring the same construct

> Werts–Linn–Joreskog ρc coefficients . . . All of the refined scales have high values of both reliability indices.
>
> (Ahire and Dreyfus, 2000)

CONSTRUCT VALIDITY

Construct validity refers to the degree to which a measure represents and acts as the concept being measured. While content validity refers to the degree to which the meaning of a set of items represents the domain of the concept under investigation, the construct validity refers to the degree to which the scores obtained from using a set of items behave as expected (i.e. load only one underlying factor, correlate quite highly between them, correlate strongly with alternative measures of the same concept, correlate significantly with measures of constructs theoretically associated, though less than with measures of the same construct, do not correlate with measures of unrelated concepts, etc.). Obviously without content validity it is impossible to have construct validity.

Out of all the different properties that can be assessed concerning a measure, construct validity is the most complex and, yet, the most critical to substantive theory testing (Bagozzi et al., 1991). The notions of construct validity and content validity are sometimes presented in such a way that it is not possible to discriminate between them. This situation generates some confusion within the OM community, so that recently some OM researchers have avoided the use of the term 'construct validity' even though they had performed a very thorough measurement validation. If this notion has to be used in OM, then it deserves further refinement, taking into account its recent developments in other social sciences disciplines (see for example the notion of validity as a unified concept proposed by Messick (1995)).

Construct unidimensionality is the first property to check in assessing construct validity. It should even precede the assessment of reliability. 'It is a matter of logical and empirical necessity that a variable be unidimensional' (Bagozzi, 1980:126). A multidimensional measure (i.e. a measure comprised of indicators which represents more than one construct) 'cannot, by definition, be considered a variable and hence must not be treated as such in one's theory' (Bagozzi, 1980:126). From an empirical perspective, 'when a measure of one variable improperly includes empirical indicators that are related to another variable, we are in a sense combining two variables A and B to form a new variable C. Serious problems arise regarding the interpretation of association between C and other variables' (O'Leary-Kelly and Vokurka, 1998).

A measure must satisfy two conditions in order to be considered unidimensional. 'First, an empirical indicator must be significantly associated with an underlying latent variable i.e., the empirical representation of a construct, and, second, it can be associated with one and only one latent variable (Hair et al., 1992; Phillips and Bagozzi, 1986; Anderson and Gerbing, 1982)' (O'Leary-Kelly and Vokurka 1998).

Assessing unidimensionality is an established practice in OM. This may be performed both with exploratory factor analysis (see Saraph et al., 1989; Flynn et al., 1994) and with confirmatory factor analysis (see Ahire et al., 1996). Factor analysis can be performed on items belonging to a single summated scale or items of several summated scales (Flynn et al., 1990; Birnbaum et al., 1986).

> The unidimensionality goodness of fit index indicates the extent to which the scale items are strongly associated with each other and represent a single concept . . . All of the scales exhibited high satisfactory unidimensionality.
>
> (Ahire and Dreyfus, 2000)

Convergent and divergent validity. Campbell and Fiske (1959) proposed two aspects of construct validity, namely convergent and divergent validity. *Convergent validity* refers to the degree to which multiple attempts to measure the same concept (e.g. different measures or different items) are in agreement. The idea is that scores obtained by two or more measures of a same thing co-vary highly if they are good measures of the same thing. *Discriminant validity* refers to the degree to which measures of different concepts (or items belonging to different measures) are distinct. The idea is that, if two or more concepts are distinct (i.e. have a content domain that does not overlap), then good measures of these concepts (or items belonging to different measures of these concepts) should not correlate too strongly.

> The use of measures that lack convergent and discriminant validity can lead to numerous problems in the interpretation of the results of a study. For example, the finding of a significant relationship between variables that lack convergent validity might be attributable to the methods used to measure the latent variables, not to any 'true' relationship between them (Fiske, 1982). Similarly, if we use measures of two latent variables, x and y, that fail to demonstrate discriminant validity, we cannot conclude that the measures are reflecting two unique constructs; in this case it would be inappropriate to analyze x and y as separate latent variables.
>
> (O'Leary-Kelly and Vokurka, 1998)

Convergent and discriminant validity can be tested through the multitrait–multimethod (MTMM) matrix method (the traditional way) or the confirmatory factor analysis (CFA) method. For details see Bagozzi et al. (1991) and O'Leary-Kelly and Vokurka (1998).

Testing for convergent and discriminant validity is a practice increasingly applied in OM. The trend is to assess them through CFA on items belonging to measures of different constructs (see for example Koufteros, 1999).

> We report the Bentler–Bonett normed fit index (Δ) as a measure of convergent validity for each scale. All of the scales exceed the threshold of 0.90 for this index.
>
> Finally, the high scale correlations warranted careful assessment of discriminant validity of the constructs . . . Discriminant validity of constructs can be assessed in different ways. First, adequate discriminant validity is established when the Cronbach reliability coefficient of each of the scales is adequately larger than the average of its correlations with other constructs . . . Second, statistically distinct scales exhibit interscale correlations that are adequately different from 1.0 . . . Third, if the percent variance extracted, PVE, by the scale items of a construct is consistently greater than the squared interscale correlations of the construct, additional evidence for the discriminant validity of the construct

with respect to all other constructs is established . . . Finally, nested measurement models involving pairs of different constructs (one with a perfect correlation and one with correlation free to vary) can be run and χ^2 difference tested for significance. If the χ^2 difference statistic is significant for 1 df, the two constructs are statistically distinct . . . The discriminant validity results . . . confirm that they adequately pass all of the aforementioned tests of discriminant validity.

(Ahire and Dreyfus, 2000)

CRITERION-RELATED VALIDITY

When an instrument is intended to perform a prediction function, validity depends entirely on how well the instrument correlates with what it is intended to predict (a criterion).

(Nunnally, 1978:111)

Criterion-related validity is established when the measure differentiates subjects on a criterion it is expected to predict. Establishing concurrent validity or predictive validity can do this. Concurrent validity is established when the scale discriminates subjects who are known to be different. Predictive validity is the ability of the measure to differentiate between subjects as to a future criterion (e.g the future attainment of certain 'quality conformance' level which is caused by a change in the level of the 'use of statistical process control').

Rungtusanatham and Choi (2000) show that in OM criterion-related validity has been tested using multiple correlations (e.g. Saraph et al., 1989), canonical correlations (e.g. Flynn et al., 1994) and LISREL (e.g. Ahire et al., 1996).

Furthermore, we tested criterion-related validity of the exogenous and intermediate endogenous constructs of the model . . . We assessed the criterion-related validity of the input and intermediate outcome constructs using two additional numerical measures of operational quality, namely, overall rating of product quality within the industry and percentage of repeat customers. The overall rating of product quality . . . exhibits statistically significant correlations . . . with each construct . . . Percentage of repeat customers also indicates statistically significant correlations with each construct . . . Finally, the correlations of the external quality construct (the final endogenous construct) with product quality rating . . . and percent repeat customers . . . further confirm the convergent validity of this critical outcome construct.

(Ahire and Dreyfus, 2000)

When a test, conducted to assess an aspect of construct validity or criterion-related validity, does not support the expected result, either the measurement instrument or the theory could be invalid. It is a matter of researcher judgement to interpret the obtained results adequately.

4.5.4.3 Steps in Assessing Validity and Reliability

Developing valid and reliable measures is a process parallel to that aimed at building and testing a theory. Here, measures go through a process of developing and testing (see for example the framework for developing multi-item measures provided by Malhotra and Grover (1998) and Menor and Roth (2007)). The aim is not only to build an instrument that allows for testing a specific theory, but also to have an instrument which is reusable for other theories. Eventually this instrument may be used in practice for self-evaluation and benchmarking purposes.

When developing measures in a pilot-testing phase or in exploratory research, cut-off levels (e.g. for Chronbach's α) are less stringent and, due to small sample sizes, assessments (e.g. of unidimensionality) are of an exploratory nature (Nunnally, 1978). When testing measures, cut-off levels are set at higher values, confirmatory methods should be used and all the various relevant aspects of validity and reliability should be considered. If an already-developed measure is used in a modified form, then the measure quality should be re-assessed and contrasted with the one of the original measures.

Measure quality assessment, therefore, takes place at various stages of survey research: before data collection, in pilot testing, in ad hoc analyses to validate the measure and, finally, after data collection, for hypothesis testing. At all of these stages measures may be refined and items may be eliminated or modified. The elimination of an item requires the researcher to return to content validity assessment and redo all of the subsequent tests (Rungtusanatham and Choi, 2000). Examples of application are provided by Parasuraman et al. (1988) and Saraph et al. (1989).

4.5.4.4 Advancement in Measurement Quality Assessment

Some research deals with samples that exhibit high heterogeneity. For example we may have big and small companies or plants placed in different countries. International marketing research and international business research advise that in these cases measurement equivalence should be assessed before pooling data or before comparing subgroups.

This issue has been reported in some OM works (e.g. Ahire and Dreysus, 2000; Rungtusantaham et al., 2005). Recently some prescriptions for OM research regarding when we can pool data in the context of highly heterogeneous samples have been provided (Rungtusantamam et al., 2007). Over the coming years we may expect advancement of this aspect of measurement quality.

4.6 Survey Execution

4.6.1 Redoing Activities on a Larger Scale

At the end of pilot testing, either the researcher can proceed with theory testing or will have to revise the survey questionnaires, the survey administration process, or both. In the latter case, the researcher would have to go back to the issues raised in sections 4.3 and 4.4. It follows that the researcher should move to the survey execution phase only when all relevant issues have been addressed. Ideally, data collection problems and measurement problems should have been reduced to the minimum level. Therefore, at the survey execution stage the researcher has the opportunity to direct attention elsewhere until the data have been returned.

Fundamentally, the researcher in this phase has to repeat the pilot-testing activities with a large sample:

- Approaching companies/respondents and collecting data
- Controlling and reducing the problems caused by non-respondents
- Performing data input and cleaning
- Treating missing data (recalling respondents, estimating/replacing data)
- Assessing measurement quality
- Providing feedback to respondents

Providing feedback to companies/respondents is an ethical obligation (if promised) and should be done to motivate their present and future involvement. This feedback could be a standard summary report, personalized feedback, an invitation to meetings where results are communicated, or something else that could be useful to the respondents.

4.6.2 Handling Missing Data

Handling missing data should be a key concern during data collection. 'When statistical models and procedures are used to analyse a random sample, it is usually assumed that no sample data is missing. In practice, however, this is rarely the case for survey data' (Anderson et al., 1983). Missing data cannot be overlooked, as they have a negative impact on statistical power and may cause biased estimates in several ways (Roth et al. 1999). Useful reviews of how to handle missing data are provided by Anderson et al. (1983), Roth (1994) and, with specific reference to OM, Tsikriktsis (2005).

Two questions must be addressed concerning missing data (Tsikriktsis, 2005). First, how much of the data is missing? As the percentage of missing data increases, not only does statistical power decrease dramatically, but also different techniques to treat missing data lead to increasingly different results (under 10% little difference, close to 20% considerable difference, over 30–40% high difference). The second question is whether the pattern of missing observations is random or not. One method to assess the randomness is to split the set of observations into two subsets: one with missing data for the variable and the other with valid values of the variable. If patterns of significant difference are found between the two subsets on other variables of interest, this would indicate that missing data are not the result of a random process.

The best approach to dealing with missing data is to prevent their occurrence in the first place by increasing respondent involvement, giving them clear instructions in the questionnaire as well as supporting and recalling respondents to ensure completeness after administering the questionnaire. However, in spite of all of these efforts some data, unavoidably, will be missing. Three broad strategies can be adopted: 1) deletion; 2) replacement based on estimation; 3) model-based strategy. Deletion simply omits from analyses observations with missing data. Deletion may be listwise (an entire observation is deleted if it has a missing value in one variable) or pairwise (the observation is deleted only from those statistical analyses that require the missing data). When data are missed randomly, a deletion strategy leads generally to unbiased results, but (especially if listwise) decreases statistical power. Replacement based on estimation, the second strategy, estimates the missing observation, subsequently replaces the missing data with the estimate and, finally, proceeds with a statistical analysis of the data set. Replacement procedures are of four types: mean-based, regression-based, model-based and hotdeck imputation (a missing value is replaced with the actual score from a similar case in the amended dataset). The third strategy (model-based) provides explicit modelling of missing data, thus allowing an open analysis and critique. It is the best solution with missing data that are definitely non-random. Tsikriktsis (2005) describes synthetically the different missing data treatment procedures, presenting advantages, disadvantages, context of utilization and references to studies that apply them.

Tsikriktsis examined 103 survey-based articles from the Journal of Operations Management (JOM) between 1993 and 2001. He found that:

> First, 67% of the articles did not mention anything about whether there were missing data and, if there were, how they were treated . . . Second, authors are not explicit about their treatment of missing data. Only 4 out of 45 articles that were coded as having missing data have clearly stated the technique used (listwise deletion in all four cases) . . . Third, {authors do not mention the presence of missing data, either because they take it for granted or} in order to avoid potential comments from reviewers . . . Fourth, on average 13% of the data were missing. Such a high percentage of missing data could have catastrophic implications for statistical power . . . Overall, most advanced methods, such as imputation and model-based procedures, were never used, or, if they have been used, they have not been reported . . .

Overall, we recommend the following to OM researchers who are dealing with missing data. First, they should understand the reasons that lead to missing data and make an effort to avoid/minimize missing data . . . Second, researchers should not always fall for listwise deletion that provides a 'quick and easy fix'. Despite the fact that listwise deletion is a 'conservative' technique that results in researchers 'making it harder for themselves' . . ., it also reduces statistical power and accuracy more than many other techniques . . . Finally, authors should be very explicit about how they handle missing data in their manuscripts (method used, why, etc.).

(Tsikriktsis, 2005)

4.7 Data Analysis and Interpretation of Results

Data analysis can be divided into two phases: preliminary data analysis and hypothesis testing. These phases are described below and the most commonly used data-analysis methods are presented briefly. The objective here is to provide some information to complete the overview of the theory-testing survey research process. However, this issue deserves a more extensive discussion and the reader is encouraged to address this issue in more depth in statistical manuals and with statisticians.

Before getting into the details of the analysis, we should briefly look at the kind of data analyses that have been used in OM. Scudder and Hill (1998) analysed the method used in 477 OM empirical research articles published during the period 1986–1995 in the 13 main journal outlets for OM research. They found that 28% of articles did not use any statistical data-analysis method (almost all of these articles were based on case studies), while some articles used more than one data-analysis method. Furthermore, they found that 72% of articles used descriptive statistics, 17% regression/correlation, 9% means testing, 7% data reduction (principal component analysis, etc), 4% analysis of variance (ANOVA) and multivariate analysis of variance (MANOVA), and 3% cluster analysis.

4.7.1 Preliminary Data Analysis

In order to acquire knowledge of the characteristics and properties of the collected data, some preliminary data analyses are conducted usually before performing measurement quality assessment or tests of hypotheses. Carrying out such analyses before assessing measurement quality gives preliminary indications of how well the coding and inputting of data have been done, how good the scales are and whether there is a suspicion of poor content validity or systematic bias. Before testing hypotheses, it is useful to check the assumptions underlying the tests and to get a feeling for the data, in order to better interpret the results of the tests.

The discovery of errors, outliers, absence of normality and absence of variance homogeneity leads to a number of actions. These actions may entail the modification of data (error correction, outlier deletion or modification or replacement, observation deletion, variable transformation) to make them suitable for subsequent analyses. Sometimes, however, the problems are so serious that variables should be deleted and the planned analyses should be changed. The need for such actions should not be underestimated. Outliers, for example, bias the mean and inflate the standard deviation and can lead both to type I and type II errors.

The knowledge acquired in this preliminary data analysis may influence the discussion of the results and the conclusions. The deletion of certain outliers may introduce a clear restriction on the generalizability of results, which in turn requires a detailed identification and description of these outliers. The description of demographic variables may better characterize the sample under investigation and these characterizations may be important when discussing the generalizability of results.

Preliminary data analysis is performed by checking central tendencies, dispersions, frequency distributions, correlations. It is good practice to calculate 1) the frequency distribution of the demographic variables, 2) the mean, standard deviation, range and variance of the other dependent and independent variables, and 3) an inter-correlation matrix of the variables. Table 4.13 gives some of the most frequently used descriptive statistics in preliminary data analysis. Table 4.14 presents some of the most common

Table 4.13 Descriptive Statistics used in Preliminary Data Analysis

Type of analysis	Explanation	Relevance
Frequencies	Refers to the number of times various subcategories of certain phenomenon occur	Generally obtained for nominal variables
Measures of central tendencies	Mean (the average value), median (half of the observations fall above and the other half fall below the median) and mode (the most frequently occurring value) characterize the central tendency (or location or centre) of a set of observations	To characterize the central value of a set of observations parsimoniously in a meaningful way
Measures of dispersion	Measures of dispersion (or spread or variability) include the range, the standard deviation, the variance and the interquartile range	To concisely indicate the variability that exists in a set of observations
Measures of shape	The measures of shape, skewness and kurtosis describe departures from the symmetry of a distribution and its relative flatness (or peakedness), respectively.	To indicate the kind of departures from a normal distribution

Table 4.14 Techniques Used to Perform Preliminary Data Analysis

Technique	Explanation	Relevance
Frequency tables	To array data from highest to lowest values with counts, percentages, percentage adjusted for missing values, and cumulative percentages	Useful to inspect the range of responses and their repeated occurrence Not particularly informative with interval–ratio scales
Barcharts and piecharts	To represent graphically the basic information of frequency tables	Appropriate for relative comparisons of nominal data
Histograms	To show the frequency of different scores (or score intervals of equal length)	Useful to identify outliers and to get a first feeling of departures from normality Optimal for continuous variables
Boxplots	To show graphically median, spread and inter-quartile range of scores	Useful to have a detailed picture of the main body, tails and outliers of the distribution
Scatterplots	To show relationships between two (or three) variables	Useful to identify outliers Useful to get a feeling of the presence and the form of association between variables
Crosstabulations	The cells of these tables contain combination of count, row, column, and total percentages	Useful to perform preliminary evaluation of relationships involving nominally scaled variables

techniques available in statistical packages to perform the preliminary data analysis. Some statistical packages (for example SAS and SPSS) provide tools for exploratory or interactive data analysis which facilitate preliminary data-analysis activities through emphasis on visual representation and graphical techniques.

4.7.2 Analysing Data for Hypothesis Testing

Significance tests can be grouped into two general classes: parametric and non-parametric. Generally, parametric tests are considered more powerful because their data are typically derived from interval and ratio measurements whose likelihood model (i.e. the distribution) is known, except for some parameters. Non-parametric tests are used with nominal and ordinal data. Experts in non-parametric testing claim that non-parametric tests are comparable in terms of power (Hollander and Wolfe, 1999). However, in social science at the moment parametric techniques are considered 'the tests of choice if their assumptions are met. Some of the assumptions for parametric tests include: 1) the observations must be independent (that is, the selection of any one case should not affect the chances for any other case to be selected in the sample); 2) the observation should be drawn from normally distributed populations; 3) these populations should have equal variance; 4) the measurement scales should be at least interval so that arithmetic operations can be used with them' (Emory and Cooper, 1991). The researcher is responsible for assessing whether the assumptions of the chosen test are satisfied or not and should provide evidence of having performed such checks. It should be remembered, however, that some parametric tests are not affected seriously by violations of assumptions, while for others a departure from assumptions may threaten result validity. Non-parametric tests have fewer and less stringent assumptions. They do not require normally distributed populations or homogeneity of variance. Some of them require independent cases, while others are deliberately designed for analyses with related cases. Therefore, when the population distribution is undefined, or violates assumption of parametric tests, non-parametric tests must be used.

In order to choose the significance test, at least three questions should be considered (Emory and Cooper, 1991): 1) does the test involve one sample, two samples or k samples? 2) If two or k samples are involved, are the individual cases independent or related? 3) Is the measurement scale nominal, ordinal, interval or ratio? Additional questions may arise once answers to these ones are known. For example, what is the sample size? If there are several samples, are they of equal size? Have the data been weighted? Have the data been transformed? The answers can complicate the selection, but once a tentative choice is made, most standard statistics textbooks will provide further details. Decision trees provide a more systematic means of selecting techniques. One widely used guide from the Institute for Social Research (Andrews et al., 1976) starts with a question about the number of variables, nature of variables and level of measurement. It continues with more detailed questions, thus providing indications concerning over 130 solutions.

Table 4.15 gives examples of some parametric tests and Table 4.16 gives examples of non-parametric tests.

In any applied field, such as OM, most tools are, or should be, multivariate. Unless a problem is treated as a multivariate problem in these fields, it is treated superficially. Therefore, multivariate analysis (simultaneous analysis of more than two variables) is, and will continue to be, important in OM. Table 4.17 presents some of the more established multivariate techniques as well as some of the emerging ones (for more details see Hair et al., 1992).

4.7.3 Linking Measure Quality Assessment to Hypothesis Testing

Section 4.5 highlighted that measurement quality assessment can be done in an exploratory way when pilot testing. Further, it deserves confirmatory

Table 4.15 Examples of Parametric Tests

Test	When used	Function
Pearson correlation	With interval and ratio data	To test hypothesis which postulates significant positive (negative) relationships between two variables
t-test	With interval and ratio data	To see whether there is any significant difference in the means for two groups in the variable of interest. Groups can be either two different groups or the same group before and after the treatment
Analysis of variance (ANOVA)	With interval and ratio data	To see whether there are significant mean differences among more than two groups. In order to see where the difference lies, tests like Sheffe's test, Duncan Multiple Range test, Tukey's test and student-Newman-Keul's test are available

Table 4.16 Examples of Non-parametric Tests (adapted from Sekaran, 1992:279)

Test	When used	Function
Chi-squared (χ^2)	With nominal data for one sample or two or more independent samples	Test for equality of distributions
Cochran Q	With more than two related samples measured on nominal scale	Similar function as χ^2, it helps when data fall into two natural categories
Fisher exact probability	With two independent samples measured on nominal scale	More useful than χ^2 when expected frequencies are small
Sign test	With two related samples measured on ordinal scale	Test for equality of two groups distributions
Median test	With one sample	To test the equality in distribution under the assumption of homoschedasticicity
Mann-Witney U test	With two independent samples on ordinal data	Analogue to the two independent sample t-tests with ordinal data
Kruskall-Wallis one-way ANOVA	With more than two independent samples on an ordinal scale	An alternative to one-way ANOVA with ordinal data
Friedman two-way ANOVA	With more than two related samples on ordinal data	Analogue to two-way ANOVA with ranked data when interactions are assumed absent
Kolmogorov-Smirnov	With one sample or two independent samples measured on ordinal scale	Test for equality of distribution with ordinal scale

Table 4.17 Main Multivariate Analysis Methods

Multivariate technique	When used	Function
Multiple regression	When a single, metric, dependent variable is presumed to be related to one or more, metric, independent variables	To predict the changes in the dependent variable in response to changes in the several independent variables
Multiple discriminant analysis	When the single, dependent variable is dichotomous (e.g. male–female) or multidichotomous (e.g. high–medium–low) and, therefore, non-metric	To understand group differences and predict the likelihood that an entity (individual or object) will belong to a particular class or group based on several, metric, independent variables
Multivariate analysis of variance (MANOVA) Multivariate analysis of covariance (MANCOVA)	When an experimental situation (manipulation of several, non-metric, variables) is designed to test hypotheses concerning the variance in group response on two or more metric-dependent variables	To simultaneously explore the relationship between several, categorical, independent variables (usually referred to as treatments) and two or more, dependent, metric variables
Canonical correlation	An extension of multiple regression analysis	To simultaneously correlate several, metric, independent variables and several, dependent, metric variables
Structural equation modelling	When multiple, separate regression equations have to be estimated simultaneously	To simultaneously test the measurement model (which specifies one or more indicators to measure each variable) and the structural model (the model which relates independent and dependent variables)
Factor analysis	When several, metric variables are under analysis and the researcher wishes to reduce the number of variables to manage or find out the underlying factors	To analyse interrelationships among a large number of variables and to explain these variables in terms of their common underlying dimensions (factors)
Cluster analysis	When metric variables are present and the researcher wishes to group entities	To classify a sample of entities (individuals or objects) into a smaller number of mutually exclusive subgroups based on the similarities among the entities

analyses when doing the analyses with the data which will be used to test hypotheses. However this is not enough to be very accurate in the analysis. Traditionally, in fact, procedures to assess measure validity–reliability are 'applied independently of statistical procedures to test causal hypotheses . . . {The consequence is that} whereas construct validation procedures typically establish the presence of significant amounts of measurement and/or method error, contemporary hypothesis-testing procedures assume it away entirely' (Bagozzi and Phillips, 1982). Measurement and method error can cause 'spurious confirmation of inadequate theories, tentative rejection of adequate theories, and/or distorted estimates of the magnitude and relevance of actual relationships' (Bagozzi and Phillips, 1982). Structural equation modelling (SEM) provides an instrument to test measurement quality and to consider it while testing the hypotheses.

SEM is a powerful but complex technique. An example of its application in OM can be found in Koufteros (1999). SEM is receiving increasing attention within OM but it should be properly applied. Shah and Goldstein (2006) present the implications of overlooking fundamental assumptions of SEM and ignoring serious methodological issues. They provide guidelines for improving future applications of SEM in OM research.

4.7.4 *Interpreting Results*

The choice and the application of an appropriate statistical test is only one step in the analysis of data for theory testing. In addition, the results of the statistical tests must be interpreted. When interpreting results, the researcher moves from the empirical to the theoretical domain. This process implies considerations of inference and generalization (Meredith, 1998).

In making an inference on relations between variables, the researcher could incur a statistical error or an internal validity error. The statistical error (see type I and type II errors discussed in section 4.4.3) can be taken into account by considering the issues of statistical power, significance level, sample size and effect size. The internal validity error mistakenly attributes the cause of variation to a dependent variable. For example, the researcher could infer that variable A causes variable B, while there is an unacknowledged variable C which causes both A and B. The link that the researcher observes between A and B is, therefore, spurious. 'POM researchers, in the absence of experimental designs, should try to justify internal validity. This can be done informally through a discussion of why causality exists or why alternate explanations are unlikely' (Malhotra and Grover, 1998:414).

Even in the situation when data analysis results are consistent with the theory at the sample level, the researcher should be careful in inferring that the same consistency holds at the population level, because of the previously discussed issues of sampling, response rate and response bias. A further aspect of result interpretation concerns the discussion of potential extension of the theory to other populations. The degree to which the study's results can be generalized across populations, settings and other similar conditions constitutes the external validity of the study (Davis, 2005).

4.8 What Information should be Reported in Articles

In the article reporting the results of a survey-based study the researcher should provide, in a concise but complete manner, all the information which allows reviewers and readers to 1) understand what has been done, 2) critically evaluate what the work has achieved, and 3) replicate the work or compare the results with similar studies. To understand what information is to be included, one can refer to Verma and Goodale (1995), Malhotra and Grover (1998), Forza and Di Nuzzo (1998), Hensley (1999), Rungtusanatham et al. (2003). The main points to consider are summarized in Table 4.18.

All of the information listed in Table 4.18 is necessary if the article has a theory-testing purpose, but it is generally useful also when the article is of descriptive or exploratory nature. Providing this information may make survey shortcomings evident. Serious journals and reviewers, however, greatly appreciate those authors who present the limitations of their research: a survey-based paper without a serious discussion of research limitations appears somewhat suspicious to them. The reason is that, while a research with fatal flaws cannot be accepted for publication, no research is without limitations. A honest and capable researcher should mention such limitations, thus paving the way to further research and avoiding definitive acceptance of results whose validity is, to some extent, questionable.

Providing all of the required information is difficult and, probably, not feasible in a single paper. In fact, over the last few years we have witnessed more and more papers that split the outcomes of a survey-based study in two or more articles focused, respectively, on concept formalization, measure development and testing of the main hypotheses. In my opinion, this trend will lead to a broader-based and stronger theoretical foundation of OM survey-based research.

Exploratory, descriptive and theory-testing survey research are, all of them, important and widely used in OM. Therefore, in concluding this chapter it is useful to outline the different requirements of the various types of survey. Obviously, if a particular requirement is relaxed, then there is no longer the need to provide detailed information concerning that requirement. Table 4.19 summarizes the differences in requirements among different survey types.

4.9 Summary

The chapter has presented and discussed the various steps of the survey research process. For each step, it has provided responses to the following questions: 1) What is it about? 2) Why should it be done? 3) What is suggested to be done? Examples of applications in OM and more general

Table 4.18 Information to Include in the Report

Main issues	Detailed points
Theoretical base	Name and definitions of constructs, relations between variables, validity boundary of the relations, unit of analysis, previous literature on each of these points
Expected contribution	Purpose of the study (whether it is exploration, description, or hypothesis testing), research questions/ hypotheses, types of investigation (causal relationships, correlations, group differences, ranks, etc.)
Sample and data collection approach	Sampling process, source of population-frame, justification of sample frame, a priori sample, resulting sample, response rate, bias analysis Time horizon (cross-sectional or longitudinal), when and where data have been collected, type of data collection (mail, telephone, Web, personal visit), pilot testing, contact approach, kind of recall
Data pre-treatment	Missing data analysis and treatment, outliers analysis and treatment, data pooling (putting together observations from different subpopulations), scale transformation, data standardization
Measurement	Description of measure construction process, reference/ comparison to similar/identical measures, description of respondents, list of respondents for each measure, description of the data aggregation process (from informants to unit of analysis), measure pre-testing, adequacy to the unit of analysis, adequacy to the respondents, face validity, construct unidimensionality, reliability, convergent and divergent validity, predictive validity, appendix with the measurement instrument, description of the measurement refinement process including information on techniques used
Data analysis	Description of the techniques used, evidence that the technique assumptions are satisfied, statistical power, results of the tests including level of significance, interpretation of the results in the context of the hypotheses
Discussion	Discusses what the substantiation of the hypotheses means in terms of the present research and why some of the hypotheses (if any) may not have been supported Consider through intuitive but appropriate and logical speculations how inadequacies in the sampling design, the measures, the data collection methods, control of critical variables, respondent bias, questionnaire design and so on affect the results, their trustability and generalizability

Table 4.19 Requirement Differences among Survey Types (adapted from Pinsonneault and Kraemer, 1993)

Survey type Element/dimension	Exploratory	Descriptive	Theory testing
Unit(s) of analysis	Clearly defined	Clearly defined and appropriate for the questions/ hypotheses	Clearly defined and appropriate for the research hypotheses
Respondents	Representative of the unit of analysis	Representative of the unit of analysis	Representative of the unit of analysis
Research hypotheses	Not necessary	Questions clearly stated	Hypotheses clearly stated and theoretically motivated
Representativeness of sample frame	Approximation	Explicit, logical argument; reasonable choice among alternatives	Explicit, logical argument; reasonable choice among alternatives
Representativeness of the sample	Not a criterion	Systematic, purposive, random selection	Systematic, purposive, random selection
Sample size	Sufficient to include the range of the interest phenomena	Sufficient to represent the population of interest and perform statistical tests	Sufficient to test categories in the theoretical framework with statistical power
Pre-test of questionnaires	With subsample of sample	With subsample of sample	With subsample of sample
Response rate	No minimum	Greater than 50% of targeted population and study of bias	Greater than 50% of targeted population and study of bias
Mix of data collection methods	Multiple methods	Not necessary	Multiple methods

reference literature are referenced throughout the chapter. Table 4.20 summarizes the questions that the researcher should ask at the various steps of survey research in order to enhance the quality of the process.

By following the guidelines provided in this chapter, the researcher should be able to execute survey research that will meet the main requirements of a scientific research project as outlined by Sherakan (1992):

Table 4.20 Questions to Check the Quality of an Ongoing Survey Research

Survey phase	Check questions to assure survey research quality
Prior to survey research design	1. Is the unit of analysis clearly defined for the study? 2. Are the construct operational definitions clearly stated? 3. Are research hypotheses clearly stated?
Defining the sample	4. Is the sample frame defined and justified? 5. What is the required level of randomness needed for the purposes of the study? 6. What is the minimum sample size required for the planned statistical analyses? 7. Can the sampling procedure be reproduced by other researchers?
Developing measurement instruments	8. Are already-developed (and preferably validated) measures available? 9. Are objective or perceptual questions needed? 10. Is the wording appropriate? 11. In the case of perceptual measures, are all the aspects of the concept equally present as items? 12. Does the instrumentation consistently reflect that unit of analysis? 13. Is the chosen scale compatible with the analyses which will be performed? 14. Can the respondent place the answers easily and reliably in this scale? 15. Is the chosen respondent(s) appropriate for the information sought? 16. Is any form of triangulation used to ensure that the gathered information is not biased by the respondent(s) or by method? 17. Are multi-item measures used (in the case of perceptual questions)? 18. Are the various rules of questionnaire design (see above) followed or not?
Collecting data	19. What is the response rate and is it satisfactory? 20. How much is the response bias? 21. Are data cleaned of errors or inconsistent answers? 22. Could missing data affect results? 23. Is it possible to pool data or treatments are necessary?
Assessing measure quality	24. Is face validity assessed? 25. Is field-based measure pre-testing performed? 26. Is reliability assessed? 27. Is construct validity assessed? 28. Is pilot data used for purifying measures or are existing validated measures adapted? 29. Is it possible to use confirmatory methods?
Analysing data	30. Is the statistical test appropriate for the hypothesis being tested? 31. Is the statistical test adequate for the available data?

(Continued Overleaf)

Table 4.20 (Continued)

Survey phase	Check questions to assure survey research quality
	32. Are the test assumptions satisfied?
	33. Do outliers or influencing factors affect results?
	34. Is the statistical power sufficient to reduce statistical conclusion error?
Interpretation of results	35. Do the findings have internal validity?
	36. Is the inference (both relational and representational) acceptable?
	37. For what other populations could results still be valid?

- *Purposiveness*: the researcher has been guided by and communicates a specific aim or purpose for the research
- *Rigour*: a strong theoretical base and a sound methodology are needed to collect the appropriate information and to interpret it adequately, that is, to do research in a trusted manner
- *Testability*: the researcher can reliably infer whether or not the data support conjectures and has controlled for what can influence the results
- *Replicability*: it is possible to repeat the study exactly. If controlled repetition of replicable studies is performed, conjectures will neither be supported (or discarded) merely by chance nor due to method differences
- *Precision and confidence*: refer on the one hand to how close the findings are to 'reality' and, on the other, to the probability that estimations are correct
- *Objectivity*: the conclusions are based on all the relevant facts and are not influenced by the researcher's subjective values
- *Generalizability*: refers to the applicability of the research findings to settings different from the studied one
- *Parsimony*: the use of a small number of variables and relationships among variables to describe and explain a phenomenon generally makes research frameworks more manageable and useful

Notes

1 This chapter is based on Forza, C. (2002) Survey research in operations management: a process based perspective. *International Journal of Operations and Production Management*, 22 (2): 152–194.
2 The concept of 'content validity' has been controversial in social indicators research. This kind of validity deserves further consideration by OM researchers in the context of recent developments in its conceptualisation (Sireci, 1998).

References and Bibliography

Survey and Empirical Methods in Operations Management

Amoako-Gyampah, K. and Meredith, J.R. (1989) 'The operations management research agenda: an update', *Journal of Operations Management*, 8 (3): 250–262.

Amundson, S.D. (1998) 'Relationships between theory-driven empirical research in operations management and other disciplines', *Journal of Operations Management*, 16 (4): 341–359.

Barnes, D. (2001) 'Research methods for the empirical investigation of the process of formation of operations strategy', *International Journal of Operations and Production Management*, 21 (8): 1076–1095.

Boyer, K.K. and Pagell, M. (2000) 'Measurement issues in empirical research: Improving measures of operations strategy and advanced manufacturing technology', *Journal of Operations Management*, 18 (3): 361–374.

Boyer, K.K., Olson, J.R., Calantone, R.J. and Jackson, E.C. (2002) 'Print versus electronic surveys: a comparison of two data collection methodologies', *Journal of Operations Management*, 20: 357–373.

Collins, R.S. and Cordon, C. (1997) 'Survey methodology issues in manufacturing strategy and practice research', *International Journal of Operations and Production Management*, 17 (7): 697–706.

Dangayach, G.S. and Deshmukh, S.G. (2001) 'Manufacturing strategy: literature review and some issues', *International Journal of Operations & Production Management*, 21 (7): 884–932.

Davies, A.J. and Kochhar, A.K. (2002) 'Manufacturing best practice and performance studies: a critique', *International Journal of Operations and Production Management*, 22 (3): 289–305.

Filippini, R. (1997) 'Operations management research: some reflections on evolution, models and empirical studies in OM', *International Journal of Operations and Production Management*, 17 (7): 655–670.

Flynn, B.B., Sakakibara, S., Schroeder, R.G., Bates, K.A. and Flynn, E.J. (1990) 'Empirical research methods in operations management', *Journal of Operations Management*, 9 (2): 250–284.

Forza, C. (2002) 'Survey research in operations management: a process based perspective', *International Journal of Operations and Production Management*, 22 (2): 152–194.

Forza, C. and Di Nuzzo, F. (1998) 'Meta-analysis applied to operations management: summarizing the results of empirical research', *International Journal of Production Research*, 36 (3): 837–861.

Forza, C. and Vinelli, A. (1998) 'On the contribution of survey research to the development of operations management theories', in P. Coughlan, T. Dromgoole and J. Peppard (eds), *Operations Management: Future Issues and Competitive Responses*, 183–188, Dublin: School of Business Studies.

Frohlich, M.T. (2002) 'Techniques for improving response rates in OM survey research', *Journal of Operations Management*, 20: 53–62.

Gupta, S., Verma, R. and Victorino, L. (2006) 'Empirical research published in production and operations management (1992–2005): trends and future research directions', *Production and Operations Management Journal*, 15 (3): 432–448.

Handfield, R.B. and Melnyk, S.A. (1998) 'The scientific theory-building process: a primer using the case of TQM', *Journal of Operations Management*, 16: 321–339.

Hensley, R.L. (1999) 'A review of operations management studies using scale development techniques', *Journal of Operations Management*, 17 (2): 343–358.

Ho, D.C.K., Au, K.F. and Newton, E. (2002), 'Empirical research on supply chain management: a critical review and recommendations', *International Journal of Production Research*, 40 (17): 4415–4430.

Ketokivi, M.A. and Schroeder, R.G. (2004) 'Perceptual measures of performance: fact or fiction?', *Journal of Operations Management*, 22: 247–264.

Malhotra, M.K. and Grover, V. (1998) 'An assessment of survey research in POM: From constructs to theory', *Journal of Operations Management*, 16 (17): 407–425.

Meredith, J.R. (1998) 'Building Operations Management theory through case and field research', *Journal of Operations Management*, 16 (4): 441–454.

Meredith, J.R., Raturi, A., Amoako-Jampah, K. and Kaplan, B. (1989) 'Alternative research paradigms in operations', *Journal of Operations Management*, 8 (4): 297–326.

O'Leary-Kelly, S.W. and Vokurka, R.J. (1998) 'The empirical assessment of construct validity', *Journal of Operations Management*, 16 (4): 387–405.

Pannirselvam, G.P., Ferguson, L.A., Ash, R.C. and Siferd, S.P. (1999) 'Operations management research: an update for the 1990s', *Journal of Operations Management*, 18 (1): 95–112.

Roth, A.V., Schroeder, R.G., Huang, X. and Kristal, M.M. (2008) *Handbook of Metrics for Research in Operations Management*, Thousand Oaks (CA): Sage.

Rungtusanatham, M.J. (1998) 'Let's not overlook content validity', *Decision Line*, July: 10–13.

Rungtusanatham, M.J. and Choi, T.Y. (2000) 'The reliability and validity of measurement instrument employed in empirical OM research: Concepts and definitions', Phoenix (AZ): Arizona State University—Working Paper of Department of Management.

Rungtusanatham, M.J., Choi, T.Y., Hollingworth, D.G., Wu, Z. and Forza, C. (2003) 'Survey research in operations management: historical analyses', *Journal of Operations Management*, 21: 475–488

Rungtusanatham, M., Ng, C. H., Zhao, X. and Lee, T. S. (2007) 'Pooling data across transparently different groups of key informants: measurement equivalence and survey research', *Decision Science*, 38 (4): 115–145.

Saraph, J.V., Benson, P.G. and Schroeder, R.G. (1989) 'An instrument for measuring the critical factors of quality management', *Decision Science*, 20 (4): 810–829.

Scudder, G.D. and Hill, C.A. (1998) 'A review and classification of empirical research in operations management', *Journal of Operations Management*, 16 (1): 91–101.

Shah, R. and Goldstein, S.M. (2006) 'Use of structural equation modeling in operations management research: looking back and forward', *Journal of Operations Management*, 24: 148–169.

Tsikriktsis, N. (2005) 'A review of techniques for treating missing data in OM survey research', *Journal of Operations Management*, 24: 53–62.

Van Donselaar, K. and Sharman, G. (1997) 'An innovative survey in the transportation and distribution sector', *International Journal of Operations and Production Management*, 17 (7): 707–720.

Verma, R. and Goodale, J.C. (1995) 'Statistical power in operations management research', *Journal of Operations Management*, 13 (2): 139–152.

Vokurka, R.J. and O'Leary-Kelly, S.W. (2000) 'A review of empirical research on manufacturing flexibility', *Journal of Operations Management*, 18 (4): 485–501.

Wacker, J.G. (1998) 'A definition of theory: research guidelines for different theory-building research methods in operations management', *Journal of Operations Management*, 16 (4): 361–385.

Wacker, J.G. (2004) 'A theory of formal conceptual definitions: developing theory-building measurement instruments', *Journal of Operations Management*, 22: 629–650.

Whybark, D.C. (1997) 'GMRG survey research in operations management', *International Journal of Operations and Production Management*, 17 (7): 686–696.

Examples of OM Articles Based on Survey Research

Ahire, S.L. and Dreyfus, P. (2000) 'The impact of design management and process management on quality: an empirical investigation', *Journal of Operations Management*, 18 (5): 549–575.

Ahire, S.L., Goldhar, D.Y. and Waller, M.A. (1996) 'Development and validation of TQM implementation constructs', *Decision Sciences*, 27 (1): 23–56.

Anderson, J.C., Rungtusanatham, M. and Schroeder, R.G. (1994) 'A theory of quality management underlying the Deming management method', *Academy of Management Review*, 19 (3): 472–509.

Anderson, J.C., Rungtusanatham, M., Schroeder, R.G. and Devaraj, S. (1995) 'A path analytic model of a theory of quality management underlying the Deming Management method', *Decision Sciences*, 26 (5): 637–658.

Boyer, K.K., Olson, J.R., Calantono, R.J. and Jackson, E.C. (2002) 'Print versus electronic surveys: a comparison of two data collection methodologies', *Journal of Operations Management*, 20 (4): 357–373.

Birnbaum, P.H., Farh, J-L and Wong, G.Y.Y. (1986) 'The job characteristics model in Hong Kong', *Journal of Applied Psychology*, 71 (4): 598–605.

Corbett, L.M. and Whybark, D.C. (2001) 'Searching for the sandcone in the GMRG data', *International Journal of Operations and Production Management*, 21 (7): 965–980.

Flynn, B.B., Schroeder, R.G. and Sakakibara, S. (1994) 'A framework for quality management research and an associated measurement instrument', *Journal of Operations Management*, 11 (4): 339–366.

Flynn, B.B., Schroeder, R.G. and Flynn, E.J. (1999) 'World class manufacturing: an investigation of Hayes and Wheelwright's foundation', *Journal of Operations Management*, 17: 249–269.

Flynn, B.B., Schroeder, R.G., Flynn, E.J., Sakakibara, S. and Bates, K.A. (1997) 'World-class manufacturing project: overview and selected results', *International Journal of Operations and Production Management*, 17 (7): 671–685.

Forza, C. (1995) 'Quality information systems and quality management: A reference model and associated measures for empirical research', *Industrial Management and Data Systems*, 95 (2): 6–14.

Forza, C. and Filippini, R. (1998) 'TQM impact on quality conformance and customer satisfaction', *International Journal of Production Economics*, 55 (1): 1–20.

Handfield, R.B. and Melnyk, S.A. (1998) 'The scientific theory-building process: A primer using the case of TQM', *Journal of Operations Management*, 16 (4): 321–339.

Husseini, M.S.M. and O'Brien, C. (2004) 'Strategic implications of manufacturing performance comparisons for newly industrialising countries', *International Journal of Operations and Production Management*, 24 (11): 1126–1148.

Klassen, R.D. and Jacobs, J. (2001) 'Experimental comparison of web, electronic and mail survey technologies in operations management', *Journal of Operations Management*, 19 (6): 713–728.

Koste, L.L. and Malhotra, M.K. (1999) 'A theoretical framework for analyzing the dimensions of manufacturing flexibility', *Journal of Operations Management*, 18: 75–93.

Koste, L.L., Malhotra, M.K. and Sharma, S. (2004) 'Measuring dimensions of manufacturing flexibility', *Journal of Operations Management*, 22: 171–196.

Koufteros, X.A. (1999) 'Testing a model of pull production: a paradigm for manufacturing research using structural equation modelling', *Journal of Operations Management*, 17 (4): 467–488.

Lambert, D.M. and Harrington, T.C. (1990) 'Measuring nonresponse bias in customer service mail surveys', *Journal of Business Logistics*, 11 (2): 5–25.

Lawshe, C.H. (1975) 'A quantitative approach to content validity', *Personnel Psychology*, 28 (4): 563–575.

Menor, L.J. and Roth, A.V. (2007) 'New service development competence in retail banking: construct development and measurement validation', *Journal of Operations Management*, 25: 825–846.

Narasimhan, R. and Kim, S.W. (2002) 'Effect of supply chain integration on the relationship between diversification and performance: evidence from Japanese and Korean firms', *Journal of Operations Management*, 20: 303–323.

Parasuraman, A., Zeithaml, V.A. and Berry, L.L. (1988) 'SERVQUAL: a multiple-item scale for measuring consumer perceptions of service quality', *Journal of Retailing*, 64 (1): 12–40.

Rungtusanatham, M. (2001) 'Beyond improved quality: the motivational effects of statistical process control', *Journal of Operations Management*, 19 (4): 653–673.

Rungtusanatham, M., Anderson, J.C. and Dooley, K.J. (1999) 'Towards measuring the SPC implementation/practice construct: some evidence of measurement quality', *International Journal of Quality and Reliability Management*, 16 (4): 301–329.

Rungtusanatham, M., Forza, C., Balaji, K., Salvador, F. and Nie, W. (2005) 'TQM across Multiple Countries: Convergence Hypothesis versus National Specificity Arguments', *Journal of Operations Management*, 23 (1): 43–63.

Salvador, F. and Forza, C. (2004) 'Configuring products to address the customization-responsiveness squeeze. A survey of management issues and opportunities', *International Journal of Production Economics*, 91 (3): 273–291.

Ward, P.T., Leong, G.K. and Boyer, K.K. (1994) 'Manufacturing proactiveness and performance', *Decision Sciences*, 25 (3): 337–358.

Research Methods in Business and Social Sciences

Anderson, J.C. and Gerbing, D.W. (1982) 'Some methods for respecifying measurement models to obtain unidimensional construct measurement', *Journal of Marketing Research*, 19: 453–460.

Bagozzi, R.P. (1980) *Causal Models in Marketing*. New York: Wiley.

Bagozzi, R.P. and Phillips, L.W. (1982) 'Representing and testing organizational theories: a holistic construal', *Administrative Science Quarterly*, 27 (3): 459–489.

Bagozzi, R.P., Yi, Y. and Phillips, L.W. (1991) 'Assessing construct validity in organizational research', *Administrative Science Quarterly*, 36 (4): 421–434.

Baroudi, J.J. and Orlikowski, W.J. (1989) 'The problem of statistical power in MIS research', *MIS Quarterly*, 13 (1): 87–106.

Carmines, E.G. and Zeller, R.A. (1990) *Reliability and Validity Assessment*, New York: Sage.

Cohen, J. (1960) 'A coefficient of agreement for nominal scales', *Educational and Psychological Measurement*, 20 (1): 37–46.

Cronbach, L.J. (1951) 'Coefficient Alpha and the internal structure of tests', *Psychometrika*, 16 (4): 297–334.

Dansereau, F. and Markham, S.E. (1997) 'Level of analysis in personnel and human resources management', in K. Rowland and G. Ferris (eds) *Research in Personnel and Human Resources Management*, vol. 5, Greenwich: JAI Press.

Davis, D. (2005) *Business Research for Decision Making*, 6th edn, Belmont, CA: Brooks/Cole Thomson Learning.

Dubin, R. (1978) *Theory Building*, New York: The Free Press.

Emory, C.W. and Cooper, D.R. (1991) *Business Research Methods*, Homewood, IL: Irwin.

Hardesty, D.M. and Bearden, W.O. (2004) 'The use of expert judges in scale development. Implications for improving face validity of measures of unobservable constructs', *Journal of Business Research*, 57: 98–107.

Hinkin, T.R. (1995) 'A review of scale development practices in the study of organisations', *Journal of Management*, 21 (5): 967–988.

Kerlinger, F.N. (1986) *Foundations of Behavioral Research*, 3rd edn, New York: Harcourt Brace Jovanovich College Publishers.

Lazarsfeld, P.F. (1935) 'The art of asking why', *National Marketing Research*, 1: 26–38.

Messick, S. (1995) 'Validity of psychological assessment', *American Psychologist*, 50 (9): 741–749.

Miller, D.C. (1991) *Handbook of Research Design and Social Measurement*, London: Sage.

Nunnally, J.C. (1978) *Psychometric Theory*, 2nd edn, New York: McGraw-Hill.

Nunnally, J.C. and Bernstein, I.C.H. (1994) *Psychometric Theory*, New York: McGraw-Hill.

Payne, S.L. (1951) *The Art of Asking Questions*, Princeton, NJ: Princeton University Press.

Phillips, L.W. and Bagozzi, R.P. (1986) 'On measuring organizational properties of distribution channels: methodological issues in the use of key informants', *Research in Marketing*, 8: 313–369.

Robinson, W.S. (1950) 'Ecological correlations and the behaviours of individuals', *American Sociological Review*, 15 (June): 351–350.

Roth, P.L., Switzer, F.S. and Switzer, D.M. (1999), 'Missing data in multiple item scales: a Monte Carlo analysis of missing data techniques', *Organizational Research Methods*, 2 (3): 211–232.

Sekaran, U. (1992) *Research Methods for Business*, New York: John Wiley & Sons.

Simon, H. (1980) 'The behavioral and social sciences', *Science*, 209: 72–78.

Sireci, S.G. (1998) 'The construct of content validity', *Social Indicators Research*, 45: 83–117.

Straub, D.W. (1989) 'Validating instruments in MIS research', *MIS Quarterly*, 13 (2): 147–169.

Survey in Business and Social Sciences

Alreck, P.L. and Settle, R.B. (1985) *The Survey Research Handbook*, Homewood, IL: Irwin.

Anderson, A.B., Basilevsky, A. and Hum, D.P.J. (1983) 'Missing data' in Rossi, P.H., Wright, J.D. and Anderson, A.B., *Handbook of Survey Research*, 415–494, New York: Academic Press.

Babbie, E. (1990) *Survey Research Methods*, Belmont, CA: Wadsworth.

Biemer, P.P., Groves, R.M., Lyber, L.E., Mathiowetz, N.A. and Sudman, S. (1991) *Measurement Errors in Surveys*, New York: Wiley.

Birnbaum, M.H. (1999) 'Testing critical properties of decision making on the Internet', *American Psychological Society*, 10 (5): 399–407.

Converse, J.M. and Presser, S. (1986) *Survey Questions. Handcrafting the Standardized Questionnaire*, New York: Sage.

Dillman, D.A. (1978) *Mail and Telephone Surveys: The Design Method*, New York: John Wiley & Sons.

Dillman, D.A. (2007) *Mail and Internet Surveys: The Tailored Design Method*, 2nd edn, Hoboken, NJ: John Wiley & Sons.

Fowler, Jr F.J. (1993) *Survey Research Methods*, New York: Sage.

Greer, T.V., Chuchinprakarn, N. and Seshadri, S. (2000) 'Likelihood of participating in mail survey research—business respondents' perspectives', *Industrial Marketing Management*, 29 (2): 97–109.

Karweit, N. and Meyers, Jr E.D. (1983) 'Computers in survey research' in Rossi, P.H., Wright, J.D. and Anderson, A.B., *Handbook of Survey Research*, 379–414, New York: Academic Press.

Oppenheim, A.N. (1992) *Questionnaire Design, Interviewing and Attitude Measurement*, New York: Pinter.

Peter, J.P. (1979) 'Reliability: A review of psychometric basics and recent marketing practices', *Journal of Marketing Research*, 16 (1): 6–17.

Peter, J.P. (1981) 'Construct validity: a review of basic issues and marketing practices', *Journal of Marketing Research*, 18 (2): 133–145.

Pinsonneault, A. and Kraemer, K.L. (1993) 'Survey research methodology in management information systems: an assessment', *Journal of Management Information Systems*, 10 (2): 75–106.

Rea, L.M. and Parker, R.A. (1992) *Designing and Conducting Survey Research*, San Francisco, CA: Jossey-Bass.

Rossi, P.H., Wright, J.D. and Anderson, A.B. (1983) *Handbook of Survey Research*, New York: Academic Press.

Roth, P.L. (1994) 'Missing data: a conceptual review for applied psychologists', *Personnel Psychology*, 47 (3): 537–560.

Roth, P.L. and BeVier, C.A. (1998) 'Response rates in HRM/OB survey research: norms and correlates, 1990–1994', *Journal of Management*, 24 (1): 97–118.

Sudman, S. (1983) 'Applied sampling' in Rossi, P.H., Wright, J.D. and Anderson, A.B., *Handbook of Survey Research*, 144–194, New York: Academic Press.

Swab, B. and Sitter, R. (1974) 'Economic aspects of computer input-output equipment' in House W.C. (ed), *Data Base Management*, New York: Petrocelli Books.

Wilson, E.J. (1999) 'Research practice in business marketing—a comment on response rate and response bias', *Industrial Marketing Management*, 28 (3): 257–260.

Statistical Methods

Andrews, F.M., Klem, L., Davidson, T.N., O'Malley, P.M. and Rodgers, W.L. (1976) *A Guide for Selecting Statistical Techniques for Analysing Social Science Data*, Ann Arbor, MI: Institute for Social Research.

Hair, Jr J.F., Anderson, R.E., Tatham, R.L. and Black, W.C. (1992) *Multivariate Data Analysis*, New York: Maxwell MacMillan.

Hollander, M. and Wolfe, D.A. (1999) *Nonparametric Statistical Methods*, 2nd edn, New York: Wiley.

McClave, J.T. and Benson, P.G. (1991) *Statistics for Business and Economics*, New York: Macmillan.

Sharma, S. (1996) *Applied Multivariate Techniques*, New York: Wiley.

5 Case Research in Operations Management[1]

Chris Voss

Chapter Overview

- When to use case research
- Developing the research framework, constructs and questions
- Choosing cases:

    - How many cases?
    - Longitudinal or retrospective
    - Case selection
    - Sample controls

- Developing research instruments and protocols
- Conducting the field research:

    - Field data collection
    - Conducting interviews
    - Reliability and validity

- Data documentation and coding
- Data analysis, hypothesis development and testing:

    - Within-case analysis
    - Searching for cross-case patterns
    - Hypothesis testing and development

5.1 Introduction

Case research has consistently been one of the most powerful research methods in OM, particularly in the development of new theory. To cope with the growing frequency and magnitude of changes in technology and managerial methods, OM researchers have been calling for greater employment of field-based research methods (Lewis, 1998). Pure case research, that is research based on analysis of a limited number of cases to which, at best, only limited statistical analysis can be applied, is widely used in Europe but is less common in North American OM (Drejer et al., 1998). However, there is an increasing number of case research based papers appearing; Barratt et al. (2007) list over 180 papers published in four top US OM journals that use case research.

There are several challenges in conducting case research: it is time consuming, it needs skilled interviewers, and care is needed in drawing generalizable conclusions from a limited set of cases and in ensuring rigorous research. Despite this, the results of case research can have very high impact. Unconstrained by the rigid limits of questionnaires and models, it can lead to new and creative insights, development of new theory and have high validity with practitioners—the ultimate users of research. Through triangulation with multiple means of data collection, the validity can be increased further. Many of the breakthrough concepts and theories in OM, from lean production to manufacturing strategy, have been developed through case research. Finally, case research enriches not only theory, but also the researchers themselves. Through conducting research in the field and being exposed to real problems, the creative insights of people at all levels of organizations, and the varied contexts of cases, the individual researcher will personally benefit from the process of conducting the research. Increasingly new ideas are being developed, not by distant academics, but by those working in close contact with multiple case studies—management consultants! It is important that case research is conducted and published because it is not only good at investigating how and why questions, but also it is particularly suitable for developing new theory and ideas and can also be used for theory testing and refinement. It is also important that case research is conducted well, so that the results are both rigorous and relevant. Case research is not an excuse for 'industrial tourism'—visiting lots of organizations without any preconceived ideas as to what is being researched.

OM differs from most other areas of management research, in that it addresses both the physical and human elements of the organization, e.g. Hayes and Wheelwright's (1984) structural and infrastructural elements of manufacturing strategy. In addition to the 'hard' elements of the area, many OM researchers focus on the human elements of the productive system and the arrangements of the physical elements to support this. There is a particular tradition of this kind of research in Scandinavia, where case research is widely used in such research (see Chapter 2, section 2.1.4). Case research is widely used in other management disciplines, notably organizational behaviour and strategy. Yin (1994) has described in detail case research design, and Glaser and Strauss (1967) described the grounded theory method. Case research has its roots in the broader field of social sciences, in particular ethnographic studies and anthropology. In this chapter, we will draw on the experience of these disciplines as well as that of researchers in operations and technology management. In particular, we will draw on the work of Eisenhardt (1989) and Eisenhardt and Graebner (2007), who brought together much of the previous work on building theory from case research. Our intention is to provide a roadmap for designing, developing and conducting case-based research and also to describe some recent examples of case-based research in the field of operations and technology management.

Most of the research conducted in the field of OM is based on rationalist[2] research methods, primarily statistical survey analysis and mathematical modelling. However, since '. . . the explanation of quantitative findings and the construction of theory based on those findings will ultimately have to be based on qualitative understanding' (Meredith, 1998), case research is very important for our field. The key steps in conducting case research are shown in the text box on the first page, and are explored in the rest of this chapter.

5.2 When to Use Case Research

> A case study is a history of a past or current phenomenon, drawn from multiple sources of evidence. It can include data from direct observation and systematic interviewing as well as from public and private archives. In fact, any fact relevant to the stream of events describing the phenomenon is a potential datum in a case study, since context is important.
>
> (Leonard-Barton, 1990)

A case study is a unit of analysis in case research. It is possible to use different cases from the same firm to study different issues, or to research the same issue in a variety of contexts in the same firm. Case research is the method that uses cases studies as its basis. Meredith (1998) cites three outstanding strengths of case research put forward by Bebensat et al. (1987):

- The phenomenon can be studied in its natural setting and meaningful, relevant theory can be generated from the understanding gained through observing actual practice
- The case method allows the questions of *why, what* and *how*, to be answered with a relatively full understanding of the nature and complexity of the complete phenomenon
- The case method lends itself to early, exploratory investigations where the variables are still unknown and the phenomenon not at all understood

Case studies can be used for different types of research purposes such as exploration, theory building, theory testing and theory extension/refinement. The link between purpose, research questions and research method is outlined in Table 5.1 (see also Chapter 3, sections 3.6–3.7).

- *Exploration*: in the early stages of many research programmes, exploration is needed to develop research ideas and questions. Many doctoral theses begin with one or more case studies in order to generate a list of research questions that are worth pursuing further (e.g. Frohlich, 1998)

- *Theory building*: a particular area where cases are strong is theory building. 'Nothing is so practical as a good theory' (Van De Ven, 1989). Theory can be considered as being made up of four components: definitions of terms or variables, a domain (the exact setting in which the theory can be applied), a set of relationships and specific predictions (Wacker, 1998). A theory may be viewed as a system of constructs and variables in which constructs are related to each other by propositions and the variables are related to each other by hypotheses (Bacharach, 1989). Without theory, 1) it is impossible to make meaningful sense of empirically generated data, 2) it is not possible to distinguish positive from negative results, and 3) empirical research merely becomes 'data-dredging' (Handfield and Melnyk, 1998). If we are to ground theory on data, then a large and rich amount of primary data is needed, case studies are a prime source of this (McCutcheon and Meredith, 1993). Cases are particularly useful when there is uncertainty in the definition of constructs (Mukherjee et al., 2000)
- *Theory testing*: despite its limited use for theory testing, case study research has been used in the OM field in order to test complicated issues such as strategy implementation (e.g. McLachlin, 1997; Boyer and McDermott, 1999; Pagell and Krause, 1999). When case study research is used for theory testing, it is typically used in conjunction with survey-based research in order to achieve triangulation. This is the use and combination of different methods to study the same phenomenon, so as to avoid sharing the same weaknesses (Campbell and Fiske, 1959; Cook and Campbell, 1979; Jick, 1979)
- *Theory extension/refinement*: case studies can also be used as a follow-up to survey-based research in an attempt to examine more deeply and validate previous empirical results. For example, Meredith and Vineyard (1993) and Hyer et. al. (1999a) conducted case studies, which resulted in extending the fields of advanced manufacturing technology (AMT) and cell system design, respectively

Overall, OM is a very dynamic field in which new practices are continually emerging. Case research provides an excellent means of studying emergent practices, an example being a study of product, customer involvement and quality information, by Finch (1999). Case research both builds on theory and is an excellent means for development of theory in OM (McCutcheon and Meredith, 1993). Table 5.2 summarizes some recent articles in the field of OM using case studies. These illustrate the different uses of case research. A more complete listing of recent articles can be found in Barratt et al. (2007).

Table 5.1 Matching Research Purpose with Methodology (a modification of original work by Handfield and Melnyk, 1998)

Purpose	Research question	Research structure
Exploration		
Uncover areas for research and theory development	Is there something interesting enough to justify research?	In-depth case studies Unfocused, longitudinal field study
Theory building		
Identify/describe key variables Identify linkages between variables Identify 'why' these relationships exist	What are the key variables? What are the patterns or linkages between variables? Why should these relationships exist?	Few focused case studies In-depth field studies Multi-site case studies Best-in-class case studies
Theory testing		
Test the theories developed in the previous stages Predict future outcomes	Are the theories we have generated able to survive the test of empirical data? Did we get the behaviour that was predicted by the theory or did we observe another unanticipated behaviour?	Experiment Quasi-experiment Multiple case studies Large scale sample of population
Theory extension/ refinement		
To better structure the theories in light of the observed results	How generalizable is the theory? Where does the theory apply?	Experiment Quasi-experiment Case studies Large-scale sample of population

5.3 The Research Framework, Constructs and Questions

> No matter how small our sample, or what our interest, we have always tried to go into organisations with a well defined focus.
>
> (Henry Mintzberg, 1979)

The starting point for case research is the research framework and questions. Case study research has been recognized as being particularly good for examining the *how* and *why* questions (Yin, 1994). Such questions can lead both to theory testing, but more importantly to theory development. In theory-building research, no matter how inductive the approach, we need to have a prior view of the general constructs or categories we intend to study, and their relationships. Miles and Huberman (1994) suggest doing this

Table 5.2 Examples of Case-Based Research in Operations Management

Study	Research questions	No. of cases	Other methods	Purpose
Åhlström et al. (1998)	Why is diagnostic benchmarking used? How is diagnostic benchmarking used or not used by companies to improve manufacturing performance?	15	Longitudinal study, survey	Theory extension
Akkermans and Vos (2003)	What are the root causes and associated countermeasures of the amplification phenomenon in service supply chains?	1		Theory development
Boyer and McDermott (1999)	Is there strategic consensus in operations strategy across different organizational levels?	7	Survey	Theory testing
Choi and Hong (2002)	What does a supply chain look like and how does it behave?	8	Mapping supply chain network	Theory building
Hyer et al. (1999b)	What are the significant elements in a comprehensive cell design process and how are they related? How will the application of socio-technical systems (STS) principles influence and enhance a cell system design? Of the elements in the comprehensive cell system design, which ones appear to be the most significant determinants of sustainable success?	1		Theory refinement
Lamming et al. (2000)	How are different types of supply networks created and operated?	16	Survey	Theory building
McLachlin (1997)	Which management initiatives are necessary for just-in-time (JIT) implementation?	6	Survey, interviews, direct observation	Theory testing
Meredith and Vineyard (1993)	How can we better understand the role of manufacturing technology in the firm's business strategy?	3		Theory refinement *(Continued Overleaf)*

Table 5.2 (Continued)

Study	Research questions	No. of cases	Other methods	Purpose
Narasimhan and Jayaram (1998)	What are the unique aspects of Service Operations that lead to differences in the way a reengineering project should be carried out in a service context?	1		Theory building
Pagell and Krause (1999)	Is there a relationship between the firm's external environment and its internal level of operational flexibility? Do firms that align their level of operational flexibility with the level of uncertainty in the external environment exhibit superior performance compared to firms that do not have alignment?	30	Survey	Theory testing
Pil and Rothenberg (2003)	How do efforts to enhance environmental performance enable other types of manufacturing improvements?	17	Survey of 42 plants	Theory testing
Sousa and Voss (2001)	Are quality management practices contingent on a plant's manufacturing strategy?	5		Theory development
Voordijk et al. (2006)	What is the applicability of Fines' three-dimensional modularity concept as a tool to describe and analyse the alignment of product, process and supply chain architectures?	3		Theory testing
Zomerdijk and de Vries (2007)	How does distinction between contact and non-contact activities influences the design of service delivery systems?	5	3 delivery systems per case	Theory refinement

through construction of a *conceptual framework* that underlies the research. Such a framework explains, either graphically or in narrative form, the main things that are to be studied—the key factors, constructs or variables—and the presumed relationships amongst them. Building a conceptual framework will force the researcher to think carefully and selectively about the constructs and variables to be included in the study.

The next vital step in designing case research is the initial research question behind the proposed study. This may precede, or follow directly from, the conceptual framework. Even if at this stage the question(s) are tentative, it is important to have as well-defined a focus as possible at the start, to guide the collection of data. There is a range of question types, many of which postulate some form of causal relationship (Miles and Huberman, 1994) (Table 5.3).

For example, Tyre and Orlikowski (1994) in a study of process technology adaptation defined two research questions: What is the pattern of technology adaptations in organizations? and What organizational forces help explain the patterns of adaptation over time? In theory-testing research we can see also the following sorts of propositions:

Concept A is a sufficient condition for concept B
Concept A is a necessary condition for concept B
There is a deterministic relationship between concept A and concept B
                                                    (Dul and Hak, 2008)

A further set of examples of research questions in studies using cased-based research is shown in Table 5.2. In case research, the amount of data that can potentially be collected is vast; therefore the stronger the research focus, the easier it is both to identify potential cases and to design research protocols.

Underlying the research question is likely to be one or more constructs, for example technology adaptation in the example given above. Eisenhardt (1989) argues that a priori specification of constructs is valuable because 'it permits researchers to measure constructs more accurately. If these constructs

Table 5.3 Question Types (Smith, 1987)

Question type	Example of general form
Causal	Does X cause Y?
Non-causal	What is X?
Non-causal—policy	What does 'Y' mean?
Non-causal—evaluation	What makes W good?
Non-causal—management	Is X more cost effective than Z?

prove important, then researchers have a firmer empirical grounding for the emergent theory.'

When conducting case-based research it is not uncommon for the research question to evolve over time and for the constructs to be modified, developed or abandoned during the course of the research. This can be a strength, as it can allow the development of more knowledge than if there were just a fixed research question. Again, over time the research may shift from theory building to theory testing. This should be recognized on the one hand, but not used as an excuse for inadequate specification of research questions or constructs. Case research otherwise risks degenerating into a 'fishing expedition', where the observer is hoping to catch valuable insights that in turn will lead to research questions.

5.4 Choosing Cases

There is a wide set of choices in conducting case research. These include how many cases are to be used, case selection and sampling.

5.4.1 What is the Ideal Number of Cases?

For a given set of available resources, the fewer the case studies, the greater the opportunity for depth of observation. Single in-depth case studies are often used in longitudinal research (see also Chapter 6). Examples include Narasimhan and Jayaram (1998) who used a longitudinal study of a single case to examine reengineering in service operations, and Karlsson and Åhlström (1995) who studied implementation of JIT in a single company over a period of time. Another example of a single case study is Schonberger (1982), whose highly influential book on Japanese manufacturing practices was based on in-depth study of a single Japanese run factory in the US. There is no clear definition of what is a single case study or unit of analysis. Single cases may sometimes involve the opportunity to study several contexts within the case (Mukherjee et al., 2000). A study of a single firm may involve a number of different cases. For example many operations are organized on a multi-site basis and studying a set of these can help control the variables studied (see section 5.4.3.1, Sample Controls). As a result the number of cases studied can be different from the number of firms.

Single cases have limitations. The first is the limits to the generalizability of the conclusions, models or theory developed from one case study. When only one case is used, there may also be other potential problems (Leonard-Barton, 1990). These include the risks of misjudging of a single event, and of exaggerating easily available data. These risks exist in all case research, but are somewhat mitigated when events and data are compared across cases. Multiple cases may reduce the depth of study when resource is constrained, but can both augment external validity, and help guard against observer bias. The multi-case studies in Table 5.2 involve 3 to 30 cases.

5.4.2 Longitudinal or Retrospective Cases?

A second choice in case selection is whether to use retrospective or current cases. In many cases this may be an artificial distinction. For example when researching current case studies, it is usually necessary to collect some archival and/or historical data. Retrospective cases allow for more controlled case selection, for example it is possible to identify cases that reflect either success or failure only in retrospect.

Longitudinal case research can be particularly valuable. One of the most difficult, but most important things we try to identify in research is the relation between cause and effect. The longer the period over which phenomena are studied, the greater the opportunity to observe at first hand the sequential relationships of events. However, as Leonard-Barton (1990) points out there are problems with historical data. For example, participants may not recall important events and even if they do, their recollection may be subject to bias. A particular problem is post-rationalization, the interpretation of events in a different manner than they would have at the time. For example the respondent may place interpretations on events, or justify decisions with arguments or knowledge that was not available at the time. Similarly, what is described in archive data, such as minutes of meetings, may not reflect the whole truth, difficult or controversial items may not be recorded. Karlsson and Åhlström (1995, 1997) point out that the researcher who wishes to conduct a longitudinal field study of a process faces the problem of access. They see the clinical perspective as one means of overcoming the access problem. This method is characterized by active participation in formulating and observing organizational change (see Chapter 6, section 6.3). As a result, researchers are able to gain access to rich data denied to other approaches. The main difference from consulting is that the clinical researcher is interested in the results of the interventions and in drawing generalizable conclusions from these results. The consultant is more interested in giving recommendations and implementing them. The factors governing these choices are summarized in Table 5.4.

5.4.3 Case Selection and Sampling

If multiple case studies are to be used for research, then a vital question is the case selection or sampling. Miles and Huberman (1994) state that sampling involves two actions. The first is setting boundaries that define what you can study and connect directly to the research questions. The second step is creating a sample frame to help uncover, confirm, or qualify the basic processes or constructs that underpin the study.

The traditional way of sampling is to identify a population, and then to select a random or stratified sample from that population (see Chapter 4). However, in case research we often build a sample of cases by selecting cases according to different criteria (Eisenhardt, 1989; Yin 1994). When building

Table 5.4 Choice of Number and Type of Cases

Choice	Advantages	Disadvantages
Single cases	Greater depth	Limits on the generalizability of conclusions drawn. Biases such as misjudging the representativeness of a single event and exaggerating easily available data
Multiple cases	Augment external validity, help guard against observer bias	More resource needed, less depth per case
Retrospective cases	Allow collection of data on historical events	May be difficult to determine cause and effect, participants may not recall important events
Longitudinal cases	Overcome the problems of retrospective cases	Have long elapsed time and thus may be difficult to do

theory from case studies, case selection using replication logic rather than sampling logic should be used. Each case should be selected so that it either:

- Predicts similar results (a literal replication); or
- Produces contrary results but for predictable reasons (a theoretical replication)

Miles and Huberman (1994) suggest three kinds of instances that have great payoff in case research. First, if you can find a typical or representative case—can you find another one? Second the negative or disconfirming instance and finally, the exceptional or discrepant instance. Another selection criterion is to identify polar types, cases with sharply contrasting characteristics that will highlight the differences being studied. For example, a sample might be constructed of organizations that have high and low performance on certain dimensions, while controlling for performance on others.

An example of theoretical sampling is that of Åhlström et al. (1998), who examined the impact of benchmarking interventions on process improvement. They wished to study the impact of starting point on the outcome of benchmarking. The underlying proposition being that the nature of the process would vary from those firms with high levels of 'best' practice to those with low levels and from those who had high levels of operational performance and low operational performance. From a potential sample set of over 1,000 cases on which they had data, they pre-selected a convenience sample of cases where access was likely to be easy. Within this sample they then selected cases based on different starting points at the time of benchmarking. On a matrix of high existing practice and high existing operational performance, they chose cases from each quadrant of the matrix, and a fifth set from companies in the middle. This design facilitated examination of how company context impacts on the effective use of benchmarking. Not all researchers use theoretical or literal sampling in case research. An example in OM research is Pagell and Krause (1999), who studied manufacturing flexibility. They used a convenience sample of 30 case studies.

Sampling plans are likely to evolve over a research project. Miles and Huberman (1994) suggest a number of tests to apply to a sampling plan:

- Is it relevant to the conceptual frame and research questions?
- Will the phenomena to be studied appear? Can they appear?
- Is it one that enhances generalizability?
- Is it feasible?
- Is it ethical in terms of informed consent, potential benefits and risks and relationships with informants?

5.4.3.1 Sample Controls

When selecting cases it is also important to consider what are the parameters or factors that define the population and are to be held constant across the sample. Controls rely on the *selection* of the phenomena during the study's experimental design stage for their control. This allows particular factors (e.g. managerial policies, inventory systems) to be, in essence, 'held constant' while others (e.g. costs, defect rates) are left free to vary as they would naturally (Meredith, 1998). For example, Sousa (2000) controlled for quality maturity, Voss (1984), in developing a sample of a single application software area, applied tests of independence to ensure that the software had been developed without input from one of the other organizations. Leonard-Barton (1990), in a study of technology transfer, used three dimensions to control for irrelevant sources of variance originating *within* the firm. First, the technologies selected had all passed some baseline tests of technical feasibility. This provision eliminated from the study any cases in which the failure to transfer to users occurred simply because the technology was technically infeasible. Second, all the technologies selected altered the work environment in some obvious way. Third, the transfer stages included in the study were consistently defined across projects. One powerful way of thinking of multi-case research, particularly in the context of theory testing, is the distinction between comparative case studies and parallel single case studies where the same proposition is tested independently (replicated) in each of the cases. In theory testing we are testing some form of proposition concerning the relationship between concept A and concept B. To be able to test this we must select a sample in which either the dependent or independent concept/variable is held constant across cases (Dul and Hak, 2008).

It is important to apply tests to validate the controls and to ensure that each case meets the sample criteria. The researcher should have the courage to discard cases that do not fit their research design and sample structure.

5.5 Developing Research Instruments and Protocols

Typically the prime source of data in case research is structured interviews, often backed up by unstructured interviews and interactions. Other sources of data can include personal observation, informal conversations, attendance at meetings and events, surveys administered within the organization, collection of objective data and review of archival sources. The reliability[3] and validity of case research data will be enhanced by a well-designed research protocol (Yin, 1994). A protocol contains, but is more than, the research instrument(s). It will also contain the procedures and the general rules that should be used in using the instrument(s), and indicate from whom or from where different sets of information are to be sought. The core of the protocol is the set of questions to be used in interviews. It outlines the subjects to be covered during an interview, states the questions to be asked and indicates the specific data required. A commonly used format is the funnel model. This starts with broad and open-ended questions first, and as the interview progresses the questions become more specific and the detailed questions come last. The protocol serves both as a prompt for the interview and as a checklist to make sure that all topics have been covered. In addition, it is often useful to send an outline of the protocol in advance, so that the interviewee(s) are properly prepared. A well-designed protocol is particularly important in multi-case research. When developing the research protocol and instruments it is important to address triangulation (McCutcheon and Meredith, 1993). Case research data is not just collected by interview. Frequently questionnaires are also used in collecting data within and across cases (for questionnaire design see Chapter 4).

Case research in OM differs from case research in the wider social science field in that researchers are interested in analysing the manufacturing and service processes and systems of the plant (Hill et al., 1999). Thus research design in OM should pay attention to what processes and systems are to be studied, the methods for studying them and the operating data to be collected from them.

As with questionnaires, case research protocols need piloting either in a pilot case or in initial interviews within an organization.

5.5.1 Single or Multiple Respondents and Viewpoints

In designing case research a key question is what should be the number of respondents? If a set of questions can be reliably answered by one 'key informant', then the research process should focus on identifying these and validating that this person(s) is indeed one. However, when there are questions for which no one person has all the required knowledge, or the events being studied may have different interpretations or viewpoints, how and why questions may be subject to different interpretations. In such cases the researcher may consider interviewing multiple respondents, or using a follow-up survey with multiple respondents. In addition, it is also important to recognize that informants are prone to subjectivity and biases. Where this is an issue, the research design should not rely on self-report as the only evidence.

In research design, we must consider the trade-off between efficiency and richness of data. On the one hand, by asking the same question to a number of people, we may enhance the reliability of our data, and by going beyond formal interviews we can collect much valuable data. On the other hand, it can be very time consuming. Leonard-Barton (1990), in reporting on a multiple set of case-based research studies, found that in a longitudinal in-depth study, she was able to observe many critical events and follow a research thread over a 3-year period. She also points out that in this sort of research, a large sample size per se may not be as important as in survey research. She gives as an example a pilot study of 25 people followed up with 145 personal interviews. These interviews added bulk, not depth to the research database. In summary, the researcher should be seeking multiple viewpoints particularly where there is likely to be subjectivity and bias, but be wary of committing too much time and resource.

5.6 Conducting the Field Research

5.6.1 Who to Contact

In researching case-based data, it is important to seek out the person(s) who are best informed about the data being researched. This person is often known as the principle informant. However, in gaining access to an organization, this person may not be known and/or may not be the most appropriate prime contact. An ideal prime contact should be someone senior enough to be able to open doors where necessary, to know who best to interview to gather the data required and to provide senior support for the research being conducted. Gaining access is often a sequential process. The first step is writing to or calling a potential prime contact. As case research requires time and commitment from the organization, it is important that the value and relevance of the research, and the time and resource required is outlined at this stage. In many cases, going through an organization such as an industry or technical association can provide an accelerated way of doing this, as well as providing the opportunity to select a well-structured and controlled sample. Pointing out the mutual benefits to potential participants can be helpful. The organization may find it useful and interesting to have an issue analysed in a systematic way.

Having gained agreement, the next step is to set up the research meetings. For simple research, this can usually be done with a letter outlining the areas that are being investigated, the nature of the people that you would like to interview, and objective and/or archival data that you would like to collect. For more complex case research, set-up visits to the case organization will probably be necessary. The time required for case research at a site can vary from one or two carefully structured short visits, to a full ethnographic study—in-depth involvement with the organization over an extended period of time, often years.

5.6.2 *Field Data Collection*

An underlying principle in collection of data in case research is that of triangulation, the use and combination of different methods to study the same phenomenon. Such methods can include interviews, questionnaires, direct observations, content analysis of documents and archival research. Reliability of data will also be increased if multiple sources of data on the same phenomenon are used. Two examples in OM research illustrate this. Boyer and McDermott (1999) studied strategic consensus in operations strategy. They performed semi-structured interviews on-site in seven plants, with either the Plant Manager, Vice President of Operations or President of each firm. Issues relating to the historical development of the firm, its main competition, main markets, structural (e.g. AMT) and infrastructural (e.g. worker training) investments were explored in these discussions. Interviews typically ranged from 1–2 hours in duration. In addition, the survey questions were discussed and elaborated upon, and any questions relating to the content of the survey were answered. Discrepancies between survey responses and interview discussion were noted and clarified. To augment the on-site interviews and surveys, tours of the manufacturing facility were arranged. These tours allowed for a visual check and comparison of each firm's efforts in areas such as AMT adoption, layout, degree of worker empowerment and training, and level of technology relative to others in the industry. In general, these plant tours provided an opportunity for verification and clarification of survey and interview responses, as well as providing the researchers with a feel for the overall work environment and systems. A further example is a study by Hyer et al. (1999b) of cell design:

> 'Data sources for the study included participant observation, structured and unstructured interviews of key participants, formal debriefing sessions following major design activities, and reviews of a wide array of relevant operational data and other documentation (meeting minutes, status reports, internal white papers, hard copies of electronic messages, and so forth). Although most of the data were qualitative in nature, quantitative data on organisational performance also were collected. This use of multiple measures drawn from different data sources is, as McCutcheon and Meredith (1993) point out, one way of improving both the validity and reliability of case study findings.'

5.6.3 Conducting Interviews

Much, but not all field data will be collected through interviews. The effectiveness of case research will, in part, be dependent on the skills of the interviewer. Leonard-Barton (1990) compares the necessary interviewing skills with those of an investigative reporter. One needs to keep previous interviewee responses in mind while simultaneously probing with the current informant, and to be very aware of the significance of what is left unsaid as well as what is said, and so on. Yin (1994) lists a set of skills required by the field researcher:

- To be able to ask good questions and interpret the answers
- To be a good listener and not be trapped by preconceptions
- To be adaptable and flexible, to see newly encountered situations as opportunities not threats
- To have a firm grasp of the issues being studied
- To be unbiased by preconceived notions, and thus receptive and sensitive to contradictory evidence

There are many ways in which an interview can be conducted and evidence gathered. Interviews can be unstructured, focused with more structure or highly structured resembling a questionnaire. Alternatively evidence can also be gathered by direct observation of meetings, processes etc. This could be formal process analysis or casual observation. Another form of evidence collection is participant observation, also described as the clinical method (Schein, 1987). Interviews may be with a single interviewee or with a group. The latter allows debate, but may also be dominated by a, possibly senior, individual.

5.6.4 Single or Multiple Investigators

Interviews are usually conducted by a single investigator, but as Eisenhardt (1989) points out, the use of multiple investigators can have advantages. They can enhance the creative potential of the teams and convergence of observations increases confidence in the findings. If interviews are done by two people or a team, investigators may either take notes independently or one may take the lead interview role, while the other takes a lead data collection role. In studies involving a large number of sites where multiple singe interviewers are used, it is important that early interviews are done in pairs or teams. This increases the probability of a common approach being used in all sites and allows inter-rater reliability to be checked. Inter-rater reliability can be defined in terms of the degree to which raters agree or disagree on the rating or interpretation of the evidence presented to them:

$$\text{Reliability} = \frac{\text{number of agreements}}{\text{total number of agreements} + \text{disagreements}}$$

For an example of the use of inter-rater reliability in OM, see Ritzman and Safizadreh (1999). For a fuller discussion see Demaree and Wolf (1984).

5.6.5 Collecting Objective Data

The fact that case research is often associated with qualitative data should not deter the researcher from seeking out objective data. Indeed, case research provides the opportunity for researchers to collect such data with greater accuracy and reliability than in survey research, as they can have direct access to the original data sources on performance and operating data.

5.6.6 Administering Questionnaires

As discussed earlier, triangulation through the use of different methods of data collection can strengthen the validity of research. It is not uncommon for researchers to administer questionnaires within organizations being studied. This can increase the efficiency of data collection and/or allow for data to be collected from a wider sample of respondents. For example Leonard-Barton (1990), in the case-based research study mentioned earlier, conducted a telephone survey of 46 unit managers, and administered a series of questionnaires to about 100 sales representatives.

5.6.7 Recording the Data

The research protocol should provide a strong foundation for documentation of the evidence gathered in case research. There are divided views on whether tape recorders should be used in interviews. They certainly provide accurate rendition of what has been said. Where exactness of what people have said is important, then taping will be a benefit (Yin, 1984:85). If interviews are more focused on objective data, as is often the case in OM research, then the benefits of taping are reduced. On the negative side transcribing tapes is very time consuming, it often takes place some time after the interview, can be seen as a substitute for listening and may inhibit interviewees.

Whatever method is used to transcribe data, it is important there are good and accurate records and minutes of research interviews and meetings. In addition, that there is feedback and checking of the data. This is an important, if slow activity—'obtaining agreement that the story had been accurately (and completely) presented was the most time consuming part of the studies' (Leonard-Barton, 1990). Feedback and checking typically involves presenting the case description or written up record of the data to the organization for verification. Keeping additional field notes is an important part of field research. Field notes are a running commentary about what is happening in the research, involving both observation and analysis; preferably separate from one another (Eisenhardt, 1989). Even prior to formal data analysis, it is important that the field researcher is sensitive to the emergence of patterns observed in the field. In case research, there is an overlap between data collection and data analysis. However it is important that these two processes are kept separate so that there is clarity in the conduct and presentation of the data analysis. In addition to the formal collection of data, it is often useful to record ideas, impressions etc., as soon as they occur, and certainly before formal analysis takes place. Many researchers use field notes—writing down impressions when they occur—in order to push their thinking.

5.6.8 Seeking Convergence and Clarification

In the field there is a number of things that a researcher should be paying attention to. The first is looking for convergence of views and information about events and processes. It is not uncommon to find differing or incomplete views. In such cases, it is important to challenge, to revisit the issue and to seek other sources of data to clarify the information. Inevitably, on reflection and analysis there will be many uncertainties and gaps. In addition, during research in later cases it may become clear that some important areas of questioning may have been missed. There are several tactics for dealing with this. One is to revisit earlier cases and to review notes and evidence that may have been forgotten that could address the gaps. Another is to conduct interviews over a period of time, at least on 2 separate days. Prior to the final day all the data that has been collected can be reviewed to identify gaps and areas needing clarification. These can then be addressed.

5.6.9 Determining Sequence (Cause and Effect)

One of the main advantages of case research is that it increases the chance of being able to determine the link between cause and effect, something that is difficult in survey research. It is therefore important to try to determine the sequence of events and the links between them. This is not always an easy task as interviewees often attribute a cause and effect after the event, which may not actually match the actual links. If historical data are being collected, rather than real-time observation, it is important to use multiple sources and cross-check carefully before attributing cause and effect. It can be very helpful to construct a timeline of key events being studied.

5.6.10 Challenges of Observer Bias

A researcher will enter the field, bringing with them a strong interest in an area and potentially strong biases. It is reported that students of innovation are notoriously prone to a strong 'pro-innovation' bias (Leonard-Barton, 1990). Similarly, it is likely that students of manufacturing strategy or JIT will have strong biases towards these areas as well. Personal biases can shape what you see hear and record. In addition, the researcher may become an advocate, not an observer. There are a number of ways of countering this. One is to use multiple interviewers. Each can then review what is observed by the other. If a structured research protocol is used, then inter-rater reliability can be assessed. It is important that researchers recognize their biases, but also that they do not overreact. The use of tape recording can contribute towards reduction of observer bias, especially if the evidence is presented verbatim rather than summarized.

5.6.11 When to Stop

In case research, there is often the temptation to do 'just one more case' or 'just one more interview' to test some of the emerging theory or to get greater insight into the research questions. Knowing when to stop is an important skill of a case researcher. It may be time to stop when you are in danger of not having enough time to complete the analysis and write up in the time available. It may also be when there are diminishing returns from incremental cases or interviews. Most importantly the time to stop is when you have enough cases and data to satisfactorily address the research questions.

Field research with case studies is an iterative approach, which frequently involves multiple methods of data collection, multiple researchers and an evolution of concepts and constructs. This can be illustrated in OM research in a study of cell design by Hyer and Brown (1999a):

> During the past two years, we have visited over 15 firms with the express purpose of exploring what works and what does not work in manu-facturing cells. Using a standard set of questions, we asked operations managers to relate stories about cells they have implemented and to highlight the outcomes that have resulted from the changes they made. From this very rich set of stories, we uncovered consistent patterns that ultimately led us to reformulate our thinking about cells. Throughout the process, our definitions and their underpinnings evolved with each new or return plant visit, serving to reinforce or reshape our emerging theory. Our approach was consistent with the prescriptions for case study research of Eisenhardt (1989) in that we intentionally selected theoretically useful cases, used multiple (two) investigators, considered qualitative and quantitative data, and allowed the study to change course as themes emerged.
>
> (Hyer and Brown, 1999a)

5.7 Reliability and Validity in Case Research

As mentioned previously, it is particularly important to pay attention to reliability and validity in case study research. Reliability and validity have a number of dimensions.

Construct validity is the extent to which we establish correct operational measures for the concepts being studied. If the construct as measured can be differentiated from other constructs, it also possesses *discriminant validity* (Leonard-Barton, 1990). Construct validity can be tested by:

- Observing whether predictions made about relationships to other variables are confirmed
- Using multiple sources of evidence (similar results are evidence of convergent validity)
- Seeing if a construct as measured can be differentiated from another (evidence of discriminant validity)
- Seeking triangulation that might strengthen construct validity

Internal validity is the extent to which we can establish a causal relationship, whereby certain conditions are shown to lead to other conditions, as distinguished from spurious relationships (Yin, 1994:35). *External validity* is knowing whether a study's finding can be generalized beyond the immediate case study. *Reliability* is the extent to which a study's operations can be repeated, with the same results (Yin, 1994:36). For a general discussion on validity and reliability see Chapter 4.

Yin (1994) has outlined how some of these might be addressed as shown in Table 5.5. In addition, qualitative data often provide a good understanding of the why, a key to establishing internal validity—what is the theoretical relationship and why this happens. Multiple cases have higher external validity than single cases.

5.8 Data Documentation and Coding

Once data are collected they should be documented and coded. A key issue in analysing case research is the volume of data.

5.8.1 Documentation

The necessary first step is a detailed write-up of each case and unit of analysis following the research protocol structure. Where appropriate this will involve transcription of tape recordings. Ideally this should be done as soon as possible after the case visit, both to maximize recall and to facilitate follow-up and filling of gaps in the data.

An example in OM research is a study of JIT manufacturing by McLachlin (1997):

Table 5.5 Reliability and Validity in Case Research (Yin, 1994:33)

Test	Case study tactic	Phase of research in which tactic occurs
Construct validity	Use multiple sources of evidence	Data collection
	Establish chain of evidence	
	Have key informants review draft case study report	Data collection Composition
Internal validity	Do pattern matching or explanation building or time-series analysis	Data analysis
External validity	Use replication logic in multiple-case studies	Research design
Reliability	Use case study protocol	Data collection
	Develop case study database	Data collection

> For each site visited, the raw data, originally grouped by informant, was recorded electronically, coded with standard codes, and grouped by construct category. For each construct, summary paragraphs and associated ratings were derived using all available evidence, qualitative and quantitative. The condensed information was placed in a summary display for the particular plant.
>
> (McLachlin, 1997)

Documentation can include typing up of notes and/or transcription of tapes. This produces a *case narrative*. Other documentation can include gathering together documents and other material collected in the field or through other sources. It should also include documenting ideas and insights that arose during or subsequent to the field visit. Accuracy of the documentation can be increased by letting key informants review draft reports. There is an increasing number of tools available for textual analysis of qualitative data. These allow on-screen coding of documents and exploration of patterns and relationships of words and phrases. These can be particularly useful when tape recorded interviews are transcribed.

5.8.2 Coding

Central to effective case research is the coding of the observations and data collected in the field. It is important to try to reduce data into *categories* (Glaser and Strauss, 1967; Miles and Huberman, 1994). The existence of good documentation of observations and multiple sources of evidence allows a chain of evidence to be established. *Incidents* of phenomena in the data are *coded* into *categories*. By comparing each incident with previous incidents in the same category, the researcher develops theoretical *properties* of categories and the *dimensions* of these properties.

Many researchers have followed the coding scheme suggested by Strauss and Corbin (1990). They propose three steps. The first step is open coding—data are fragmented or taken apart. Concepts are the basic building blocks of theory and open coding is an analytical process by which concepts are identified and are developed in terms of their properties and dimensions. Individual observations, sentences, ideas, events are given names, and then regrouped into *sub-categories* which in turn can be grouped as *categories*. The next step is axial coding—the putting together the data in new ways. The objective of this step is to regroup and link categories with each other in a rational manner. The final step is selective coding—selecting a core category and relating it to other categories.

An example of this in OM research is a study of black box engineering by Karlsson et al. (1998). One of the drivers of doing good data documentation and coding is to improve reliability. They state:

> In order to improve reliability, i.e., demonstrating that the data collection procedures can be repeated with the same results, data from interviews, open discussions, and observations exist in three forms:
>
> - Directly taken field notes (from interviews and observations);
> - Expanded typed notes made as soon as possible after the fieldwork. This includes comments on problems and ideas that arise during each stage of the fieldwork and that will guide further research);
> - A running record of analysis and interpretation (open coding and axial coding).
>
> (Karlsson et al., 1998)

When coding constructs based on case research, it is often prudent to limit the number of categories. 'For testing propositions, the magnitude of each construct was either the existence or the non-existence of a condition, based on high, neutral, and low ratings. The purpose of having a neutral range, for which no conclusions would be drawn, was to avoid making mistakes between high and low ratings' (McLachlin, 1997). Miles and Huberman (1994) suggest three concurrent stages to be followed: data reduction, data display and conclusion drawing/verification. Having now addressed data reduction, we can examine the next two stages, which can be seen as the analysis stage.

Coding and Analysing Data Using Software Packages

There is an increasing number of packages that can be very helpful in analysing interviews, field notes, textual sources and other types of qualitative data. These include NVivo, NU★DIST and ATLAS.ti. Data can be coded using a pre-defined code list that can be expanded during the analysis to capture emerging themes. Coding interviews and using software can contribute to more systematic analysis procedures and guard against information-processing biases. Although these are valuable tools, it must remembered that they are tools and not a substitute for thought. There is always a danger of too much coding, not enough reflection. Each tool comes with comprehensive guides on their use and further understanding of how to use such software packages can be found in Richards (1999) and Lewins and Silver (2007).

5.9 Analysis

Eisenhardt (1989) suggests two steps in analysis: analysis within case data, and searching for cross-case patterns.

5.9.1 Analysing Data—Within Cases

Having developed detailed case descriptions and coded the data, the first step is to analyse the pattern of data within cases. A very useful and common starting point is to construct an array or display of the data. A display is a visual format that presents information systematically so that the user can draw valid conclusions. Displays can be simple arrays, but might also be event listings, critical incident charts, networks, time ordered matrices, taxonomies etc. (Miles and Huberman, 1994). The overall idea is to become intimately familiar with each case as a stand-alone entity, and to allow the unique patterns of each case to emerge before you seek to generalize across cases (Eisenhardt, 1989). This in turn gives the researcher the depth of understanding that is needed for cross-case analysis.

Once an array or display has been constructed, then the researcher should begin looking for explanation and causality. Miles and Huberman present a number of ways of analysing case data. One is the case dynamics matrix. This displays a set of forces for change and traces the consequential processes and outcomes. Another form of analysis is making predictions and then using the case data to test them. This might consist of gathering, in tabular form, the evidence supporting and evidence working against a prediction and examining it. When visiting case researchers, it is not uncommon to see a wall completely covered with such displays. A third method is the causal network. A causal network is a 'display of the most important independent and dependent variables in a field study and of the relationships among them' (Miles and Huberman, 1994:153). Causal networks are associated with analytic texts describing the meaning of the connections among factors. This has been used in OM by Sousa (2000), following Miles and Huberman's (1994) guidelines:

> The working blocks were the codes, researcher comments, interim case
> summaries and the displays constructed in the data reduction stages. In

the whole process, several tactics for generating meaning were used such as noting patterns, seeing plausibility, clustering, counting, making contrasts/comparisons, subsuming particulars into the general, noting relations between variables, finding intervening variables, building a logical chain of evidence and making conceptual coherence (Miles and Huberman, 1994, pp. 245–262). As more knowledge became available during the course of the field work and associated conceptualisation, recurrent patterns of interaction between variables within the orienting research framework started to emerge, both within and across cases. Some variables looked connected, while others looked random or unconnected. These patterns guided guesses about directions of influence among sets of variables. Initial versions of the causal networks were amended and refined as they were successively tested against the data collected in the field. During this process, I actively looked for negative evidence opposing the emerging relationships as well as rival explanations. In addition, I received feedback from informants on the networks' emerging relationships. In order to reduce the effect of the researcher on the behaviour of informants, this was done towards the later stages of the data collection when a certain rapport had already been established with the informants. At these later stages, the relationships to be tested were also clearer. This process led to five individual networks whose relationships received support from the data. In parallel, the five individual case networks were compared with each other in order to identify similarities and differences. These comparisons resulted in the extraction of relationships that were found to replicate across cases, abstracting from the peculiarities of individual cases and generalising them to a broader theory. This resulted in the building of general (cross-case) causal networks embodying generalisable explanations that were empirically grounded in the five individual case networks.

(Sousa, 2000)

An example of one of Sousa's causal networks is shown in Figure 5.1.

5.9.2 Analysing Data—Searching for Cross-case Patterns

The systematic search for cross-case patterns is a key step in case research. It is also essential for enhancing the generalizability of conclusions drawn from cases. There is a wide variety of methods and tools available for this. As with within-case analysis, the simplest and often most effective method is to construct an array. Typically this involves the construction of very large spreadsheets or charts, and in turn refining these, for example summarizing in two-by-two cells. Having constructed an array, a simple but very effective analytical approach is to pick a group or category and to search for within-group similarities or differences. A similar approach is to select pairs of cases and to look for similarities and differences, including subtle ones. Miles and

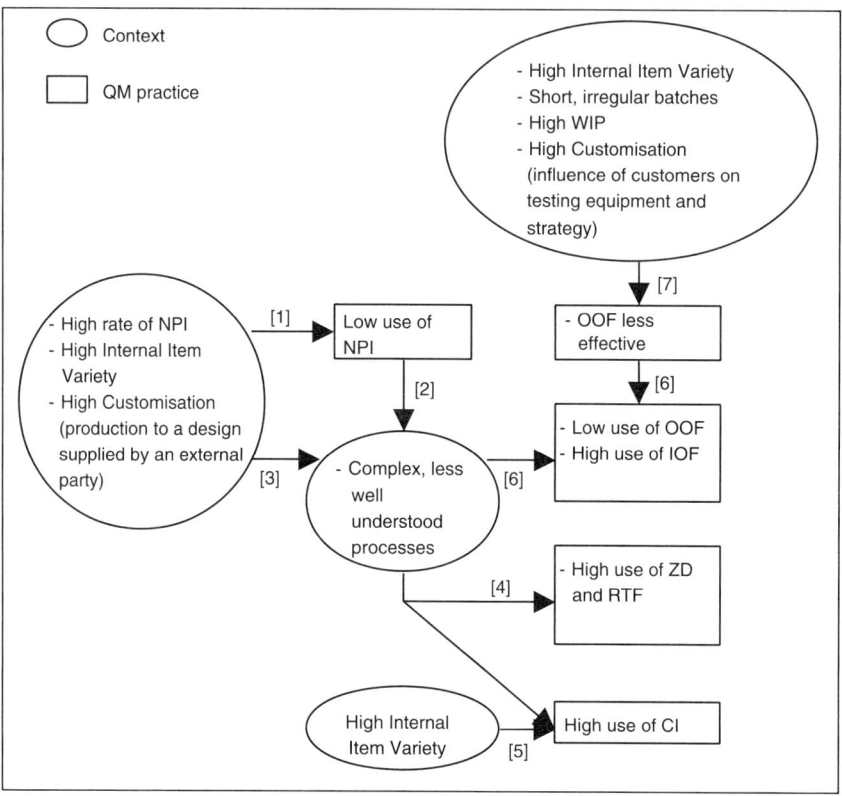

Figure 5.1 Example of Causal Network Analysis (adapted from Sousa and Voss, 2001). The research variables are shown in boxes or circles and the relationships among them are shown by arrows. Each arrow (labelled 1 to 7) represents a different connection. The text below the figure describes the meaning of the connections among variables in the network. Constructs are: QM = quality management, OOF = overall process off-line feedback, IOF = in process off-line feedback, NPI = formalized new product introduction process, ZD = zero defects process, RTF = real time feedback, CI = changeover inspection.

Huberman (1994) suggest a number of approaches to facilitate cross-case analysis. The first is partially ordered displays. These are appropriate for first-cut analysis 'to see what the general territory looks like'. They suggest that further displays can be constructed by organizing by concept, by case or by time. Within these, they describe many ways of structuring the data, including constructing and summing indices, two variable matrices, contrast tables that compare extreme cases or exemplars with other, scatterplots and sequence analysis.

With well-coded and quantified case data, continuous measures or data ordered in sequences can be developed. This lends itself to simple analysis such as graphing and more sophisticated statistical tests. There are a number of non-parametric statistical tests such as the Spearman's R and Kendall's Tau that can be used to test and explore patterns, even with relatively small sample sizes (SPSS, 2007). Where large numbers of cases have been used, then the standard analytical procedures of survey research can be used.

Cross-case analysis should also seek to increase the internal validity of the findings. As argued above, the use of multiple data sources or triangulation is important in case research. Deliberately seeking confirmation from multiple data sources leads to more reliable results. As Eisenhardt (1989) points out, we are poor processors of information. We tend to leap to conclusions based on a limited set of data, be overly influenced by individuals such as elite respondents, ignore basic statistical properties and inadvertently drop conflicting evidence. Cross-case analysis is an attempt to counter this.

5.9.3 Hypothesis Development and Testing

Case research is used for both hypothesis testing and theory development. In most case research there will be some initial hypotheses, which can be directly tested using the case data, in particular with larger case sample sizes. However, in much case research the focus is also on theory development and on shaping and developing new hypotheses from the data as well as testing the initial ones. Wacker (1998) puts forward a four-step general procedure for theory building: definition of variables; limiting the domain; relationship (model building); and finally theory prediction and empirical support. The process of theory testing involves measuring constructs and verifying relationships (Eisenhardt, 1989).

5.9.4 Shaping Hypotheses

During the process of case research, overall themes, concepts and possibly relationships between variables will begin to emerge. This is an iterative process, whereby the emergent themes, frameworks or hypotheses are compared with data from each case. This will iterate towards theory that provides a close fit. During this there will be a parallel process of refining the definition of the constructs using evidence that measures the construct in each case. At this stage we are likely to have new or refined hypotheses and constructs that allow us to verify the emergent relationship.

5.9.5 Testing Hypotheses

If replication logic has been used in case selection then cases that confirm an emergent relationship enhance confidence in the hypothesis or theory. Cases that disconfirm may at first seem problematical. However to the researcher seeking to develop and test theory, they provide the opportunity to refine and expand the theory. When the data seem to support hypotheses, case research allows the researcher to go one step further and examine the underlying reasons in each case as to why things are happening. What are the theoretical reasons for the observed relationships?

There are many different approaches. One is to propose alternative theories and use cases to test the fit of each theory. For example Orlikowski (1992) identified three alternative theoretical models relating technology to the organization. She conducted in-depth case studies of five projects at various stages of their life cycles. She then ascertained the fit or lack of fit of each model to the case data. From this she was able to propose a revised theoretical model. A new approach to analysis of case data is first to frame the propositions to be tested as sufficient or necessary conditions. Then these propositions can be tested using set theoretic logic (Goertz, 2006; Dul and Hak, 2008). These methods, are yet to be applied in OM research, but have the advantage of being able to address both the small samples often found in case research and to evaluate alternative paths (equifinality).

5.9.6 Enfolding Literature

In theory development research, it is important to review the emergent theory against the existing literature. This research must be built on existing theory. It is not an excuse to say that 'this precise issue has not been studied before'. There is always some relevant literature to refer to. Reviewing emergent theory involves asking what is similar, what is different and why (Eisenhardt, 1989). It is very important to address literature that conflicts with the findings. Not to do so reduces confidence in the findings, and doing it may force you into more creative thinking and deeper insights. Literature discussing similar findings will help tie together underlying similarities. Overall effective enfolding of literature increases both the quality and the validity of the findings.

5.9.7 Writing up the Research

Case research will ultimately only have a strong impact if it is written up well. First it is important that the methodology is well defined and justified. This includes justification of the methods used, and the number of cases used, stating what is the unit of analysis, and clearly stating how the researcher got from their data and field notes to their conclusions (Barratt et al., 2007). Eisenhardt and Graebner (2007) present some valuable guidelines about theory-building research. It is important to begin with strong grounding in related literature that identifies a research gap and to justify why theory-building methods are more appropriate than theory-testing methods. Next, a critical aspect is presenting the evidence from which the theory of interest was inducted. In single cases this may be through a relatively complete rendering of the 'story' behind the case. In multi-case research, space limitations often mean that there is a trade-off between theory and empirical richness. One way to address this is to develop a theory in sections or by distinct propositions in such a way that each is supported by empirical evidence. The use of tables and other devices that summarize the related case evidence is central to signalling the depth and detail of empirical grounding. Their final guideline is about presenting the emergent theory. There is no one right way of doing this. They recommend sketching the emergent theory at the beginning of the paper, then in the body of the paper link each proposition to the supporting empirical evidence for each construct and the relationships between them. When this is done the propositions will mostly be consistent with the cases and there is effectively pattern matching between theory and data. It is crucial to write the underlying theoretical arguments that provide the logical link between the constructs within a proposition. This should thus convey a clear theoretical argument to the reader.

Finally in writing up case research a valuable approach is to study how others have done this in OM.

5.10 Summary

This chapter has set out a step-by-step approach for conducting case research in OM. Though this has been set out as sequential steps, anyone who has conducted case research will know that they are both parallel and iterative. The research question may be revisited during case analysis, constructs refined and redefined during field research and analysis and so on. It is important to recognize this, and also to have the courage to bring the research to a firm conclusion, and resist the temptation to continually and incrementally improve the findings.

- There are several challenges in conducting case research:
    - It is time consuming, it needs skilled interviewers, and care is needed in drawing generalizable conclusions from a limited set of cases and in ensuring rigorous research
    - Despite this, the results of case research can have very high impact. Unconstrained by the rigid limits of questionnaires and models, it can lead to new and creative insights, development of new theory and have high validity with practitioners
- Case studies can be used for different types of research purposes such as exploration, theory building, theory testing and theory extension/refinement:
    - *Exploration*: in the early stages of many research programmes, exploration is needed to develop research ideas and questions
    - *Theory building*: a particular area where cases are strong is theory building. 'Nothing is so practical as a good theory'
    - *Theory testing*: despite its limited use for theory testing, case study

research has been used in the OM field in order to test complicated issues such as strategy implementation

- ○ *Theory extension/refinement*: case studies can also be used as a follow-up to survey-based research in an attempt to examine more deeply and validate previous empirical results

- Important choices in case selection are single or multiple cases and retrospective or longitudinal cases:

  - ○ Single cases give greater depth but limits on the generalizability of conclusions drawn and biases such as misjudging the representativeness of a single event and exaggerating easily available data
  - ○ Multiple cases augment external validity and help guard against observer bias but more resources are needed and they may give less depth per case
  - ○ Retrospective cases allow collection of data on historical events but it may be difficult to determine cause and effect since participants may not recall important events
  - ○ Longitudinal cases overcome the problems of retrospective cases but have long elapsed time and thus may be difficult to do

- It is important to apply tests to validate the controls and to ensure that each case meets the sample criteria:

  - ○ When selecting cases it is important to consider what are the parameters or factors that define the population and are to be held constant across the sample
  - ○ Controls rely on the *selection* of the phenomena during the study's experimental design stage for their control. This allows particular factors (e.g. managerial policies, inventory systems) to be, in essence, 'held constant' while others (e.g. costs, defect rates) are left free to vary as they would naturally

- There is a set of skills required by the field researcher:

  - ○ To be able to ask good questions and interpret the answers
  - ○ To be a good listener and not be trapped by preconceptions
  - ○ To be adaptable and flexible, to see newly encountered situations as opportunities not threats
  - ○ To have a firm grasp of the issues being studied
  - ○ To be unbiased by preconceived notions, and thus receptive and sensitive to contradictory evidence

- An underlying principle in collection of data in case research is that of triangulation, the use and combination of different methods to study the same phenomenon:

  - ○ Such methods can include interviews, questionnaires, direct observations, content analysis of documents and archival research

- Reliability of data will also be increased if multiple sources of data on the same phenomenon are used

- Central to effective case research is the coding of the observations and data collected in the field. It is important to try to reduce data into *categories*

    - The first step is open coding—data are fragmented or taken apart. Concepts are the basic building blocks of theory and open coding is an analytic process by which concepts are identified and are developed in terms of their properties and dimensions. Individual observations, sentences, ideas, events are given names, and then regrouped into *sub-categories* which in turn can be grouped as *categories*
    - The next step is axial coding—putting together the data in new ways. The objective of this step is to regroup and link categories with each other in a rational manner
    - The final step is selective coding—selecting a core category and relating it to other categories

- There are two steps in the analysis: analysis of within-case data, and searching for cross-case patterns. Key issues for the within-case analysis are the following:

    - A very useful and common starting point is to construct an array or display of the data. A display is a visual format that presents information systematically so that the user can draw valid conclusions
    - Once an array or display has been constructed, then the researcher should begin looking for explanation and causality. One way is the case dynamics matrix. This displays a set of forces for change and traces the consequential processes and outcomes. Another form of analysis is making predictions and then using the case data to test them. This might consist of gathering, in tabular form, the evidence supporting and evidence working against a prediction and examining it. A third method is the causal network. A causal network is a 'display of the most important independent and dependent variables in a field study and of the relationships among them'

- The systematic search for cross-case patterns is a key step in case research. It is also essential for enhancing the generalizability of conclusions drawn from cases. There is a wide variety of methods and tools available for this:

    - As with within-case analysis, the simplest and often most effective method is to construct an array. Typically this involves the construction of very large spreadsheets or charts, and in turn refining these, for example summarizing in two-by-two cells
    - Having constructed an array, a simple but very effective analytical

approach is to pick a group or category and to search for within group similarities or differences

○   A similar approach is to select pairs of cases and to look for similarities and differences, including subtle ones

Most of the research conducted in the field of OM is based on statistical survey analysis and mathematical modelling. However, '. . . embracing a field investigation technique such as case studies is bound to make the individual researcher, and the field in general richer and better prepared to solve real OM problems' (McCutcheon and Meredith, 1993). We hope that this chapter will help OM researchers conduct case research with the appropriate rigour, which, when combined with relevance, makes case-based research a very powerful methodology.

Notes

1 This chapter is based on Voss C.A., Frohlich M. and Tsikriktsis N. (2002), 'Case research in operations management', *International Journal of Operations and Production Management*, 22, 2, 195–219.
2 The main characteristic of rationalist research is that the phenomenon being studied exists 'out there', independent of the research context or beliefs and assumptions of the researcher. Thus the relationships and observations are considered to be independent of the theories used to explain them and can hence be studied, manipulated at will, and controlled as needed by the researcher.
3 *Reliability* is the degree to which a measure is free from random error components (i.e. what you intended to measure is actually being measured). *Validity* is the extent to which a measure only reflects the desired construct without contamination from other systematically varying constructs (DeVellis, 1991).

References and Bibliography

Åhlström P.A., Blackmon K. and Voss C.A. (1998), 'Diagnostic benchmarking and manufacturing improvement', in Coughlan P., Dromgoole T. and Peppard J. (eds.), *Operations management—future issues and competitive responses*, University of Dublin, 7–12.

Akkermans H. and Vos B. (2003), 'Amplification in service supply chains: an exploratory case study from the telecom industry', *Production and Operations Management*, 12, 2, 204–223.

Baccarach S.B. (1989), 'Organisational theories: some criteria for evaluation', *Academy of Management Review*, 14, 4, 496–515; quoted in Wacker op.cit.

Barratt M., Choi T.Y. and Li M. (2007), *State of Inductive Case Studies in Operations Management*: Working paper, W.P. Carey School of Business; Arizona State University.

Boyer K.K. and McDermott C. (1999), 'Strategic consensus in operations strategy', *Journal of Operations Management*, 17, 289–305.

Campbell D.T. and Fiske D.W. (1959), 'Convergent and discriminant validation by the multitrait—multimethod matrix', *Psychological Bulletin*, 56, 2, 81–105.

Choi T.Y. and Hong Y. (2002), 'Unveiling the structure of supply networks: Case studies in Honda, Acura, and DaimlerChrysler', *Journal of Operations Management*, 20, 5, 469.

Cook T.E. and Campbell D.T. (1979), *Quasi-Experimentation: design and analysis issues for field settings*, Boston: Houghton Mifflin.

Demaree R.G. and Wolf G. (1984), 'Estimating within-group inter-rater reliability with and without response bias,' *Journal of Applied Psychology*, 69, 1, 85–98.

DeVellis R.F. (1991), *Scale development: theory and applications*, Newbury Park, CA: Sage Publications.

Drejer A., Blackmon K. and Voss C. (1998), 'Worlds apart?—a look at the operations management area in the US, UK and Scandinavia', *Scandinavian Journal of Management*, 16, 45–66.

Dul J. and Hak T. (2008), *Case study methodology in business research*, Oxford: Butterworth Heinemann.

Edmondson A.C. and McManus S.E. (2007), 'Methodological fit in management research', *Academy of Management Review*, 32, 4, 1135–1179.

Eisenhardt K.M. (1989), 'Building theory from case study research', *Academy of Management Review*, 14, 4, 532–550.

Eisenhardt K.M. and Graebner M.E. (2007), 'Theory building from cases: opportunities and challenges', *Academy of Management Journal*, 50, 1, 25–32.

Finch BJ. (1999), 'Internet discussions as a source for consumer product customer involvement and quality information: an exploratory study', *Journal of Operations Management*, 17, 535–556.

Frohlich M. (1998), *The implementation of advanced manufacturing technologies: An empirical study of surface mount technology*, Unpublished DBA Thesis, Boston University.

Glaser B.G. and Strauss A.L. (1967), *The discovery of grounded theory: strategies for qualitative research*, New York: Aldine De Gruyter.

Goertz G. (2007), *Social science concepts—a user's guide*, Princeton Press.

Handfield R.S. and Melnyk S.A. (1998), 'The scientific theory-building process: a primer using the case of TQM', *Journal of Operations Management* 16, 321–339.

Hayes R.H. and Wheelwright S.S. (1984), *Restoring our competitive edge: competing through manufacturing*, New York: Wiley.

Hill T., Nicholson A. and Westbrook R. (1999), 'Closing the gap: a polemic on plant-based research in operations management', *International Journal of Operations and Production Management*, 19, 2, 139–156.

Hyer N.L. and Brown K. (1999a), 'The discipline of real cells', *Journal of Operations Management*, 17, 557–574.

Hyer N.L, Brown K.A. and Zimmerman S. (1999b), 'A socio-technical systems approach to cell design: case study and analysis', *Journal of Operations Management*, 17, 179–203.

Jick T.D. (1979), 'Mixing qualitative and quantitative methods: triangulation in action', *Administrative Science Quarterly*, 24, 602–611.

Karlsson C. and Åhlström P. (1995), 'Change processes towards lean production: the role of the remuneration system', *International Journal of Operations and Production Management*, 15, 11, 80–99.

Karlsson C. and Åhlström P. (1997), 'Changing product development strategy—a managerial challenge', *Journal of Product Innovation Management*, 14, 473–484.

Karlsson C., Nellore R. and Söderquist K. (1998), 'Black box engineering: redefining the role of product specifications', *Journal of Product Innovation Management*, 15, 534–549.

Lamming R.C., Johnsen T.E., Zheng J. and Harland C.M. (2000), 'An initial classification of supply networks', *International Journal of Operations and Production Management*, 20, 5/6, 675–691.

Leonard-Barton D. (1990), 'A dual methodology for case studies: synergistic use of a longitudinal single site with replicated multiple sites', *Organisation Science*, 1, 1, 248–266.

Lewins A. and Silver C. (2007), *Using software in qualitative research: a step-by-step guide*, London: Sage Publications.

Lewis M.W. (1998), 'Iterative triangulation: a theory development process using existing case studies', *Journal of Operations Management*, 16, 455–469.

McCutcheon D. and Meredith J. (1993), 'Conducting case study research in operations management', *Journal of Operations Management*, 11, 3, 239–256.

McLachlin R. (1997), 'Management initiatives and just-in-time manufacturing', *Journal of Operations Management*, 15, 271–292.

Meredith J. (1998), 'Building operations management theory through case and field research', *Journal of Operations Management*, 16, 441–454.

Meredith J. and Vineyard M. (1993), 'A longitudinal study of the role of manufacturing technology in business strategy', *International Journal of Operations and Production Management*, 13, 12, 4–24.

Miles H. and Huberman M. (1994), *Qualitative data analysis: a sourcebook*, Beverly Hills, CA: Sage Publications.

Mintzberg H. (1979), 'An emerging strategy of "direct" research', *Administrative Science Quarterly*, 24, 590–601.

Mukherjee A., Mitchell W. and Talbot F.B. (2000), 'The impact of new manufacturing technologies and strategically flexible production', *Journal of Operations Management*, 18, 139–168.

Narasimhan R. and Jayaram J. (1998), 'Reengineering service operations, a longitudinal case study', *Journal of Operations Management*, Dec, 7–22.

Orlikowski W. (1992), 'The duality of technology, rethinking the concept of technology in organisations', *Organization Science*, 3, 3, 2.

Pagell M. and Krause D.R. (1999), 'A multiple-method study of environmental uncertainty and manufacturing flexibility', *Journal of Operations Management*, 17, 307–325.

Pil F.K. and Rothenberg S. (2003), 'Environmental performance as a driver of superior quality', *Production and Operations Management*, 12, 3), 404.

Richards L. (1999) *Using NVivo in qualitative research*, London: Sage Research.

Ritzman L.P. and Safizadeh M.H. (1999), 'Linking process choice with plant level decisions about capital and human resources,' *Production and Operations Management*, Muncie, Winter.

Schein E.H. (1987), *The clinical perspective in fieldwork*, Newbury Park: Sage.

Schonberger R. (1982), *Japanese manufacturing techniques*, New York: The Free Press.

Smith N.L. (1987), 'Towards a justification of claims in evaluation research', *Evaluation and Programme Planning*, 10, 209–314, quoted in Miles and Huberman (1994) op. Cit.

Sousa R. (2000), '*Quality management practice: universal or context dependent? An empirical investigation*' unpublished PhD thesis, London Business School.

Sousa R. and Voss C.A. (2001). Quality management: universal or context dependent? *Production and Operations Management*, 10, 4, 383.

SPSS (2007), *'SPSS exact tests'*, http://www.spss.com/exact_tests/

Strauss, A. and Corbin, J. (1990), *Basics of qualitative research: grounded theory procedures and techniques*, Newbury Park, CA: Sage Publications.

Tyre W. and Orlikowski W.J. (1994), 'Windows of opportunity: temporal patterns of technological adaptation in organizations', *Organization Science*, 59, 1, 98–118.

Van De Ven A.H. (1989), 'Nothing is quite as practical as a good theory', *Academy of Management Review*, 14, 4, 486–489.

Voordijk H., Meijboom B. and de Haan, J. (2006), 'Modularity in supply chains: a multiple case study in the construction industry', *International Journal of Operations & Production Management*, 26, 6, 600.

Voss C.A. (1984), 'Multiple independent invention and the process of technological innovation', *Technovation*, 2, 169–184.

Voss C.A., Frohlich M. and Tsikriktsis N. (2002), 'Case research in operations management', *International Journal of Operations and Production Management*, 22, 2, 195–219.

Wacker J.G. (1998), 'A definition of theory: research guidelines for different theory building research methods in operations management', *Journal of Operations Management*, 16, 361–385.

Yin R. (1994), *Case study research*, Beverly Hills: Sage Publications.

Zomerdijk L.G. and de Vries J. (2007), 'Structuring front office and back office work in service delivery systems', *International Journal of Operations & Production Management*, 27, 1, 108.

6 Longitudinal Field Studies

Pär Åhlström and Christer Karlsson

Chapter Overview

- *Introduction to the longitudinal field study*—describing what the longitudinal field study is and how it is a special form of case research
- *Setting up the longitudinal field study*—choosing the appropriate research questions, gaining access to data and setting up the study
- *Setting up the longitudinal field study as clinical research*—conducting the research through simultaneously contributing to an organization and to knowledge
- *Collecting data in the longitudinal field study*—dealing with the peculiarities and challenges of collecting longitudinal data
- *The mechanics of analysing longitudinal field data*—developing ways of analysing the overwhelming amount of data often collected in longitudinal field studies
- *Building theory from longitudinal field studies*—developing and reporting on the findings of the longitudinal field study
- *Evaluating theory from longitudinal field studies*—ensuring reliable and valid results from a longitudinal field study

---

This chapter deals with longitudinal field studies, in-depth studies of change processes inside organizations. The longitudinal field study is a case study, since it seeks to study a phenomenon in its natural setting. However, the longitudinal field study has a number of features which requires treating it separately from case research, which we covered in Chapter 5. As a research strategy, longitudinal field studies are best used in the early stages of research programmes, for exploration and theory building. Longitudinal field studies are particularly useful for studying processes of change and development in organizations. This chapter will explain the nature of longitudinal research, particularly focusing on how it is different from case research. The chapter will also provide a description of how to design, execute and report longitudinal field studies.

6.1 Introduction to the Longitudinal Field Study

In this section, the longitudinal field study is introduced. Particular focus is on what the longitudinal field study is and why it is considered a special type of case research.

6.1.1 Longitudinal versus Cross-sectional Research

In defining what we mean by a longitudinal field study, we first need to make a distinction between longitudinal research and cross-sectional research. Cross-sectional research implies studying a phenomenon at a specific point in time. For instance, we may conduct cross-sectional case studies to discern how companies use benchmarking to improve their manufacturing processes. The research concerns the companies' current usage of benchmarking and thus refers to a specific point in time. The specific point in time we are interested in can be historical. For instance, we can use case research to investigate how companies make decisions regarding capacity extensions. To do this, we select a number of companies that have made capacity extensions. We then study the decision process behind these extensions, in retrospect.

Conducting longitudinal research implies studying a phenomenon over time. Longitudinal research can be seen as a number of cross-sectional snapshots of a phenomenon, taken over time. An example will illustrate this. Suppose we are interested in using case studies to study how companies improve their manufacturing process over time. Having selected a number of companies, we visit them regularly over a period of time, for instance once every 3 months for a period of 2 years. During each visit we enquire about various aspects of how the manufacturing process has been improved since our last visit and any future plans for manufacturing improvement.

With longitudinal research being the study of a phenomenon over time using multiple observations, then one could argue that we have a longitudinal study if we have two snapshots. However, we would normally require a bit more of a study for it to qualify as a longitudinal study. Exactly how many snapshots are required is not possible to say beforehand, since it depends on many different things, most importantly the research question.

6.1.2 The Difference of Timing—the Longitudinal Field Study is a Real-time Study

Within the domain of longitudinal studies, what further characterizes the longitudinal field study is timing. The issue of timing can be seen as a choice along a continuum with two end-points: retrospection or real time. In retrospective studies we attempt to discern what has happened by asking respondents to recollect historical events. In real-time studies we study current events. Longitudinal field studies imply that the researcher studies change processes as they unfold, in real time.

Real-time studies overcome a major weakness of retrospective research—the difficulty of determining cause and effect from reconstructed events (Leonard-Barton, 1990). In retrospective research, respondents tend to reinterpret things from a new perspective and can therefore not always give an accurate account of the past (Becker and Geer, 1957). Respondents can also be vague about the timing of events or be reluctant to talk about political issues, believing it unwise to dredge up old problems (Leonard-Barton, 1990).

It is important to note here that the difference in timing lies along a continuum. The purest form of a longitudinal field study would be daily participant observation. This is seldom feasible for the researcher. This means that longitudinal field studies can contain an element of retrospection. One of the key characteristics of longitudinal field studies still remains—that the researcher is present in the organization. For instance, we may be in place at a company every other week. Part of the data we collect when we are present thus refers to past events. But the error introduced by the respondents interpreting events is likely to be smaller than if we visit the company once every 3 months. A longitudinal study involving a series of multiple interviews about recent events offers the obvious benefit of proximity in time to current events. This increases the likelihood that the researcher can determine the sequence and nature of events accurately (Leonard-Barton, 1990).

Longitudinal field studies share important characteristics with ethnography, the study of cultures. The ethnographic approach is that of anthropology and sociology, using participant observation. This approach allows a fieldworker to use the culture of the setting to account for the observed patterns of human activity (Van Maanen, 1979). Crucial in ethnography is long residence and participant observation (Sanday, 1979). The ethnographer becomes part of the situation being studied in order to feel what it is like for the people in that situation. He or she becomes immersed in the everyday life of the observed, for an extended period of time (Barley, 1990).

6.1.3 Longitudinal Field Studies in Operations Management

OM literature does not contain many longitudinal field studies, a feature it shares with other fields, such as organization theory (Miller and Friesen, 1982) or strategic management (Pettigrew, 1990). There are longitudinal studies on organizations, but not in organizations. One of the main reasons for this is that they imply significant researcher commitment and organizational access (Van de Ven, 1993).

Within OM, broadly defined, three longitudinal studies stand out. We will use them throughout the chapter as illustrations of good practice in conducting longitudinal field studies. The three studies are:

- The Minnesota Innovation Research Programme (Van de Ven et al.,

1989). This landmark work involved a large team of researchers over 5 years. It is not a single project but rather many research projects guided by a common research framework, all employing the longitudinal field study method. The level of detail in which the methods applied are described, for instance by Van de Ven and Poole (1990), makes it a good role model for any researcher interested in longitudinal field studies. The studies have also spawned a great deal of prestigious publications

- Leonard-Barton's work on the implementation of technology (see for instance Leonard-Barton, 1988). This study contains an interesting combination of a longitudinal field study and several retrospective cases. The employed methodology has been well described in Leonard-Barton (1990), and is a good example of well-conducted case research, which employs the longitudinal field study as one part

- Our own work on the implementation of lean production (at length reported in Åhlström, 1997). This study is a 2.5 year longitudinal field study of one company, adopting lean production. Our insights from performing this study are the backbone of the chapter

As we proceed, we will come back to these studies at various points. They are used partly as illustrations of good practice and partly as illustrations of the steps in the process of setting up and conducting a longitudinal field study.

6.1.4 Longitudinal Field Studies—to Generate Theories of Change Processes

Given the scarcity of longitudinal field studies—when should we use them? Longitudinal field studies are most suitable for generating theory, not testing theory. By using longitudinal field studies, the researcher can get close enough to the studied phenomena to discover the forces most crucial to the object of inquiry. The researcher can also remain close to the studied phenomena for long enough to discover the causal links among events and constructs. It is scarcely possible to imagine a more fertile basis for generating theory (Miller and Friesen, 1982).

A basic assumption throughout this book is that the phenomenon being researched dictates the terms of its own dissection and exploration (Leonard-Barton, 1990). This obviously applies to longitudinal field studies as well. They are not suitable for all types of research questions. In fact, since longitudinal field studies are a special form of case research, the use of longitudinal field studies is further restricted to certain types of phenomena. The benefits of longitudinal real-time studies make them particularly useful for studying processes of change and development in organizations (Barley, 1990; Van de Ven, 1993).

During processes of change, the tendency to reinterpret things from a new perspective is probably more prevalent, since the change process almost by definition means that things are changing, and probably so is the perspective of the person being interviewed. During such transformations, organization members will find it difficult or impossible to remember former actions, outlooks, or feelings. Reinterpreting things from his or her new perspective, an interviewee cannot give an accurate account of the past, for the concepts in which he or she thinks about it have changed and with them perceptions and memories (Becker and Geer, 1957). Hence, the use of longitudinal field studies to study processes of change.

The contribution of longitudinal field studies is therefore likely to be theories, models and hypotheses of change processes. The topic of concern for these change processes can of course vary. We return to our example studies:

- A process theory of innovation—focusing on explaining the temporal order and sequence of steps that unfold as an innovative idea is transformed and implemented into a concrete reality (Van de Ven and Poole, 1990)
- A theory on the nature of the innovation process during the internal development of equipment, processes and software tools (Leonard-Barton, 1988)
- A theory on the sequence between different improvement initiatives whilst adopting lean production (Åhlström, 1997)

6.2 Setting up the Longitudinal Field Study

In setting up the longitudinal field study, several issues are necessary to consider. The first concerns defining an appropriate research question. Then it is a matter of selecting an organization or several to study. After these initial considerations follow the tasks of gaining access to relevant data and putting together a framework for data collection. Finally, we discuss the demands that longitudinal field studies put on the researcher, which need to be considered as well.

6.2.1 Defining an Appropriate Research Question for Longitudinal Field Studies

Longitudinal field studies are particularly suited for the following research question: 'How does organizational change emerge, develop, grow, or terminate over time?' (Van de Ven and Huber, 1990). This question is concerned with describing and explaining temporal sequences of events that unfold as an organizational change occurs. The explanations are sought in terms of some underlying mechanisms that cause events to happen and the particular circumstances or contingencies when these mechanisms operate. Within OM, several types of changes can be considered suitable for using longitudinal field studies, for instance the process of adopting lean production (Åhlström, 1997) or the implementation of new technology (Leonard-Barton, 1988).

This conceptualization of research questions suited for applying longitudinal field studies rests on a specific definition of the process of change. The term 'process' is here taken to mean: a sequence of incidents, stages, events or activities that describe how things change over time (Van de Ven, 1993). The term 'process', as it is used here, represents a development view of how change unfolds. The central focus is on progressions (i.e. the nature, sequence and order) of activities or events that an organizational entity undergoes as it changes over time. This usage of process is important to keep in mind, since there are many different usages of the term, particularly in OM.

Within this view of change processes, it is possible to further specify the types of change processes that constitute good candidates for longitudinal field studies. First of all, the change process has to be reasonably limited in time. In an ideal world, one would like to study a change process throughout its entire life, from beginning to end (Van de Ven and Poole, 1990). To permit the study to be conducted within a reasonable time frame, this requirement places restrictions on the process to be studied. The restrictions placed are particularly apparent for a doctoral student who is under time pressure to finalize his or her thesis. All research involves compromises of different kinds, but it is always good to know what the ideal is (Czarniawska-Joerges, 1992).

In designing the study, it is important to ensure that the study is not dependent on the change process being studied having run its entire length, for two reasons. First, it is not always easy to determine exact end-points for change processes. Since change is increasingly becoming a part of organizational life, determining when exactly a change processes has ended is not a trivial task. Second, it is not uncommon for change processes to be stretched out in time, beyond the point in time they were originally set out to end. Therefore, the research question has to be put in such a way and the research structured so that interesting results are yielded regardless of whether the change process has finished or not. There are great risks involved in the research relying on the change process having run its course. This risk also involves relying on a particular outcome of the change process. The research question needs to be put in such a way that no matter what the outcome is, something valuable comes out of the research.

Another demand we can put on a change process for it to be amenable to a longitudinal field study is that the process needs to be observable. This requirement is very much related to the size of the organization and the unit of analysis. In terms of size, it is easier to observe change processes in reasonably small organizations. For instance, observing the process of adopting lean production at a company with 400 employees is easier than observing it at a company with 4,000.

Regarding unit of analysis, the challenge is to define it at such a way that it is amenable to observation. This is seldom a problem within OM, since much of the changes the field is concerned with are fairly operational, or at a not too abstract level. For example, in her study, Leonard-Barton (1990) observed the 'internal development of equipment, processes and software tools'. The types of changes that can be more difficult to observe in a longitudinal field study are strategic changes, occurring at a higher level of abstraction, involving multiple organizational units. Although these types of change processes are not impossible to study through longitudinal field studies, many of the benefits of the method are diminished. Of course, this assumes that a single researcher, and not a team of researchers, is carrying out the longitudinal field study.

Note finally that size and unit of analysis are related to each other. The larger the organization, the more important it is to choose a unit of analysis that is observable. Conversely, in a smaller organization, it can be possible to observe even more strategic and high-level change processes.

6.2.2 Demands on the Longitudinal Field Study Case

During the selection of organizations to study when conducting longitudinal field studies, it is important to keep a few considerations in mind. The first consideration concerns numbers. Conducting a longitudinal field study is very demanding in terms of the time and effort the researcher needs to spend on being in the organization. The amount of effort naturally depends on the extent of the researcher's engagement in the organization. However, in general, it is very difficult to manage to study more than one organization, at least for a single researcher.

Studying only one organization obviously leads to disadvantages in terms of generalization. The properties of the chosen case will also have a profound impact on the outcome of the study. An important question therefore becomes whether or not the case is representative of the specific type of phenomenon that is studied? The answer to this question will affect the degree to which the findings can be considered to have general value (Berg, 1981). We will return to the topic of generalization towards the end of the chapter.

Using a single case study is also subject to other potential biases, such as misjudging the representativeness of a single event, exaggerating the salience of a datum because of its ready availability, or biasing estimates because of unconscious anchoring (Leonard-Barton, 1990). These are biases related to the observer, which need to be safeguarded against. Several practices to help achieve this safeguarding will be developed later on.

One way of avoiding the shortcomings of having only one organization to study is to combine a longitudinal field study with retrospective case studies, as Leonard-Barton did. However, it is important to note that within one single organization, it is possible to study different cases, depending on how we define the unit of analysis. Assume that we are interested in studying the innovation process when developing new products. We may choose to follow several product development projects within the same organization. Thus, although we study only one organization, our study includes several cases.

The second consideration when selecting organizations to study is to choose organizations where the change process of interest is likely to be transparently observable. This is particularly important if only one organization is chosen. This recommendation is linked to the more general idea that in case research it makes sense to choose cases where the phenomenon of interest is most likely to appear, such as extreme situations and polar types (Eisenhardt, 1989).

For example, in our study, we were interested in studying the adoption of lean production by manufacturing companies (Åhlström, 1997). In particular, we were interested in the issues (or problems) that arose as companies changed their operations in accordance with lean production principles. Since only one company could be chosen for the study, due to reasons of time constraints, it was important to choose a case where the adoption process was likely to be transparently observable. The chosen company provided such an opportunity. The company's operations at the outset of the study were quite far from being lean and thus provided an opportunity to study a radical reorganization, where issues were likely to occur:

- The work organization was hierarchical, with several organizational layers between the shop floor worker and production managers
- Manufacturing was functionally organized, with assembly carried out on a production line, where each employee performed only one task
- Transportation was frequent within and between the company's two sites
- Manufacturing lead times were long and inventory high
- Internal cost of quality was high

To these more rational considerations when choosing cases to study, a final consideration needs to be added. This consideration is related to the scarcity of longitudinal field studies in general and within OM in particular. Researchers interested in performing longitudinal field studies often face limited possibilities for strategic choice (Berg, 1981). When the purpose of the study is to generate theory, the opportunities for strategic choice are also made difficult by the fact that the dimensions that could be said to govern this choice have not yet been explored. Research opportunities are not abundant and if one is given the possibility to conduct a longitudinal field study, one must often seize the opportunity (Czarniawska-Joerges, 1992). The possible amount of advance planning and consideration on the appropriateness of the research object should not be exaggerated (Stymne, 1970).

6.2.3 Gaining Access to Relevant Data

Having selected an organization to study, the next important step in the research design is for the researcher to find a suitable vantage point from where to gather data. Within OM, taking a managerial perspective is often relevant since research questions often concern how various change processes can be managed (Van de Ven, 1993). In her study, Dorothy Leonard-Barton was interested in how to manage the implementation of new technology (Leonard-Barton, 1988). It was therefore necessary for her to place herself within the managers' temporal and contextual frames of reference. The focus was then primarily on the actions and perceptions of managers over time.

A guiding principle for field work in general is that the researcher's account of the studied scene should build on information provided by the most knowledgeable members of that scene (Van Maanen, 1979). The aim for the researcher is to collect data from the change process to promote a rich, full understanding of the context and the process from the perspective of someone who has lived through the events (Leonard-Barton, 1990). There is often a need to find ways of gaining access to the relevant management level of the company. Access to the management levels of the organization gives the researcher a chance to assess the impact of high-level decisions on a lower level (Schein, 1987). A researcher who only gains access to the lower levels of the organization has to infer decisions taken higher up in the organization.

On a more practical level, different types of project meetings are often good places to gain access to relevant data. Under the assumption that the study concerns a change process, participating in project meetings associated with the change process is an economical way of gaining access to data. The key is to gain the access which permits the researcher to be kept informed when events occur that affect the study (Leonard-Barton, 1990).

Data can also be collected through interaction with managers at relevant levels and in relevant functional areas, depending on the research focus. The study of organizational change processes often needs to take into account the organizational context of the change process (Pettigrew, 1985). The researcher therefore needs to collect data from a broad array of organizational functions and levels, not focusing too narrowly. The research design needs to slice vertically though the organization, enabling the researcher to obtain data from multiple levels and perspectives (Leonard-Barton, 1990).

Related to the question of from where to look is the question of whether or not to structure the research in different phases, sequences or stages. It can be tempting to divide the research process into neat stages. However, when researchers use a priori stages or phases to design their research and collect data, their results can easily become self-fulfilling prophesies (Van de Ven, 1993).

6.2.4 The Importance of a Framework for Data Gathering

Not focusing too narrowly does not mean the longitudinal field researcher should avoid focus; on the contrary. Without a research focus it is easy to become overwhelmed by the volume of data. The risk of starting without a framework is also that the data collected will not be relevant for the final analysis (Miles, 1979).

Before going into the field the longitudinal field researcher needs a framework. The framework is not to be taken from pre-formulated theoretical propositions, which may bias and limit the findings (Eisenhardt, 1989). The framework is more like a telescope, pointed towards the organization to direct the researcher's attention towards some aspects of the organization (Berg, 1974). It is important to remember that any research framework specified beforehand needs to be tentative in this type of research. Both constructs and research question may shift during the research (Eisenhardt, 1989).

What is then the content of a framework? Naturally, it is impossible to say, since it is entirely dependent on the research question. However, it is important here to distinguish between the conceptual part of the framework and the more practical part. The following examples illustrate the point.

Researchers in the Minnesota Innovation Research Program were interested in studying innovation processes. To this end, they used a framework consisting of a set of categories or variables to describe innovation development (which will be described later in the chapter). These categories were viewed as sensitizing categories, for conducting exploratory theory-building research. Assumptions and definitions of these concepts changed substantially and became progressively clearer with field observations over time.

In our study, we were interested in studying the adoption of lean production (Åhlström, 1997). We then utilized a definition of lean production as the basis for a framework, or starting point in data collection. With the framework in mind, attention was directed towards the adoption process: the order and sequence of events as the organization adopted lean production.

With these two examples, we have illustrated the more conceptual part of a framework for data collection. The starting point is thus the research question, which is used to focus data collection. The result is in the form of a conceptual framework. These concepts are seldom directly observable, which means that a more practical part needs to be added to the conceptual part of the framework, where concepts are made operational. This helps the researcher to know what exactly to look for while in the field.

It is beneficial beforehand to explicitly define what to look for while in the field. The reason is that spending a significant amount of time in the field compounds the need for having limited the range of behaviour to observe (Turner, 1981). Observation needs to be systematic, selecting particular aspects of behaviour to observe (Scott, 1965). We also need to choose a unit of observation (Leonard-Barton, 1990). For instance, are we interested in observing comments of individuals involved in the change process or the major outcomes of various project meetings held in the change process?

Ultimately, what the longitudinal field researcher is interested in is events. Events require careful definition and vary with the subject being investigated. Only by being clear about the subject and conceptual categories does the researcher know 'what' events/activities to record, and 'where' to look for them. This is particularly important since it is often difficult to identify critical data in a longitudinal field study, whilst one is in the midst of the research (Leonard-Barton, 1990). It is important to keep in mind that events are constructs; conceptual categories that are not directly observable, but are indicated by observable incidents (Van de Ven and Poole, 1990). Exactly how these observable incidents are defined, of course, depends on the particular research question.

In our research we have found it fruitful to use a modified version of the critical incident technique (Flanagan, 1954) as a starting point. In this technique, an incident is defined as: 'any observable human activity that is sufficiently complete in itself to permit inferences and predictions to be made about the person performing the act' (Flanagan, 1954:327). A few modifications of this definition can be made:

- Speech acts can be included in the definition of acts. Acts are not confined to something being done; acts also refer to something being said
- Incidents can include non-acts. This is in line with Leonard-Barton (1990:258) who found it necessary to inquire 'about critical individuals' lack of action as well as about their overt actions'

How do we know that incidents are critical, being worthy of observation? Again, the research question is an important indicator. But the original definition of the critical incident technique serves as a useful starting point, where critical incidents are 'effective or in-effective with respect to attaining the general aims of the activity' (Flanagan, 1954:338).

Following on with our own example, we used the following decision rule during the collection of data: incidents were considered critical when they indicated events that either facilitated or impeded the process of adopting lean production. With the process view of manufacturing improvement taken in the study, the factors influencing the success and failure of the adoption process were of essence (Voss, 1988). When looking for the critical incidents two major types of questions were used:

1 For the observable incidents, we asked ourselves: 'Does it affect the adoption of lean production? If it does, then how?' The observable incidents comprised both acts (something which was done) and remarks (something which was said)

2   When searching for the covert incidents, we asked ourselves: 'If something should be done, why isn't it?'

These two questions cover most of the decision rules used for observing critical incidents. To the decision rules were added some 'subjective judgements' (Van de Ven and Poole, 1990). Some personal judgements were necessary to decide whether an incident was to be classified as critical or not. Thus, it is not possible to give an exact account of the types of incidents that were noted down. Having observed a critical incident, it is important to note down the relevant information concerning the incident as quickly as possible (Van de Ven and Poole, 1990):

- The type of action or behaviour that occurred
- Type of incident
- The names of the actors involved in the incident
- Time and place for the incident
- Circumstances surrounding the incident

6.2.5 Demands on the Researcher Conducting Longitudinal Field Studies

Longitudinal field studies are not for everyone. The special characteristics of these types of studies place demands on the researcher, demands which do not fit everyone. Before considering conducting a longitudinal field study, the researcher is well advised to consider the following (see also Leonard-Barton, 1990):

- The research skills needed resemble those of an investigative reporter. Attention to detail is paramount. One needs to use both ears attentively while simultaneously asking the right questions, keeping the previous interview or observation in mind. One also needs to be very aware of the significance of what is left unsaid as well as what is said. These observations must then be recorded, categorized and later coded
- One must really enjoy field work. The longitudinal field study may require as much time on fostering and maintaining relationships with the organization as on the actual data gathering. Further, in order to observe critical events, one must often spend an inordinate amount of time on non-critical ones. The researcher therefore needs to enjoy spending time in an actual organization. It is easier to make single phone-based interviews, than having to confront the same people, day after day
- The analysis of data collected in a longitudinal field study is a particularly challenging task. For the analysis task, the researcher requires a high tolerance for ambiguity, as one systematically iterates from a huge amount of qualitative data towards clarity

6.3 Setting up the Longitudinal Field Study as Clinical Research

A major obstacle towards conducting longitudinal field studies is the problem of gaining access to organizations. Organizations often have a need to keep their inner functioning hidden from observers. Observers may also get in the way or organization members do not want to share personal conflicts, stress and setbacks (Sofer, 1961). Gaining access to an organization is likely to be more of a problem the longer the study of the organization is. The researcher who wishes to conduct a longitudinal field study thus faces a problem of access, which is not to be underestimated (Leonard-Barton, 1990; Van de Ven, 1993). One way of dealing with the access problem is through setting up the longitudinal field study as clinical research.

6.3.1 Using Clinical Research to Gain Access in Longitudinal Field Studies

Utilizing clinical research can be a fruitful way of gaining access to organizations in order to conduct longitudinal field studies. The principal characteristic of clinical research is that the researcher participates in and studies organizational change from within the organization. The aim is to contribute both to the advancement of knowledge and to the practical concerns of the organization (Stymne, 1970). The model for clinical research is taken from clinical medicine. An active working relationship is sought with the organization on its day-to-day problems. In this relationship, the researcher accepts a fully professional role with responsibility for helping in solving problems that arise (Jaques, 1951).

Clinical research offers a possibility to overcome the problem of access, since the organization receives something in return for allowing the researcher access. Clinical research also has the benefit of giving access to data not usually available for research (Stymne, 1970). Since the members of the organization have a reason for having the researcher present, they are less likely to conceal data (Schein, 1987). By participating in the organization and interacting with people for an extended period of time, the researcher can get close to the organization. Being close to data enhances the possibility of discovering the forces most crucial to the inquiry, which provides a fertile basis for generating theory (Miller and Friesen, 1982).

6.3.2 The Researcher Effect in Clinical Research

A clinical researcher will affect the studied organization, since it is the nature of the methodology. In fact, all forms of inquiry into organizations entail intervention. Just by asking people questions, we (hopefully) start to make them think, possibly about things they had not thought of before (Schein, 1987). Even within physics, there is Heisenberg's uncertainty principle, which means that scientific research involves an interaction between the scientist and the object of observation (Morgan, 1983). The interaction between the observer and the observed is compounded in organizational inquiry: 'in the organizational context, the quest for objectivity, in the sense of freedom from influence by the research process, is probably hopeless' (Schön, 1983:127). A more appropriate kind of objectivity has to do with the researcher's awareness of his or her effect on others.

As a clinical researcher, you need to be aware of what you do in the organization and how this is received. Such awareness is the best remedy against self-confirming hypotheses and irresponsible interventions (Czarniawska-Joerges, 1992). The researcher must also attempt to assess the nature and extent of his or her effect on the studied phenomena (Sofer, 1961). The in-depth nature of the access achieved in clinical research will increase the familiarity the researcher gains with the company. This familiarity will help making assessments of the effects of any interventions and facilitate discussions with organization members regarding the effects the researcher has on the organization.

6.3.3 Defining Research Issues Beneficial for Both Research and Practice

The first requirement on the clinical longitudinal field study is to define research issues that are of interest both to the company and the researcher. Processes of change provide an interesting opportunity here, since they often are of interest both in theory and in practice.

The field of OM lacks studies of the process of implementing new tools and practices. Existing literature tends to focus on the content of the tools and practices and ignores the problems associated with implementing new tools and practices. Literature on organizational change, although naturally being strong on the change process, often ignores the content and context of change. Thus, studying change processes associated with OM is a fruitful area for research. The fit with longitudinal field studies is apparent here.

However, for companies it is not sufficient to get the final report of the longitudinal field study. Companies are interested in obtaining more short-term benefits of the relationship with the researcher, particularly if the company is funding the research. Short-term benefits can be provided in several different ways in the clinical research design, for instance in the form of:

- Analyses of current practices at the company. The researcher can make investigations of current practices at the company, analyses which can be used as input to the change process
- Theoretical input into the change process. The researcher can often provide input from literature into the change process. Although the change process itself, or parts of it, is the object of study in longitudinal

field studies, there are often many opportunities to provide theoretical input to a company
- Support in the change process. The researcher can also take on the role of providing support in the change process, for instance when problems arise or when actions are taken as part of the change process

6.3.4 Agreeing on Concurrent Knowledge Development

A second requirement of the clinical longitudinal field study is to ensure that the researcher gets the opportunity to develop knowledge as the change process is unfolding. Clinical research entails a balancing act between the scientific and the practical aspects of the collaboration. The balancing act concerns the researcher's interest to study a change process and the company's interest to receive support in the change process. The following are examples of measures that can be taken to help the researcher in this balancing act:

- Make the dual expectations explicit in the contract between the researcher and the company. That is, make sure to include the need for time for the researcher to conduct concurrent theoretical development
- Choose a research design that allows the researcher to regularly spend time away from the organization. This is necessary for the researcher to be able to analyse data and read up on theory on the phenomenon being studied. Time away from the company also gives the researcher the necessary distance to avoid the dangers of getting too close to the studied organization
- Choose a research question that is of interest to both the company and the researcher. A research question that both parties are interested in helps to ensure that the time the researcher spends in the organization is of benefit to both the company and the researcher

An example will illustrate what we mean by a research question that is of interest both to the company and to the researcher (see Åhlström, 1997). In this study, both parties were interested in the process of adopting lean production. The company was interested in keeping the adoption process as smooth as possible and the researchers' interest was in the issues that arose in the process.

6.3.5 Defining and Organizing Involvement for the Researcher

A third and final requirement on the design of a clinical longitudinal field study is that the researcher gets involved in the organization in a way that supports both the research and the more practical side of the collaboration. In particular, there is a need to find a role in the organization that increases the chances of making observations in line with the research question. The role should at the same time permit the researcher to contribute to the organization.

Since it is probably not uncommon that clinical research is conducted in teams of more junior and more senior researchers, as in the case of a PhD process, the researchers can take on different roles. This is beneficial both for the research side and the more practical side of the collaboration. For example, in the study we conducted (Åhlström, 1997), the agreement with the company was that we would be given access to the adoption process in return for providing input from research into the process. Our role as researchers would be twofold:

1   The more junior researcher would participate in the daily activities of the projects that were part of the adoption of lean production and was therefore appointed secretary for these projects
2   The more senior researcher would visit the company approximately 1 day per month, to give various forms of input to the adoption process, often in the form of seminars

The usage of two researchers with slightly different roles in the company can facilitate the assessment of the effects of the researchers' interventions. The more passive researcher will get opportunities to assess the effects of the more active researcher's interventions. In the analysis these effects can be treated as if generated by any person coming from within or outside the company.

6.4 Collecting Data in the Longitudinal Field Study

The longitudinal field researcher has at his or her disposal the same toolbox of methods for data collection as any case researcher, which are described in Chapter 5. However, due to the nature of the research approach, the longitudinal field researcher is likely to rely heavily on participant observation. This method is often complemented by more informal interviews and studies of documents. As always, using different data collection methods can help the researcher triangulate evidence; using the strength of one method to compensate for the weaknesses of another (Jick, 1979).

6.4.1 Main Method for Collecting Data is Participant Observation

The participant observer collects data by participating in the organization. Participant observation allows the researcher to record action as it occurs, without relying on the willingness or ability of respondents to describe their actions (Scott, 1965). What exactly this means is nicely captured in the following:

> The participant observer gathers data by participating in the daily life of the group or organization he studies. He watches people he is studying to see what situations they ordinarily meet and how they behave in them. He enters into conversations with some or all of the participants in these situations and discovers their interpretations of the events he has observed.
>
> (Becker, 1958:652)

Participant observation gives the researcher a possibility of learning the language of the group under study (Becker and Geer, 1957). Any social group will to some degree have a culture differing from that of other groups. These differences will find expression in a language whose nuances are peculiar to that group and fully understood only by its members. In interviewing we cannot fully understand this language, and we often do not understand that we do not understand and are thus likely to make errors in interpreting what is said to us. Participant observation provides a situation in which the meaning of words can be learned with great precision through the study of their use in context.

When the researcher participates in the daily activities of the people in the organization, he or she can become aware of the full meaning of hints. Participant observation is thus helpful in reading the cues that are an important part of communication (Czarniawska-Joerges, 1992). The quality of the observations that are made tend to increase if the researcher can gain the informal status of an employee. The rapport gained through being seen as an employee is valuable, since information is not withheld from the researcher for being an outsider.

The role a participant observer can take in the field can be seen as positions on a continuum (Schwartz and Schwartz, 1955). At one end of the continuum is the passive observer and at the other end the active observer. The passive participant observer attempts not to interact with the organization's members. This has benefits in terms of maintaining objectivity. However, passive participant observation may exclude the researcher from some arenas, for being an outsider.

The active participant observer uses himself or herself as the principal instrument of observation and interpretation (Sanday, 1979). Participating actively in the organization, the researcher builds an ever-growing fund of impressions that give an extensive base for interpretation and analysis (Becker and Geer, 1957). By experiencing the life of and sharing the perspectives of the subject group, the researcher can use his or her own feelings and attitudes as clues in interpreting the behaviour of those observed (Scott, 1965). The researcher's experiences of the situation can also be used in the analysis (Smircich, 1983).

The choice of being an active or passive participant observer in part depends on the research approach employed. If the study is being conducted as clinical research, the role naturally tends to lie towards the active end of the continuum. But even if the longitudinal field study is not conducted as clinical research, it will be difficult for the researcher who participates in an organization over an extended period of time, not to participate actively in the organization (Schwarz and Schwarz, 1955). What is important when active participation is used is to meticulously note down in the field notes one's own actions and any observable effects on the organization and its members. These notes then need to be considered in the analysis.

Even if the research is being conducted as clinical research, there will be plenty of opportunities for the longitudinal field researcher to conduct more passive participant observation. Just by spending time at the company, the researcher will be able to collect data that can prove useful for the analysis. Conversations can be overheard, non-verbal cues read, and who spoke to who, about what, can be observed.

6.4.2 Dealing with the Risks Associated with Participant Observation

The main risk of participant observation as a method for collecting data is the danger of 'going native'. The participant observer who has gone native gets totally immersed in the studied organization and loses the perspective necessary for a researcher. Losing the perspective means the researcher finds little that requires explanation (Scott, 1965).

One way of dealing with the risk of going native is to temporarily withdraw from the field. By allowing the researcher to withdraw regularly from the field back to the academic environment, the risk of going native can to some extent be avoided. During the periods in the academic environment, the researcher reads literature, writes up field notes and discusses with colleagues. These activities help raise the level of abstraction on what has been observed while in the field, which helps to avoid the risk of losing perspective.

The researcher remaining cognisant of being a researcher can also reduce the risk of going native. This may sound like a truism, but our experience is that that the difference between working in an organization and studying it, even if it is part of clinical research, is large enough that the risk of going native is not to be overstated.

Participant observation is also associated with emotional difficulties. These kinds of problems accompany all methods, but are especially salient when researchers use themselves as research tools in longitudinal participant observation (Barley, 1990). Meeting your respondents day after day is more difficult than making a few visits or using the telephone. Conducting a longitudinal field study is like moving into a new culture with accompanying feelings of alienation (Czarniawska-Joerges, 1993). Apart from affecting the researcher, the emotional difficulties associated with participant observation may have effects on the data that are collected. If you work long enough in one place, you tend to become involved with the observed emotional life (Schwartz and Schwartz, 1955). One negative effect this involvement could have is that the researcher finds that his or her concern with protecting and developing good relations with people in the organization interferes with the collection of data (Scott, 1965). The best advice here is simply for the researcher to be aware of this danger and avoid it as far as possible.

6.4.3 Complementary Data Gathering using Interviews and Documents

The longitudinal field researcher is also likely to use interviews as a data collection method. Often these interviews will tend to be informal, bordering on conversations, part of the process of observation (Zelditch, 1962). For instance, by engaging in conversations with organization members the researcher can gain a deeper understanding of the change process being studied. During interaction with organization members, the researcher can probe for what they feel of their current situation and the changes that are taking place.

There will be occasions when the conversations are more formalized and are more like informant interviews. These can, for instance, be used to collect data from the periods the researcher is not present at the company. Interviews can also be valuable in finding explanations to observed behaviour. The informants used for interviews can be seen as 'surrogate observers': persons who were in a situation that enabled them to observe significant events (Scott, 1965). The researcher in the field cannot possibly be everywhere, all the time (Zelditch, 1962).

More formalized interviews can of course be used, using a structured interview protocol. The same type of guidelines for conducting these applies in longitudinal field studies as in any case study. A major reason for not conducting more formalized interviews can be that they may interrupt the rapport the researcher has achieved. Being seen as an employee, rather than as a researcher, is of importance for the quality of the data obtained; using more formalized interviews may threaten the rapport gained.

A final source of data for the longitudinal field researcher is documents, such as meeting protocols, official statements, leaflets and newsletters. Documents can be useful for many types of data, in particular to keep track of events taking place before the start of the study and events that the researcher was not able to observe. The danger with documents is that they cannot always be taken at face value (Scott, 1965). Documents may not contain enough information to be of any real value or be biased in the sense they do not reflect what was said in a meeting. Documents are also subject to the dangers of selective survival (Pettigrew, 1990). The content of documents therefore needs to be cross-checked with informant interviews whenever possible.

6.4.4 *Keeping Field Notes and Other Data Records*

Participant observation requires diaries (Czarniawska-Joerges, 1992). The participant observer needs to note what is observed as accurately as possible (Van Maanen, 1979). Good notes are rich in detail and provide full or complete explanations. Good notes describe and explain the context of a comment or event and identify all actors, preferably by position, role and location in the organization under study (Martin and Turner, 1986).

Pen and paper are most likely to be used for taking field notes. The field notes then need to be transcribed using a word processor. The workload of transcribing the field notes should not be underestimated: it takes almost as much time for a researcher to type notes as the original contact. The need for transcribing notes as soon as possible after the observation is perhaps self-evident. Despite this need, at times the transcription cannot be done immediately. The researcher in the field always faces a fear of having missed something important. To overcome this fear, emphasis tends to be put on data collection. Unfortunately, as more data are collected, the easier it is to become late with transcription (Miles, 1979).

The more covert observations that the participant observer makes should not be noted down immediately. There is a great risk in the researcher jeopardizing the rapport he or she has achieved by constantly taking notes of what people say. Instead, the researcher needs to memorize the most important points of what was said and write these points down as soon as possible. The longitudinal field researcher is likely to notice that the skill in memorizing observations increases over time, since one is often forced to practise the skill of observing without taking notes.

The rapport gained with organization members is also the reason why pen and paper are likely to be most useful in taking field notes. Using a computer may work, but could act against the researcher and the informal status that has been gained. It is hard to make general recommendations; it is best for the individual researcher to rely on his or her own judgement.

The rapport is also the reason that using a tape recorder during data collection may not be a good idea. The risk of missing something has to be weighed against the advantage of not disturbing too much. There is also a more pragmatic side to the choice of using a tape recorder. Transcribing tape recordings of an extended period of interaction with organization members is an awesome task.

To facilitate the analysis task, it is advisable to set up a good system for keeping track of all the documents that tend to accumulate during longitudinal field studies. Field notes, diaries, meeting protocols and other types of documents that the researcher is likely to hoard as part of the study tend to accumulate over time, creating vast amounts of data. Our own experience shows that a good way of organizing the field notes and other data records is to keep them in the order of observation date, possibly using databases.

6.5 Analysing Longitudinal Field Data

Analysing qualitative data is a challenging task (Huberman and Miles, 1983). The challenge is to order and analyse an overwhelming amount of descriptive data (Barley, 1990). For some, the result is 'death by data asphyxiation—the slow and inexorable sinking into the swimming pool which started so cool, clear and inviting and now has become a clinging mass of maple syrup' (Pettigrew, 1990:281). The central difficulty in analysing qualitative data is that methods are not well formulated (Miles, 1979). Methods for analysis are particularly lacking for researchers interested in processes of change in organizations. Researchers undertaking process studies have therefore been forced to develop their own methods through trial and error (Van de Ven and Huber, 1990).

The analysis process described below concerns the activities that take place when the fieldwork is completed. The activities constitute the mechanics of the analysis process, in the sense that the activities are the time-consuming and more mechanical part that precedes the theory-building part. The mechanics of analysing longitudinal field data is in essence a question of data reduction.

6.5.1 Data Reduction as Analysis

Data reduction is at the core of the task of analysing qualitative data (Miles and Huberman, 1984). To help the qualitative researcher cope with the data overload that he or she encounters, qualitative data need to be reduced for any analysis to occur. Data reduction not only allows analysis, it also is analysis, since the choice of a reduction strategy or heuristic will determine what kind of analysis is possible. We therefore need to put two demands on the data reduction methods (Huberman and Miles, 1983):

1   They need to reduce the data without unduly distorting or oversimplifying them
2   They need to leave room for a wide range of alternative analytic approaches, not locking in the researcher

The steps described below are guidelines to help the longitudinal field researcher with the task of analysing data. They have proved fruitful in earlier studies. Note, however, that each researcher will probably have to develop his or her own analysis methods depending on the particular circumstances surrounding the study. In doing so, it is important to note that analysis, in the form of data reduction, occurs at all points during a study, from design through data collection, analysis and write-up.

6.5.2 Writing a Narrative of the Change Process

The starting point for the analysis is a story that narrates the sequence of events in the change process. Before writing such a narrative, it is very useful to read through all the collected material to gain familiarity with it. The material needs to be read with an open mind at this stage, trying not to single out different aspects of the material for further elaboration. However, the material needs to be read with the research question in mind. Having read the material several times, the researcher can then type it up as a narrative in one document, compiling field notes, documents and interview protocols. Having all the collected material as one document will give the researcher a better grasp of the change process before starting the more detailed analysis.

If the researcher has been careful in recording the observations made during the study, the narrative will basically be a compilation of all field notes and documents, sorted in chronological order. The narrative needs to include all events that took place in the studied change process, transcribed as closely from the original sources as possible. Whatever interpretation the researcher makes of the material at this stage of the analysis needs to be kept out of the narrative and be added as comments.

6.5.3 Dividing the Narrative for Further Analysis

In the second stage of the analysis, the narrative exposing the studied change process needs to be divided to permit further analysis. The division is done to arrive at the basic element of information—the datum. A datum is to be entered into a data file for analysing temporal event sequences in the change process (Van de Ven and Poole, 1990). A qualitative datum can be defined as: (1) a bracketed string of words capturing the basic elements of information, (2) about a discrete incident or occurrence (the unit of analysis), (3) that happened on a specific date, which is (4) entered as a unique record in a qualitative data file and (5) is subsequently coded and classified as an indicator of a theoretical event.

The qualitative datum in a process study can be termed an 'incident'. It is important here to distinguish between an incident (which is a raw datum) and an event (which is a theoretical construct). Whereas an incident is an empirical observation, an event is not directly observed; it is a conceptual construct in a model that explains the occurrence of incidents. For each event one can choose any number of incidents as indicators that the event has happened.

Thus a qualitative datum is a bracketed string of words about a discrete incident. Explicit decision rules are needed to bracket raw words. These decision rules of course need to reflect the purpose and focus of the research. A few examples will illustrate. As with many decision rules in qualitative research, some further subjective judgements are involved in defining incidents in an operationally consistent manner.

Researchers in the Minnesota Innovation Research Program used as a rule to bracket words using their definition of incident: a major recurrent activity or change in any of the five core concepts (Van de Ven and Poole, 1990):

- People—the people involved in an incident, the roles and activities they perform at a given point in time
- Ideas—the ideas or strategies used by innovation group members to describe the content of an innovation
- Transactions—the informal and formal relationships among innovation group members, other firms and groups involved in the incident
- Context—exogenous events outside of the innovation unit in the larger organization and industry, which affected the innovation
- Outcomes—evidence of results of the innovation, being positive, negative or mixed/neutral

When each incident was identified, the bracketed string or words required to describe it included: date of occurrence, the actor(s) or object(s) involved, the action or behaviour that occurred, the consequence (if any) of the action and the source of the information.

In our study, an incident was defined as an occurrence that either facilitated or impeded the process of adopting lean production. The starting point for defining the incidents was the narrative and in particular the experiences of the actors involved in the adoption process, expressed through their language. The incidents were defined by reading the narrative a number of times and bracketing the incidents each time a transition in meaning in the narrative was experienced. An incident was therefore not necessarily equal to one sentence in the narrative. The number of sentences could vary and it was the basic meaning of the incident that was of interest.

6.5.4 Coding Incidents

As a third step in the analysis, the incidents need to be coded into qualitative event constructs. The list of incidents is, in itself, not particularly useful for further analysis. Therefore, the next step is to code incidents into theoretically meaningful events. It is important here to note the nature of codes:

> A code is an abbreviation or symbol applied to a segment of words . . . in order to classify the words. Codes are categories . . . They are retrieval and organizing devices.
>
> (Miles and Huberman, 1984:56)

Providing explicit recommendations on how to create codes is impossible. However, it is possible to outline a few guidelines on the nature of codes. At one extreme the codes can be taken from theory or at the other extreme derived from the data. Which of these two extremes is chosen depends on the nature of the research, whether it is theory-generating or theory-testing. Given that longitudinal field studies tend to be conducted to generate theory, an approach where codes are derived from data is likely to be used.

It is important to note here, that even though the data is used as a starting point for creating codes, it is the researcher who creates the codes. This applies even in the most extreme case of using the data to creating the codes. At this extreme end, the starting point for devising codes is the experiences of the individuals—what actors perceived as being important—expressed through their language. The terms individuals use comprise the fundamental material and the coding task is that of meaningfully abstracting from this material (Normann, 1980).

In the less extreme case of creating codes, the researcher is likely to use a combination of the data and theory to create codes. Nevertheless, the same applies—it is the researcher who creates the codes, using the data as an important or perhaps the most important, source of inspiration. This lies within the nature of theory-building research.

Since it is the researcher who designs the coding system, it does not necessarily correspond to the way in which participants see the incidents. It is still necessary to test empirically whether the researcher's classifications are consistent with practitioners' common perceptions of events. If the evidence indicates inconsistency, researchers can still sustain claims about the meaning of the incident from their theoretical position, but no claims about the social reality of the event are appropriate (Van de Ven and Poole, 1990).

6.5.5 Entering Incidents in a Database

To include the full meaning of an incident, each incident can be coded on more than one dimension of an event (Van de Ven and Poole, 1990). One way to organize these multidimensional data into a format to analyse change processes is to array them on multiple tracks that correspond to conceptually meaningful categories. Within each conceptual track a number of more specific codes is possible, depending on the particular questions being addressed by the researcher.

It is useful for the further analysis to code and enter the incidents in a database or using a software program such as NudIST©. Using a database will give the researcher an opportunity to keep track of all incidents in an efficient manner. It is useful to describe the incidents fully enough to avoid the need for backtracking to the notes to recall details (Martin and Turner, 1986). Using a database will enable the researcher to search for all incidents with a certain code, to see how the code was used.

The definition of the codes used for the coding process needs to be kept separate in a database. Using a database will facilitate going back to the codes' definition when necessary. A database will also make it possible to modify the definition to take into account new information, should it become necessary. This is in line with the inductive way in which most longitudinal field studies are designed. We are interested in developing theory, not testing theory.

6.5.6 Sorting and Recoding to Separate Important Events

With the coded incidents as a basis, the analysis of the data can now continue. Before coming to the stage of the analysis where patterns are sought, inferences made and cause and effect are determined, an intermediate stage may often be necessary. In this stage the list of incidents is scrutinized carefully, incidents are sorted and perhaps recoded. The aim is to separate out the important events from the less important.

Whether this intermediate stage is necessary or not and the exact nature of the stage depends on many different things. It is therefore very difficult to make general recommendations here. However, the researcher will most likely realize whether this intermediate stage is necessary or not. The research question that the research is trying to answer will have a big impact on whether an intermediate stage is needed or not.

The need for an intermediate stage and its nature will also depend on how focused the data collection was in the first place. The importance of focusing data collection was stressed earlier in the chapter. It is at this stage of the analysis the researcher will start getting the benefit of a focused data collection. Or conversely, if the data collection has not been that focused, using a conceptual framework as a starting point, this stage of the analysis can become very cumbersome indeed.

What particularly determines whether the intermediate stage is necessary or not, is the complexity inherent in the coded incidents. This complexity is partly a function of both the research question and how focused data collection was. The complexity is also determined by the amount of time the researcher spent in the organization and how much data were collected. The number of incidents is one indicator of the complexity inherent in the coded incidents.

The intermediate stage of the analysis aims at separating out the important events from the less important. This can be done in different ways. A fruitful way of working can be to start by sorting the incidents in various ways, reading and re-coding them. This process essentially means that the researcher switches between the whole and the parts; between a string of incidents and an individual incident. The rationale for switching between the whole and the parts is that coding an incident is easier when each incident is seen in relation to other incidents.

A tool in this stage of the analysis is to use printouts of all the incidents sorted in different ways. Several different rounds of recoding are probably necessary, each round with the incidents sorted in different ways, depending on the research question. Each round needs to share two characteristics: it should involve a search for incidents indicating recurring events and an elimination of those incidents that do not indicate recurring events. At least one of the rounds should have the incidents sorted in chronological order.

The importance of separating out important events retrospectively should not be underestimated. What may have seemed important during data collection is not necessarily important in the retrospective analysis: 'time itself sets a frame of reference that directly affects our perceptions of change' (Van de Ven, 1993:318). Therefore the retrospective analysis is often to be trusted more than the initial assessment of an incident's importance. This does not invalidate the initial judgement made during data collection, but the whole picture is needed to be able to relate the details to it. For instance, not all incidents that were collected will have a significant effect. This is particularly valid for those incidents that were related to individuals that turned out to have only ephemeral roles in the studied change process (Leonard-Barton, 1990).

Graphical techniques are also useful tools in the intermediate stage of the analysis. After several rounds of sorting and re-coding, the researcher may still have hundreds or even thousands of incidents left for further analysis. With this number of incidents, it is easy to get lost in detail if only text is used. Remember the old adage: 'a picture says more than a thousand words'.

Exactly how graphical techniques can be used is of course highly dependent on the research question. One way of working is to convert lists of incidents to graphical displays consisting of a timeline with an 'X' marking each incident. These timelines often need to be created at different levels of analysis, for instance for each event. The displays are useful for assessing the importance of different events, since the displays give an overview of the change process. It is important to note that it is not simply a matter of assessing the importance of an event and excluding incidents based on simple counting. Both the graphical displays and printouts of the incidents need to be used, together with the researcher's judgement and insights gained during the fieldwork.

Regardless of what tools are used, this intermediate stage is likely to lead to reduced complexity in the further analysis. Incidents are re-coded; events may be taken out or merged. It is here useful to exclude incidents from analysis technically through a code in the database. The actual incidents should still be kept for reference in the further analysis.

6.6 Building Theory from Longitudinal Field Studies

After having gone through the more mechanical side of the analysis task, the more creative part follows. It is at this stage that the collected data are used as the basis to develop theory, hypotheses or models. Giving general recommendations exactly on how to proceed here is naturally impossible. What we can offer are some general guidelines. The difficulty of explicitly describing exactly how analysis takes place is compounded by the fact that interpretation and analysis begin in the field and continue throughout the whole process (Berg, 1981). The researcher should not expect to proceed in a linear fashion from raw data to final theory. The process is self-consciously and intentionally non-linear and iterative (Martin and Turner, 1986).

An important part of the analysis is going on when data are still being collected (Barley, 1990). The researcher conducting a longitudinal field study builds an overgrowing fund of impressions, many of them at the subliminal level, which give an extensive base for the interpretation and analytic use of data (Becker and Geer, 1957). While collecting data, the researcher needs to write down whatever impressions occur; to react to rather than to sift out what may seem important (Eisenhardt, 1989). When noting down the impressions it is useful to let them stand out in the field notes, so that impressions are not mixed with observations.

6.6.1 Seeking Underlying Mechanisms through Sequences and Patterns

In building theory from longitudinal field studies, it is important to remember that the basis for the analysis task is the events indicated by the incidents. Thus, the incidents are the raw material for the analysis, but what we are interested in are the events underlying the incidents. Concerning the level of analysis and interpretation, a differentiation can be made between surface and in-depth interpretations (Berg, 1981). Surface interpretations deal with the easily apparent and observable, whereas in-depth interpretations deal with the underlying latent structures and processes.

Key to identifying underlying mechanisms in longitudinal field data is sequence analysis (Van de Ven and Poole, 1990). Sequence analysis is concerned with determining temporal order and relationships and patterns among events. This pattern will gradually evolve during the analysis process, not suddenly emerge (Berg, 1981). The coded data that were the outcome of the previous, more mechanical, stage of the analysis are scanned for sequences. The pattern is, in a sense, generated as the researcher works with the data. Once a sequence or patterns of events is found to exist, one can turn to questions about what the causes or consequences are of the events within the process pattern (Van de Ven and Huber, 1990). These are the underlying mechanisms, the in-depth interpretations.

6.6.2 Techniques for Identifying Sequences and Patterns

In determining sequences and patterns, the researcher is greatly helped by using different techniques for data analysis. The objective should be for the longitudinal field researcher to avoid relying exclusively on subjective eye-balling and anecdotal information in qualitative data (Van de Ven and Poole, 1990). The intention is not to make the analysis process standardized and mechanical, but to combine the rich insights that are gained during the field work with more systematic techniques. Two types of techniques are highly useful for the longitudinal field researcher—graphical and quantitative techniques.

Graphical techniques are simply visual models that help the researcher visualize data, patterns and sequences (Berg, 1981). These can range from simple figures to complex displays of relationships between events and constructs, covering several square metres. It is difficult to give general advice, apart from noting that a graphical display is an indispensable way for the researcher to gain an overview over large amounts of qualitative data. For the longitudinal field researcher, displaying the pattern of coded incidents in various ways is often very fruitful. Regardless of how the displays are made, it is important to note that the display modes chosen will inevitably condition the processes and conclusions of the analysis (Huberman and Miles, 1983). One piece of advice is therefore to use a variety of display modes.

The longitudinal field researcher can make also good use of traditional quantitative analytical methods in order to find regularities or patterns that might be hidden in the material. Included among these quantitative tools is simple counting, which enables researchers to remove nagging doubts about the accuracy of their impressions about the data (Silverman, 1993). The data can also be subjected to more rigorous statistical treatment. Van de Ven and Poole (1990) recommend transforming qualitative codes into quantitative dichotomous categories, using one for presence or zero for absence of a qualitative incident. This will permit applying various statistical methods to examine time-dependent patterns of relation among event constructs. Regardless of approach chosen, our position is that quantitative methods should be seen as tools by means of which hidden information might be washed out of the data, information that makes sense only when related to the interpretation made by the researcher.

6.6.3　Comparing the Emerging Theory with Literature

When the longitudinal field researcher is analysing the data, the concepts that are used to describe and explain the process of change are generally derived from and grounded in the data, and not from a preconceived theoretical framework. However, this does not deny the value of theoretical concepts derived from existing frameworks. On the contrary, existing concepts and theories are very valuable for connecting the concepts that are developed with a wider theoretical framework. Most important of all, existing theories can be used as creative devices in the search for sequences and patterns (Berg, 1981).

An essential feature of theory building is comparison of the emergent concepts, theory or hypotheses with existing literature (Eisenhardt, 1989). This involves asking what is this similar to, what does it contradict, and why. A key to this process is to consider a broad range of literature, particularly since longitudinal field studies tend to rest on few cases:

- Literature that discusses similar findings in different contexts is important since it ties together underlying similarities in phenomena normally not associated with each other. The result is often a theory with stronger internal validity and wider generalizability
- Literature which conflicts with the emergent theory is equally important to consider. Taking conflicting literature into account strengthens the confidence in the findings and forces the researcher into more creative thinking

The importance of creative thinking should not be underestimated. Building theory is not only a mechanical process, which takes the researcher from raw data to models and hypotheses. When building theory, researchers design, conduct and interpret imaginary experiments (Weick, 1989). If we are to develop knowledge that is really new, then we do not know the answer in advance. The significant discovery requires a high degree of uncertainty and ambiguity at the outset (Daft, 1983). Theory building involves a significant degree of guess work, the making up and revising of hypotheses in disciplined thought experiments.

The way theory is developed from longitudinal field studies shares an important characteristic with all case research—it is subjected to the myth that the theory-building process is limited by the researcher's preconceptions. In general, just the opposite tends to be true:

> The constant juxtaposition of conflicting realities tends to 'unfreeze' thinking, and so the process has the potential to generate theory with less researcher bias than theory built from incremental studies or armchair, axiomatic deduction.
>
> (Eisenhardt, 1989:546)

However, there are also some weaknesses, most importantly that the longitudinal field researcher gets stuck in details and is unable to raise the level of generality of the theory. The researcher must also avoid the idiosyncrasies of a particular case.

6.6.4 Presenting the Developed Theory

The final challenge for the longitudinal field researcher is to present the huge amount of rich data that have been collected, so that the presentation provides evidence for the developed theory (Huberman and Miles, 1983). In this respect, the challenges are the same as for any case research, see Chapter 5. The challenges are frequently compounded due to the often large amounts of data that are collected in longitudinal field studies. Critical in writing up longitudinal field studies is to illustrate to the reader how the author arrived at the conclusions (Åhlström, 2007). Few general recommendations can be made here. It is up to the individual researcher to use his or her own judgement and inventive abilities to find ways to present the data. The use of graphical techniques can be strongly recommended. Graphs can offer a means to survey the whole corpus of data ordinarily lost in qualitative research. Instead of taking the researcher's word for it, the reader has a chance to gain a sense of the data (Silverman, 1993).

The graphs can be complemented with illustrations from the huge amount of rich qualitative data the researcher is likely to have collected, for instance through excerpts from the database of incidents. The main purpose of the excerpts should be to introduce to the reader parts of the researcher's own learning process, in reaching the conclusions, to facilitate the reader's learning process (Normann, 1980). The use of excerpts should not be seen as a way of proving a point. All usage of interview excerpts is subject to subjective choice. The use of shorter excerpts can often be chosen in favour of a lengthy narrative of the adoption process, since a narrative does not always add enough value to the reader's understanding.

6.7 Evaluating Theory from Longitudinal Field Studies

An important premise for evaluating the research findings derived from longitudinal field studies is that the value of research findings must be seen in relation to the way in which they were derived (Berg, 1981). Therefore, we first need to discuss the qualitative nature of the inquiry that characterizes the longitudinal field study. Qualitative research is normally contrasted with quantitative research based on which techniques have been used for data collection and analysis. Proponents of quantitative research, in this technique-based view, stress the importance of reliability, validity and accurate measurement before research outcomes can contribute to knowledge (Daft, 1983). Objectivity is another concept celebrated by quantitative researchers (Kirk and Miller, 1986).

However, distinguishing qualitative from quantitative research, based on which techniques are used for data collection and analysis, cannot absorb the diversity of uses to which the qualitative label applies (Van Maanen, 1983). Qualitative researchers are more interested in the meaning, rather than the measurement, of organizational phenomena (Daft, 1983). Qualitative research is best seen as an approach rather than a set of techniques (Morgan and Smircich, 1980). Nothing excludes the qualitative researcher from using data collection and analysis techniques considered 'quantitative', such as statistical techniques (Daft, 1983).

The standards used for judging quantitative studies are inappropriate for judging qualitative studies (Agar, 1986). This does not mean that no standards are applicable to qualitative research; qualitative research is not less scientific than quantitative research (Silverman, 1993). It is a matter of using different ways of ensuring reliability and validity in qualitative research. We must ensure that the longitudinal field study is not done as 'industrial tourism'. Rigour must be applied both in research design, data collection and analysis.

The description of reliability and validity ordinarily provided by quantitative researchers needs to be modified to fit qualitative research (Kirk and Miller, 1986). A qualitative approach requires the reader to be able to make judgements about components of the research process leading to the final product (Strauss and Corbin, 1990). Qualitative research is scientific in that the collection, analysis and reporting of data are done systematically, with care and discipline (Smircich, 1983). The researcher's task is in no small part to convince the reader the findings are reasonable, drawn from material that has been processed by methods that can be explicitly described.

6.7.1 Increasing Reliability through a Systematic Research Process

Reliability for a quantitative researcher means that if another researcher replicates a study, the same results would be obtained (Yin, 1989). In a longitudinal field study, this demand is probably very hard, or even impossible, to live up to. So many things come in between the ability to exactly replicate the findings. For a researcher conducting longitudinal field studies, reliability therefore translates to demands on the research process: 'reliability depends essentially on explicitly described observational procedures' (Kirk and Miller, 1986:41). Two aspects of data collection are particularly relevant: making the observations and writing up field notes.

While collecting data, the researcher needs to pay continual and careful attention to the details of his or her adventures in the field (Van Maanen, 1979). There is first of all a need to separate first- and second-order concepts. First-order concepts are the facts of the investigation and second-order concepts are the theories the researcher uses to organize and explain the facts. During data collection, the researcher needs to be careful not to mix the observations with the interpretation of the observations. In the field notes this may for example be done through using different typefaces. During the analysis process, the interpretation of coded incidents needs to be kept away from the actual observations, for instance through being entered in a separate field of the database.

During the field work there is also a need to pay constant attention to the distinction between observational and presentational data (Van Maanen, 1979). Observational data refer to observed activity. Presentational data concern those appearances informants strive to maintain or enhance. Making the separation between the two types of data is an analytical task to be carried out while in the field, although the line separating the two types is not always distinct. Both types of data are useful, since the intentionally subjective picture given by presentational data can be an extremely important asset, since it provides the researcher with additional information on the organization being studied (Berg, 1981).

Longitudinal observation facilitates the task of separating observational data from presentational data, since people will find it difficult to monitor their behaviour for a long period of time (Barley, 1990). Through spending a significant amount of time in the field and participating in daily interaction, the longitudinal field researcher will gain knowledge of how to read the cues that are part of communication, which helps in separating observational from presentational data.

A final detail to pay attention to while conducting the fieldwork is whether informants speak the truth, as they know it (Van Maanen, 1979). There may be different reasons why false information is given. Informants may want to mislead the researcher. Informants may also themselves be misled or wrong about their own matters. To overcome both these reasons for not speaking the truth, the researcher needs to rely on the information provided by the most knowledgeable members of the organization (Van Maanen, 1979). Who these informants are is very much linked to the research question. A benefit of clinical research if employed in a longitudinal field study is that informants are less likely to conceal the truth since the researcher is there to help (Argyris, 1968).

The reliability of longitudinal field studies is also increased through proper field notes (Kirk and Miller, 1986). There is a need to 'conduct research as if someone were always looking over your shoulder' (Yin, 1989:45). Information on how and in what contexts field notes were recorded is needed (Silverman, 1993). Apart from the observation, the following information needs to be noted, at a minimum: when the observation was made, in what forum and which actors were present. Furthermore, field notes must conform to two requirements (Kirk and Miller, 1986). First, they must be legible and chronologically ordered. Second, although the field notes do intrinsically involve the observer, the field notes must differentiate between what people said and the researcher's interpretation.

Finally, the researcher needs to be able to demonstrate as clearly as possible how he or she reached the conclusions. This requires the researcher to as carefully and accurately as possible document and describe the analytical processes that lead from data to final analysis (Huberman and Miles, 1983). The description particularly needs to be of the data reduction procedures described earlier, the more mechanical side of the analysis task. Although this would not necessarily lead to replicability, it does allow the reader to follow how the researcher arrived at his or her conclusions.

6.7.2 Increasing Validity through the Research Design and Coding Process

Validity for the quantitative researcher is whether the instrument measures what it is supposed to measure (Yin, 1989). There are several ways to increase the validity of longitudinal field studies. First it is important to note that the research design itself is a way of increasing validity. Given that longitudinal field studies are used for researching change processes in organizations, the research design increases validity: making real-time observations increases the validity of a study compared with retrospective research (Leonard-Barton, 1990).

Longitudinal field studies can be validated by triangulation: using multiple methods and sources of data (Silverman, 1993). Apart from participant observation, interviews and documents, studies within OM can often benefit from using quantitative measures of performance outcomes. These measures can be used to help determine effects of the change process that is being studied. When collecting data using multiple methods, one way of increasing validity is to transcribe the field notes as soon as possible (Schwartz and Schwartz, 1955).

For the qualitative observation, the issue of validity is to a certain degree a question of whether or not the researcher is calling what is measured by the right name (Kirk and Miller, 1986). This means that the coding process employed in the longitudinal field study has implications for validity. Codes developed after data collection are less likely to be biased by the researcher's own fantasies, since the categories emerge from and remain closer to the data (Barley, 1990). Participant observation helps increase the validity of the coding procedure. The participant observer has tested partial analyses for a period of time prior to the actual coding (Glaser and Strauss, 1967). During data collection, the researcher acts on tentative conclusions based on his or her current understanding of the situation. If this understanding is invalid, the researcher will sooner or later find out about it (Kirk and Miller, 1986). Validity can also be increased by respondent validation; feeding back the research findings to the studied organization's members research and see whether it provides them with a meaningful explanation (Berg, 1981). However, there are risks associated with respondent validation. One risk is that individuals recognize themselves in the material, despite necessary attempts to cover up the data. It can also be that the respondents do not agree with the researcher's interpretation. This can lead to demands on the researcher to change the interpretation. At the very least, this process is time-consuming and can in some environments lead to threats of legal action (compare Miles, 1979).

Related to respondent validation is whether the research results can be communicated to and understood by other people (Normann, 1980). Are the findings understandable to individuals who have some familiarity with the phenomena under study (Turner, 1983)? One way of validating the research findings is by letting colleagues experienced in the study's focus read and comment on the research results.

To complement these more traditional ways of validating qualitative research, simple counting procedures or statistical techniques can be used (Silverman, 1993). The methods of generalizing to a larger population are a way of increasing the validity of a study's findings.

6.7.3 Generalizing from Longitudinal Field Studies

The ability to generalize has widely been considered a barrier for case studies, particularly for single case studies (Yin, 1989). Single case studies resulting from longitudinal field studies obviously cannot be generalized in the statistical sense. Statistical generalization is, however, not the aim.

The ability to generalize is related to the way in which corroboration takes place (Spencer and Dale, 1979). Quantitative studies rely on multiplicative corroboration; a multiplication of evidence (Pepper, 1942). Qualitative studies, on the other hand, rely on a structure of evidence; structural corroboration (Spencer and Dale, 1979). The persuasive force in structural corroboration comes from assembling a mass of evidence converging on the same point (Pepper, 1942).

An example illustrates the difference between the two methods of corroboration. Suppose I want to find out if a chair is strong enough to hold my weight. I can ask several people of my approximate weight to sit on the chair, one at a time. If the chair holds these people, it should be strong enough to hold my weight. The problem has been solved through multiplicative corroboration.

Another way of solving the problem of the chair's strength is by examining the relevant facts about the chair. What kind of material is it made of? Are the chair's legs thick enough? How is the chair joined together? Have the makers of the chair got a reputation for making solid chairs? Putting all this evidence together, it is possible to conclude whether the chair is strong enough to hold my weight. This process of giving evidence is structural corroboration.

Using structural corroboration to generalize from a longitudinal field study can be done by comparing the findings with something outside the study (Berg, 1981). The general value of the findings will increase if they can be supported by observations from other organizations or from other theoretical frameworks. It is here that the comparison with existing theory plays an important role, a comparison taking place during the analysis of data.

When discussing generalization, one needs to bear in mind that generalization from case studies takes place towards theory, not towards samples and universes (Yin, 1989). The value of in-depth single case studies lies in their capability to be used for developing and refining concepts and frameworks which can be generalized (Pettigrew, 1985). Results of in-depth studies of single organizations can also be cumulative (Miller and Mintzberg, 1983). Therefore, we agree with Herbert Simon, a pioneer of research on organizations:

> If we are concerned about the imprecision of case studies as research data, we can console ourselves by noting that a man named Darwin was able to write a very persuasive (perhaps even correct) book on the

origin of species on the basis of a study of the Galapagos Islands and a few other cases.

(Simon, 1991:128)

Apart from theoretical generalization, there is a more practical side to the issue of generalization. Researchers in OM are often interested in arriving at conclusions with potential practical applicability. When generalizing from single cases to the practical arena, it is the receivers of the information that must determine whether or not it applies to their own situation (Kennedy, 1979). Although one may be a bit unaccustomed to the notion of leaving generalization up to the practitioner, it is not an uncommon occurrence in other fields, such as law and clinical medicine.

6.8 Examples of Important Longitudinal Studies

As discussed in section 6.1.3, like other academic fields, OM does not contain many longitudinal field studies conducted inside organizations. Within OM, broadly defined, three longitudinal studies stand out:

- The Minnesota Innovation Research Programme (Van de Ven et al., 1989). This landmark work involved a large team of researchers over 5 years. It is not a single project but rather many research projects guided by a common research framework, all employing the longitudinal field study method. The level of detail in which the methods applied are described, for instance by Van de Ven and Poole (1990), makes it a good role model for any researcher interested in longitudinal field studies. The studies have also spawned a great deal of prestigious publications
- Leonard-Barton's work on the implementation of technology (see for instance Leonard-Barton, 1988). This study contains an interesting combination of a longitudinal field study and several retrospective cases. The employed methodology has been well described in Leonard-Barton (1990), and is a good example of well-conducted case research, which employs the longitudinal field study as one part
- Our own work on the implementation of lean production (at length reported in Åhlström, 1997). This study is a 2.5 year longitudinal field study of one company, adopting lean production

In addition to these three studies, those interested in conducting longitudinal field studies can also consult the work of Andrew Pettigrew. Although in another academic field, Pettigrew has over a long period of time, together with various other scholars, conducted longitudinal research on organizations. A few sample references are Pettigrew, 1985, 1990 and 1992.

6.9 Summary

- **Introduction to the longitudinal field study**. Longitudinal field studies are in-depth studies of change processes inside organizations. They are case studies, with two features distinguishing them. First, longitudinal research implies studying a phenomenon over time. Second, the longitudinal field study is a real-time study of an organizational phenomenon, with the researcher being present in the organization often for long periods of time. Often they are used for generating theories of change processes, since they enable the researcher to better observe cause and effect. OM, like many other fields, does not contain many longitudinal field studies, primarily because they require a significant commitment and organizational access

- **Setting up the longitudinal field study**. Research questions suitable for longitudinal field studies concern how organizational changes emerge, develop, grow or terminate over time. Organizations suitable for longitudinal field studies are those where the change process is likely to be transparently observable, but they are not always easy to find. Before entering the field, a framework for data gathering is critical. Data need to be gathered from a position in the organization, where organization members are likely to be most knowledgeable about the change process being studied. Because of the nature of longitudinal field studies, the researcher attempting them needs skills resembling those of an investigative reporter, where attention to detail is paramount

- **Setting up the longitudinal field study as clinical research**. One important reason behind the relative lack of longitudinal field studies is the difficulty of gaining access to organizations. To gain access, a longitudinal field study can be set up as clinical research. In clinical research, the researcher participates in and studies organizational change. Defining research issues that are beneficial both for theory and practice is critical in clinical research. Different kinds of change processes can provide a fruitful basis for achieving practical and theoretical benefits. The clinical research needs to be set up to create involvement of the researcher while at the same time allowing the researcher to develop theory as the change process is unfolding

- **Collecting data in the longitudinal field study**. The longitudinal field researcher has at his or her disposal the same toolbox of methods for data collection as any case researcher. However, the longitudinal field researcher is likely to rely heavily on participant observation. To deal with the risk of going native, it is important to regularly withdraw from the field back to the academic environment. Participant observation requires careful and meticulous note taking, together with a system to organize the collected data. Participant observation is often complemented by more informal interviews and studies of documents

- **Analysing longitudinal field data**. Analysing longitudinal field data is a challenging task due to the often huge amounts of data being collected and the lack of well-defined methods for data analysis. A certain amount of invention is therefore critical, central to which is a process of data reduction. The more mechanical side of the analysis process starts with the writing of a narrative of the change process. The narrative is then divided into basic units of information, or incidents, using explicit decision rules. The third step of the analysis process is to code incidents, for retrieval and organizing purposes. To help keep track of the coded incidents, databases are useful tools. The incidents are finally sorted and recoded, for instance using graphical techniques

- **Building theory from longitudinal field studies**. The more creative part of the analysis process, the generation of theory, starts while the researcher is still in the field. Therefore field notes should distinguish observations from the interpretation of them. The starting point for building theory is the incidents, but we are interested in the mechanisms and events underlying them. The analysis requires identifying sequences and patterns in the events, for instance using graphical techniques. The theory thus developed needs to be constantly compared with existing theory. Finally, presenting longitudinal field studies is a real challenge, requiring a certain amount of innovation from the researcher

- **Evaluating theory from longitudinal field studies**. The evaluation of longitudinal field studies needs to be made in relation to how the findings are derived. The longitudinal field researcher is more interested in the meaning of phenomena, rather than their measurement; but rigour is still very important. To increase the reliability, the researcher needs to adhere to a systematic research process. Validity is enhanced through the research design and through a systematic coding process. Generalization in longitudinal field studies is always towards theory, not samples, since they tend to rely heavily on a few cases

References and Bibliography

Agar, M. H. (1986), *Speaking of Ethnography*, Sage University Paper series on Qualitative Research Methods, Volume 2, Sage, Beverly Hills, California.

Åhlström, P. (1997), *Sequences in the Process of Adopting Lean Production*, EFI, Stockholm.

Åhlström, P. (2007), 'Presenting Qualitative Research: Convincing through Illustrating the Analysis Process', *Journal of Purchasing and Supply Management*, Vol. 13, No 3, pp. 216–218.

Argyris, C. (1968), 'Some Unintended Consequences of Rigorous Research', *Psychological Bulletin*, Vol. 70, No. 3, pp. 185–197.

Barley, S. R. (1990), 'Images of Imaging: Notes on Doing Longitudinal Field Work', *Organization Science*, Vol. 1, No. 3, pp. 220–247.

Becker, H. S. (1958), 'Problems of Inference and Proof in Participant Observation', *American Sociological Review*, Vol. 23, pp. 652–660.

Becker, H. S. and Geer, B. (1957), 'Participant Observation and Interviewing: A Comparison', *Human Organization*, Vol. 16, No. 3, pp. 28–32.

Berg, C. (1974), *Samrådssystemet: En klinisk undersökning i ett växande företag* (The Participation System: A Clinical Study of a Growing Company. in Swedish), EFI, Stockholm.

Berg, P-O. (1981), *Emotional Structures in Organizations: A Study of the Process of Change in a Swedish Company*, Studentlitteratur, Lund.

Clark, P. A. and Ford, J. R. (1970), 'Methodological and Theoretical Problems in the Investigation of Planned Organisational Change', *Sociological Review*, March, pp. 29–52.

Czarniawska-Joerges, B. (1992), *Exploring Complex Organizations: A Cultural Perspective*, Sage, Newbury Park, California.

Czarniawska-Joerges, B. (1993), *The Three-Dimensional Organization: A Constructionist View*, Studentlitteratur, Lund.

Daft, R. L. (1983), 'Learning the Craft of Organizational Research', *Academy of Management Review*, Vol. 8, No. 4, pp. 539–546.

Eisenhardt, K. M. (1989), 'Building Theories from Case Study Research', *Academy of Management Review*, Vol. 14, No. 4, pp. 532–550.

Flanagan, J. C. (1954), 'The Critical Incident Technique', *Psychological Bulletin*, Vol. 51, No. 4, pp. 327–358.

Glaser, B. G. and Strauss, A. L. (1967), *The Discovery of Grounded Theory: Strategies for Qualitative Research*, Aldine de Gruyter, New York.

Huberman, A. M. and Miles, M. B. (1983), 'Drawing Valid Meaning from Qualitative Data: Some Techniques of Data Reduction and Display', *Quality and Quantity*, Vol. 17, pp. 281–339.

Jaques, E. (1951), *The Changing Culture of a Factory: A Study of Authority and Participation in an Industrial Setting*, Tavistock, London.

Jick, T. D. (1979), 'Mixing Qualitative and Quantitative Methods: Triangulation in Action', *Administrative Science Quarterly*, Vol. 24, No. 4, pp. 602–611.

Kennedy, M. M. (1979), 'Generalizing from Single Case Studies', *Evaluation Quarterly*, Vol. 3, No. 4, pp. 661–678.

Kirk, J. and Miller, M. L. (1986), *Reliability and Validity in Qualitative Research*, Sage, Beverly Hills, California.

Leonard-Barton, D. (1988), 'Implementation as Mutual Adaption of Techonology and Organization', *Research Policy*, Vol. 17, pp. 251–267.

Leonard-Barton, D. (1990), 'A Dual Methodology for Case Studies: Synergistic Use of a Longitudinal Single Site With Replicated Multiple Sites', *Organization Science*, Vol. 1, No. 1, pp. 248–266.

Martin, P. Y. and Turner, B. A. (1986), 'Grounded Theory and Organizational Research', *The Journal of Applied Behavioral Science*, Vol. 22, No. 2, pp. 141–157.

Miles, M. B. (1979), 'Qualitative Data as an Attractive Nuisance: The Problem of Analysis', *Administrative Science Quarterly*, Vol. 24, No. 4, pp. 590–601.

Miles, M. B. and Huberman, A. M. (1984), *Qualitative Data Analysis: A Sourcebook of New Methods*, Sage, Beverly Hills, California.

Miller, D. and Friesen, P. H. (1982), 'The Longitudinal Analysis of Organizations: A Methodological Perspective', *Management Science*, Vol. 28, No. 9, pp. 1013–1034.

Miller, D. and Mintzberg, H. (1983), 'The Case for Configuration', in Morgan, G. (Ed.), *Beyond Method: Strategies for Social Research*, Sage, Newbury Park, California, pp. 57–73.

Morgan, G. (1983), 'Research as Engagement: A Personal View', in Morgan, G. (Ed.), *Beyond Method: Strategies for Social Research*, Sage, Newbury Park, California, pp. 11–18.

Morgan, G. and Smircich, L. (1980), 'The Case for Qualitative Research', *Academy of Management Review*, Vol. 5, No. 4, pp. 491–500.

Normann, R. (1980), *A Personal Quest for Methodology* (Fourth Edition), SIAR Dokumentation, Stockholm.

Pepper, S. C. (1942), *World Hypotheses*, University of California Press, Berkeley, California.

Pettigrew, A. M. (1985), 'Contextualist Research and the Study of Organisational Change Processes', in Mumford, E. et al. (Eds.), *Research Methods in Information Systems*, North Holland, Amsterdam, pp. 53–78.

Pettigrew, A. M. (1990), 'Longitudinal Field Research on Change: Theory and Practice', *Organization Science*, Vol. 1, No. 3, pp. 267–292.

Pettigrew, A. M. (1992), 'The Character and Significance of Strategy Process Research', *Strategic Management Journal*, Vol. 13, pp. 5–16.

Rapoport, R. N. (1970), 'Three Dilemmas in Action Research', *Human Relations*, Vol. 23, pp. 499–513.

Sanday, P. R. (1979), 'The Ethnographic Paradigm(s),' *Administrative Science Quarterly*, Vol. 24, No. 4, pp. 527–538.

Schein, E. H. (1987), *The Clinical Perspective in Fieldwork*, Sage, Newbury Park, California.

Schwartz, M. S. and Schwartz, C. G. (1955), 'Problems in Participant Observation', *American Journal of Sociology*, Vol. 60, pp. 343–353.

Schön, D. A. (1983), 'Organizational Learning', in Morgan, G. (Ed.), *Beyond Method: Strategies for Social Research*, Sage, Newbury Park, California, pp. 114–128.

Scott, W. R. (1965), 'Field Methods in the Study of Organizations', in March, J. G. (Ed.), *Handbook of Organizations*, Rand McNally, Chicago, Illinois, pp. 261–304.

Silverman, D. (1993), *Interpreting Qualitative Data*, Sage, London.

Simon, H. A. (1991), 'Bounded Rationality and Organizational Learning', *Organization Science*, Vol. 2, No. 1, pp. 125–134.

Smircich, L. (1983), 'Studying Organizations as Cultures', in Morgan, G. (Ed.), *Beyond Method: Strategies for Social Research*, Sage, Newbury Park, California, pp. 160–172.

Sofer, C. (1961), *The Organization from within: A Comparative Study of Social Institutions Based on a Sociotherapeutic Approach*, Tavistock, London.

Spencer, L. and Dale, A. (1979), 'Integration and Regulation in Organizations: A Contextual Approach', *Sociological Review*, Vol. 27, No. 4, pp. 679–702.

Strauss, A. and Corbin, J. (1990), *Basics of Qualitative Research: Grounded Theory Procedures and Techniques*, Sage, Newbury Park, California.

Stymne, B. (1970), *Values and Processes: A Systems Study of Effectiveness in Three Organizations*, Studentlitteratur, Lund.

Turner, B. A. (1981), 'Some Practical Aspects of Qualitative Data Analysis: One Way of Organising the Cognitive Processes Associated With the Generation of Grounded Theory', *Quality and Quantity*, Vol. 15, pp. 225–247.

Turner, B. A. (1983), 'The Use of Grounded Theory for the Qualitative Analysis of Organizational Behaviour', *Journal of Management Studies*, Vol. 20, No. 3, pp. 333–348.

Van de Ven, A. H. (1993), 'An Assessment of Perspectives on Strategic Change', in

Zan, L., Zambon, S. and Pettigrew, A. M. (Eds.), *Perspectives on Strategic Change*, Kluwer Academic Press, Dordrecht, pp. 313–325.

Van de Ven, A. H., Angle, H. L. and Poole, M. S. (1989), *Research on the Management of Innovation*, Ballinger, Cambridge, MA.

Van de Ven, A. H. and Huber, G. P. (1990), 'Longitudinal Field Research Methods for Studying Processes of Organizational Change', *Organization Science*, Vol. 1, No. 3, pp. 213–219.

Van de Ven, A. H. and Poole, M. S. (1990), 'Methods for Studying Innovation Development in the Minnesota Innovation Research Program', *Organization Science*, Vol. 1, No. 3, pp. 313–335.

Van Maanen, J. (1979), 'The Fact of Fiction in Organizational Ethnography', *Administrative Science Quarterly*, Vol. 24, No. 4, pp. 539–550.

Voss, C. A. (1988), 'Implementation: A Key Issue in Manufacturing Technology: The Need for a Field of Study', *Research Policy*, Vol. 17, pp. 53–63.

Weick, K. E. (1989), 'Theory Construction as Disciplined Imagination'; *Academy of Management Review*, Vol. 14, No. 4, pp. 516–531.

Yin, R. K. (1989), *Case Study Research: Design and Methods* (Revised Edition), Sage, London.

Zelditch, M. Jr. (1962), 'Some Methodological Problems of Field Studies', *American Journal of Sociology*, Vol. 67, pp. 566–576.

7 Action Research[1]

Paul Coughlan and David Coghlan

Chapter Overview

- Action in operations management
- What is action research?
- Characteristics of action research
- Origins of action research
- What is needed before entering into action research?
- Designing an action research project
- Implementing action research
- Action research skills
- Generating theory through action research
- Quality in action research
- Writing an action research dissertation

7.1 Introduction

Action research is a generic term, which covers many forms of action-orientated research. It indicates diversity in theory and practice among action researchers, so providing a wide choice for potential action researchers as to what approach might be appropriate for their research question. The outcomes of action research are both an action and research-based knowledge which contrast with traditional positivist science, which aims at creating knowledge only. Action research has applicability to unstructured or integrative issues. It has broad relevance to practitioners and can contribute to theory. This chapter explores the themes and challenges facing OM researchers as they attempt to learn from the applied activity that characterizes the practice of OM.

7.2 Action in Operations: See the Layout, Hunt the System

In operations, something happens. Inputs are converted into outputs and there is a commercial connection between the operations and commercial performance. The manager, as an operations manager, has a role as part of the operational system and the process of operational improvement depends upon on the manager's understanding of the system. Hayes et al. (2005), for example, propose that a broadly based, diffused improvement programme is built around a '. . . common philosophy that fosters activities such as:

- Examining the organization's own past experience in the attempt to extract useful information and ideas
- Seeking out and learning from the experiences and best practices of other companies
- Experimenting systematically with new ideas and approaches
- Communicating important information throughout the organization (across functional, business and geographic lines)' (p.330)

They suggest that the sustainability of such a programme requires that management '. . . surround the improvement activities . . . with a web of supporting activities and policies' (p.330) such as creating a climate to encourage and sustain improvement, measuring and rewarding improvement efforts, providing supportive and stable human resources, eliminating things that impede improvement, sharing information and establishing and maintaining a portfolio of potential projects.

From the above activities, the roles of the operations manager as a researcher and of the researcher working with the operations manager emerge. When working together, both the operations manager and the researcher need to take action—to experiment systematically—and to observe the workability of the operation, to infer the manageability of the operation and to evaluate the viability of the operation as run in this way, as a route towards identifying areas for improvement. In effect, the operations management and improvement challenge is condensed down to a single statement—see the layout, hunt the system—and it is in this statement that the link to action research emerges. Alastair Nicholson introduced this statement into his teaching of operations management at London Business School in the early 1990s. It is as relevant today as then. In 'seeing the layout and hunting the system', the manager and researcher together are looking for where in the specification, coordination, pacing, rationing, inspection and change systems that trade-offs have been and can be made if the operation is to improve. Here, there is a need for a comprehensive and accurate database on which technical and managerial decisions can rely. From this database, the manager and researcher together can identify operational performance data (on quality, cost, dependability, flexibility and speed) and financial performance data (profit, sales and cost trends). The manager and researcher can examine the significance of the operational data in relation to the financial data before attributing these data to the way in which the operations resources (capacity, supply network, process technology, development and organization) are structured and run. Then the manager and researcher can consider the impact of changes in the operations resources on operational performance, and attempt to predict how these changes might show up in revenues and costs.

Based on this analysis, the manager and the researcher together can begin to see how the operation might be re-configured to work better, and where an improvement in operational performance (delivery time, rejects, utilization of particular resources etc.) might lead to a financial improvement in terms of revenue generation, cost reduction or cost containment. In particular, the manager and researcher may ask:

- What operational actions could yield improvement in these operational variables?
- What financial improvement could follow from an improvement in the operational variables, e.g. would delivery improvement generate more sales?
- How would that improvement show up in the financial statements?
- How soon?
- What other negative/positive knock-on effects would result from the improvement?

This section has outlined the centrality of active involvement in the operation as a means of understanding the operation as an organized contest between the physical organization of the operations resources, the progressing of the work through the system and the performance required of it. This need to structure this active involvement leads on to an outline of action research and how action research is an appropriate methodology for OM research (Coughlan and Coghlan, 2002).

7.3 What is Action Research?

Action research may be defined as:

> . . . an emergent inquiry process in which applied behavioural science knowledge is integrated with existing organizational knowledge and applied to solve real organizational problems. It is simultaneously concerned with bringing about change in organizations, and developing self-help competencies in organizational members and adding to scientific knowledge. Finally, it is an evolving process that is undertaken in a spirit of collaboration and co-inquiry.
>
> (Shani and Pasmore, 1985:439)

This definition expands upon one of the well-recognised early definitions in the area:

> Action research aims to contribute both to the practical concerns of people in an immediate problematic situation and to the goals of science by joint collaboration within a mutually acceptable ethical framework.
>
> (Rapoport, 1970:499)

7.3.1 Characteristics of Action Research

Gummesson (2000) lays out ten major characteristics of action research, each of which has implications for the execution of action research and the action researcher. We present and discuss each in the context of OM:

- *Action researchers take action.* Action researchers are not merely observing something happening; they are actively working at making it happen. In OM, the actions, for example, may be in the areas of process modification, methods improvement, workforce organization, capital-for-labour substitution, product modification, materials substitution or supplier change.
- *Action research always involves two goals*: to solve a problem and to contribute to science. These are the dual imperatives of action research (McKay and Marshall, 2001). Action research is about research *in* action and does not postulate a distinction between theory and action. Hence the challenge for action researchers is to engage *in* both taking action and contributing to practice, and standing back from the action and reflecting on it as it happens in order to contribute theory to the body of knowledge. In OM, for example, the problem (or opportunity) may be to develop the ability to gain strategic advantage by extending innovation to a significant part of the organization. The contribution to practice may be the achievement of a sustainable advantage over the competition. The contribution to knowledge may be an understanding of how different paths to improvement foster different organizational capabilities.
- *Action research is interactive.* In action research, the action researcher and the client personnel are co-researchers working to resolve or to improve the client's issue, and to contribute to the body of knowledge (Shani et al., 2008). As action research is a series of unfolding and unpredictable events, the co-researchers need to work together and to be able to adapt to the contingencies of the unfolding story. In OM, the client personnel may be staff within the organization or supplier personnel within the supply network. Their interaction may depend on the nature of the commercial agreement governing exchanges between the parties.
- *Action research aims at developing holistic understanding* during a project and recognizing complexity. As organizations are dynamic socio-technical systems, action researchers need to have a broad view of how the system

works and to be able to move between formal structural and technical and informal people subsystems (Nadler and Tushman, 1984; Pasmore, 2001). In OM, the action researcher works with organizational systems and requires an ability to work with dynamic complexity (Senge, 1990) arising from multiple causes and effects over time.

- *Action research is fundamentally about change.* Action research is applicable to the understanding, planning and implementation of change in operations. Over time, an operation in a competitive environment has to improve along many competitive dimensions including cost, quality, flexibility, dependability and speed (Slack and Lewis, 2002). As action research is fundamentally about change, knowledge of and skill in the dynamics of organizational change are necessary. Such knowledge informs how an operation, as a large system, recognizes the need for change, articulates a desired outcome from the change and actively plans and implements how to achieve that desired future (Beckhard and Harris, 1987; Nadler, 1998; Coghlan and Brannick, 2005). Such knowledge also includes how change moves through a system (Coghlan and Rashford, 2006) and the dynamics of organizational politics (Buchanan and Badham, 1999).

- *Action research requires an understanding of the ethical framework*, values and norms within which it is used in a particular context (Morton, 1999; Walker and Haslett, 2002; Coghlan and Shani, 2005). In action research, ethics involves authentic relationships between the action researcher and the members of the client system as to how they understand the process and take significant action (Coghlan and Brannick, 2005). Values and norms that flow from such ethical principles typically focus on how the action researcher works with the members of the organization. In OM, people, and not just systems and procedures, are the focus of managerial attention. Actions taken impact directly and indirectly on the roles, responsibilities, accountabilities and actionabilities of people and, so, cannot be treated without ethical considerations. Ethical dilemmas arise both in the imbalance of power in the organization and in the action research process of influencing by persuasion (Rusaw, 2001).

- *Action research can include all types of data gathering methods.* Action research does not preclude the use of data gathering methods applied in traditional research. Qualitative and quantitative tools, such as interviews and surveys are commonly used. However, data collection tools are themselves interventions and generate data. For example, a survey or interview may generate feelings of anxiety, suspicion, apathy and hostility or create expectations in a work force. If action researchers do not attend to this and focus only on the collection of data, they may miss significant data that may be critical to the success of the project, or they may confound the data they think that they are gathering. What is important, then, in action research is that the planning and the use of these tools be well thought through in advance with the members of the organization and be clearly integrated into the action research design. In OM, differing kinds of data emerge in such operations decision areas as capacity, supply networks, process technology and product development. For example, in relation to capacity, relevant data may include not just how fast capacity expansion or reduction might be pursued, but also the potential knock-on effects for staff motivation of such changes.

- *Action research requires a breadth of pre-understanding* of the corporate environment, the conditions of business, the structure and dynamics of operating systems and the theoretical underpinnings of such systems. Pre-understanding refers to the knowledge the action researcher brings to the research project. Action researchers in OM, therefore, need to have not only knowledge of operations and the level of contribution of operations to the competitive strategy of the firm (Hayes and Wheelwright, 1984), but also a broader knowledge of organizational systems and the dynamics of the operation in its contemporary business environment. Such a need for pre-understanding signals that an action research approach is inappropriate for researchers who, for example, think that all they have to do to develop theory is just to go out into the field.

- *Action research should be conducted in real time*, though retrospective action research is also acceptable. While action research is a 'live' case study being written as it unfolds, it can also take the form of a traditional case study written in retrospect, when the written case is used as an intervention into the organization in the present. In such a situation the case performs the function of a 'learning history' and is used as an intervention to promote reflection and learning in the organization (Kleiner and Roth, 1997). In service OM, for example, the simultaneity of production and consumption make it necessary to engage with the situation in real time in order to develop the necessary understanding.

- *The action research paradigm requires its own quality criteria*. Action research should *not* be judged by the criteria of positivist science, but rather within the criteria of its own terms. Levin (2003) argues that the contribution of action research to scientific discourse is not a matter of sticking to the rigour–relevance polarity but of focusing on vital arguments relating to participation, real-life problems, joint-meaning construction and workable solutions. In OM, for example, research into a problem of materials substitution may demand the participation of manufacturing, engineering and purchasing staff from within the organization, and complementary supplier staff from outside. To the extent that their collaborative efforts towards a workable solution—the identification and qualification of a new or substitute material—are integrated and joint-meaning construction is facilitated, then the research may be deemed of high quality.

7.3.2 The Origins of Action Research

Action research has many roots, some of which are in the tradition of organizational renewal that developed in western industrial economy over the past 50 years. Other roots lie outside of this setting and are grounded in emancipatory movements (Greenwood and Levin, 2007). Action research is seen now as a family of approaches, rather than as a single unitary concept where there is only one way of conducting it. For instance, action research in the context of organizational improvement necessarily embodies different emphases than action research undertaken in the context of social exclusion. The family of approaches is grounded in the ten major characteristics presented above and variation occurs through context and emphasis.

Action research originated primarily in the work of Kurt Lewin and his colleagues and associates. In the mid 1940s, Lewin and his associates conducted action research projects in different social settings. Through the following decades, action research in organizations grew into what became recognised as organization development (OD), particularly in the US (French and Bell, 1999). One of the best known early organizational action research projects was a study of resistance to change in an industrial plant (Coch and French, 1948). The researchers were essentially addressing the question of how to introduce technological change into the company where there was strong resistance to change. They set up two approaches to introducing the change—representative participation and total participation in discussing the implementation. Using these two approaches they were able to show differing effects of each approach on productivity and on the acceptance of the change. The results indicated that productivity increased faster and further beyond previous levels in groups where total participation was used as a means of introducing the change.

The socio-technical work of the Tavistock Institute originated in the UK in the field of coal mining and then extended to other industries in India, Sweden and the US (Trist and Murray, 1993; Pasmore 2001; Weisbord, 2004). The learning from these research initiatives is that social and technical perspectives on work are interdependent and that organizational and work design need to optimize both.

Action research in the Scandinavian tradition typically focuses on structural issues in working life and regional development. It focuses on relationships, both in the workplace and between social partners in regional development, whose central process for building relationships is democratic dialogue (Fricke and Totterdill, 2004).

7.3.3 Contrasts with Positivist Science

Action research can be contrasted with positivist science (Susman and Evered, 1978) (Table 7.1). The aim of positivist science is the creation of universal knowledge or covering law, while action research focuses on knowledge in action. Accordingly, the knowledge created in positivist science is universal while that created through action research is particular, situational and out of praxis. In action research the data are contextually embedded and interpreted. In positivist science findings are validated by logic, measurement and the consistency achieved by the consistency of prediction and control. In action research, the basis for validation is the conscious and deliberate enactment of the action research cycle. The positivist scientist's relationship to the setting is one of neutrality and detachment while the action researcher is immersed in the setting. In short, the contrast of roles is between that of detached observer in positivist science and that of an actor and agent of change in action research (see also chapter 3, section 3.4.2 on research philosophy).

This section has outlined the boundaries, historical roots and comparative characteristics of action research. As Riordan (1995:10) expresses it:

> . . . (action research) is a kind of approach to studying social reality without separating (while distinguishing) fact from value; they require a practitioner of science who is not only an engaged participant, but also incorporates the perspective of the critical and analytical observer, not as a validating instance but as integral to the practice.

7.4 What is Needed Before Entering into Action Research

Before entering into action research, the researcher needs to position the proposed research in relation both to the research programme and to the needs of the organization.

Table 7.1 Comparison of Positivist Science and Action Research

	Positivist science	*Action research*
Aim of research	Universal knowledge Theory building and testing	Knowledge in action Theory building and testing in action
Type of knowledge acquired	Universal Covering law	Particular Situational Praxis
Nature of data	Context free	Contextually embedded
Validation	Logic, measurement Consistency of prediction and control	Experiential
Researcher's role	Observer	Actor Agent of change
Researcher's relationship to setting	Detached, neutral	Immersed

7.4.1 Positioning in Relation to the Academic Programme

When the action researcher is enrolled in an academic programme, such as one leading to a master's or a doctorate, it is useful to note that typically there are two action research projects co-existing in parallel (Coghlan and Brannick, 2005).

First there is the core action research project (Zuber-Skerritt and Perry, 2002), which is the project on which the student action researcher is working within the organization. This project has its own identity and may proceed, irrespective of whether or not it is being studied. There is also the thesis action research project (Zuber-Skerritt and Perry, 2002). This involves the action researcher's inquiry into the organizational project. This distinction is useful as it is the thesis project which will be submitted for examination, rather than the core project. While the core project may be unsuccessful as reflected in the thesis project, the researcher's inquiry into the lack of success may merit the academic award the student action researcher is pursuing.

7.4.2 Positioning in Relation to the Needs of the Organization

Essentially, three things are needed to position the action research in relation to the needs of the organization: a real issue, access and a contract. A *real issue* must be of both research and managerial significance upon which a group or organization is embarking, which has an uncertain outcome and which the group or organization is willing to subject to rigorous inquiry, particularly the analysis and implementation of action. As action research is what we might term a 'live' case in real time, the action researcher has to *gain access* and to be contracted as an action researcher (Schein, 1995, 2008; Gummesson, 2000). This *contract* involves the key members of the organization who recognize the value of the action research approach and are willing to have the action researcher working with them in relation to real-life problems, joint-meaning construction and workable solutions. Developing the contract, a key element of the pre-step (defined in the following section), and execution of the contract requires access. Here, access involves recognition of the different stakeholders of the problem (or opportunity), their differing expectations and inter-relationships; interaction with the stakeholders in real time; and confidence that they can be relied upon to engage in joint exploration of the problem (or opportunity).

For example, Middel et al. (2005) described the application of an action learning and action research approach in collaborative improvement (CoI) within an extended manufacturing enterprise (EME) in the Netherlands. Over a period of 1.5 years, five CoI initiatives within the EME were started in the area of quality, change order management and manufacturing. The initiatives were multi-disciplinary and required the involvement of different functional departments from all the companies, such as purchasing, engineering, sales, quality and production. The suppliers selected to participate represented different kinds of relationship and delivered different kind of products. This meant that information and communication could pass freely throughout the whole group without running the risk of giving or losing sensitive information to competitors. The underlying reason for the selection of these suppliers was that the suppliers were perceived as highly involved in collaboration and were dedicated partners in assembling and delivering product to the market.

Similarly, in an action research study of process improvement in product development, Coughlan and Brady (1995) sought to increase awareness of areas of management choice. The expectations of the five participating firms guided the specific emphases in the project. For example, one firm stated:

> We want to understand how we can achieve cycle time reduction (getting it right first time will be a subset of this). To do this we need to understand the detail of the product development process. . . . {We} need a facilitator {the researchers} to provide the structure for analysing the process. We will then analyse the data ourselves to identify what we need to do to achieve cycle time reduction.
>
> (p.43)

The other firms stated their expectations in similar terms. In addition to defining their expectations, the firms also agreed to a code of conduct, derived from the International Benchmarking Clearing House (1992). The key elements of this code included: keep it legal; be willing to give what you get; respect confidentiality; keep information internal; use benchmarking contacts only; don't refer without permission; be prepared from the start; understand expectations; act in accord with expectations; be honest; follow through with commitments. Together with the expectations, this code formed the basis for the contract between the researchers and the firms. This contract was 'psychological', as motives, goals and the locus of control, as well as business arrangements were agreed.

7.5 Designing an Action Research Project

As with any research project, designing an action research project confronts the researcher with issues of framing the issue, determining its scope, gaining access and negotiating an appropriate role.

7.5.1 Framing the Issue

Framing and selecting an issue is a complex process (Coghlan and Brannick, 2005). The complexity of issue identification and selection illustrates that the search for an appropriate issue to study is difficult. There may appear to be a wide and diverse set of issues all vying for research attention. Some issues may be blatantly obvious while others may go unnoticed unless attempts are made to uncover organizational members' perceptions of key issues. Not every issue will volunteer itself automatically for resolution. It is human perception that makes the difference thus leading us to conclude that organizational actors' interpretations are pivotal in this whole process.

7.5.2 Determining the Scope

For the action researcher the questions of who selects the scope of the project, who provides access and who is involved in it are critical, as they are in any research project. It is common that action researchers have a project steering group, which enables them to manage the project, by:

- Having a team with which to work in planning, implementing and evaluating; and
- Building insider knowledge of the organization (Bartunek and Louis, 1996).

This group also acts as a learning group and reflects on the emergent learning from the project (Bushe and Shani, 1991). In a growing number of settings, the action research is constructed as collaborative research between the organization and the researcher (Adler et al., 2004; Shani et al., 2008).

7.5.3 Gaining Access

For the action researcher working towards a master's or a PhD, access may come through the university and more specifically through the academic supervisor with whom the researcher has a mentoring relationship. Two types of access are relevant: primary and secondary. Primary access refers to the ability to get into the organization and to contract to undertake action research. Secondary access refers to access to specific areas within the organization or specific levels of information and activity.

7.5.4 Negotiating a Role for the Action Researcher

Roles are patterns of behaviour which individuals expect of others performing specific functions or tasks. For the action researcher there is potential role ambiguity and role conflict as different expectations from the organization and the university may make different and conflicting demands on the action researcher (Coghlan and Shani, 2005). Hence, there is the need for clear contracting as discussed above. Action researchers may play one of two roles in an action research project: outside agent and insider. The two roles are related but different.

More commonly, action researchers are *outside agents* who act as facilitators of the action and reflection within an organization. Here, it is useful to talk about the action researcher and the client system, that is, those within the organization who are engaging in the action research in collaboration with the action researcher. In this role, the action researcher is acting as an external helper to the client system, working in a facilitative manner to help the clients inquire into their own issues and create and implement solutions (Schein, 1995, 2008). This role contrasts with the expert model as in the doctor–patient model (Schein, 1999) where patients go to doctors for expert diagnosis and prescriptive direction.

There is also a growing incidence of action research being done from within organizations by *insiders*, as when practising managers undertake action research projects in and on their own organizations (Coghlan, 2001, 2003; Coghlan and Brannick, 2005). This role is increasingly common in the context of managers participating in academic programmes. In such contexts the manager takes on the role of researcher in addition to their regular organizational roles and may both manage the project and study it at the same time. In this role, the insider action researcher should find access, both primary and secondary, easier. The other participants are likely to include subordinates and colleagues who need to buy-in to the project. In addition, the manager is likely to have a personal stake in the outcome of the project.

7.6 Implementing Action Research

There are many versions of the action research cycle. In Figure 7.1, we present an action research cycle comprising a pre-step and four basic steps—diagnosing, planning action, taking action and evaluating action (Coghlan and Brannick, 2005).

7.6.1 Pre-Step: Context and Purpose

The action research cycle unfolds in real time and begins with an under-standing of the context of the project. Having knowledge of business and organizations is a prerequisite for engaging in action research in business

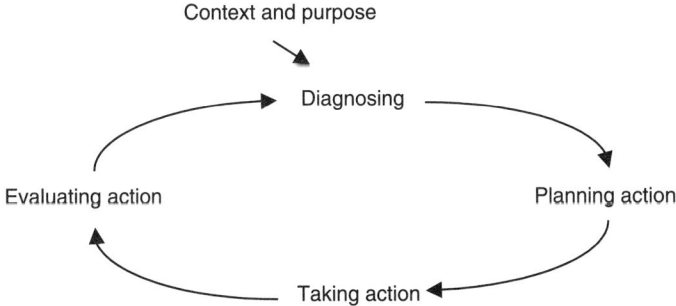

Figure 7.1 The Action Research Cycle. (Coghlan and Brannick (2005:22), reproduced with permission).

organizations (Gummesson, 2000). The pre-step is characterized by two questions:

- What is the rationale for action?
- What is the rationale for research?

7.6.1.1 What is the Rationale for Action?

The action research cycle unfolds in real time and requires a clear rationale for action. This requirement helps to establish clarity through a number of initiatives undertaken by the key members of the organization. The *first initiative* is to develop an understanding of the context of the action project, in particular the necessity and desirability of the project. The *second initiative* is to identify the economic, political, social and technical forces driving the need for action and to analyse the source, potency and nature of the demands these forces are making on the system. A *final initiative* in this pre-step is establishment of collaborative relationships with those who have ownership or need to have ownership of the project. In an OM research setting for example, the context of the action project may be defined in terms of the prototyping stage in the development process of a new product. The economic and technical forces driving the need for action to change the approach to prototyping may include competitive comparisons, customer surveys and costs of quality. The potency of the competitive demands on the prototyping system may challenge the underlying attributes of the product and the overall product development strategy for the firm. The ownership of the product and process technologies held both within the firm and in the supply base, may define collaborative relationships of relevance to the project.

7.6.1.2 What is the Rationale for Research?

The complementary question is to ask what the rationale for the research is and, in particular, the rationale for the thesis action research project (Zuber-Skerritt and Perry, 2002). This questioning involves asking why this action project is worth studying, how action research is an appropriate methodology to adopt and what contribution to knowledge it is expected to make. In the OM example introduced above, relating to prototyping, an action project to change the involvement of suppliers in prototyping may be worth studying because of the complex issues associated with earlier involvement of suppliers in the development process. The appropriateness of action research may be defended in relation to the longitudinal process involved in developing the relationship with and trust of, and in, the supplier in order to effect the changes proposed. The contribution to knowledge may be defined in terms of the greater insights into the concept of early supplier involvement. Correspondingly, it is essential to the pre-step that action researchers in OM begin with a basic knowledge of the theory and practice of OM.

7.6.2 Main Steps

7.6.2.1 Diagnosing

Diagnosing involves naming what the issues are, however provisionally, as a working theme—such as increasing the information content of proto-types—on the basis of which action will be planned and taken. As diagnosis involves the articulation of the theoretical foundations of action—such as seeing prototyping as a manufacturing process in its own right—it needs to be done carefully and thoroughly. While the diagnosis may change in later iterations of the action research cycle, any such changes need to be recorded and articulated clearly, showing how events have led to alternative diagnosis and presenting the evidence and rationale for the new diagnosis on which further action is to be based. It is important that the diagnosing step be a collaborative venture, that is, that the action researcher engages relevant others in the process of diagnosis—such as the design engineers, manufacturing engineers and supplier/guest engineers—and not be the expert who does the diagnosis apart from others.

Data are central to diagnosis and data are generated in different ways. There are what are sometimes referred to as 'hard' data. These are data that are gathered through performance statistics such as capacity utilization, first-pass yield or customer returns. Then there are what are commonly referred to as 'soft' data, such as customer expectations and perceptions of functionality. These are data gathered through observation, discussion and interview. The supposed 'softness' lies in the largely subjective nature of these data and, as a result, they may be more difficult to interpret.

While data are gathered through formal mechanisms, such as discussed above, data are also generated through the process of inquiry itself. For the action researcher, data generation comes through active involvement in the day-to-day organizational processes relating to the action research project. Not only are data generated through participation in and observation of teams at work, problems being solved, decisions being made and so on, but also through the interventions which are made to advance the action project. People's responses to these interventions generate further data. For example, hesitancy to adopt a particular course of action may illustrate reticence to novelty or an underlying attitude that hitherto was hidden. Accordingly, the action researcher has to be sensitive to and able to work in the context of, and to address, such hesitancy. Some of these observations and interventions are made in formal settings—meetings and interviews; many are made in informal settings—over coffee, lunch and other recreational settings.

In action research, directly observable behaviour is an important source of data for the action researcher (Schein, 1999). Observations of the dynamics of customer–supplier groups at work—for example, the directionality of their communications, the behaviour of the team leader, the use of economic power, the freedom accorded to sub-groups to investigate alternative scenarios, the norms of trust and respect for intellectual property rights, the collaborative nature of problem solving and decision making, the integrative relations with other groups both within and outside the immediate frame of the project (such as the cost accountants)—provide the basis for inquiry into the underlying assumptions and their effects on the work and life of these groups. In dealing with directly observable phenomena in the organizations with which they are working, the critical issue facing the action researcher is how to be helpful to the client system and, at the same time, how to inquire in what is being observed. Observation and inquiry into how the systemic relationship (for example between the individual, the team, the inter-departmental group, the organization and the suppliers) operates is critical to the complex nature of organizational problem solving and issue resolution (Coghlan and Rashford, 2006).

The action researcher takes the data and feeds them to the client system with a view to making them available for analysis. Sometimes the action researcher has collected the data and does the reporting; at other times, the organization itself has gathered the data and the action researcher facilitates or participates in the feedback meetings.

The critical aspect of data analysis in the diagnostic step is that it is collaborative—both the researcher and members of the client system (for example, the management team, the supplier, a customer group etc.) do it together. This collaborative approach is based on the assumption that clients know their organization best, know what will work, and, ultimately, will be the ones to implement, own and follow through on whatever actions will be taken. Hence, their involvement in the analysis is critical. The criteria and tools for analysis need to be talked through and ultimately need to be directly linked to the purpose of the research and the aim of the interventions.

7.6.2.2 Planning Action

Planning action follows from the analysis of the context and purpose of the project, the framing of the issue and the diagnosis, and is consistent with them. It may be that this action planning focuses on a first step or a series of first steps. As Beckhard and Harris (1987) advise, key questions arise around:

- What needs to change?
- In what parts of the organization?
- What types of change are required?
- Whose support is needed?
- How commitment is to be built?
- How resistance is to be managed?

These questions are critical and need to be answered as part of the change plan.

Again we emphasize the importance of collaboration in planning action. In the same vein and for the same reasons as the data-gathering step, action planning is a joint activity. The project steering group and the senior management set out both who does what and an appropriate time schedule.

Continuing the example of prototyping, the management group may identify that the timing of the introduction of a manufacturing perspective into the prototyping process needs to change. This change involves not just the manufacturing group, but also the designers, technicians and purchasers. The types of change required may include sharing of information, development of alternative design solutions, re-definition of work practices and contracting earlier with suppliers. The proposed changes may be of such significance that the support of the board may be needed. As such, the early involvement, not just of the management group but also the HR specialists or the board may be necessary to build commitment and to manage resistance.

7.6.2.3 Taking Action

The client implements the planned action. This action involves making the desired changes and following through on the plans in collaboration with relevant key members of the organization. In the prototyping example, the initial action may focus on a specific product module. The selection of the particular module may be with a view to providing the greatest insight into the issues while not putting the whole development project at risk of delay or non-completion. The term of the planned action may extend over one or more design iterations, taking some weeks or months.

7.6.2.4 Evaluating Action

Evaluation involves reflecting on the outcomes of the action, both intended and unintended, a review of the process in order that the next cycle of planning and action may benefit from the experience of the cycle completed. In the prototyping example, the intended consequences may include a higher level of 'launch' quality with greater conformance to specification and correspondingly lower costs of rejects. The unintended consequences may include the need for staff to increase their appreciation of the technical issues faced by their upstream and downstream colleagues, and their anticipation of those issues in the design decisions and feedback.

Such evaluation is the key to learning. Without evaluation actions can go on and on regardless of success or failure, errors can proliferate and ineffectiveness and frustration increase. The outcomes of the action, both intended and unintended, are examined with a view to seeing:

- If the original diagnosis was correct
- If the action taken was correct

- If the action was taken in an appropriate manner
- What feeds into the next cycle of diagnosis, planning and action

So, as Figure 7.2 illustrates, the cyclical process continues as the project moves from cycle to cycle (McKay and Marshall, 2001).

7.7 Meta Learning

The notion of meta learning, that is learning about learning, is central to the two action research projects which we discussed earlier and which are operating in parallel—the core action research project and the thesis action research project (Zuber-Skerritt and Perry, 2002; Coghlan and Brannick, 2005). We will discuss the role of meta learning in relation to these two projects.

7.7.1 Meta Learning in the Core Action Research Project

While the action researchers are engaging in the cycles of the core action research project, they need to be diagnosing, planning, taking action and evaluating about how the action research project itself is going and what they are learning. They need to be inquiring continually into each of the four

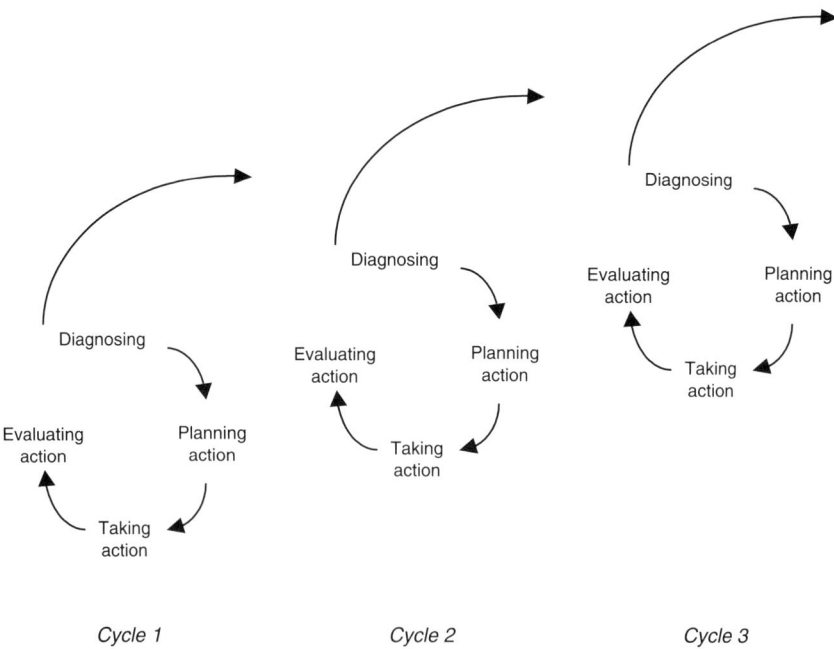

Figure 7.2 Continuing Cycles of Action Research. (Coghlan and Brannick (2005:24), reproduced with permission).

main steps, asking how these steps are being conducted and how they are consistent with each other and, so, shaping how the subsequent steps are conducted. Argyris (2003) argues that this inquiry into the steps of the cycles themselves is central to the development of actionable knowledge, that is, knowledge that can serve simultaneously the needs of a living system and the scientific community. It is the dynamic of this reflection on reflection that incorporates the learning process of the action research cycle and enables action research to be more than everyday problem solving. Hence it is learning about learning, in other words, meta learning.

Meta learning is grounded in the process of reflection of which there are many forms. Reflection is the process of stepping back from experience to process what the experience means, with a view to planning further action. Of relevance here is Coghlan and Brannick's (2005) use of Mezirow's three forms of reflection—content, process and premise—in an action research context. *Content* reflection is where the researchers think about the issues, what is happening. *Process* reflection is where they think about strategies, procedures and how things are being done. *Premise* reflection is where they critique underlying assumptions and perspectives. In action research, all three forms of reflection are critical. When content, process and premise reflections are applied to the action research cycle, they form the meta cycle of inquiry (Figure 7.3).

Returning to our prototyping example, the *content* of what is diagnosed,

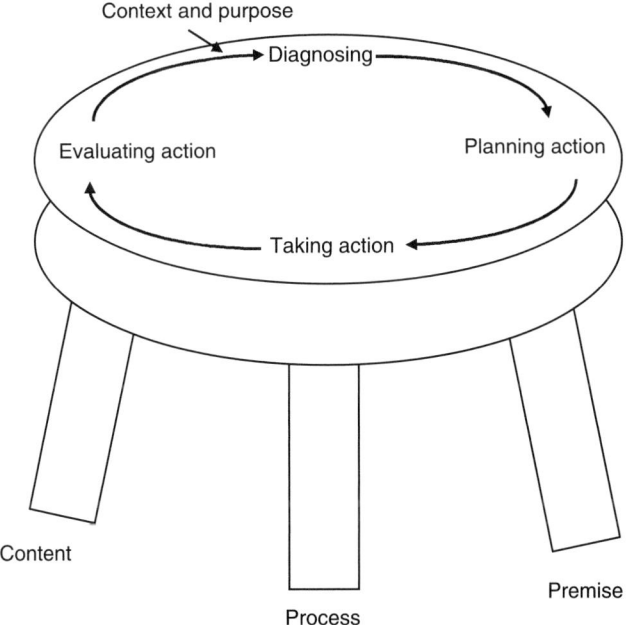

Figure 7.3 Meta-Cycle of Action Research. (Coghlan and Brannick, (2005) p. 26. Reproduced with permission).

planned, acted on and evaluated is studied. Here, seeing prototyping as a process transforming ideas and early stage specifications into information-intensive platforms for use by designers and manufacturing is relevant. The planning of the integration of differing functional perspectives into the process and the specific nature of their interventions is of interest. Emerging from this content focus is the opportunity to consolidate key insights consistent with the research aims.

The *process* of how diagnosis is undertaken, how action planning flows from that diagnosis and is conducted, how actions follow and are an implementation of the stated plans and how evaluation is conducted are critical foci for inquiry. In the prototyping example, the way in which the stakeholders in the initiative work together in evolving cycles of experimentation are of interest. For example, the process may begin as a pilot concentrating on a specific product module, selected for its representation of the breadth of issues faced at the broader product level. This pilot may engage upstream and downstream groups and suppliers in the development of a more inclusive process, with the potential to inform the redesign of the broader prototyping process.

There is also *premise* reflection, which is inquiry into the unstated, and often taken for granted, underlying assumptions which govern attitudes and behaviour. Here, the prototyping initiative may challenge the underlying attitudes in the organization towards and between differing functional groups. For example, there are acknowledged cultural differences between manufacturing engineering and design engineering groups (Francis and Winstanley, 1992). Yet, such differences may remain unquestioned until and unless subjected to premise reflection. The result may be a broadening or a refocusing of the research initiative on other, but related, issues.

7.7.2 *Meta Learning in the Thesis Action Research Project*

For those action researchers who are writing a dissertation, the meta cycle is the focus of the dissertation. The dissertation is an inquiry into the action project and, hence, action researchers need to describe both the core and thesis action research projects in a way that demonstrates the quality of rigour of the inquiry. Returning to the three forms of reflection, described earlier, *content* reflection would challenge the contribution of the work to the academic and managerial communities.

The *process* reflection is where the action researchers think about the research strategies, data generation procedures and how the researchers dealt with the inevitable difficulties and opportunities which can arise in the course of an action research project. Such reflection, different to that on content, is also a contribution to actionable knowledge.

Premise reflection is where the action researchers critique their underlying assumptions on the role of research in action on the development of actionable knowledge and outcomes for managers and researchers.

Let us return one last time to the prototyping example. If, as part of the initiative to improve the prototyping process, the researcher had called a meeting of stakeholders and that few of those who had accepted the invitation showed up, what assumptions would this event challenge? Action research takes a holistic view of the organization and, so, the assumption of the isolation of the prototyping process from the political and cultural dynamics of the organization is challenged by the non-attendance. There may be a shared view that, as past attempts to manage this issue had failed, the issue was, essentially, intractable. Or, there may have been a reluctance to engage in an attempt to address the issues, given the likely 'political' fallout from the honesty required. In this instance, the assumption that the prototyping initiative could be studied only within its own technical terms is unfulfilled and the premise shifts to include political and cultural dynamics of the organization.

7.8 Action Research Skills

Action research is a challenging approach to research because it requires confident and experienced researchers to cope with the uncertainty of the unfolding story and to be able to work as researchers exposed to the reality of organizational change in real time. For the inexperienced action researcher it is important to be part of a team with experienced researchers and to learn through an 'apprenticeship' model (Eden and Huxham, 1996).

To work as an action researcher in organizations requires skills in diagnosis, intervention in relation to issues and problems in organizations, learning in action and journal keeping.

7.8.1 Diagnosis

Diagnosis may be defined as investigations that draw on concepts, models and methods in order to examine the current state of an organization and to help find ways to solve problems and to enhance organizational effectiveness (Coghlan and Brannick, 2005). Correspondingly, OM action researchers need to have a basic knowledge of the theory and practice of OM. From this knowledge, they should be able to select, adapt and operationalize suitable frameworks and instruments as appropriate to help make sense of the current situation and to predict outcomes. In addition, and with the awareness that their underlying assumptions may be challenged as the research progresses, they should be aware that frameworks and instruments from other areas of research, such as organizational studies, may become relevant.

7.8.2 Intervention

Action research involves core skills at engaging with others in a process of inquiry and action. Inquiry can be focused outward (e.g. what is going on in the organization, in the team?) or inward (e.g. what is going on in me?). In his articulation of the dynamics of helping, Schein (1999) describes a typology of inquiry, which provides a useful framework for the action researcher in working with members of the client system:

- *Pure inquiry*, where the action researcher prompts the elicitation of the story of what is taking place and listens carefully and neutrally. She asks, 'What is going on?', 'Tell me what happened'
- *Exploratory diagnostic inquiry*, where the action researcher begins to manage the process of how the client analyses the content by exploring reasoning, actions and emotional processes. Here, the action researcher may ask, 'Why do you think this happened?', 'What did you do?', 'What are you going to do?', 'How do you feel about this?'
- *Confrontive inquiry*, where the action researcher, by sharing her own ideas, challenges the client to think from a new perspective. These ideas may refer to content and process. Examples of confrontive questions would be, 'Have you thought about doing this . . .?', 'Have you considered that . . . might be a solution?'

This typology of inquiry provides the basis for explicit training and education necessary for action researchers to develop key interpersonal inquiry and helping skills. These intervention skills enable action researchers to work at engaging with members of a client system, helping *them* to identify issues, diagnose what they think is causing the issues, plan, implement and evaluate action, and learn from the experience.

7.8.3 Learning in Action

Learning in action is grounded in the inquiry-reflection process. Coghlan and Brannick (2005) have described the learning cycle in terms of experiencing, reflecting, interpreting and taking action. Reflection is the critical link between the concrete experience, the interpretation and taking new action. As Raelin (2000) discusses, it is the key to learning as it enables action researchers to develop an ability to uncover and make explicit to themselves what they planned, discovered and achieved in practice. Raelin also argues that reflection must be brought into the open so that it goes beyond their privately held taken-for-granted assumptions and helps them to see how their knowledge is constructed. In action research, reflection is the activity that integrates action and research.

Action researchers are themselves instruments in the generation of data. When action researchers engage in the action research cycles with others and try to understand and shape what is going on, they are also engaging in their own experiential learning cycle activities. Further, some of the core skills of the action researcher are in the areas of self-awareness and sensitivity to what they observe, supported by the conceptual analytical frameworks on which they base their observations and interpretations. When they inquire into what is going on, when they show people their train of thought and put forward hypotheses to be tested, when they make suggestions for action, they are generating data. People's responses to these interventions generate further data.

7.8.4 Journal Keeping

Journal keeping is a significant mechanism for developing reflective skills. Action researchers note their observations and experiences in a journal and, over time, learn to differentiate between different experiences and ways of dealing with them. McNiff et al. (1996) describe some of the useful functions of a journal or research diary:

- A systematic and regularly kept record of events, dates and people
- An interpretative, self-evaluative account of the researcher's personal experiences thoughts and feelings, with a view to trying to understand her own actions
- A useful way of dumping painful experiences
- A reflective account where the researcher can tease out interpretations
- An analytic tool where data can be examined and analysed

Journal keeping enables integration of information and experiences which, when understood, help the action researchers understand their reasoning processes and consequent behaviour and, so, anticipate experiences before embarking on them (Raelin, 2000). Regular journal keeping imposes a discipline on the action researchers and captures their experience of key events close to when they happen and before the passage of time intervenes to change perception.

7.9 Generating Theory through Action Research

Checkland and Holwell (1998) point out that the aim of action research is to enact a process that is recoverable by anyone wishing to scrutinize the research. So, it is not enough to express the generality drawn out of action research through the design of tools, techniques and models. Rather, the basis for their design must be explicit and shown to be related to theory.

Action research demands an explicit concern with theory that is generated from the conceptualization of the particular experience in ways that are intended to be meaningful to others. Accordingly, theory generated through action research has three characteristics: it is situation specific, emergent and incremental:

- When faced with a genuine need to take action there are settings that are more amenable to theory generation than to theory testing. Action research does not lend itself to repeatable experimentation—each intervention will be different to the last. Action research projects are *situation specific* and do not aim to create universal knowledge

- Action research generates *emergent* theory, in which the theory develops from a synthesis of the understanding which emerges from the data and from the use in practice of the body of theory which informed the intervention and research intention (Eden and Huxham, 1996). In contrast to positivist science, where the theory to be tested is defined from the outset, theoretical understanding in action research unfolds through reflection on implementation and outcomes

- Theory generation, as a result of action research, is *incremental*, moving from the particular to the general in small steps (Eden and Huxham, 1996). An action research project unfolds through a series of events as the designated issue is confronted and members of the organization attempt resolution with the help of the action researcher. The enactment of the cycles of planning, taking action and evaluating can be anticipated but cannot be designed or planned in detail in advance. The philosophy underlying action research is that the stated aims of the project lead to planning the first action, which is then evaluated. So the second action cannot be planned until evaluation of the first action has taken place

7.10 Quality in Action Research

Action research does not have to justify itself in relation to alternative epistemologies and research approaches (Susman and Evered, 1978; Aguinis, 1993). It must be justified within its own terms, particularly those which argue that the reflection and data generation and the emergent theories cannot be captured readily by alternative approaches (Schein, 1987; Eden and Huxham, 1996). Accordingly, there is a reluctance to use the term 'validity' in relation to action research, since that term has connotations from positivist science; instead, 'quality' is preferred (Reason and Bradbury, 2001).

Levin (2003) suggests four criteria for judging the quality of action research: participation, real-life problems, joint-meaning construction and workable solutions. With regard to *participation*, how well does the action research reflect the cooperation between the action researcher and members of the organization? With regard to *real-life problems*, is the action research project guided by a concern for real-life practical outcomes, and is it governed by constant and iterative reflection as part of the process of organizational change and improvement? With regard to *joint-meaning construction*, is the process of interpreting events, articulating meaning and generating understanding a collaborative process between the action researcher and members of the organization? Finally, with regard to *workable solutions*, does action research engage in significant work, does sustainable change come out of the project?

The process of exploration of the data must demonstrate a high degree of method and orderliness in reflecting about and holding on to the emerging theoretical content of each episode and the process whereby issues are planned and implemented (Eden and Huxham, 1996). In order to maintain quality, action researchers must consciously and deliberately enact the action research cycles, testing their own assumptions and subjecting their assumptions to public testing (Argyris et al., 1985). Accordingly, action researchers need to combine advocacy with inquiry, that is to present their inferences, attributions, opinions, viewpoints as open to testing and critique. This combination involves illustrating inferences with relatively directly observable data and making reasoning both explicit and publicly testable in the service of learning. Here, for example, Argyris et al. (1985:258–261) provide seven rules for inference testing:

1   Combine advocacy with inquiry
2   Illustrate your inferences with directly observable data
3   Make your reasoning explicit and publicly test for agreement at each inferential step
4   Actively seek disconfirming data and alternative explanations
5   Affirm the making of mistakes in the service of learning
6   Actively inquire into your own impact in the learning context
7   Design ongoing experiments to test competing views

7.11 Writing an Action Research Dissertation

For action researchers writing a dissertation, the dissertation is an inquiry into the action project. As a report, it is a structured, scholarly piece of writing which should describe the thesis action research cycle and demonstrate the quality of the action research. There are many elements of structure (Coghlan and Brannick, 2005; McNiff et al., 1996). For example, the structure of the action research dissertation or report may deal with:

* Purpose and rationale of the research
* Context
* Methodology and methods of inquiry
* Story and outcomes
* Self-reflection and learning of the action researcher
* Reflection on the story in the light of the experience and the theory
* Extrapolation to a broader context and articulation of usable knowledge

Each of these elements has been dealt with earlier in this chapter. Some may merit a chapter in the dissertation, while others may merit treatment in a number of chapters. For example, the story might be spread over several chapters in the dissertation, depending on its length and complexity and the extent of the research process. Yet, all such chapters should treat these elements clearly and formally.

7.12 Conclusions

There are many definitions of OM. For example, OM may be seen as concerned with the way organizations produce goods and services (Slack et al., 2001). More generally, the concerns are with the relationship between financial results (such as the accounting system reports), operational activity and the operating structure. Operating problems arise in the forms of poor designs, production bottlenecks, poor worker performance and methods, poor product quality and late delivery. Usually, there are several internal views on the opportunities for making improvements that can realize the potential of the operation. *En route* to improvement, there are lots of internal snags to slow and to confound the process of improvement.

This chapter has presented an in-depth review of action research as a valid methodology for research in OM. It has highlighted the need, nature and process of conceptually based collaboration among managers and researchers around intellectually interesting and managerially relevant operational realities faced by managers. The set of iterative action research cycles yields unique insights that can deepen understanding, improve practice and extend theory.

Action research, then, is an approach to research that does not distinguish between research and action; it addresses the theme of *research in action*. Accordingly, compared with other approaches to research it is an imprecise, uncertain and sometimes unstable activity, as life is. It works at gathering data with the community of practitioners who want to improve organizations and communities. Regretfully, it has often become a glib term for involving clients in research and has lost its role as a powerful conceptual tool for generating actionable knowledge. Action research is a form of science, which differs from, say, experimental physics, but is genuinely scientific in its emphasis on careful observation and study of the effects of human behaviour on human systems as they manage change. Delivering quality and rigorous action research demands a holistic attention to a number of key issues, particularly the enactment of the cycles of planning, implementation and evaluation, the quality of participation in the client system, the development of emergent theory from the action and the contribution to the client system and continuous learning.

7.13 Summary

- **Action in OM** In operations, something happens. The operations manager as researcher, or the researcher working with the operations manager, needs to take action, to observe, to infer and to evaluate the operation in order to generate actionable knowledge

- **What is action research?** Action research aims to contribute both to the practical concerns of people in an immediate problematic situation and to the goals of science by joint collaboration within a mutually acceptable ethical framework
- **Characteristics of action research:**

  o Action researchers take action
  o Action research always involves two goals: to solve a problem and to contribute to science
  o Action research is interactive
  o Action research aims at developing holistic understanding
  o Action research is fundamentally about change
  o Action research requires an understanding of the ethical framework
  o Action research can include all types of data gathering methods
  o Action research requires a breadth of pre-understanding
  o Action research should be conducted in real time
  o Action research should *not* be judged by the criteria of positivist science, but rather within the criteria of its own terms

- **Origins of action research.** Action research has many roots, some of which are in the tradition of organizational renewal
- **What is needed before entering into action research?** Before entering into action research, the researcher needs to position the proposed research in relation both to the research programme and to the needs of the organization
- **Designing an action research project.** Designing an action research project confronts the researcher with issues of framing the issue, determining its scope, gaining access and negotiating an appropriate role
- **Implementing action research.** An action research cycle comprises a pre-step and four basic steps—diagnosing, planning action, taking action and evaluating action
- **Action research skills.** An action researcher requires skills in diagnosis, intervention in relation to issues and problems in organizations, learning in action and journal keeping
- **Generating theory through action research.** Theory generated through action research has three characteristics: it is situation specific, emergent and incremental
- **Quality in action research.** There are four criteria for judging the quality of action research: participation, real-life problems, joint-meaning construction and workable solutions
- **Writing an action research dissertation.** The structure of the action research dissertation may deal with:

  o Purpose and rationale of the research
  o Context
  o Methodology and methods of inquiry

- ○ Story and outcomes
- ○ Self-reflection and learning of the action researcher
- ○ Reflection on the story in the light of the experience and the theory
- ○ Extrapolation to a broader context and articulation of usable knowledge

Note

1 This chapter is based on Coughlan, P and Coghlan, D. (2002) Action Research for Operations Management, *International Journal of Production and Operations Management*, Vol.22, No.2, pp. 220–240.

References and Bibliography

Adler, N., Shani, A.B. (Rami) and Styhre, A. (2004), *Collaborative Research in Organizations*. Sage, Thousand Oaks.

Aguinis, H. (1993), 'Action research and scientific method: Presumed discrepancies and actual similarities', *Journal of Applied Behavioral Science*, Vol.29, pp. 416–431.

Argyris, C. (2003), 'Actionable knowledge', in Tsoukas, T. and Knudsen, C. (eds.) *The Oxford Handbook of Organisation Theory*. Oxford: Oxford University Press, pp. 423–452.

Argyris, C., Putnam, R. and Smith, D. (1985), *Action Science*. Jossey-Bass, San Francisco.

Bartunek, J.M. and Louis, M.R. (1996), *Insider/Outsider Team Research*. Sage, Thousand Oaks, CA.

Beckhard, R. and Harris, R. (1987), *Organizational Transitions: Managing Complex Change*. 2nd edition. Addison-Wesley, Reading, MA.

Buchanan, D. and Badham, R. (1999), *Power, Politics and Organizational Change: Winning the Turf Game*. Sage, London.

Bushe, G.R. and Shani, A.B. (1991), *Parallel Learning Structures*. Addison-Wesley, Reading, MA.

Checkland, P. and Holwell, S. (1998), 'Action research: Its nature and validity', *Systems Practice and Action Research*, Vol.11, No.1, pp. 9–21.

Coch, L. and French, J. (1948), 'Overcoming resistance to change', *Human Relations*, Vol.11, pp. 512–532.

Coghlan, D. (2001), 'Insider action research: Implications for practising managers', *Management Learning*, Vol.32, No.1, pp. 49–60.

Coghlan, D. (2003), 'Practitioner Research for Organizational Knowledge: Mechanistic- and Organistic-oriented Approaches to Insider Action Research', *Management Learning*, Vol.34, No.4, pp. 451–463.

Coghlan, D. and Brannick, T. (2005), *Doing Action Research in Your Own Organization*. 2nd edition. Sage, London.

Coghlan, D. and Rashford, N. (2006), *Organizational Change and Strategy: An Interlevel Dynamics Approach*. Routledge, Abingdon, Oxon.

Coghlan, D. and Shani, A.B. (Rami), (2005) 'Roles, Politics and Ethics in Action Research Design', *Systemic Practice and Action Research*, Vol.18, No.6, pp. 533–546.

Coughlan, P. and Brady, E. (1995), 'Self-assessment and benchmarking product development in five Irish firms', *Journal of Managerial Psychology*, Vol.10, No.6, pp. 41–47.

Coughlan, P. and Coghlan, D. (2002), Action Research for Operations Management, *International Journal of Production and Operations Management*, Vol.22, No.2, pp. 220–240.

Eden, C. and Huxham, C. (1996), Action research for management research, *British Journal of Management*, Vol.7, pp. 75–86.

Francis, A. and Winstanley, D. (1992), The organization and management of engineering design in the United Kingdom. In Susman, G.I. (ed.) *Integrating Design and Manufacturing for Competitive Advantage*. Oxford University Press, New York, pp. 265–284.

French, W. and Bell, C. (1999), *Organization Development*. 6th edition. Prentice-Hall, Englewood Cliffs, NJ.

Fricke, W. and Totterdill, P. (2004), *Action Research in Workplace Innovation and Regional Development*. John Benjamins, Amsterdam.

Greenwood, D. and Levin, M. (2007), *Introduction to Action Research*. 2nd edition. Sage, Thousand Oaks, CA.

Gummesson, E. (2000), *Qualitative Methods in Management Research*. 2nd edition. Sage, Thousand Oaks, CA.

Hayes, R.H., Pisano, G., Upton, D. and Wheelwright, S. (2005), *Pursuing the Competitive Edge*. Wiley, New York.

Hayes, R.H. and Wheelwright, S.C. (1984), *Restoring Our Competitive Edge: Competing Through Manufacturing*. Wiley, New York.

International Benchmarking Clearing House (1992) *Benchmarking Code of Conduct*. American Productivity and Quality Center, Houston, TX.

Kleiner, A. and Roth, G. (1997), 'How to make experience your company's best teacher', *Harvard Business Review*, September–October, pp.172–177.

Kolb, D. (1984), *Experiential Learning*. Prentice-Hall, Englewood Cliffs, NJ.

Levin, M. (2003), 'Action Research and the Research Community', *Concepts and Transformation*, Vol.8, No.3, pp. 275–280.

McKay, J. and Marshall, P. (2001), The dual imperatives of action research, *Information Technology and People*, Vol.14, No.1, pp. 46–59.

McNiff, J., Lomax, P. and Whitehead, J. (1996), *You and Your Action Research Project*. Routledge, London.

Middel, R., Coughlan, P. Coghlan, D. and Brennan, L. (2005) The Application of Action Learning and Action Research in Collaborative Improvement within the Extended Manufacturing Enterprise. In Kotzab, H., Seuring, S., Müller, M., Reiner, G. (eds.): *Research Methodologies in Supply Chain Management*. Physica, Heidelberg, 2005, p. 365–380.

Morton, A. (1999), Ethics in action research, *Systemic Practice and Action Research*, Vol.12, No.2, pp. 219–222.

Nadler, D. (1998), *Champions of Change*. Jossey-Bass, San Francisco.

Nadler, D. and Tushman, M. (1984), 'A congruence model for diagnosing organisational behavior'. In D.A Kolb, I.M. Rubin, and J.M. McIntyre, *Organizational Psychology, Readings on Human Behavior in Organizations*. 4th edition. Prentice Hall, Englewood Cliffs, NJ, pp. 587–603.

Pasmore, WA (2001) 'Action research in the workplace: The socio-technical perspective'. In P. Reason and H. Bradbury, (eds.) *Handbook of Action Research*. Sage, London, pp. 38–47.

Rapoport, R.N. (1970), 'Three dilemmas of action research', *Human Relations*, Vol.23, pp. 499–513.

Raelin, J. (2000), *Work-Based Learning*. Prentice-Hall, Upper Saddle, NJ.

Rashford, N. S. and Coghlan, D. (1994), *The Dynamics of Organizational Levels*. Addison-Wesley, Reading, MA.

Reason, P. and Bradbury, H. (2001), *Handbook of Action Research*. Sage, Thousand Oaks, CA.

Riordan, P. (1995), 'The philosophy of action science', *Journal of Managerial Psychology*, Vol.10, No.6, pp. 6–13.

Rusaw, A.C. (2001), 'Ethical dilemmas of action research: A typological analysis'. In M.A. Rahim, R.T. Golembiewski, and K.D. MacKenzie (eds.) *Current topics in management*, vol. 6. Oxford: Elsevier, pp. 51–66.

Schein, E.H. (1987), *The Clinical Perspective in Fieldwork*. Sage, Thousand Oaks.

Schein, E.H. (1995), 'Process consultation, action research and clinical inquiry, are they the same?' *Journal of Managerial Psychology*, Vol.10, No.6, pp. 14–19.

Schein, E.H. (1999), *Process Consultation Revisited, Building the Helping Relationship*, Addison-Wesley, Reading, MA.

Schein, E.H. (2008), 'Clinical Inquiry/Research', in P. Reason and H. Bradbury (eds.) *Handbook of Action Research*. 2nd edition. Sage, London.

Senge, P. (1990), *The Fifth Discipline*. Doubleday, New York.

Shani, A.B. (Rami) and Pasmore, W. (1985), 'Organisation Inquiry: Towards a New Model of the Action Research Process', in D.D. Warrick (ed.) *Contemporary Organisation Development: Current Thinking and Applications*. Scott Foresman, Glenview, IL.

Shani, A.B (Rami), Mohrman, S.A., Pasmoire, W.A., Stymne B and Adler N. (2008), *Handbook of Collaborative Management Research*. Sage, Thousand Oaks, CA.

Slack, N., Chambers, S. and Johnston, R. (2001), *Operations Management*. 3rd Edition. Financial Times—Prentice Hall, Harlow.

Slack, N. and Lewis, M. (2002), *Operations Strategy*. Financial Times—Prentice Hall, Harlow.

Susman, G. and Evered R. (1978), 'An assessment of the scientific merits of action research', *Administrative Science Quarterly*, Vol.23, pp. 582–603.

Trist, E. and Murray, H. (1993), *The Social Engagement of Social Science. A Tavistock Anthology. Volume II, The Socio-Technical Perspective*. University of Pennsylvania Press, Philadelphia.

Walker, B. and Haslett, T. (2002) 'Action research in management—ethical dilemmas', *Systemic Practice and Action Research*, Vol.15, No.6, pp. 523–533.

Weisbord, M.R. (2004), *Productive Workplaces Revisited*. San Francisco: Jossey-Bass.

Zuber-Skerritt, O. and Perry, C. (2002), 'Action research within organisations and university thesis writing', *The Learning Organisation*, Vol.9, pp. 171–179.

8 Modelling and Simulation

J. Will M. Bertrand and Jan C. Fransoo

Chapter Overview

- Modelling and simulation using quantitative models: making causal relationships explicit
- An historical overview of how modelling and simulation research has evolved out of scientific management, management consulting and military applications, and what are its strengths and weaknesses for understanding and solving OM problems
- Modelling and simulation characterized as descriptive or prescriptive research, and as axiomatic or empirical research
- How to perform research in OM using modelling and simulation in steps to be taken, and demonstrated in an example, both in descriptive and prescriptive scientific problem settings
- The relevance of research using modelling and simulation for understanding and solving real-life OM problems

---

8.1 Introduction

Quantitative modelling has been the basis of most of the initial research in operations, labelled as operational research in Europe, and was the basis of initial management consulting and operations research in the US. Initially, quantitative modelling in operational research was oriented very much towards solving real-life problems in OM rather than towards developing scientific knowledge. Later however, especially in the US, a strong academic research line in operations research emerged in the 1960s, working on more idealized problems and thus building scientific knowledge in OM. During that same period, much of this research lost its empirical foundations, and research methods have been primarily developed for these more or less theoretical research lines, leaving the more empirically orientated research lines for more than 30 years in the blue with regard to research methodology.

Recently, however, this tide has turned, and the need to develop explanatory and predictive theory regarding operational processes and OM has become apparent. Articles have been published that formulate requirements for theory development in OM (Amundson, 1998; Schmenner and Swink, 1998; Wacker, 1998) or that try to connect the knowledge generated along the various research lines into a more general theoretical framework (Melnyk and Handfield, 1998b). The ideas in this chapter are based on Bertrand and Fransoo (2002).

In this chapter, we will give an overview of quantitative model-based research in OM, focusing on research methodology. OM is defined as the process of design, planning, controlling and executing operations in manufacturing and service industries. Our emphasis will be on model-based quantitative research, i.e. research where models of causal relationships between control variables and performance variables are developed, analysed or tested. Performance variables can be either physical variables, such as inventory position or utilization rate, or economic variables, such as profits, costs or revenues. We will distinguish between empirical and axiomatic research, and furthermore between descriptive and prescriptive research. We address the problem of assessing the academic quality of research work in this arena and present guidelines for doing so. In this paper, academic quality is defined as the rigour with which the standard for good academic research for the type of research conducted has been adhered to. To distinguish these types, we present a typology of model-based quantitative OM research, and present research guidelines for each of these types. In constructing our arguments, we will build on learnings from operations research and OM research from the past century and on research from a selected number of other academic disciplines.

In this chapter, we will use the following working definition to distinguish quantitative model-based research in OM from other research in OM:

Quantitative models are based on a set of variables that vary over a specific domain, while quantitative and causal relationships have been defined between these variables.

The rest of this chapter is organized as follows. In section 8.2, we will give a short overview of the origins and historical development of quantitative model-based research in OM, highlighting the strong and weak points of this type of research. Next, in section 8.3, we give the major characteristics of model-based empirical and axiomatic research. Section 8.4 discusses in detail how the various types of quantitative model-based research in OM can be conducted. In section 8.5, we discuss briefly the issue of relevance of model-based research; an issue that is often a source of debate. We conclude in section 8.6.

8.2 Origins and Development of Model-based Research in Operations Management

8.2.1 Scientific Management

Scientific management (Taylor, 1911) can be considered as the root of the development of quantitative OM. In fact scientific management was not a science, but the application of systematic methods to the study of managerial problems on the shop floor. In line with the dominant mindset in the scientific arena in those days, scientific management applied analytical techniques to operational processes, analysing the activities needed, identifying the smallest building blocks needed to achieve desired results, eliminating unnecessary activities and grouping and sequencing activities such that maximum use of resource was achieved. The attention around business process re-engineering in the 1990s can be considered as a revival of scientific management, but applied to a wider set of processes.

The essence of scientific management was the analysis of instances of real-life operational processes, based on systematic observations and measurements of these process instances, and the redesign of these processes in order to improve quality and productivity. As such, scientific management did not produce generic scientific knowledge about real-life operational processes. Its claim was that applying the methods of scientific management to existing operational processes would improve their performance. Scientific management therefore was not a science but an engineering profession; it was a systematic working method to achieve something. However, unlike engineering professions such as mechanical engineering and chemical engineering, scientific management lacked the underlying generic scientific knowledge about operational processes. Nevertheless, despite this lack of scientific foundations, the scientific management approach was extremely successful in improving operational processes. This illustrates the power of learning by doing and copying; a method of working facilitated by the emergence of the consultancy profession.

8.2.2 Business Schools and Idealized Problems: Operations Research

Scientific management laid the basis of the profession of management consultancy in the US during the interbellum. Simultaneously, business school education emerged and quantitative models were introduced in these educational programmes. In order to teach the methods and techniques from scientific management and management consultancy at these schools, the type of problems encountered in real life were simplified and formulated in general terms. Only those aspects of the problems were included that were assumed relevant from the perspective of the method and technique dealt with, and the problem was formulated independently of any particular instance of the problem in industry.

These are what we call *idealized problems*. Examples of such idealized operations management problems are inventory control problems, sequencing and scheduling problems, routing problems, statistical quality control problems and maintenance problems. Note that a model is always an abstraction from reality in the sense that not the complete reality is included. An idealized model is a model where, in addition, the abstraction from reality has been further extended so that essential trade-offs become very explicit, functions become one- or two-dimensional, differentiable, etc, in order to make the model tractable for mathematical analysis.

It will be clear from this description that these idealized OM problems were not intended as scientific models of real-life managerial problems, in the sense that the models could be used to explain or predict the behaviour or performance of real-life operational processes. They were just *partial* models of problems that operations managers may encounter. The models were partial because all aspects of the problem that were not related to the method or technique used were left out, the implicit assumption being that these aspects would not affect the effectiveness of the problem solutions based on these models. It was left to the practitioner to include these aspects into the solution based on his knowledge of reality and of the partial model of the problem. Operational processes can be very complex systems that are difficult to model scientifically from a performance point of view. This is because the performance of an operational process—generally measured in terms such as in product quality, production efficiency, cost and in delivering speed and flexibility—can be affected by many different elements in the process. For instance, machine conditions in a factory may affect quality and volume of output; however the actual impact of machine conditions on the factory output may also depend on the knowledge, motivation and training of the personnel, and on the information systems and performance measurement systems used by management. An important shortcoming of the idealized problems is therefore that the effect of the human factor on the performance of the operational process is largely neglected. As a result, implementing problem solutions based on these models often turned out to be a tedious process, and frequently failed.

It is important to realize that the models that were (and in fact are still) taught in the business school were aimed at creating insights and not at direct application. Neither were the models developed as scientific models of operational processes, i.e. models that can be used to explain or predict the output or performance of the process as a function of process characteristics, process states and inputs to the process. The professors teaching these models however conducted research, *operations research*, to further study the models, and increase their complexity. Analysis of these idealized operational management problems has generated valuable knowledge about and insight into their solution. Starting from small-scale simple problem formulations, research has been conducted on analysing the problem and finding optimal or near optimal solutions. The problems were formulated in mathematical terms, and mathematical techniques were used for analysis and solution. Gradually the complexity of the problem formulations studied was increased, making use of progress made in mathematics, statistics and computing science, leading to the development of operations research as a branch of applied mathematics and computer science. These idealized models have provided us with valuable insights in basic trade-offs, at a managerial level, but cannot be characterized as explanatory or predictive models of operational processes.

Operations research can be considered as part of the quantitative research in OM. However, the scientific aspect of operations research does not pertain to the modelling of operational processes, but to the analysis of the mathematical aspect-model of the process and the quality of the mathematical solutions. In operations research hardly any attention is paid to the scientific modelling of operational processes, that is, describing the statics and dynamics of the *processes* that are the object of study in OM. Instead, an operations research methodology has been developed mainly dealing with technique-orientated modelling of *problem* instances and implementing of solutions derived from the model. An example of this operations research methodology is the well-known hierarchical planning approach (Hax and Meal, 1975), where the problem is formulated in terms of a set of hierarchically positioned mathematical programming models.

8.2.3 Complex and Multidisciplinary Problem Instances: Operational Research

Independent from the development of operations research in the US, during WWII in the UK, operational research developed as another branch of quantitative modelling in OM (see, e.g. Keys (1991) for an excellent overview of this development). In operational research, teams of researchers with different disciplinary backgrounds, in close co-operation with the problem owner, work on developing a simple but sufficiently valid model of the problem, derive solutions to the problem based on this simple model, and test and implement the solution under problem-owner leadership. The operational research approach intends to include all aspects of operational processes that are relevant for explaining the behaviour and actual performance of the process, including the knowledge, views and attitudes of the people at the operational level and the managerial level (see, e.g. Ackoff (1957) for an explanation of this phenomenon). However, the operational research approach also does not produce scientific knowledge about operational processes, since it is only interested in explaining and improving the performance of one specific operational process instance. Operational research studies are rich in terms of modelling the various aspects and details that are considered relevant for the problem at issue. This relevance is determined exclusively by the team consisting of problem owner(s) and researchers. Operational research studies generally lack in construct validity (for definitions and a discussion on construct validity in OM, we refer to O'Leary-Kelly and Vokurka (1998) and Yin (1994:34)). Operational research can be viewed as a straightforward extension of the scientific management approach to solving operational process problems. The extension that operational research provides is the concept of working in multidisciplinary teams in close cooperation with and reporting to the problem owner(s).

8.2.4 *Influential Work from Quantitative Modelling*

Because of the developments described above in the USA and in the UK, which took place between roughly 1920 and 1960, quantitative scientific models of operational processes were virtually non-existent. With scientific models, we mean models which can be used to predict the behaviour or performance of operational processes, and which can be validated empirically in an objective way. That does not mean however, that the knowledge reported in the operations research and operational research literature is of no value. In fact, the operations research literature contains valuable knowledge about aspects of operational processes and operational research literature contains valuable knowledge about problem instances. The fact that models were either particular to a specific problem instance (as in operational research) or not validated in reality (as in operations research) does not imply that the work conducted by these researchers has not been used. Two examples of work from the operations research community that developed in the research tradition outlined in section 8.2.2 have had a significant impact in industry. The first achievement is the development of powerful short-term forecasting techniques, based on statistical analyses of historical data of the variables to be forecasted. These results have been consolidated in the work of Box and Jenkins (1976). It is interesting to note that their approach is based on discerning patterns in historical data that can be used to predict future data. This approach does not seek causal relationships to explain past behaviour or predict future behaviour, but considers the process that generates the data as a black box. The second achievement is in the area of inventory control where a large amount of idealized inventory control problems have been studied and solved to optimality or good approximate solutions. This work has been consolidated in the work by Zipkin (2000). Inventory control theory may well be the most frequently applied part of idealized models in operations research.

Despite the rather underdeveloped scientific state of the field, in the last two decades of the twentieth century methods and techniques developed by operations research started to have a serious impact on the design and control of operational processes. This especially pertains to highly automated operational processes, or operational processes and operational decision problems where the impact of the human factor is negligible. A prominent field of successful application of mathematical optimization techniques is in the general area of static allocation problems. In those problems the objective is to optimize the allocation of a resource, such as in cutting stock problems (see Cheng et al. (1994) for an overview) and vehicle routing problems (see Ball et al. (1995) for a comprehensive overview and Lenstra et al. (2001) for recent additions).

Apart from the impact of the work in forecasting, inventory modelling and mathematical optimization, three other streams of work have had significant impact in real life. They can however be distinguished from the work mentioned above by the fact that the work has been validated extensively within the research process. These three exceptions are industrial (system) dynamics, queuing theory and the research on the learning curve.

In the 1950s at MIT, J.W. Forrester developed a theoretical model of the interactions between flows of resources, materials and information in operational processes, which was able to explain the dynamic behaviour of these processes. The industrial dynamics models of Forrester are scientific theoretical models of operational processes, as they can explain and predict the dynamic behaviour and performance of the processes, and can be validated empirically (Forrester, 1961). In this respect, the work of Forrester was a major breakthrough, which has led to a general methodology for modelling dynamic systems known as system dynamics (Sterman, 2000).

The second important major achievement in theoretical model-based research in operations research is queuing theory (Buzacott and Shantikumar, 1993). Queuing theory provides us with a firm basis for understanding the performance of an operational process from its resource structure and the variability in order arrivals and resource availability (e.g. Hopp and Spearman, 2001). Just like industrial dynamics provides a theoretical framework for understanding the dynamic or non-stationary behaviour of industrial systems from the feedback characteristics of the system, queuing theory provides a theoretical framework for understanding the steady-state or stationary behaviour of the system from the variability in orders and resources.

Finally, we mention the work around the so-called 'learning curve' (see Yelle (1979) for a review) and the modelling efforts by operations researchers of this phenomenon. The learning curve models the empirical finding that frequent repetition of an operation leads to a decrease in the time needed for the execution of the operation. The basic learning curve asserts that the relation of unit labour hours or production costs to the total number of items produced is linear in the logarithms of these variables. Note that the learning curve was discovered when observing data from real-life processes (Wright (1936) as referred to by Muth (1986)). As such, it was not a causal model, but a phenomenon that occurred in a systematic way. Later, efforts have been made to develop explanatory and predictive models (e.g. Muth, 1986). These models relate existing theory from areas such as psychology and organizational behaviour to the observed power function in empirical learning curve studies and describe causal quantitative relationships.

8.2.5 Analysis of Industry Breakthroughs in Relation to Quantitative Models

In the 1970s and 1980s operations research was already an established field as far as mathematical analysis was concerned. Major achievements have been realized in the field of mathematical programming and other areas of discrete optimization. However, in those days, apart from the exceptions discussed above, its impact on the design and control of real-life operational processes was very limited. In the early 1970s, articles were published stating that operations research society was mainly talking to itself. In the late 1970s, one of the founding fathers of operations research, R. Ackoff, wrote an article stating that 'the future of operations research is past' (Ackoff, 1979), expressing his frustration over the tremendous amounts of resources spent on analysis of problems that had only a weak relation to real-life operational processes. Their lack of impact on the management of operational processes could be attributed to the fact that many of the models and solutions provided were not recognized by managers as having close correspondence to the problems they struggled with. Therefore, the real breakthrough developments took place in industry and were not driven by theoretical findings. We will give three examples to elaborate on this statement.

In the 1970s, much time in industry was spent on introducing information technology for the control of manufacturing processes, especially MRP (material requirements planning) systems (Wight, 1974). At the first instance, the operations research community did not consider these systems to be of any importance. However, the MRP systems evolution was a carrying wave for APICS, the American Production and Inventory Control Society, to start a real crusade to reduce inventories, increase efficiency and increase delivering performance in American industry. The Society organized professional education, launched its own journals, and was highly successful in terms of membership and getting the profession (production and inventory control) to a higher level. Initially, scientists did not play an important role in this development. Eventually, however, the MRP system was adopted as a 'way of working' and operations research theorists started to analyse MRP-related problems, thereby creating insights into the working of MRP systems, but again without much impact on the profession.

A similar phenomenon was observed in response to the introduction of Japanese manufacturing techniques, as in the Toyota Production System (Schonberger, 1982). In the Toyota factories in Japan, in the 1950s and 1960s a way of organizing manufacturing processes had evolved which was quite different from the processes used in the West. The Japanese put an emphasis on reliable machines, reliable products (quality) and flexibility, both in terms of machine set-ups and resource flexibility. The result was a manufacturing system that was not only more efficient than those used in the West, but at the same time more flexible, more easy to control and could deliver high-quality product. In short, their operational processes were superior to those used in the West. Studying the Toyota Production System the West has learned the lessons, and consequently used just-in-time techniques, total quality management and total productive maintenance. In response, the operations research community shifted its attention to new operational process problems, including elements of e.g. just-in-time manufacturing, and started to analyse these new problems, producing insight into the characteristics of these new manufacturing techniques.

Another example is the use of workload control to manage throughput time in complex production systems. Workload control was already advocated as 'input–output control' by Wight in his book on MRP (Wight, 1974) and is now widely known as CONWIP (Hopp and Spearman, 2001). In the 1970s and 1980s, two research groups involved in empirical research in industry observed independently that workload control dramatically improved both throughput and throughput time (Bertrand and Wortmann, 1981; Wiendahl, 1987). The observed improvements could not be explained by conventional operations research models. The conventional way for operations research to model a complex production system is an open queuing network model. Analysis of open queuing network models reveal no improvement when applying workload control; on the contrary, the performance deteriorates if workload control is applied. However, in many real-life production situations workload control was adopted as an effective management tool and eventually operations research theorists have picked it up as a research topic. Later research showed that workload control does improve performance under the assumption that management can influence the arrival of new orders to the system (Hopp and Spearman, 2001), thus closing the queuing network. However, the improvements observed in industry by Wiendahl (1987) were obtained without such control on new customer orders. Recent survey and field study research (Schmenner, 1988; Holmström, 1994; Lieberman and Demeester, 1999) contains indications that one of the assumptions underlying the conventional queuing network models might be wrong. Other types of queuing network models might explain what is observed in real-life operational processes (Bertrand and Van Ooijen, 2002).

8.2.6 Implications for Current Modelling Research in OM

In current model-based research in OM, the clear impact of both operations research and operational research can still be observed. Much of the model-based research has a strong focus on model-based analysis and managerial insight of simplified models and solution methodologies for complex but single-aspect formalized models. Within those studies, validation of the models is typically not addressed. Below, we will discuss this axiomatic type of research further. Also, more case-orientated model development is published in a number of selective journals. In these studies, validation in the methodological sense is not conducted, but models are implemented and performance differences are measured.

The discussion above suggests that model-based research can become more effective by becoming more empirical. Model-based empirical research studies models that are closer to real-life operational processes. In fact, models are studied which can be validated at real-life processes, and in some cases even the results of the analysis are tested in real life. In such a way, feedback is obtained regarding the quality of the model used for and the quality of the solutions obtained from the analysis. In this way, theoretical quantitative research is combined with empirical quantitative research. For fine examples of such research, we refer to Inman (1999) and DeHoratius and Raman (2000). In the next section, both theoretical quantitative research and empirical quantitative research are discussed more extensively and explicitly and are positioned in a general quantitative modelling OM research.

8.3 Methodologies in Quantitative Modelling

8.3.1 *Method and Methodology*

Research methodology in quantitative modelling in OM has traditionally not been perceived as an issue. There are a couple of explanations for this. The main point is that most of the reported work on methodology in OM has been on empirical research methodology. We refer to the other chapters of this volume, where overviews are given on action science (action research), longitudinal research, surveys and case studies. Methodology articles specifically addressing the domain of quantitative modelling in empirical research have however not appeared in the academic literature. Keys (1991) addresses this in his monograph on some methodological issues in the field of operational research, as do Ackoff and Sasieni (1968) in their seminal book on operations research. It is important to realize that their work is not so much concerned with the research methodology in an academic sense. They are more interested in the method used by operations/operational researchers when solving relevant and specific problems, which, as discussed above, is distinct from the academic/scientific research methodology that we are addressing in this chapter. In this chapter we focus on research that is aimed to obtain generic results towards theory building in OM rather than results of solutions for specific problems without this generic contribution.

Quantitative model-based research can be classified as a rational knowledge generation approach (see Meredith et al., 1989). It is based on the assumption that we can build objective models that explain (part of) the behaviour of real-life operational processes or that can capture (part of) the decision making problems that are faced by managers in real-life operational processes. It is important to stress that the relationships between the variables are described as causal, meaning that it is explicitly recognized that a change of value a in one variable will lead to a change of $f(a)$ in another variable. In other types of quantitative research, such as survey research, relationships are also defined between the variables that are under study. However, generally in survey research the range over which the variables vary is not always defined explicitly, and the relationship between the variables is usually not causal, and in most cases not quantitative. With 'quantitative' in this observation, we mean that the extent to which the dependent variable changes when a specified change in the independent variable occurs, is quantitative. An important consequence of the fact that relationships are causal and quantitative, is that the models can be used to predict the future state of the modelled processes rather than be restricted to explaining the observations made. Within the model, all claims are therefore unambiguous and verifiable. It is important to realize that this is not valid for claims that pertain to the world outside the model. For the world outside, unambiguous and verifiable predictions are very hard to make. Consequently, we can distinguish two distinct classes of model-based OM research: axiomatic quantitative modelling research and empirical quantitative modelling research.

8.3.2 Axiomatic Research

The first class of research is primarily driven by the (idealized) model itself. We will denote this type of research as axiomatic, in line with the terminology introduced by Meredith et al. (1989). In this class of research, the primary concern of the researcher is to obtain solutions within the defined model and make sure that these solutions provide insights into the structure of the problem as defined within the model. Axiomatic research produces knowledge about the behaviour of certain variables in the model, based on assumptions about the behaviour of other variables in the model. It may also produce knowledge about how to manipulate certain variables in the model, assuming desired behaviour of other variables in the model, and assuming knowledge about the behaviour of still other variables in the model. Formal methods are used to produce this knowledge. These formal methods are developed in other scientific branches, mainly mathematics, statistics and computer science. In fact, theoretical model-based OM research relies heavily on results obtained in mathematics, statistics and computer science. As a result, the types of models that are studied in this research line are largely determined by the available methods and techniques in mathematics, statistics and computer science, such as combinatorial optimization and queuing theory. In fact, the researchers look at the operational process or the operational decision problem, through the looking glass of the mathematical models that can be analysed. Researchers in this line are trained in, for instance, decision theory, dynamic programming, mathematical optimization, Markov processes or queuing theory.

Typically, axiomatic research is prescriptive, although descriptive research, aimed at understanding the process that has been modelled, is also present. Prescriptive research is primarily interested in developing policies, strategies and actions, to improve over the results available in the existing literature, to find an optimal solution for a newly defined problem or to compare various strategies for addressing a specific problem. Almost all articles in the (US-based) operations research domain fall into this prescriptive area (e.g. allocation theory and inventory theory). Research in the area of queuing and game theory typically is descriptive in nature and in most cases model driven. Descriptive research is primarily interested in analysing a model, which leads to understanding and explanation of the characteristics of the model.

The axiomatic model-based research line has been very productive and a vast body of model-based knowledge has been developed over the last 50 years. This knowledge is regularly consolidated in monographs and books. Good recent examples of such books are:

- *Stochastic Models of Manufacturing Systems* (Buzacott and Shantikumar, 1993)
- *Logistics of Production and Inventory* (Graves et al., 1993)
- *Supply Chain Management* (De Kok and Graves, 2003)
- *Local Search in Combinatorial optimization* (Aarts and Lenstra, 1997)

8.3.3 Empirical Research

The second class of model-based research is primarily driven by empirical findings and measurements. In this class of research, the primary concern of the researcher is to ensure that there is a model fit between observations and actions in reality and the model made of that reality. This type of research can also be both descriptive and prescriptive. Descriptive empirical research is primarily interested in creating a model that adequately describes the causal relationships that may exist in reality, which leads to understanding of the processes going on. Examples of this type of research is the industrial dynamics research conducted by Forrester in the 1950s (e.g. Forrester, 1961) and the research on clock speed in industrial systems by Fine, Mendelson, and Pillai in the 1990s (Fine, 1998; Mendelson and Pillai, 1998). Prescriptive empirical quantitative research is primarily interested in developing policies, strategies and actions to improve the current situation. This area of research is very small. Some prescriptive claims have been made within quantitative empirical articles (e.g. Blocher et al., 1999), but the verification procedure is usually not very strong. As with any research with a longitudinal design where a change action is made during the research, it is very hard to assess which changes in performance are due to the specific action and which are due to other changing circumstances. In empirical OM research, controlling all relevant variables is impossible.

In contrast with axiomatic quantitative research, empirical quantitative model-based research has not been very productive. Empirical model-based research reports on the applications of theoretical research results in real-life operational processes. Researchers working in this line should have much knowledge about the relevant characteristics of the operational process under study. However, OM still lacks a well–defined, shared methodological framework for identifying and measuring the relevant characteristics of real-life operational processes. For instance, important factors in a queuing model of an operational process are the capacity of the resources, the processing times of the operations and the arrival rate of work orders. There is no objective, situation-independent and generally accepted procedure that, observing a specific operational process by means of a queuing model, is used for measuring the capacity of the resources, the processing times of the operations and the arrival rate of the orders. Of course, in each application in a real-life situation, this construct problem is dealt with in some way or another; however, this is always done in a subjective and situation-dependent way that is seldom explicitly reported in publications. For that reason, it is difficult to judge the scientific value of the results reported in these publications. However, given the fact that quantitative model-based research is a rational, objective, scientific approach, it must develop an objective, rational way to deal with the problems encountered, when doing empirical research.

8.3.4 General Differences between Axiomatic and Empirical Research

The discussion above leads to a classification as shown in Table 8.1.

Each of these four research types leads to different contributions to the general research questions in OM. Note that in large-scale research projects several of these research types could be combined. In addition, research methodology varies across the different types of quantitative model-based research.

In the axiomatic domain, the discussion on methodology is largely absent. Instructions for referees in journals publishing this type of work do not mention the methodology issue. Rather, they focus on mathematical correctness (referring to the earlier mentioned fact that the line of reasoning must be unambiguous) and in some cases on a judgment of the referee on relevance of the problem. Reisman and Kirschnick (1994) further distinguish within the axiomatic research between what they call pure theory articles and those axiomatic articles that are tested using synthetic data. They do not address the methodology issue in their article. A special case is axiomatic research that uses computer simulation. Generally speaking, methodology is an issue in articles based on computer simulation. The methodology relies

Table 8.1 Classification of Quantitative (Model-based) OM Research Types

	Descriptive	*Prescriptive*
Empirical	ED	EP
Axiomatic	AD	AP

largely on statistics theory in experimental design and analysis, and has been well established in books such as Kleijnen and Van Groenendaal (1992) and Law and Kelton (2000).

An early contribution to the methodology discussion in OM is the seminal article by Mitroff et al. (1974). Mitroff et al.'s model is presented in Figure 8.1. The model is based on the initial approach used when operational research emerged as a field; this approach consists of a number of phases:

* Conceptualization
* Modelling
* Model solving
* Implementation

In the conceptualization phase, the researcher makes a conceptual model of the problem and system he is studying. The researcher makes decisions about the variables that need to be included in the model, and the scope of the problem and model to be addressed. In the next phase, the researcher actually builds the quantitative model, thus defining causal relationships between the variables. After this, the model-solving process takes place, in which mathematics usually plays a dominant role. Finally, the results of the model are implemented, after which a new cycle can start. Mitroff et al. argue that a research cycle can arguably begin and end at any of the phases in the cycle, if the researcher is aware of the specific parts of the solution process that he is addressing and, consequently, of the claims he can make based on the results of his research. Additionally, they put forward the notion of shortcuts in the research cycle that are often applied and that lead to less than desirable research designs. For instance, they distinguish the <modelling—model solving—narrow feedback> cycle, and comment that many researchers

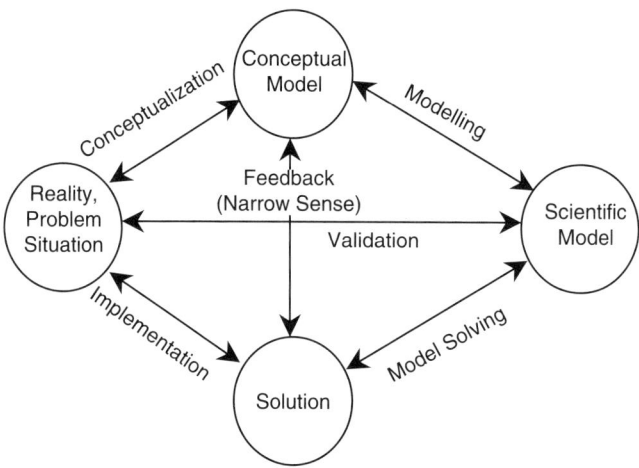

Figure 8.1 Research Model (Mitroff et al., 1974).

following this cycle tend to mistake the model-solving process for implementation. Alternatively, they name the <conceptualization—narrow feedback—implementation> cycle, which tends to mistake conceptualization for modelling, and thus distinguishing a flaw that characterizes some of the non-quantitative research. Mitroff et al.'s model is very helpful in identifying a specific methodological path that a specific article is following, and relating it to the validity of the claims that are made in the article.

As such, each of the four research types identified in the previous section can be positioned in this model. Since we are discussing quantitative model-based research, the 'scientific model' is a central issue in all four types.

In axiomatic descriptive (AD) research, the modelling process is central. The researcher takes a conceptual model—mostly from the literature—and makes a scientific model of this. Further, the researcher does some analyses on this scientific model to gain insight into the behaviour of this model. The researcher typically does not move into the model-solving phase. This extension is made in axiomatic prescriptive research, where the model-solving process is the central research process reported. In many axiomatic prescriptive (AP) articles, the modelling process is also included, and the results of the model are fed back to the conceptual model. This leads to the <modelling—model solving> shortcut. Mitroff et al. call this feedback in the narrow sense, and cite as the most common flaw that the researcher mistakes this feedback for implementation and puts forward the scientific claim accordingly.

In empirical descriptive (ED) research, the researcher typically follows a cycle <conceptualization—modelling—validation>. It is interesting to note that the main risk that Mitroff et al. notice is an overconcern with validation, i.e. the researcher wants to make a perfect fit between the model and reality. Earlier in this chapter, we noticed that reality in OM cannot be fully captured and an over-axiomatic approach in empirical research should therefore be avoided. Finally, the most complete form of research is empirical prescriptive (EP), where the entire <conceptualization—modelling—model solving —implementation> cycle is conducted. As discussed above, in many cases, this research builds upon earlier published research that is in the AD category and has already developed paths for the <modelling—model solving> stages.

8.4 How to Conduct Quantitative Research in Operations Management

In this section, we will discuss more specifically how to conduct axiomatic quantitative research and how to conduct empirical quantitative research in OM. In the axiomatic research domain, we will distinguish between analytical and numerical axiomatic research and axiomatic research using simulation. For each of the research types, we will present an example that demonstrates the research methodology in more detail. For axiomatic research, these are examples from studies on job shops. Therefore, we will first explain some basics of job shops and job shop research.

8.4.1 Background

In this section, we will demonstrate the three types of model-based research also at a particular problem area in OM. This problem area is the control of production in complex, job shop-like production systems. The term job shop characterizes production systems that can produce a large variety of products with each product having low demand, or even being a one-of-a-kind product. Such production systems use a large set of technologies, with each technology organized as a work centre, each consisting of similar machines and similar operators. Production is in small batches, and production orders for products have different routings of varying length along the work centres. Job shops generally supply components to assembly shops for complex end products. Demand for components is highly variable, which results in highly varying demand for capacity, both at the work centre level and at the aggregate level.

Job shop production systems are notorious for the high work-in-process that is needed for their economic operation, their long lead times and their difficulty in predicting the completion times of the released production orders. In the early days of OM research, queuing phenomena were already recognized as a root cause of these characteristics, and queuing models have been used to explain the steady state and dynamic behaviour of job shop production systems.

Queuing theory is a branch of applied mathematics and is one of the tools in the toolbox of researchers that perform model-based research. OM researchers doing model-based research generally do not contribute to queuing theory, but use results from queuing theory to improve their understanding of the behaviour of production systems, and to find ways to improve the performance of these systems. Over the past century, queuing theory has developed into a very rich body of knowledge with many application areas. In this chapter we do not assume the reader to have any foreknowledge about queuing theory, and our only aim is to demonstrate the nature of model-based research at the hand of OM systems and OM problems where queuing occurs. Therefore, we only use the simplest possible queuing models. We refer readers that are interested in queuing theory to e.g. Kleinrock (1975), and readers interested in the application of queuing theory to production processes to e.g. Hopp and Spearman (2001). Before demonstrating the three types of model-based research at the hand of research on job shop-like production systems, we therefore first present a few basic queuing concepts and a simple queuing result for the benefit of the non-informed reader.

Queuing occurs wherever an order (customer) arrives at a machine (server) and finds it occupied, for instance with the execution of another order. Basic concepts in queuing theory are:

- Arrival process: the arrival process defines the time that elapses between arrivals of successive orders

- Server process: the server process defines the time that it takes for the server to process an order

Queuing theory generally defines these concepts in probabilistic terms; that is, it defines the probability density function of the time between two consecutive order arrivals, and the probability density function of the time from start to finish of the processing of an order on the server. If the server is uninterruptedly available, queuing theory provides a very elegant result for the probability density function of number of orders at a single server, under the following conditions:

- The order inter-arrival times follow a stationary exponential probability density function with parameter λ
- The order processing times follow a stationary exponential probability density function with parameter μ
- Order inter-arrival times and order processing times are uncorrelated
- Orders are processed in order of arrival

This queuing system is known as the $M/M/1$ queue. The ratio $\rho = \mu / \lambda$ is known as the utilization of the server. An important result for the $M/M/1$ queue states that on the condition that $\rho < 1$, the probability of having n orders in the systems (in process plus in queue) at an arbitrary point in time is equal to:

$$p(n) = \rho\, p(n - 1), \text{ with } p(0) = 1 - \rho$$

8.4.2 Axiomatic Descriptive Research—Analytical and Numerical

As discussed above, we distinguish two types of analytical research in OM. The first type of research, axiomatic descriptive, aims at creating managerial insights into the behaviour of operational processes and their control. The second type of research, axiomatic prescriptive, aims at developing rules and tools for managerial decision making. The borderline between these two types is not always very sharp, since insights into how to control a process may directly lead to decision rules. We first discuss axiomatic descriptive research aiming at creating managerial insights; a demonstration of this type of research is given in section 8.4.2. Section 8.4.4 contains some comments that indicate research elements specific to prescriptive research.

8.4.2.1 Conceptual Modelling

Axiomatic quantitative OM research starts with a condensed description of the characteristics of the operational process or the operational decision problem that is going to be studied. This corresponds with the conceptual model in Figure 8.1. The conceptual model description should use as much as possible concepts and terms that are accepted as standards published in scientific OM literature on the subject under study. Generally, what is studied is a variant of a process or a problem that has been studied before. Therefore, in the conceptual model description reference is given to generally accepted anchor articles that contain descriptions of the general characteristics of the process or problem studied in the research line in which the current research fits (e.g. economic lot sizing, queuing or inventory control). In addition, references are given to the recent articles that study processes or problems that are closely related to the process or problem under study. In this way, the process or problem under study is clearly positioned in the scientific literature. Note that studying a process can be considered as descriptive, whereas studying a problem can be considered as prescriptive research. In axiomatic research, it is also necessary to describe all assumptions that underlie the conceptual model.

The scientific relevance of the research is mainly determined by what the research intends to contribute by the existing literature. We can distinguish two types of contribution. The first type of contribution is the study of a new variant of the process or problem, using well-known solution techniques. The second type of contribution is to study a process or problem that has been studied before, but provides a new, or in some respects better, solution to the problem, either by applying new types of solution techniques to the problem or by achieving better results with accepted solution techniques.

8.4.2.2 Scientific Modelling

The second phase in axiomatic quantitative research is the specification of the scientific model of the process or problem. The scientific model must be presented in formal, mathematical terms, such that either mathematical or numerical analysis is possible, or computer simulation can be carried out. In addition, the relationships in the model should be explained, and possibly related to earlier work in which similar relations have been developed. The scientific quality of the model is determined by various characteristics, including its innovative formulation, the compactness of the model and the degree to which the model can be studied analytically. Any description of a scientific model should discuss the additional assumptions that are introduced when developing the scientific model from the conceptual model.

Analytical research aimed at managerial insights does not try to provide the manager with a direct answer to his question; instead, it constructs an idealized model of the problem, ensuring that an answer for the idealized problem can be found with the analytical methods and tools available. At this point the analytical OM researcher has to answer the validity questions regarding his modelling assumptions. Since he deals with idealized models, validity in this context does not mean that his model needs to be a true representation of any real-life occurrence of the model of system that he is studying. Validity here means that the model captures *some* of the characteristics of each of the real-life occurrences of the model that is being studied.

Validity can be claimed in three ways. First, the researcher may refer to scientifically accepted axiomatic descriptions of the system studied that contain evidence of the occurrence of the characteristics in real life. Second, the researcher may refer to published empirical research that shows the existence in real life of the characteristics captured in the model. Third, the researcher may simply refer to earlier published research that uses the same modelling assumptions. The idea behind this is that, once a modelling assumption has been accepted as being valid for a certain class of production systems, this assumption can be used in all future research about this class of production systems.

Models used in analytical research are usually small scale, that is, the characteristics of the system are studied at a small-scale model. The reason for this can be twofold: first, problems may exist where results obtained for a small scale can be scaled up to larger models. In this case, it is efficient to study a small-scale model. Second, high dimensional models may be analytically intractable; therefore, results can only be obtained for small-scale models. The difficulty with the obtained results is, of course, that it is uncertain to what extent the managerial insight from the small-scale model also applies at a larger scale.

8.4.2.3 *Analysis, Solution and Proofs*

Researchers analyse the scientific model using algebraic techniques, numerical techniques, or use computer simulation. Thus researchers in this field must be well educated in mathematical analysis, numerical analysis or computer science. The objective of using algebraic techniques is to develop so-called 'closed-form solutions'. Closed-form solutions are expressions in which all variables can be related and only simple mathematical function can be included. For more complex problems this is often not possible, but an expression can be developed which can be computed numerically (for instance by using a computer algorithm). For many problems, even this is not possible, and in those cases computer simulation is used as a research tool. Where computer simulation is used, knowledge is also needed about experimental design and statistical analysis. The scientific quality of the research is mainly determined by the 'optimality' of the result, given the scientific model. In case of prescriptive research, 'optimality' pertains to the extent to which the result can be proven the best possible solution for the problem given. In case of descriptive research, 'optimality' pertains to the extent to which the results can be proven to provide exact characteristics of the process given.

Proofs can generally only be delivered with mathematical analysis. Therefore, in axiomatic research a strong mathematical background is needed for doing high-quality research. This is also needed to be able to judge which scientific problem formulations, given the current state of mathematical knowledge, are good problems, that is, problems for which high-quality results can be obtained. High-quality solutions result from insight into what might be a solution, in combination with a mathematical proof of the quality of the solution. Criteria for the correctness of the proof are found in the branch of mathematics used in the research. This is not discussed in this chapter. Intuition plays an important role, both in finding a solution and in proving the correctness of the solution. Thus, good research is not just the result of analytical skills or applying a methodology, but also the result of good intuition in combination with analytical skills and a good methodology.

8.4.2.4 Insights

After providing the analysis and developing the solution, the researcher needs to deduce managerial insights from the analysis, solution and proofs. This requires the researcher to relate the scientific model to the conceptual model, and develop insights within the conceptual model assumptions. In many cases, these insights will be somewhat speculative, since the conceptual model assumptions are generally less strict than the assumptions in the scientific model. An example would be that to construct a specific proof, an additional assumption may be needed about the probability density function of demand. Strictly speaking, the results from the analysis can then only be applied to managerial insights under the same restrictive assumption. In most of the journals, however, it has been accepted that some degree of speculation on assessing the impact of assumptions is applied.

8.4.3 Demonstration of Axiomatic Descriptive Research—Analytical

To demonstrate analytical research in OM we consider a single machine job shop production system. Typical OM research questions for such a production system could be:

- What is the probability that an arbitrary order arriving at this system finds more than x orders in the system?
- What fraction of the orders would be delivered late, if each arriving order would have to be delivered within L hours after arrival? (L is the customer order lead time of the system)
- What would be the effect on the average throughput time of the orders, of increasing the capacity (working hours per day) by $y\%$?
- What would be the effect on the average throughput time of the orders, if less orders would arrive per time unit, but each order would require more processing (for instance due to an increase in batch size)?
- What would be the effect on the delivery performance, of taking into

account shop workload information when quoting lead times to customer orders?

We notice that all these questions relate to issues that a manager of a job shop has to deal with; he has to decide on capacity of the shop, the production batch sizes and the lead times assigned to customer orders.

8.4.3.1 Axiomatic Descriptive

How would an analytical researcher approach the five research questions posed above? First, assuming that he is familiar with queuing theory, he might look at the system from a queuing point of view and he might postulate that a simple $M/M/1$ queuing model represents the behaviour of the system. This postulate implies that if the two parameters of the model, the order inter-arrival time, and the order processing time, can be determined, the probability density function of the number of order in the system, can be calculated.

The answer to the first question can be found by adding up the probabilities of finding $x+1, x+2, \ldots$, orders in the system at an arbitrary point in time. This leads to:

$$P(n > x) = \sum_{n=x+1}^{\infty} (1 - p)p^n = p^{x+1}$$

The managerial insight to be gained from this result is that the probability is highly sensitive to the parameter p. As p decreases, the fraction decreases sharply, especially for large values of x. Now suppose a manager of a job shop wants to communicate a certain fixed customer order lead time to the market, and he wants to be sure that at most $y\%$ of the customer orders have to queue behind x orders or more in the system at the time they arrive. Thus he requires that $P(n>x) = p^{x+1} \leq y/100$. This means that he has to control the utilization p of the system.

Thus, if the order arrival rate is given, he should be able to influence the processing rate such that $p^{x+1} \leq y/100$; if the processing rate is given, then he should be able to influence the arrival rate such that $p^{x+1} \leq y/100$.

A second important managerial insight to be gained from this result is that short and reliable lead times come at a cost. This can be seen as follows: for any pair of values (y,x) the queuing model can be used to determine the unique value of p for which this combination of values is achieved. Now $(1-p)$ is the fraction of available capacity that is not utilized for the processing of orders. Unused capacity is a factor that adds to the average cost of production. The queuing model shows that a lower utilization allows for a decrease of the lead time, or to increase the reliability of achieving the lead time. Thus, production cost, lead times and reliability can be traded off against each other. The trade-off must be based on the relationship between these three managerial performance variables that is given by the queuing model. A detailed analysis of this type of trade-off for the $M/M/1$ job-shop model can be found in Buss et al. (1994).

It will be clear that this type of research can make management better aware of the nature of the processes that they manage. However, it is left to the manager to integrate this knowledge into his mental model of the operational process as a whole, and to use it in making decisions of all kinds. This requires that the manager is sufficiently familiar with the basic concepts from queuing theory. He needs this knowledge in order to be able to interpret his own operational process in term of queuing theory concepts, and to translate the insights gained from the model analysis into action to be taken.

Insufficiently educated management is still one of the roadblocks to a better use of available scientific knowledge from analytical OM research. An excellent overview of queuing based models that can be used for evaluating the performance of production systems can be found in Suri et al. (1993).

8.4.4 *Axiomatic Prescriptive Research—Decision Rules*

Decision rule orientated research is more ambitious than managerial insight orientated research. Its goal is to provide the manager with decision rules that, when applied, achieve optimal or near optimal performance with respect to some criterion function. Results in this field are more difficult to obtain and modelling assumptions are often less strict. In particular, the results must be obtained for realistic large-scale models, or must be easily scalable to a realistic size.

Well-known examples of this type of research are the determination of the optimal order quantity under constant demand, fixed ordering costs and linear inventory holding costs (see e.g. Silver et al., 1998: chapter 5). Another famous example of this type of analytical research is the study of Holt et al. (1960) into the simultaneous determination of aggregate capacity levels, aggregate production levels and aggregate inventory levels for a plant. In order to achieve analytical results they assumed quadratic cost functions for changing capacity levels, for operating at a production level different from the capacity level, and for deviating from an aggregate inventory target level. Assuming knowledge about future aggregate demand over a long horizon, they could derive the decision rules for the future period capacity levels and the future period production levels that minimize total costs over the horizon. Quadratic costs functions were assumed because taking the derivative of a quadratic cost function to the future production levels and future capacity levels leads to a system of linear equalities that, with some mathematical manipulation, can be solved to optimality. The resulting decision rules give optimal results within the assumptions of the model, but are not easy to 'understand' by the decision maker. Interpreting the rationality of the decision rules requires the manager to understand the way in which the decision problem has been modelled, which is not provided by the decision rule as such. However, studying both the model and its resulting decision rules may lead to new managerial insights that can help the manager in his actual decision making, even if the decision rules themselves are not directly used.

The impact of decision rule orientated model-based research on managerial decision making is very similar to that of insight orientated model-based research. Full-fledged implementations of decision rules derived from models do occur, but are rare; for an example of an implementation of decision rules derived from a queuing-based model, refer to Lambrecht et al. (1998). However, an educated manager can gain insights into the nature of optimal decisions under specific modelling assumptions from the results of model-based research. We consider this to be the main contribution of analytical model-based research to OM decision making.

8.4.5 Axiomatic Research—Simulation

A slightly different approach is taken when the result is not obtained with mathematical analysis but with computer simulation. This technique is used where the model or problem is too complex for formal mathematical analysis. This type of research generally leads to lower scientific quality results than research using mathematical analysis, but the scientific relevance of the process or problem studied may be much higher. This is because computer simulation can deal with a much wider variety of scientific models than mathematical analysis can do. So the trade-off here often is between scientific relevance of the process or problem studied and scientific quality of the result.

8.4.5.1 Conceptual Modelling

The development of the conceptual model is similar to the conceptual modelling step in analytical research. The work may however be far more extensive since simulation models typically contain a significantly larger number of variables and relationships. Therefore, the initial conceptual model is typically far richer. Also, the objective of the model may not be limited to obtaining insights, but more extensive results may be developed, such as more specific recommendations for the situation studied.

8.4.5.2 Justification of the Research Method

Research that uses computer simulation requires a number of additional steps. A very important step in simulation research is the justification of this research method. Since the scientific quality of the results generally will be lower—rather than mathematical proofs, only results with some statistical significance can be reached—it is only justified to use this method if it can be shown that it is not possible to solve the problem in an analytical way. A well-known example here is use of computer simulation to test heuristic methods for solving combinatorial optimization problems. Articles that report on this research always contain a section in which it is demonstrated that the problem cannot be solved to optimality in polynomial time of the problem parameters. This is an accepted standard for justifying research on heuristics.

8.4.5.3 *Justification of the Heuristic or Hypothesis*

The second step is the justification of the solution or hypothesis to be tested. In research based on mathematical analysis, it is acceptable only to present the solution and the related proof. There the solution is justified by the proof. In simulation research, no proof is possible, so we need to be very careful in selecting our heuristic solution or hypothesis. Generally articles of this kind contain a section where evidence from previous research is used to reason why this heuristic might perform well, or why this hypothesis regarding the characteristics of the process might come close to the true characteristics.

8.4.5.4 *Development of the Scientific Model*

It is important to realize that the simulation model should only be developed after the hypotheses have been developed. In many cases, hypotheses are developed based on insights from (more simple) analytical models. The hypotheses drive the scientific model development in a number of ways. First, it defines what to include and what not to include in the model. Any factors that are not relevant to the hypotheses and research question should be excluded from the model in order to speed up the simulation process and to be better able to control the experiment. Since we are dealing with theoretical research on a computer model of the scientific model, there are—apart from storage, space and computer time—no limits to size and detail of the model. Simulation-based theoretical research therefore is only limited by computing power. However powerful computers are or will be, their limitations urge us to carefully decide on the complexity of the model to be investigated. Second, the hypotheses define what needs to be measured (recorded) during the simulation such that the right output can be generated.

8.4.5.5 *Experimental Design*

The next step is the set-up of the experimental design. This needs to be done very carefully and in accordance with accepted standards (Kleijnen and Van Groenendaal, 1992). All factors in the scientific model that may have an impact on the quality of the solution or results must be identified and have to be varied in the simulation over a sufficiently large range of values with sufficient detail. Thus, computer simulation articles always contain a section in which the experimental design is presented and justified. Further, the number of factors to be considered in the experimental design should be kept sufficiently low so that efficient simulation and effective data analysis are possible. Techniques exist to limit the number of experiments while not decreasing the number of factors to be considered.

8.4.5.6 Analysis of Results

The sixth step concerns the statistical analysis of the results of the computer simulations. There is a wide spectrum of statistical techniques available for this purpose, and the choice must be based on the type of research question to be answered. For performance testing, the t-statistic could be used to test the statistical significance of the difference between the performances obtained in the simulation with some benchmark, i.e. the performance of the best heuristic found in literature. For testing the sensitivity of the performance for parameter values in the model, analysis of variance could be used. Researchers involved in simulation-based theoretical research should be well trained in experimental design and statistical analysis, since the state of knowledge in this field determines what research questions can be approached with these techniques.

8.4.5.7 Interpretations of Results

The last step concerns the interpretation of the results of the analysis related to the research questions in the conceptual model. In this step the results are considered in the context of the conceptual problem description and the researchers derive conclusions about the extent to which the original questions are answered and what new questions emerge from these results.

8.4.6 Demonstration of Axiomatic Research—Simulation

Consider the job shop production system described in section 8.4.3 and assume that the order inter-arrival times are no longer exponentially distributed. This could be a job shop that produces components for a number of capital good manufacturers, where the manufacturers themselves face unit demand for components with exponential inter-arrival times, and place component orders in batches of size k at the production system. Batching is often done to decrease the total costs incurred by placing production orders, or to decrease the total time spent on setting up the machine. The production order inter-arrival times at the production system then are no longer exponential because the probability of a new production order for specific component to arrive depends on the time elapsed since the last arrival of a production order for this component. In fact, if demand for components at the manufacturer arrives with exponential inter-arrival times, demand for a batch of components of size $k>1$ arrives at the production system with Erlang distributed inter-arrival times.

Suppose the management of the job shop wants to know what the effect of the batch size is on the order throughput times. A first order estimate of this effect can be obtained by realizing that an increase in batch size results in a proportional decrease in average order inter-arrival times, and a proportional increase in average processing times, excluding set-up time. Neglecting the effects of batching on the second and higher order moments of the order inter-arrival times and the order processing times, we can use the *M/M/1* model to obtain an approximate analytical result for the order throughput time. For our single machine job shop with an average batch set up time of s time units, average order item processing time of μ time units and average order inter-arrival time of λ time units, we find:

$$\rho = (k\mu + s) \: / \: k\lambda$$

The average throughput time f is equal to the average numbers of orders in the system, times the average processing time per order:

$$f = (k\mu + s).\rho \: / \: (1 - \rho)$$

on the condition that:

$$\mu + s \: / \: k < \lambda$$

This approximation overestimates the average throughput time, since it assumes negative exponential batch inter-arrival times and negative exponential batch processing times, with coefficient of variation equal to one, whereas batching reduces the coefficient of variation in both the inter-arrival times and the processing times. Better approximations have been developed that capture the effects of batching on the coefficients of variation; see e.g. Albin (1984). Such approximations provide a so-called closed-form relationship between the average throughput time, f, and the batch size, k. A closed-form expression allows for easy evaluation of the value of f for various values of k, under different shop conditions, such as average set-up time, and average item processing time. However, we are uncertain about the magnitude of the error made by an approximation and how this error depends on shop conditions. Simulation is often used to provide information about the real relationship—given this scientific model—between the batch size and the average order throughput time. For this, a simulation programme needs to be developed. This works as follows.

We first define the different states that the system can be in, and what are the events that trigger a change of the state.

For our single machine job shop, the state is given by n, where:

$n = 0, 1, 2,$—indicates the number of orders in the system

Events that can occur are:

e_1- the arrival of a new production order at the machine
e_2- the completion of a production order on the machine

Events change the state in the following way:

$e_1 : n := n + 1$
$e_2 : n := n - 1$

Events can also generate new future events. An events list exists which can contain the time of its next occurrence for each type of event. The list is ordered according to earliest occurrence. In our model, next event occurrences are generated after the occurrence of an event according to the following rules.

Let $t_j(e_i)$ denote the time of the jth occurrence of type (e_i). The following next event occurrences are generated after an the occurrence of an event e_i

$$e_1 : \text{if } n = 0 : t_j(e_2) = t_j(e_1) + random2$$

$$: t_{j+1}(e_1) = t_j(e_1) + random1$$

$$e_2 : \text{if } n \neq 0 : t_{j+1}(e_2) = t_j(e_2) + random2$$

Random1 and *random2* have values that are each time randomly drawn from distribution functions which respectively model the inter-arrival time between consecutive production order arrivals, and the processing time of a production order on the machine. For our model this would be a drawing from a $(k, \lambda k)$ Erlang function for the inter-arrival times plus the machine set-up time, s, and a drawing from a $(k, \mu k)$ Erlang function for the processing times.

In simulation software packages, standard routines are available for generating drawings from distribution functions. For details, see Law and Kelton (2000).

A simulation consists of stepping from event to next event in the event list, executing the activities involved, generating next events to be placed in the event list, and registering the results. During a simulation, we can observe the evolution of the state of the system and perform all kinds of measurements. For instance we could add up the length of the periods during which the machine is in state n>0. This would be the total amount of time the machine has been busy with processing orders. Dividing this number by the total amount of the time elapsed gives the fraction of time that the machine has been busy. Or we could measure for each order that arrives, how much time it takes for this order to be completed. This necessitates expanding the state description of the system and adding a unique sequence number to each arriving order. This would enable us to make a list of all orders completed, with their arrival dates and completion dates. From this list we can derive statistics such as mean and standard deviation of the throughput times of the orders completed during a certain time period.

If the simulation model is a true representation of the system studied, running a simulation over a sufficiently long period can provide information about the true value of the measured variables up to any level of accuracy.

Checking the quality of the simulation model is an important phase in simulation-based research. This phase is called the 'verification of the model'. Verification is often done by running the model with parameter values for which theoretical results for the system studied are available. For instance we could run our model for batch size $k=1$ and zero set-up time. This system is the $M/M/1$ queuing model for which analytical results regarding the probability density function of the number of orders in the system as a function of inter-arrival times and processing times are available. We can run simulations for different values of inter-arrival times and processing times, measure the total time during which the system contains n orders, (for each $n \geq 0$) and, after completion of the simulation, determine the relative frequencies of these states. If the simulation model is a true representation of the system studied, the measured values from the simulation must be approximately equal to the theoretical values given by: $P(n) = (1-\rho)\rho^n$.

Another kind of theoretical knowledge that can be used for verification of the simulation model is the direction of change of certain variables, in function of a change in some system characteristics. For instance, all other things being equal, the average order throughput time should go up, if the order arrival rate increases.

Also in the verification phase, we encounter the problem of drawing conclusions from the data obtained from simulated systems. The result of a simulation always depends on the initial state of the system and the sequence of values of the random variables, and therefore is a statistical variable that shows randomness. The true value can be obtained with arbitrary precision if the simulation would run for infinite time. Any measurement of a finite simulation run must, however, be expected to deviate from the true value. The interpretation of data from simulation experiments therefore requires statistical expertise. For an overview of statistical methods and techniques to determine adequate simulation run lengths, to set up simulation experiments, and to interpret simulation data we refer to textbooks on this subject, such as Law and Kelton (2000) and Kleijnen and Van Groenendaal (1992).

Once the simulation model has been verified, the model can be used for investigation. Our research question was the dependency of the average order throughput time on the batch size. To investigate this, the following steps need to be taken:

- Determine the batch size values for which we want to obtain results. We could for instance decide to investigate the order throughput time for the batch sizes $1, 2, 3, 4, 5, 6, 7, 8, 9$ and 10

- Determine the values of other system parameters which may be expected to have an effect on the relationship between batch size and average order throughput time. For instance, we may expect that the set-up time, the average customer order inter-arrival time, λ, and the average customer order processing time, μ, all have an effect on the relationship under investigation. Formulated in a different way, we expect that for each combination of values for set-up time, inter-arrival time and processing time, a different relationship between batch size and throughput time exists

Here we face the difficult problem of choosing an adequate set of values, since all these parameters can be real-valued. Knowledge and insights about the shape of the relationship and its dependency on the parameter values are important in this phase. If, for instance, we would know that for any value of the batch size the throughput time is a continuous function or even a convex or concave function of each of the other parameter values, we could select a small but sufficiently large set of parameter values in a certain range and interpolate the results that are obtained from the simulations of the system for this set of parameter values. Mathematical analysis of the model may provide such knowledge. Another way to restrict the number of parameter combinations to be investigated is to exclude certain combinations on analytical grounds. For instance, we know that the system is unstable if the utilization of the machine is greater than or equal to one. Thus, we can constrain the combination of parameter values to the domain given by:

$$(\mu k + s) / (\lambda k) < 1$$

Knowing that for high values of the utilization the system is close to instability, and therefore very long or very many simulation runs would be needed to obtain reliable results, we might constrain the domain even further, for instance to values such that:

$$(\mu k + s) / (\lambda k) < 0.95$$

For the problem discussed in this section, this might, for instance for $k = 5$, lead to the choice of the following 12 parameter value combinations:

$$
\begin{aligned}
(\lambda, \mu, s) &= (1, 0.4, 0.5), (1, 0.6, 0.5), (1, 0.8, 0.5), \\
&= (1, 0.4, 0.3), (1, 0.6, 0.3), (1, 0.8, 0.3), \\
&= (1, 0.4, 0.2), (1, 0.6, 0.2), (1, 0.8, 0.2), \\
&= (1, 0.4, 0.1), (1, 0.6, 0.1), (1, 0.8, 0.1).
\end{aligned}
$$

Such a set of parameter values would be needed for each of the ten values of k selected earlier, leading to 120 different settings to be simulated.

For each of these 120 settings, simulations have to be run to determine estimates of the variables we are interested in. In our case, this might be the average order throughput time. Now one simulation run provides one measurement only, and each different set of starting conditions and different sequence of random numbers will produce a different measurement of the average order throughput time. An estimate of the real average order throughput time, including a reliability interval, can be obtained from a sufficiently large number of measurements. Thus for each of the 120 settings, a sufficient number of independent simulation runs must be made. For details about the design and analysis of such simulation experiments we again refer to Law and Kelton (2000). Let us assume that ten runs are needed to achieve the required estimation reliability. This implies that 1,200 simulation runs must be made for the proper investigation of the relationship between batch size and average order throughput time for the system under study.

It will be clear from this description that simulation studies can be very time consuming, and that studying a complex system using systematic computer simulation can be very cumbersome (the system we discussed in this section is quite simple).

Model-based research using computer simulation largely expands the range of systems that can be studied, but there still exist serious constraints due to limitation on computer speed and computer time. It therefore is most helpful if sufficient knowledge is available beforehand about the nature of the relationships that are to be investigated, since this would enable an efficient research design, that is, restrict the number of parameter settings to be simulated, and to allow for the interpolation or intrapolation of the estimates obtained from the simulations. This suggests that model-based research using simulation should preferably build on results from previous analytical model-based research.

8.4.7 *Model-based Empirical Research*

Quantitative model-based empirical research is concerned with either testing the (construct) validity of the scientific models used in quantitative theoretical research, or with testing the usability and performance of the problem solutions obtained from quantitative theoretical research, in real-life operational processes. In Figure 8.1, these core processes have been identified as implementation and validation. Quantitative empirical research is still in its infancy and there therefore exists much less consensus about what is good quantitative empirical research than about what is good quantitative axiomatic research.

Empirical scientific research tests and challenges the validity of theoretical models, and tests and challenges the usability and performance of the solutions of theoretical problems. Empirical scientific research should be carefully distinguished from the use of axiomatic research results in improvement projects conducted by consultants. These latter projects aim at improving the performance of an operational process by either changing its structure or its control. The use of theoretical research results in such projects is based on the belief that the underlying process models are valid and the theoretical solutions are usable and will perform well. Usually this belief is not validated during the project, although the methodological rules for the practice of operational research prescribe that the model assumptions should be checked (see e.g. Ackoff and Sasieni, 1968). It is not surprising that the assumptions in operational research projects are seldom checked, because doing so would be very time consuming and costly, due to the effort involved in collecting all the data needed for checking all the underlying model assumptions. This explains why real-life operational process improvement projects seldom produce scientific knowledge about operational processes.

As stated before, quantitative empirical research must be designed to test the validity of quantitative theoretical models and quantitative theoretical problem solutions, with respect to real-life operational processes. This is in line with the more general concept of theory-driven empirical research in OM (Melnyk and Handfield, 1998b; Handfield and Melnyk, 1998). Model-driven empirical research takes advantage of the large body of axiomatic quantitative research in OM, and designs the empirical research accordingly. Examples are the work by Fisher and Raman (1999), Inman (1999) and Zoryk-Schalla et al. (2004). The essence of their work is validating either the conceptual model or the solution proposed by axiomatic research results. Fisher and Raman (1999) analyse the accuracy of inventory records in retail and, using available models, assess the consequences of these inaccuracies on the results that have been obtained in the axiomatic studies. Inman (1999) validates the assumptions commonly made in axiomatic research about the processing times and order arrival times in production systems. Zoryk-Schalla et al. (2004) analyse the decision modelling process in advanced planning software, and compare the theoretical assessment to the empirical observations they make. Their empirical observations are driven by hypotheses that are based on the theories developed earlier in primarily axiomatic research settings.

A major problem here is that real-life operational processes are all different, although there are structural similarities within classes of operational processes. The similarities are often caused by the type of manufacturing technology used. Well-known classes of operational processes are for instance the continuous flow shop (e.g. assembly line), for high-volume production of similar products, and the job shop for low-volume production of a large variety of different products. However, depending on the work organization, the information system used, the level of education of the work force, etc., different flow lines and different job shops may have different operational process characteristics, and these characteristics may evolve over time.

Therefore empirical quantitative research should aim at validating the *basic* assumptions about the operational processes and problem characteristics for well-defined classes of operational processes, underlying the theoretical models and problems.

From these observations, we can derive the steps that need to be taken when doing empirical quantitative research.

8.4.7.1 Identification of Process or Problem Assumptions

The first step is the identification of the basic assumptions regarding the operational process underlying the theoretical models or problems. In the OM literature, we can distinguish different research streams that share common assumptions about the operations process or operational decision problem. For instance, there exists a research stream that is based on a queuing model view of the production process. We call this a basic assumption.

8.4.7.2 Identification of Process and Problem Types

The second step is that researchers should identify the type of operational process and the type of decision problem regarding this operational process, to which the basic assumptions are assumed to apply. For instance, it is assumed that decisions about the resource structure of a job shop production system should be based on a queuing model of the flow or orders along the work centres.

8.4.7.3 Development of Operational Definitions of the Process

The third step is that operational, objective criteria must be developed for deciding whether or not a real-life operational process belongs to the class of operational processes considered (i.e. a job shop) and for identifying the decision system in the operational process that represents the decision problem considered. These criteria should be objective, that is, each researcher in OM using these criteria would come to the same decision regarding the process and the decision system.

8.4.7.4 Hypotheses Development

The fourth step is to derive, from the basic assumptions, hypotheses regarding the behaviour of the operational process. This behaviour refers to variables or phenomena that can be measured or observed at the operational process in an objective way. The more different testable hypotheses are derived from the basic assumptions, the stronger the research is. Hypotheses can often be developed based on insight from axiomatic research (either analytical or simulation-based).

8.4.7.5 Measurement Development

The fifth step is to develop an objective way to do measurement or to make the observations. This very crucial step requires documentation. The reason for this is that, in operational process research, there exists no formalized construct for variables such as processing time, machine capacity, production output, production throughput time, etc., nor do generally accepted ways of measuring there variables exist. This illustrates the weak position of quantitative empirical research in OM. The situation being as it is, empirical OM researchers must develop their own way of measuring and document this carefully. This requires that the researcher knows how to identify the relevant characteristics of the operational process, and knows how to change or influence and measure the relevant characteristics of the process. Thus model-based empirical research cannot be done without a systematic approach for identifying and measuring real-life operational processes. This is what is called the conceptual modelling of a system by Mitroff et al. (1974). Conceptual models define the relevant variables of a system under study, the nature of their relationships and their measurements.

8.4.7.6 Data Collection

The sixth step consists of applying the measurement and observation systems, collecting, and documenting the resulting data. A variety of data collection methods and sources can be used, including surveys, public economic or finance data (e.g. Hendricks and Singhal, 2003), private company transactional data (e.g. Fransoo and Wiers, 2006), or observational studies (such as time and motion studies) (e.g. Van Zelst et al., in press).

8.4.7.7 Data Analysis

The seventh step is the processing of the data, which generally will include the use of statistical analysis. Here special techniques are needed since the data are not the result of an experimental design where variables in the system can be manipulated at will, but result from observations on a real-life system that cannot be manipulated in an arbitrary way. Sophisticated statistical techniques have been developed for this type of research in some branches of research in social sciences (e.g. Herzog, 1996; Marcoulides and Schumacker, 1996). When developing the hypotheses regarding the behaviour of the operational process in step 4, it should be taken into account what type of behaviour can be expected of the process under the given real-life circumstances, within the time frame that the process can be observed; the hypotheses should be restricted to behaviour in the expected range and time frame. For instance it makes no sense to develop the hypothesis that a job shop will have an average order throughput time of 60 weeks under a steady state capacity utilization of 95%, if a reliable measurement of the work order throughput time under a capacity utilization of 95% requires that the process is measured for 10,000 years. Thus, developing effective hypotheses and an efficient operational measurement system require that the researcher is quite familiar with the type of operational process and the type of decision problem concerned, and is very familiar with the statistical techniques available for analysis of field data.

8.4.7.8 Interpretation of Results

Finally, the last step in quantitative empirical research consists of the interpretation of the research results related to the theoretical models or problems that gave rise to the hypotheses that were tested. This step completes the validation process and may result in confirmation of (parts of) the theoretical model in relation to the decision problem and in relation to the operational process considered, but may also lead to (partial) rejections and suggestions for improving the theoretical models.

8.4.8 Demonstration of Model–based Empirical Research

Model-based empirical research pertains either to validating the basic assumptions underlying formal models of operational processes, or to checking the claims regarding performance that can be obtained, as predicted with the use of formal models. In this section we will demonstrate both types of research in the form of model-based empirical research carried out on the execution and control of product development projects (Van Oorschot et al., 2005; Dragut and Bertrand, 2008).

Product development projects consist of networks of design tasks. A design task is the task to determine the technical product specifications that lead to the realization of pre-specified product functionality. Design tasks are carried out by design engineers, often working together in teams managed by a project leader.

A design task essentially consists of a number of design activities, each activity referring to a specific design problem to be solved. Complex design tasks require many design activities; simple design tasks only contain a few design activities. The design activity can be considered the elementary unit for estimating the amount of time needed to carry out design tasks. The larger the number of activities needed, the larger the amount of time needed for solving a design problem. Research results from cognitive psychology (Best, 1995; Reed, 1988), suggest that the time needed by humans for solving problems can be modelled as a stochastic variable with a long-tailed distribution function that can be approximated by a negative exponential. Assuming that the time needed to perform design activities are identically distributed, it follows that the time needed for performing a design task consisting of k activities, is Erlang distributed with shape factor k.

An important aspect of the planning and control of product development projects is the estimation of the time needed for performing design tasks, and the estimation of the moment in time at which design tasks will be completed. In the company where this empirical research was carried out, the estimation of processing times and completion times was done by the engineers and their project leader. In the company, each engineer worked simultaneously on two to three design tasks and was allocated a new design task after completing a task. Upon allocation of a design task the engineer estimated the processing time of the new task, estimated the remaining processing time of the tasks on hand, added these numbers up, and divided the result by the number of hours available per week for processing design tasks. The resulting number is the estimate of the number of weeks that will elapse before completion of the new design task. (The estimated lead time of the design task.)

During execution, an engineer has to decide which of the design tasks on hand to work on. When performing a design task an engineer can detect new design activities, not identified in the initial estimation. Moreover, when performing a design task an engineer may be interrupted by another engineer that requires information or specific support for his work. The firm strongly encourages engineers to give priority to helping their colleagues out when specific information or support is needed that only they can provide. Finally when performing a design task, an engineer may encounter some difficulties and switch temporarily to another design task.

For this design tasks execution process, Dragut and Bertrand (2008) developed a formal model, based on queuing theory, for calculating the distribution function of the actual lead time of a design task; the actual lead time being defined as the time that elapses between the allocation of the design task to an engineer and the completion time of that task. The model requires parameter values for:

$N(n)$, the number of planned activities in design task n,
μ, the exponential distribution parameter of the design activity processing time,
γ, the exponential inter-arrival time of unplanned activities, and
p, the probability that the engineer will be interrupted during execution of a design task.

The model was empirically validated using data collected in the company from ten engineers working on an electronic product development project. The engineers made lead time estimates for the design tasks that were allocated to them over a period of 20 weeks. After a design task was completed, the realized lead time was noted. In total, data on 424 design tasks were collected with estimated lead times ranging from 1–8 weeks. Design tasks with equal estimated lead times are comparable in the sense that they represent situations where the engineers perceive the same total number of planned design activities to do before the newly allocated design task is completed. Comparison of the realized lead times per group of design tasks with equal estimated lead times therefore provides information of the lead time distribution as a function of estimated number of planned design activities. The data collected allows for the formation of eight such groups. Table 8.2 shows the frequency diagrams of realized lead times for the group with estimated lead time of 1 week, 3 weeks and 8 weeks.

How has validation of the model been done? First we remark that the model contains four parameters; for three of them, their value needs to be estimated from the empirical data. Thus, the empirical data have to be split up in a subset that is used for parameter estimation, and a subset that is used for model validation. Second we remark that 'Ockam's razor' must be applied. Ockam's razor refers to the rule that if one of two models, a complex one and a less complex one, have the same explanatory power, the less complex model should be adopted. Therefore validation should start with the simplest version of the model, and only proceed with a more complex one if the simpler version is rejected by the data.

Table 8.2 Frequency Diagrams of Realized Lead Times for the Group with Estimated Lead Time of 1 Week, 3 Weeks and 8 Weeks

Realized time	Estimated lead time		
	1 week	3 weeks	8 weeks
1	48	1	0
2	8	7	0
3	3	26	0
4	2	6	0
5	1	11	0
6	6	4	0
7	0	6	2
8	1	3	10
9	0	2	4
10	0	0	2
11	0	1	1
12	0	0	3
13	0	0	2
14	0	0	2
15	0	1	1
16	0	0	1
17	1	0	1
18	1	0	0
19	0	0	1
20	0	0	0
21	0	1	0
22	0	1	0
23	0	0	0
24	0	0	0
25	0	0	0

Van Oorschot et al. (2005) already checked the validity of a very simple model that assumed that completion of design tasks requires processing of a number of design activities proportional with the estimated lead time, that assumed that no new design activities will emerge, and that no interruptions will occur. They used the empirical data of design tasks with 1 week estimated lead time to estimate two parameters: the number of design activities per week estimated lead time and the average processing time per design activity; they used the other seven data sets to validate this model. The model was rejected by a goodness-of-fit test at $a = 0.01$. Thus, investigating the validity of more complex models was justified.

Dragut and Bertrand (2008) used the Kolmogorov-Smirnov goodness-of-fit test to investigate the validity of more complex models. The Kolmogorov-Smirnov test finds the greatest discrepancy between the empirical and the theoretical cumulative distribution function, which is called the D-statistic. The D-statistic is compared with the critical D-statistic for the sample size.

They first investigated a model with arrival of new design activities during execution of design tasks but without interruption of design tasks.

The empirical data with estimated lead time of 1 week was used to estimate the three parameter values $N(n)$, μ and γ, resulting in the values $N(n) = 4L$ with L the estimated lead time in weeks, $\mu = 4$ hours and $\gamma = 0.66$ arrivals per week. The model was validated on the other seven data sets. The Kolmogorov-Smirnov tests showed that the model only agreed with the data set of 2 weeks estimated lead time. For all other sets the model was rejected. Thus the introduction of the effect of interruptions in the model seems to be justified. Using again the 1 week estimated lead time data set for parameter estimation resulted in $N(n) = 4L$, $\mu = 4$ hours, $\gamma = $ one week and $p = 0.15$. Testing this model on the other seven data sets showed that the null hypothesis that the empirical distribution is in accordance with the model could not be rejected.

The scientific contribution in this example of model-based empirical research is twofold. First, the empirical data seem to corroborate the queuing model assumptions that have been used to develop the model that relates the realized design task lead time to the parameter values of the model. Second, the results of the successive tests with the different models indicate the relevance of taking into account arrival of unplanned design activities and work interruptions for explaining the distribution of the realized design task lead times.

Often model-based empirical research not only leads to corroboration or refutation of postulated formal models, but also inspires the researchers to new ideas or new hypotheses. In the example we discuss here, studying the empirical data in the light of the test results inspired the researchers to include one other effect into the model. For design tasks with estimated lead time larger than 3 weeks, the existence of a fixed delay, proportional with the estimated lead time, was postulated. The fixed lead time dependent delay was justified by the fact that every now and then engineers were faced with the need to work on a completely new design task, due to the reshuffling of the development project. The resulting model was not only accepted in all cases, but also showed a very good fit from the probability density function point of view. For details, refer to Dragut and Bertrand (2008).

8.5 Relevance

In OM, relevance is generally justified by referring to real-life situations to which the model or problem might apply. Assessing relevance has had a long history in the operations research journals. The main debate addresses the so-called 'gaps' between operations research theory and practice, bringing forward two issues:

1   Why do researchers not address more practically relevant problems, in terms of complexity, design and definitions?
2   Why do practitioners not make more use of all available tools and results that have been developed by the operations research community?

In this chapter, we will not go into this debate, but refer to other work, such as Corbett and Van Wassenhove (1993), Ormerod (1997) and Reisman and Kirschnick (1995). An important observation in these articles is that progress in operations research seems to develop along a line that Reisman and Kirschnick denote as 'ripple research'. With this, they refer to research that is conducted on small extensions of previous axiomatic research, and thus cannot bridge the gap that according to these articles apparently exists between the results of axiomatic research and the real-life need of decision makers. It should be noted that in some areas, e.g. allocation theory and inventory theory, series of small extensions have lead to very useful models that have been applied in business practice on a large scale.

The relevance issue cannot be seen apart from the fact that mathematics, statistics and computer science do not (yet) provide us with sufficiently powerful methods of analysis to address problems that come close to the complexity that is observed in most real-life operational processes. The type of models studied in operations research is therefore restricted to those models that allow the researcher to do analysis and to make scientific claims. This leads to the fact that for the axiomatic research the relevance criterion (with regard to the validity of the model versus reality) is usually applied very lightly. In many cases, relevance is motivated by referring to earlier articles addressing similar issues, or by referring to general trends in the industry, rather than tying the relevance to actual observations in reality. The model is considered 'acceptably relevant' if the modelled problem can be recognized, possibly as an aspect model of reality. We would like to add an important criterion for relevance, apart from the validity issue. This is the question whether the solution of the model assists managers in making decisions in the real world. This is the case if the aspect-model-based solution covers the most important part of the solution, and the context factors (not included in the model) are less relevant to the actual solution.

8.6 Summary

- The use of modelling and simulation for researching OM issues was discussed
- OM was defined and the quantitative modelling process that underlies the modelling and simulation research approach was characterized
- How modelling and simulation evolved out of scientific management and developed into a distinctive research approach having specific strength and weaknesses relative to other OM research approaches such as survey research, case research, action research and operational research as a special instance of action research was described
- Inventory control, forecasting, mathematical optimization and queuing theory were mentioned as examples of influential results produced by modelling and simulation research, and the major breakthroughs in industry relative to the contribution of modelling and simulation were positioned
- Modelling and simulation were characterized as descriptive or prescriptive axiomatic research and identified in their positions in the OM research model of Mitroff et al.
- Guidelines on how to conduct qualitative model-based research, both for analytical research and for simulation research were given, and the guidelines for both types were demonstrated with an example
- Finally guidelines for doing model-based empirical research were given and also this research approach was demonstrated with an example

References and Bibliography

Aarts, E.H. and Lenstra, J.K. (1997), *Local search in combinatorial optimization*, New York: Wiley.

Ackoff, R.L. (1957), 'A comparison of OR in USA and Great Britain', *Operational Research Quarterly*, 8: 88–100.

Ackoff, R.L. (1979), 'The future of operational research is past', *Journal of the Operational Research Society*, 30: 93–104.

Ackoff, R.L. and Sasieni, M.W. (1968), *Fundamentals of Operations Research*, New York: Wiley.

Albin, S.L. (1984), 'Approximating a point process by a renewal process, II: Superposition arrival processes to queues', *Operations Research*, 32, 5: 1133–1162.

Altiok, T. (1997), *Performance Analysis of Manufacturing Systems*, New York: Springer-Verlag.

Amundson, S.D. (1998), 'Relationships between theory-driven empirical research in operations management and other disciplines', *Journal of Operations Management*, 16: 341–359.

Ball, M.O., Magnanti, T.L., Monma, C.L. and Nemhauser, G.L. (Eds.) (1995), *Network Routing*, Amsterdam: North-Holland.

Bertrand, J.W.M. and Fransoo, J.C. (2002), 'Operations management research methodologies using quantitative modeling', *International Journal of Operations and Production Management*, 22, 2: 241–264.

Bertrand, J.W.M. and van Ooijen, H.P.G. (2002), 'Workload based order release and productivity: a missing link', *Production Planning and Control*, 13, 7: 665–678.

Bertrand, J.W.M. and Wortmann, J.C. (1981), *Production control and information systems for component-manufacturing shops*, Amsterdam: Elsevier.

Best, J.B. (1995), *Cognitive Psychology*, St Paul: West Publishing Company.

Blocher, J.D., Garrett, R.W. and Schmenner, R.W. (1999), 'Throughput time reduction: Taking one's medicine', *Production and Operations Management*, 8: 357–373.

Box, G.E.P. and Jenkins, G.M. (1976), *Time Series Analysis: Forecasting and Control*, 2nd Ed., San Francisco: Holden-Day.

Buss, A.H., Lawrence, S.R. and Kropp D.H. (1994), 'Volume and Capacity Interaction in facility design', *IIE Transaction*, 26, 4: 36–49.

Buzacott, J.A. and Shantikumar, J.G. (1993), *Stochastic Models of Manufacturing Systems*, New York: Prentice Hall, Englewood Cliffs.

Cheng, C.H., Feiring, B.R. and Cheng, T.C.E. (1994), 'The cutting stock problem—a survey', *International Journal of Production Economics*, 36: 291–305.

Corbett, C.J. and Van Wassenhove, L.N. (1993), 'The natural drift (What happened to operational research?)', *Operations Research*, 41: 625–640.

De Kok, A.G. and Graves, S.C., (Eds.) (2003), *Supply Chain Management: Design, Coordination and Operation* (Handbooks in Operations Research and Management Science, vol. 11), Amsterdam: North-Holland.

DeHoratius, N. and Raman, A. (2000), 'Retail performance improvement through appropriate store manager incentive design: an empirical analysis', *Working Paper*, Boston: Harvard Business School.

Dragut, A.B. and Bertrand, J.W.M. (2008), 'A representation model for the solving time distribution of a set of design tasks in New Product Development (NPD)', *European Journal of Operational Research*, 189: 1217–1233.

Fine, C.H. (1998), *Clockspeed: Winning Industry Control in the Age of Temporary Advantage*, Reading: Perseus Books.

Fisher, M.L. and Raman, A. (1999), *Tutorial: Retail operations*, presented at INFORMS Fall Meeting Philadelphia, INFORMS, Linthicum.

Forrester, J.W. (1961), *Industrial Dynamics*, Cambridge: MIT Press.

Fransoo, J.C. and Wiers, V.C.S. (2006), 'Action variety of planners: cognitive load and requisite variety', *Journal of Operations Management*, 24, 6: 813–821.

Graves, S.C., Rinnooy Kan, A.H.G. and Zipkin, P.H. (Eds.) (1993), *Logistics of Production and Inventory*, Amsterdam: North-Holland.

Handfield, R.B. and Melnyk, S.A. (1998), 'The scientific theory-building process: a primer using the case of TQM', *Journal of Operations Management*, 16: 321–339.

Hax, A.C. and Meal, H.C. (1975), 'Hierarchical integration of production planning and scheduling', in Geisler, M.A. (Ed.), *Logistics*, Amsterdam: North-Holland, pp. 53–69.

Hendricks, K.B. and Singhal, V.R. (2003), 'The effect of supply chain glitches on shareholder wealth', *Journal of Operations Management*, 21, 5: 501–522.

Herzog. T. (1996), *Research Methods in the Social Sciences*, New York: Harper Collins.

Holmström, J. (1994), 'The relationship between speed and productivity in industry networks: a study of industrial statistics', *International Journal of Production Economics*, 34: 91–97.

Holt, C.C., Modigliani, F., Muth, F. and Simon, H.A. (1960), *Planning Production Inventories and Workforce*, New York: Prentice-Hall, Englewood Cliffs.

Hopp, W.J. and Spearman, M.L. (2001), *Factory Physics*, Boston: Irwin/McGraw Hill.

Inman, R.R. (1999), 'Empirical evaluation of exponential and independence assumptions in queuing models of manufacturing systems', *Production and Operations Management*, 8: 409–432.

Keys, P. (1991), *Operational Research and Systems: The Systemic Nature of Operational Research*, New York: Plenum Press.

Kleijnen, J.P.C. and Van Groenendaal, W. (1992), *Simulation: A Statistical Perspective*, Chichester: Wiley.

Kleinrock, L. (1975), *Queuing Systems, Vol. 1: Theory*, New York: Wiley.

Lambrecht, M.R., Ivens, P.L. and Vandaele, N.J. (1998) 'ACLIPS: A capacity and lead time integrated procedure for scheduling', *Management Science*, 44, 11: 1548–1561.

Law, A.M. and Kelton, W.D. (2000), *Simulation Modeling and Analysis*, 3rd ed., New York: McGraw-Hill.

Lenstra, J.K., De Paepe, W.E., Sgall, J., Sitters, R.A. and Stougie, L. (2001), 'Computer-aided complexity classification of dial-a-ride problems', *Working Paper*, Department of Mathematics and Computing Science, Technische Universiteit Eindhoven, Eindhoven.

Lieberman, M.B. and Demeester, L. (1999), 'Inventory reduction and productivity growth: linkages in the Japanese automotive industry', *Management Science*, 45: 466–485.

Marcoulides, G.A. and Schumacker, R.E. (Eds.) (1996), *Advanced Structural Equation Modeling: Issues and Techniques*, New York: Lawrence Erlbaum.

Melnyk, S.A. and Handfield, R.B. (Eds.) (1998a), Special Issue, *Journal of Operations Management*, 16: 311–508.

Melnyk, S.A. and Handfield, R.B. (1998b), 'Preface: May you live in interesting times . . . the emergence of theory-driven empirical research', *Journal of Operations Management*, 16: 311–319.

Mendelson, H. and Pillai, R.R. (1998), 'Clockspeed and information response: Evidence from the information technology industry', *Information Systems Research*, 9: 415–433.

Meredith, J.R., Raturi, A., Amoako-Gyampah, K. and Kaplan, B. (1989), 'Alternative research paradigms in operations', *Journal of Operations Management*, 8: 297–326.

Mitroff, I.I., Betz, F., Pondy, L.R. and Sagasti, F. (1974), 'On managing science in the systems age: Two schemas for the study of science as a whole systems phenomenon', *Interfaces*, 4, 3: 46–58.

Muth, J.F. (1986), 'Search theory and the manufacturing progress function', *Management Science*, 32, 8: 948–962.

O'Leary-Kelly, S.W. and Vokurka, R.W. (1998), 'The empirical assessment of construct validity', *Journal of Operations Management*, 16: 387–405.

Ormerod, R.J. (1997), 'An observation on publication habits based on the analysis of MS/OR journals', *OMEGA*, 25: 599–603.

Reed, S.K. (1988), *Cognition: Theory and Applications*, Pacific Grove: Brooks/Cole Publishing Company.

Reisman, A. and Kirschnick, F. (1994), 'The devolution of OR/MS: Implications from a statistical content analysis of papers in flagship journals', *Operations Research*, 42: 577–588.

Reisman, A. and Kirschnick, F. (1995), 'Research strategies used by OR/MS workers as shown by an analysis of papers in flagship journals', *Operations Research*, 43: 731–740.

Schmenner, R.W. (1988), 'The merit of making things fast', *Sloan Management Review*, 30, 1: 11–17.

Schmenner, R.W. and Swink, M.L. (1998), 'On theory in operations management', *Journal of Operations Management*, 17: 97–113.

Schonberger, R. (1982), *Japanese Manufacturing Techniques: Nine Hidden Lessons in Simplicity*, New York: Free Press.

Silver, E.A., Pyke, D.F. and Peterson, R. (1998), *Inventory Management and Production Planning and Scheduling*, 3rd ed., New York: Wiley.

Sterman, J.D. (2000), *Business Dynamics: Systems Thinking for a Complex World*, Boston: Irwin/McGraw-Hill.

Suri, R., Sanders, J.L. and Kamath, N. (1993), 'Performance evaluation of production networks', Chapter 5 in Graves S.C., Rinnooij Kan, A.H.G. and Zipkin P.H. (Eds.), *Handbook in Operations Research and Management Science, Vol. 4, Logistics of Production and Inventory*, Amsterdam: North Holland.

Taylor, F.W. (1911), *The Principles of Scientific Management* (Harper & Row, New York). Reprinted as part of a collection: *Scientific Management*, Harper & Row, 1947.

Van Oorschot, K.E., Bertrand, J.W.M. and Rutte, C.G. (2005), 'Field studies into the dynamics of product development tasks', *International Journal of Production and Operations Management*, 25, 8: 720–739.

van Zelst, S., van Donselaar, K.H., van Woensel, T., Broekmeulen, R.A.C.M. and Fransoo, J.C. (2008), 'A model for store handling. potential for efficiency improvement', *International Journal of Production Economics*, in press.

Wacker, J.G. (1998), 'A definition of theory: research guidelines for different theory-building research methods in operations management', *Journal of Operations Management*, 16: 361–385.

Wiendahl, H.P. (1987), *Belastungsorientierte Fertigigungssteuerung: Grundlagen, Verfahren-saufbau, Realisierung*, Muenchen: Hanser.

Wight, O.W. (1974), *Production and Inventory Management in the Computer Age*, Boston: CBI.

Wright, T.P. (1936), 'Factors affecting the cost of airplanes', *Journal of Aeronautical Sciences*, 3: 122–128.

Yelle, L.E. (1979), 'The learning curve: historic review and comprehensive survey', *Decision Sciences*, 10: 302–328.

Yin, R.W. (1994), *Case Study Research: Design and Methods*, 2nd Ed., Thousand Oaks: Sage.

Zipkin, P.H. (2000), *Foundations of Inventory Management*, London: McGraw-Hill.

Zoryk-Schalla, A.J., Fransoo, J.C. and De Kok, A.G. (2004), 'Modeling the planning process in Advanced Planning Systems', *Information and Management*, 42: 75–87.

9 Concluding Remarks

Christer Karlsson

Chapter Overview

- Key messages from the book:

    ○ The role of research
    ○ Demands on research
    ○ The role of method
    ○ Relevance and ethics

- Summary of learning from the chapters—a brief overview
- Choosing and combining approaches—triangulation in methods:

    ○ The strength of mixtures
    ○ Different kinds of mixtures
    ○ Validity in mixed research

- Implementing good practices:

    ○ Learning from role models
    ○ Importance of contribution and rigour

- Generalization into different management areas—beyond OM

    ○ Operations across functions
    ○ Characteristics of operations and management
    ○ Conditions for generalization

- A contract with science—a researcher ethic:

    ○ Ethics and morals
    ○ Contract partners
    ○ A formal contract

- Summary
- References and bibliography

9.1 Key Messages from the Book

Research is about developing, producing and also disseminating new knowledge. There are different levels of knowledge. A high school level may be to apply and use existing formulas, an academic level may be, with the help of theory, to develop new models, while the research level may be to develop the theory.

When doing research a paramount issue will be the contribution of new knowledge to already existing knowledge. It is important that the new knowledge can be trusted as valid and reliable. For that reason the researcher will use methods that can make it probable that the receiver of the knowledge can trust the propositions generated by the research.

There are different kinds of research and different methods that can be used in different research. The methods are more or less feasible depending on the type of research and they often create different kinds of knowledge. The choice of method is not necessary a singular decision. On the contrary, combinations of methods are likely to enhance the value of the contribution when applied to different parts of the research. Often a researcher or research institute will focus not only on certain issues but may also specialize in certain types of studies and research methods.

When it comes to carrying through the research, careful planning and rigorous execution are important. Everything from literature mapping to structured analysis and synthesis must be of high standard and understandable for the receiver.

However good the methods are, there are still the issues of relevance and ethics. The research should be of value for important stakeholders. Simultaneously the research output should not create any damage to man or the environment.

It will not be possible to, with total conviction, claim that a certain piece of research is good. But the scientific community has well-established processes for assessing research, although bad pieces may get through and ideas that are too innovative may be hampered.

9.2 Summary of Learning from the Chapters— a Brief Overview

This book is both a textbook and a handbook. As such a classic summary can hardly be made. To facilitate the reader to get a comprehensive view each chapter has been designed with an introductory textbox overview of the chapter and a concluding section with brief statements of main issues from the text.

In Chapter 2 operations were described and characterized as transformation of resources into information, products and services. Operations exist throughout other functions outside the operations function itself. There are several research approaches which have a managerial focus. This book has an inclination to a European research tradition. Good research was discussed based on contribution to knowledge and rigour in process. Generally it is thought that the most significant characteristic of good research is that, methodologically, it is well done. Research is expected to provide trust-worthy knowledge since it is done by independent knowledgeable scholars trained to develop knowledge using rigorous processes. A challenge for the OM researcher is to create contributions and value for both academia and practice. This challenge will promote the often empirically based research approaches used in OM. How to think of the research contribution was analysed. Due to a cumulative character of knowledge and sequential devel-opment, different research outputs in different phases of the development of the field of knowledge will be seen. The fit between problem, method and contribution is often reached in an iterative manner. A holistic view from discussing the issues and mapping the existing knowledge via research design and structured analysis to putting the contribution in relation to knowledge was emphasized. Demands on research involve newness in contribution, research rigour and generalizability, but also relevance and ethical consider-ations. Eventually we focused on the presentation of the research and specif-ically characteristics of scientific publication. In the academic world the old saying 'Publish or perish' is increasingly relevant in global competition. If you do not publish you do not exist! Understanding criteria for reviews is important before planning the manuscript. The readers, and before that the reviewers, will ask questions such as what is the purpose of the research, what is the contribution and what does the author claim, how well is the claim supported, what is the theoretical framework and does the author know the area well enough, is the method adequate, is the report well structured and easy to follow, and is it well written? The chapter concludes with a checklist for analysing manuscripts.

In Chapter 3 we learned that designing research in OM needs to take into account the 'messy', iterative nature of a typical management research pro-ject. In the process of research the researcher will discover issues, theories, literature sources, phenomena, characteristics and variables that will not have been considered at the outset. What can be done is to manage the process by 'asking the right questions'. This is essentially what research design is all about and good research design will recognize that the research will be likely to evolve. Clear concrete steps to ensure that the process is a rigorous and reliable one can be taken. The chapter addressed these steps by concentrating on how to position the research. A key issue is to know the existing literature since research is supposed to take knowledge a step ahead of that. It is also important to have an overview of a range of research methods, to avoid being constrained by one approach or methodology. Often combinations of methods (and methodologies) are valuable. Further, the 'personality' of the researcher plays a role; there are different types of researchers and one should feel comfortable with what is done and how it is done. Finally, quality is paramount in research and it is vital to have a clear knowledge of what good research looks like and ensure steps that are taken to assure a valid and rigorous process is followed.

Chapter 4 taught us about surveys but also many basics about planning and conducting research. Before we get started we need to make clear the unit of analysis, construct definitions and hypotheses or research aim. What is it we are going to study, what is the population, the sample and the subjects? Instruments to use for measuring constructs should be developed. This activity implies a move from the theoretical to the empirical domain. It is considered so important in OM that it deserves ad hoc research projects and publications. A lot of care must be taken in selecting which observable aspects to ask for, in choosing the appropriate wording, in assessing whether the questions can be answered in a trustworthy manner, in identifying individuals who are informed and can answer, and in getting data that refers to the unit of analysis level and not to different levels. Getting data from different sources enables triangulation which enhances data validity. Then there are questions about whether satisfactory data have been received. There may be biases and systematic lack of data influencing if data is representative. There is a range of quality aspects to consider. Reliability indicates dependability, stability, predictability, consistency, accuracy and refers to the extent to which a measuring procedure yields the same results on repeated trials. Construct validity refers to the degree to which a measure represents and acts as the concept being measured. Criterion–related validity is established when the measure differentiates subjects on a criterion it is expected to predict. Then to the testing. In order to acquire knowledge of the characteristics and properties of the collected data, some preliminary data analyses are usually conducted before performing measurement quality assessment or tests of hypotheses. Significance tests can be grouped into two general classes: parametric and non–parametric. Parametric tests are generally considered more powerful because their data are typically derived from interval and ratio measurements with the likelihood model (i.e. the distribution) known, except for some parameters. Non–parametric tests are also used, usually with nominal and ordinal data. Finally results are interpreted. When interpreting results, the researcher moves from the empirical to the theoretical domain. This process implies considerations of inference and generalization.

Chapter 5 set out a step-by-step approach for conducting case research. The case method allows the questions of *why, what* and *how,* to be answered with a relatively full understanding of the nature and complexity of the complete phenomenon; and the case method lends itself to early, exploratory investigations. But case studies can be used for different types of research purposes such as exploration, theory building, theory testing and theory extension/refinement. There are several considerations regarding case selection. First the number of cases. The fewer the case studies, the greater the opportunity for depth of observation. But single cases have limitations, especially the limits to the generalizability of the conclusions, models or theory developed from one case study. A second choice in case selection is whether to use retrospective or current cases. Longitudinal case research can be particularly valuable. If multiple case studies are to be used for research, then a vital question is the case selection or sampling. When building theory from case studies, case selection using replication logic rather than sampling logic should be used. Each case should be selected so that it either predicts similar results (a literal replication), or produces contrary results but for predictable reasons (a theoretical replication). Typically the prime source of data in case research is structured interviews, often backed up by unstructured interviews and interactions. Other sources of data can include personal observation, informal conversations, attendance at meetings and events, surveys administered within the organization, collection of objective data and review of archival sources. The reliability and validity of case research data will be enhanced by a well-designed research protocol. In designing case research a key question is what should be the number of respondents? Maybe a set of questions can be reliably answered by one 'key informant'. Otherwise the researcher may consider interviewing multiple respondents, or using a follow-up survey with multiple respondents. An underlying principle in collection of data in case research is that of triangulation, the use and combination of different methods to study the same phenomenon. Much, but not all field data will be collected through interviews. Interviews can be unstructured, focused with more structure or highly structured resembling a questionnaire. Alternatively evidence can also be gathered by direct observation of meetings, processes etc. Whatever method is used to transcribe data, it is important there are good and accurate records and minutes of research interviews and meetings. Once data are collected they should be documented and coded. Documentation can include typing up of notes and/or transcription of tapes. This produces a *case narrative*. Central to effective case research is the coding of the observations and data collected in the field. It is important to try to reduce data into *categories*. Having developed detailed case descriptions and coded the data, the first step is to analyse the pattern of data within cases. A very useful and common starting point is to construct an array or display of the data. The systematic search for cross-case patterns is a key step in case research. It is also essential for enhancing the generalizability of conclusions drawn from cases. In an iterative process emergent themes, frameworks or hypotheses are compared with data from each case. This will iterate towards theory that provides a close fit. When the data seem to support hypotheses, case research allows the researcher to go one step further and examine the underlying reasons in each case as to why things are happening. What are the theoretical reasons for the observed relationships?

Chapter 6 dealt with longitudinal field studies, in-depth studies of change processes inside organizations. Longitudinal field studies are case studies but are distinguished by studying a phenomenon over time, in real time. They are particularly suitable for research questions concerning how organizational changes emerge, develop, grow or terminate over time. To gain access to organizations to conduct a longitudinal field study, it can be set up as clinical research, where the researcher participates in and studies organizational change. Before entering the field, a framework for data gathering is critical. In addition to the case study researcher's toolbox of methods for data collection, the longitudinal field researcher relies heavily on participant observation. Participant observation requires careful and meticulous note taking, together with a system to organize the collected data. Analysing longitudinal field data is a challenging task due to the often huge amounts of data being collected and the lack of well-defined methods for data analysis. The analysis requires identifying sequences and patterns in the events, for instance using graphical techniques. To increase the reliability and validity, the researcher needs to adhere to a systematic research, coding and analysis process. Generalization in longitudinal field studies is always towards theory, not samples, since they tend to rely heavily on a few cases. In the process of generalizing from longitudinal field studies, previous literature is absolutely critical.

In Chapter 7 we learned that action researchers actually take action. It can be the researcher working with the operations manager but also the operations manager can be a researcher. Action research deals with actual problematic situations, simultaneously solving problems and developing new knowledge. Doing this the research is conducted in real time with a focus on change and organizational development and there is a lot of interaction between the researcher and the organization. Doing action research puts some specific demands on the researcher who should be well positioned in academia and well regarded in practice. Preparations including gaining access and developing relations with the organization to be accepted are crucial. The action research process typically goes on in repeated cycles of observation, planning, action and evaluation. The results are typically situation-specific and incremental. Generalization may not be the key characteristic but the strength of the results lies in the deep understanding, the relevance of real problems and the construction of workable solutions that have been tested.

Chapter 8 dealt with the use of modelling and simulation for researching OM issues. The quantitative modelling process that underlies the modelling and simulation research approach was characterized. Inventory control, forecasting, mathematical optimization and queuing theory were mentioned as examples of influential results produced by modelling and simulation research. Modelling and simulation as descriptive or prescriptive axiomatic research were discussed and guidelines on how to conduct qualitative model-based research, both for analytical research and for simulation research were given. Finally guidelines for doing model-based empirical research were given.

9.3 Choosing and Combining Approaches— Triangulation in Methods

A key point in this book is that a combination of methods is a strength in creating a solid research contribution. We want to emphasize this point even if the different approaches or methods described in this book have been dealt with mainly one by one. Sometimes in these distinct chapters we have pointed at the obvious good complementary approaches. These include: doing a quantitative questionnaire study as a part of a longitudinal field research can improve quality in the project; a case study in a large questionnaire study can deepen understanding; an action research project can add to understanding relevance in surveys or multiple case studies. But mixed methods are a concept with wider meaning.

There are different types of mixes. Hence the methods can be mixed, meaning that, for example, quantitative and qualitative methods are used in combination. But there can also be a methodology perspective in which mixed methods are used as a method in itself, for example, combining different types of research questions or methods. A third perspective is paradigmatic perspective in which different world views are combined. A fourth perspective would be a practice perspective in which research procedures are combined (Creswell and Tashakkori, 2007).

The first type of mixed method we think of here is combinations of methods for collecting and analysing data, such as through surveys and case studies in which quantitative and qualitative data are dealt with. There may be different research questions that lend themselves to different approaches or a method may provide data of depth versus overview; or a quantitative method may be used for analysing qualitative data. This demonstrates the unfortunate practice of classifying research approaches as quantitative or qualitative, something we have avoided in this book. Quantitative and qualitative data and analysis thereof can be used in all approaches.

The second type of mix is combinations of methodologies. This means combining different research approaches in which there are different views on how data should be gathered, analysed and interpreted. Different perspectives become clearer the more we look at the complete research process and not only at a narrow phase such as data analysis. In this book that may be best demonstrated in the contrast between a questionnaire-based large sample survey and the action research approach. Clearly this is a perspective held throughout this book. We argue that different research approaches have different characteristics that make them more or less feasible for answering different kinds of research questions or, even more so, different research purposes.

The third type of mix is combinations of paradigms. This applies to taking different fundamental standpoints about reality and how to study it. A part of the research may be carried through in a reductionist perspective while another part is carried through with a constructivist perspective. Different standpoints may be taken regarding what is reality and what is observable.

The fourth type of mixed perspective takes its starting point in the research process. Different methods are used at different points in time and to study different phenomena following what is practicable but also feels reasonable and feasible to the researcher. This may result in a whole palette of approaches and even include innovative approaches developed to fit the temporary detailed conditions. The researcher simply chooses what for some hopefully well-argued reason is best during the circumstances. This approach can especially be found during a longitudinal field study where many different objects, actors and activities are studied in different situations over a long period of time.

Mixed methods face certain challenges concerning validity. It is sometimes claimed that mixed research demonstrates less rigour than single method approaches (Creswell and Plano Clark, 2007). One reason is the considerable distance in perspectives of validity between quantitative and qualitative research. While quantitative research tends to focus construct validity together with content and criterion validity, qualitative research tends to look at a range of concepts such as credibility, dependability, trustworthiness and others. In mixed methods research the term legitimation has appeared as an alternative (Onweugbuzie and Johnson, 2006). They introduce a whole set of legitimations including sample, weakness minimization, conversion, multiple validities, paradigmatic and political legitimation. To this can be added the design quality of the research in terms of design adequacy, suitability and consistency and the interpretative rigour in terms of consistency, distinctiveness and efficiency (Dellinger and Leech, 2007). If the reader wants to look deeper into validity in mixed research Dellinger and Leech have further developed a framework for validation of mixed research (ibid).

9.4 Implementing Good Practices

A specific aim in this book has been to describe good practices and in addition point to examples of best practices. For more detailed discussions of different methods we have to refer to specialized literature. It must be said that what is best practice depends to some extent on the perspective of the individual researcher, even if we get a good idea from the publications that have most impact.

From different best practices one may extract some general patterns of the publications:

- Research results must offer a contribution to existing knowledge
- The problem/issue together with earlier/existing knowledge must be made clear
- The approach and rigour in execution must be demonstrated
- Newness is important to get impact
- The language should preferably be easily accessible

To achieve the high level of good practice there are some rules of thumb for the research process:

- Spend considerable time on mapping, both practice and theory
- Choose issue and method integrated and related to your skills

- Use colleagues; if you are not in an institutional research team, create a virtual one
- Consult texts on methods and methodology (e.g. go back in this book)
- Develop a research manual with concrete tools
- Record everything (data and research process) constantly in a systematic way
- Use extensive communication in seminars and other forms
- Develop and use the skill of criticizing
- Redo till you are close to perfect
- Go for publication

9.5 Generalization into Different Management Areas— Beyond Operations Management

This book is primarily aimed at the field of OM. The field certainly contains many subfields and adjacent fields such as supply chain management, technology management, product development, etcetera as discussed in Chapter 2. However the book also aims at guiding research in other areas with similar issues, empirical bases and contexts. In Chapter 2 we also discussed that there are operations and there is OM in almost any function of a business or organization. The resources that are gathered, structured, processed and controlled can be human, technical or information and they may appear in organizational units dealing with marketing, manufacturing, after sales service, financial control and so on. Hence, we claimed that most of the research methods dealt with in this book apply to most of what goes on in organizations. This is said simply because most activities in most organizations are operations.

Common characteristics or commonalities lie in that we deal with managerial issues of human, technical or information resources that are gathered, structured, processed and controlled. The managerial issues may concern strategy, resources generation, organization, systems design, distribution and so on.

There are of course distinctive fields and issues in every functional area that are not operations and management. We may deal with managing sales activities but not market analysis, we may deal with managing financial services but not do financial analysis, we may deal with managing health services but not do medical analysis.

Generalizability of the methods described here lies in the characteristics of operations and the perspectives of managing them. It is not the functional area that defines the focus. For example we do not deal with production and inventory control here but with managerial issues of systems. In the same way we claim generalizability in methods also to managing operations in other functional areas than production or manufacturing or the operations function.

9.6 A Contract with Science—a Researcher Ethic

Finally we want to emphasize the need for and requests on researchers to take into consideration the research in a larger setting. The researcher must consider direct and potential effects of the research in a total global context. Go back to section 2.6 and consider some of the issues. Remember the ethical and moral aspects when planning, doing and reporting research.

The researcher should make a contract on ethics and morals. But with whom should that contract be made? There are at least three levels of stakeholders to include. The contract should at least be made with mankind, society and the environment. In the contract there may be special considerations with the poor and the vulnerable, on risk situations, if there are arms implications and other potential 'misuse' of the results.

This kind of research contract is becoming more and more common with research funders and research institutions. Some universities and business schools have their standard forms. It is for the good of the institution and the researcher together with the other stakeholders, not the least for communication with media if the research comes under attack. We see cases where the contract on research ethic is a prerequisite for both employment as a researcher and the permission of research grants. But that should of course not be necessary given the ethical issue.

9.7 Summary

- **Key messages from the book.** The role of research is to develop new knowledge and hence contribute by adding to existing knowledge. Demands on research concern both being relevant and trustworthy. Therefore clearly described good methods are important. The research must not only be relevant but also ethical
- **Choosing and combining approaches—triangulation in methods.** Mixtures of methods, methodologies and even paradigms may add to the value of research. The validity issue then becomes both more nuanced and complex
- **Implementing good practices.** Best practice is not an absolute concept but well-established research publications are an important source and especially publications with high impact. Demonstrating knowledge, contribution and rigour in carrying out research is important. Critical analysis in relevant research communities is a key activity
- **Generalization into different management areas—beyond OM.** Operations exist across functions. What is characteristic for research methods in this book come from characteristics of operations and management. The conditions for generalization of the applicability are a consequence thereof
- **A contract with science—a researcher ethic.** Research should be considered in its ethical context. There are many stakeholders in

mankind, society and the environment. A formal contract is often not only good but requested

References and Bibliography

Creswell, J. W. and Plano Clark, V. L. (2007), *Designing and conducting mixed methods research*. Thousand Oaks, CA, Sage.

Creswell, J. W. and Tashakkori, A. (2007), (editorial), Differing Perspectives of Mixed Methods Research, *Journal of Mixed Methods Research*, Vol. 1, No. 4, pp 303–308.

Dellinger, A. B. and Leech, N. L. (2007), Toward a United Validation Framework in Mixed Methods Research, *Journal of Mixed Methods Research*, Vol. 1, No. 4, pp 309–332.

Onweugbuzie, A. J. and Johnson, R. B. (2006), The validity issue in mixed research, *Research in the Schools*, 13, pp 48–63.

Ridenour, C., Newman, I., Newman, C. (2007), *Qualitative, quantitative and mixed methods research: Exploring the interactive continuum*. Carbondale, Southern Illinois University Press.

Tashakkori, A. and Teddlie, C. (2003), *Handbook of mixed methods in social & behavioral research*. Thousand Oaks, CA, Sage.

Yin, R. K. (2006), Mixed methods research: Are the methods genuinely integrated or merely parallel? *Research in the Schools*, 13, pp 41–47.

Index